Portora

The School on the Hill

a quatercentenary history: 1608-2008

Portora

The School on the Hill

a quatercentenary history: 1608-2008

Published by Portora Royal School, Enniskillen, County Fermanagh, BT74 7HA, Northern Ireland.

Copyright of this edition: Portora Royal School.

Note that the copyright of illustrations, prints and other visual material is vested in or with those who have supplied this material.
(see also Acknowledgements on page 249)

Hardback edition: ISBN: 978 0 9559971 0 5
Limited edition of 100 copies: ISBN: 978 0 9559971 1 2
Limpback edition for Portora pupils: ISBN: 978 0 9559971 2 9

This edition was written, compiled and edited by members of the Old Portora Union (London Branch).

Art direction, typesetting and imposition by members of the PRS History Project team of the Old Portora Union (London Branch).

Printed and bound in Singapore.

Visit the School's website: www.portoraroyal.co.uk

Contents

Foreword

THE RIGHT REVEREND DR WNF EMPEY,
BA, BD, DLITT, THE FORMER ARCHBISHOP
OF DUBLIN AND GLENDALOUGH

(OP, 1944-52)

- Born Dublin on 26 October 1934, the eldest son of the late Reverend Francis Fullerton Empey and Mildred May 'Mimi' Empey (née Cox).

- Entered Gloucester House in 1944 and transferred to Connacht House, Upper School, in 1948. Became House Prefect and played 1st XV rugby, gaining his colours. Captain of shooting. He took the first Portora team to Bisley to compete in Ashburton Shield for full bore rifle.

- Entered Trinity College, Dublin, and graduated in 1957. Made Deacon, 1958, and ordained Priest, 1959, as curate to St Paul's, Glenageary.

- Served six years in Canada in two parishes, the first as a Bishop's Curate, the second as a Rector. Returned as Rector of Stradbally, Co. Laois, for five years before he was appointed Dean of Limerick. Subsequently elected Bishop of Limerick in 1971, he succeeded Dr Donald Caird (S, 1954-57) as Bishop of Meath and Kildare.

- In 1996 he was elected Archbishop of Dublin, Bishop of Glendalough, Primate of Ireland and Metropolitan.

- He retired in 2002 to Carlow with his wife, Louie, to enjoy a rather more relaxed episcopal life, after more than forty years of active church ministry.

It is with pleasure that I accepted the invitation to write the Foreword to this excellent book. Despite the fact that it has been written by numerous contributors, there is a marvellous evenness in the text itself. Readers will be deeply impressed by the thoroughness of the research for each one of its different subjects. Obviously written by Old Portorans, it will be of interest to anyone remotely interested in education or indeed history.

The reader will be made conscious of movement and change, not only on the location of the School itself from Lisnaskea to Enniskillen town and finally to its present magnificent position on the hill, but also in such matters as developing the curriculum, sport and much else. We will be introduced to people in the distant past who made contributions not only to the School, but also nationally and internationally and to others who continue to do so in this 400th year of its history.

We will read of great sporting achievements such as Lloyd's magnificent Rugby XV, which defeated every team unfortunate enough to meet them, and of 'Tich' Andrews' rowing crews, which distinguished themselves over many years. Of course there were also the minor sports teams such as boxing, hockey and my own particular delight, shooting. The late General Sir Edward Jones, (Gentleman Usher of the Black Rod, UK House of Lords) was a member of my team and I well remember having to reprimand him for not cleaning his rifle properly – a future bishop dressing down a future general!

On the literary scene Portora has made a singular contribution. For such a small island, Ireland has produced myriad authors who have made their mark in the history of literature in its widest scope. Immediately, we can think of Swift, Goldsmith, Shaw, Joyce and Synge and still the list goes on to this day with the poetry of Seamus Heaney. Then there is of course Henry Francis Lyte. One wonders how many who sing his most beloved hymn 'Abide with Me' are conscious that he was an Old Portoran. Oscar Wilde and Samuel Beckett, both Old Portorans, must be added to the above list and take an honoured place in the pantheon of Ireland's literary giants.

I imagine that the last chapter on reminiscences will prompt the memories of many readers, as it certainly did for me. School life is not simply made up of study and sport but the interaction of individuals with one another and indeed the system itself when it is disregarded. The sabotage of the concert piano, for example, was carried out by a very close relative of mine.

Finally, we are most grateful to all those who contributed to this excellent work, which will be cherished by many with much appreciation.

Rathmore Lodge
Tullow
County Carlow

+ Walton N. F. Empey

September 2008

Headmaster's introduction

J Neill Morton, BA, BSSc, DASE,
MA(Ed), MA, PQH(NI)

(s, 2002-)

- Born in Belfast in 1949, educated at Annadale Grammar School. In his final year, he was appointed Head Prefect.
- Graduated from Queen's University, Belfast in English, Psychology and Sociology. Elected President of Dramsoc at the end of his first year.
- Returned to Annadale for five years, after completing a second degree. Coached School cross country teams to five Ulster and three All-Ireland Schools' titles. Formed Annadale Striders, which within ten years had become the premier Irish track and field club. Accredited coach to the NI Athletics Team at the Edmonton Commonwealth Games, 1978.
- Moved to Campbell College in 1977, to teach English. Remained for 25 years in various roles: Head of Department, Housemaster, Teacher-in-Charge of Drama, Teacher Governor, Senior Teacher and Head of Sixth Form.
- Appointed Headmaster of Portora Royal School in April 2002, and took up the post on the retirement of Richard Bennett in September 2002.

This book is a fitting publication for a great school. It is published in the final quarter of a year in which the pupils of Portora Royal School have excelled themselves. In the tradition of all past pupils, they have set benchmarks for future generations to attain. Our top students have achieved outcomes equal to those of any school and our athletes have asserted themselves to great effect. Our rugby squads have established themselves as among the best in Ulster; our 18 Eight, as reigning Irish champions, won an international regatta in Ghent. Athletics and cricket are re-established as summer sports.

The School's academic reputation was confirmed by an Inspection in February during which HM Inspectors found the teaching to range from good to excellent; they praised the excellent work within the Mathematics department and the fine progress the School had achieved in ICT provision and in the creative, visual and performing arts. They remarked on the fine pastoral provision and on the wide range of extra-curricular activities. They found the School to be 'buzzing' with life.

The commendable report from the Inspectors was testimony to the high levels of commitment of a talented group of teachers combined with the positive responses of their students. Yet it is more than just the aggregation of elements: it is Portora, a community proud of its past, confidently looking to the future.

Of course, school histories being as they are, it is likely that those who read these words will know these things already. Certainly, the contributors to this fine publication understand what makes Portora great, for even as they extol the fine building, the stunning site, the great achievements of Headmasters, teachers and Portorans, they recognise the school's propensity to adapt to changing circumstances. These adaptations have encompassed development from a free school providing religion and learning to the youth of Fermanagh to an elite boarding establishment acclaimed as the Eton of Ireland. Then in the late 20th century it returned to the original charter as the boys' (grammar) school of Fermanagh.

This is not the place to consider the challenges facing Portora in this new society that is being forged. I wish simply to state my conviction – shared by the writers herein and all those who know Portora – that we will face change and overcome challenge and remain true to ourselves.

On behalf of the larger community of the present School, I wish to express profound gratitude to those who made this book possible. It is a splendid book, aptly befitting an exceptional school.

Portora Royal School
Enniskillen
County Fermanagh

Neill Morton

September 2008

Editor's notes

It has taken two years, near enough, for this history to see the light of day. What started as a suggestion at a committee meeting of the Old Portora Union (London Branch) has taken much time and effort by a dedicated team of researchers, writers and technicians to produce.

Research into any history relies on knowing where to find the information and whom to contact. Again, Old Portorans turned out to be the most reliable and dedicated, but the School staff applied themselves, too, going through the archives to locate sometimes minor but essential items of information. I have deliberately not used individual names so far, but you can find a collective list of contributors in the Acknowledgements section, at the back of the book.

You may note strange spellings in the text of the book. These are not typing errors; they reflect how our ancestors spelled at the time of writing. We have used the original spelling when quoting from an historic document and updated it in the subsequent related text. For example, there is only one town with the name of Enniskillen, but the spelling varied over the centuries, Inniskilling being a well-known example; among past Headmasters, Dunbar and Dunbarre were the same man and Middleton and Middletoune likewise were variations on a name. Similarly, the terms Master, Headmaster, Second Master, Deputy Head or Vice Principal may seem to have been attributed to individuals in rather a random fashion; we have, however, used those titles that were in use at the particular time.

We have also adopted the practice of using bold lettering for the name of a member of staff or a pupil the first time an individual is mentioned in each chapter. Their names are usually followed by bracketed dates, which are as complete as we can find from the archives, 'S' meaning a Staff member and 'OP' an Old Portoran. This practice is followed in all chapters except chapter nine and the appendices.

We hope we have produced an informative, accurate and interesting story. It is the first attempt in 400 years to cover all aspects of scholastic life and associated activities that have affected the history of the School. Previous publications have dealt with just one or two phases of Portora life and several have relied on sources that were simply wrong, so we hope to have given readers what they want. Inevitably, more facts will emerge over the years, but they will have to wait for a future publication. Floreat Portora!

Ian Scales
Coulsdon
Surrey

September 2008

Masters of the School

The School was initially established at Ballybalfour Castle, 1618

Reverend Geoffrey Middleton, MA
1618-1626

Reverend Richard Bourke, BD, MA
1626-1661

The School probably moved to Schoolhouse Lane, Enniskillen, c1643

Thomas Dunbar, MA
1661-1692

George Bennis, MA, MD
1692-1700

Reverend John Dennis, DD, FTCD
1700-1714

Charles Grattan, MA, FTCD
1714-1745

Reverend William Dunkin, DD
1746-1763

Reverend Mark Noble, MA
1763-1795

The School transferred from Schoolhouse Lane, Enniskillen to Portora House, after construction, 1777-1779

Reverend Joseph Stock, DD, FTCD
1795-1798

Reverend Robert Burrowes, DD, FTCD
1798-1819

Reverend Andrew O'Beirne, MA, LLD
1820-1836

Reverend John Greham, MA, LLD
1836-1857

Reverend William Steele, MA, DD
1857-1891

Reverend Walter Lindesay, MA, LLD
1891-1894

Richard Biggs, LLD
1894-1904

Alaster McDonnell, MA
1904-1915

Reginald Burgess, MA
1915-1917

Reverend Edward Seale, MA
1917-1936

Ian Stuart, MA
1936-1945

Reverend Douglas Graham, MA
1945-1953

Reverend Percival Rogers, MBE, MA
1954-1973

Thomas Garrett, BA
1973-1978

Alan Acheson, BA, PhD
1978-1982

Richard Bennett, MA, Dip Ed
1983-2002

J Neill Morton, BA, BSc, DASE, MA (Ed), MA, PQH (NI)
2002-present

Chronology

1603   James Stuart, King James VI (Scotland) becomes King James I (England).

The Five Years War ends in Ireland.

Sir Arthur Chichester is appointed the Military Commander in Ireland.

1605   Chichester is appointed Lord Deputy in Ireland and remains in post until 1614.

In Dublin, Chichester discusses with his Attorney General, Sir John Davies, the disposal of lands and a simple plan for the plantation of Ulster.

1606   Chichester and Davies plan their 'Visitation to Western Ulster', stopping in Monaghan, Cavan and Fermanagh to discuss plantation settlements.

Following the 'Flight of the Earls', the Plantation scheme is considered for five counties in Western Ulster.

Lisgoole is selected as a possible site for the Shire Town of Fermanagh, along with Enniskillen.

1608   Royal Proclamation gives outline concept for a Free School to be established in each of several counties.

Enniskillen is nominated as the preferred site for the Shire Town of Fermanagh.

1609   Captain William Cole, as a Servitor, is granted lands on the island of Enniskillen. Enniskillen is confirmed as the Shire Town of Fermanagh.

1611   Cole is recommended for the position of the Constable of Enniskillen.

Enniskillen is incorporated as the Shire Town for Fermanagh, and Cole is confirmed as Constable of Enniskillen.

1614   Cole purchases the townland of Portora from Jeremy Lindsay, a Scottish undertaker. Portora Castle is constructed as a residential site with fortifications and a bawne.

James I becomes impatient with the lack of progress towards establishing all the Royal Schools; he writes to the Primate in Armagh to hasten action.

1617   Cole is knighted for services to the Crown and becomes Sir William Cole, Bart.

1618   Captain Pynnar, Inspector of Fortifications, tours Ulster and inspects fortifications at Portora, Enniskillen and Ballybalfour Castles, and reports on the progress of several plantation holdings in Ulster.

The Reverend Jeffrey Middletoune, MA, is appointed the first Master of the Free School of Fermanagh at Ballybalfour (Lisnaskea) by Letters Patent of King James I, dated 13 August 1618.

1620   The Reverend Middletoune (later known as the Reverend Geoffrey Middleton) is granted an additional Crown appointment, as Rector of Drummully in the diocese of Clogher, by a letter from the King dated 28 September 1620.

1621   The Reverend Dr James Spottiswood, DD, arrives in Dublin on 21 April 1621 from Hampton Court, to take up his appointment as Bishop of Clogher.

Later in the year he is consecrated and takes up residence at Portora Castle, courtesy of Cole. He commences a long-running feud with Lord Balfour over the siting of the Free School and lands at Ballybalfour. Further feuds ensue over other domestic matters.

1626   The Reverend Richard Bourke, BD, is appointed by King Charles I the second Master of the Free School of Fermanagh.

1627   King Charles I issues another charter to all Royal Schools, dated 15 December, granting endowments to Archbishop James Ussher for the Free School in the County of Fermanagh, stated (in error) to be at or near the town of Lisgoole.

1629   Inquisitions of Fermanagh, dated 22 January, report on Richard Boorke and the Free Schoole of the County Fermanagh, stating that there are '…three score schollers and all except 3 being Irish natives'.

Spottiswood relinquishes the lease on Portora Castle and obtains new See House at Clogher. The Cole family move into Portora Castle from Enniskillen Castle.

1640   Charles I named the five original schools as 'Royal Foundations' in 1627 and added two more which did not survive. The five original schools (Armagh, Cavan, Dungannon, Enniskillen and Rafoe) are reconfirmed as Royal Foundations by the Irish House of Lords and Parliament in a 1640 report.

1641   Rebellion and uprising in Ulster. Cole forms a local militia and Spottiswood flees to England. The Free School at Ballybalfour Castle is probably a casualty of a fire started during a local uprising by a Maguire chieftain.

1643   The probable date when the Free School for Fermanagh moves to Schoolhouse Lane, Enniskillen. The date of the actual move is uncertain. However, some historians think the move could have been as late as 1660-61, just before the arrival of Thomas Dunbar.

1661 **Thomas Dunbar, MA**, is appointed the third Master on 15 July. At this time the School is known variously as the Free School of Fermanagh or the Classical School at Enniskillen.

1673 A report on 'Publique Schooles' within the province of Ulster states: 'In the Diocese of Clogher there is a free schoole at Enniskillen endowed with lands to the yearly value of £120 per ann, whereof Mr Thomas Dunbarre is Master'.

1690 Master Thomas Dunbar, as a prominent citizen of Enniskillen, is attainted (outlawed) by the Irish Parliament because of local participation in the defeat in Fermanagh of James II's armies, during the Williamite Wars.

1692 **George Bennis, MA**, is appointed the fourth Master, with effect from 16 March. Bennis is awarded a medical degree in 1699; wishing to practise medicine, he resigns his Mastership in 1700 and becomes a doctor.

1700 **John Dennis, MD**, is appointed the fifth Master. Although Dennis is also a qualified doctor, he prefers parochial duties to medicine or teaching Classics, so he diverts to take a Doctorate in Theology. He resigns his Mastership in 1712-13, and after holding several local rectorships, he finally becomes the Vicar General of Clogher.

1714 **Dr Charles Grattan, MA, FTCD**, is appointed the sixth Master of the Free School, with effect from 5 May. Grattan holds the Mastership for over 32 years and is instrumental in building up the all-Ireland reputation of the School. His Fellowship is removed by Trinity College, Dublin, in 1713, when he refuses to take Holy Orders.

1746 **The Reverend Dr William Dunkin, DD**, is appointed seventh Master of the Free School, with effect from 6 August. He further enhances the classical scholarship of the School and continues the all-Ireland success initiated by Grattan for scholarship and competitive entry by pupils to Trinity College, Dublin.

1763 **The Reverend Mark Noble, MA**, is appointed the eighth Master by Letters Patent from George III, first in 1761 and reconfirmed in 1763.

1776 Noble then negotiates the purchase of Portora Hill from the Cole Family, and between 1777-79 constructs the central block of the present Portora façade for the sum of about £3,000.

1777 Noble seeks a third patent to cover the move from Schoolhouse Lane to Portora Hill.

1779 'The Belfast Newsletter' advertisement: 'The Free School Enniskillen lately built by Mr Noble for reception of 100 boarders. Prices are 5 guineas a quarter for boarders… and 1 guinea for day scholars'.

1795 **The Reverend Dr Joseph Stock, DD, FTCD**, an eminent Latin and Greek scholar, is appointed ninth Master. He resigns his Mastership after only three years, to become Bishop of Killala.

1798 **The Reverend Dr Robert Burrowes, DD, FTCD**, is appointed tenth Master on 24 January. A very significant scholar, he was a founding contributor to the Royal Irish Academy. He undertakes responsibility for educating Henry Francis Lyte.

1813 The Authorities appoint a Commission on 18 November charging them with 'the regulation, investigation and administration of all Royal School funds'. The Commissioners create foundation scholarships for Enniskillen Royal School from endowments previously in the hands of the Master. They also state that the current endowments are too large for the Master and decide to provide fixed salaries for the Master and staff.

1819 Burrowes petitions the Commissioners to remove boarders and to concentrate on day pupils at the School. He is frustrated by the Commissioners and resigns to become Dean of Cork.

1820 **The Reverend Dr Andrew O'Beirne, MA, LLD**, is appointed the eleventh Master and the first to be allocated a permanent salary – £500 pa.

1836 **The Reverend Dr John Greham, MA, LLD**, arrives in May from Waterford Corporation School as the twelfth Master, and the successor to O'Beirne, who had died in post.

1837 Greham immediately initiates improvements to Portora House, authorised and funded by the School Board. Side wings are constructed and the basement area is improved with new kitchens. Following disease amongst boarders, additional lavatories and sanitation facilities costing £400 are completed 1838-40. The North Wing is designed as an infirmary, and the South Wing provides additional schoolrooms and dormitories.

1845 Owing to the onset of the Famine, pupil numbers decline, with no dayboys at all at one stage.

1857 **The Reverend Dr William Steele, MA, DD**, is appointed the thirteenth Master on 23 June.

1857 Initiated by Trimble, owner of 'The Impartial Reporter', a petition is presented to Steele from the townspeople, requesting a less classical education and the introduction of more practical or commercial subjects into the curriculum.

Later, Steele starts a separate school for day pupils; it fails due to adverse reaction from the townspeople.

1863 Visit to Enniskillen and Portora, by the Lord Lieutenant, the Earl of Carlisle, who had been instrumental in the appointment of Steele as Master of Portora from Raphoe Royal School.

1885 Lord Justice Fitzgibbon's Commission is formed to investigate a complaint from the Roman Catholic (RC) community that the endowments of the Royal Schools are not sufficiently available to pupils of the RC religion. The Commission sits for a number of years and recommends that the existing endowments should be shared equally between the two communities.

1891 On 8 July the Privy Council accepts the prime recommendation of the Fitzgibbon Commission to form separate Boards for Roman Catholic and Protestant Education, to be known as Scheme 34 under the Act of 1885. Steele decides to resign, is granted a lifetime pension of £500 pa, and hands over to his Deputy Master.

The Reverend Dr William Lindesay MA, LLD, is appointed the fourteenth Headmaster, and the first to be appointed by the newly formed Protestant Board of Education for Fermanagh. The Portora buildings and site are valued at £7,000. The future administration of the School then becomes the responsibility of the Protestant Board of Education, which hands over a moiety of £3,500 to the Catholic Board of Education for Fermanagh, for their exclusive use.

1894 Dr Richard Biggs, MA, LLD, is appointed the fifteenth Headmaster on 29 October. Biggs comes from Galway Grammar School, bringing several key staff and a number of pupils with him. As a result, a number of faithful Portora masters are declared surplus and made redundant.

1899 Portora reaches the finals of Ulster Rugby for the first time, but loses to Methodist College Belfast. Portora, and in fact all the non-Belfast City Schools, complain to the various school sporting bodies that they are considerably disadvantaged by the smaller numbers from which they can select representative sporting teams.

1904 Dr Biggs collapses and dies on the oars of a skiff on 8 July, while rowing on the River Erne. Sadly missed by the townspeople, he is buried at Old Rossorry Church.

Alaster C McDonnell, Esq, MA, is appointed the sixteenth Headmaster. He is a noted rowing coach, sportsman and former Irish Rugby international.

1905 Portora wins the Ulster Schools Cup.

1908 Portora wins the Ulster Schools Cup.

1910 The Schools Inspectorate gives Portora an adverse report on many aspects of its academic programmes. McDonnell responds by founding a new Commercial Department, which, for several years, has immediate success for candidates taking Commercial Exams for Banking.

McDonnell becomes tired of criticism and departs for Eton College, Windsor.

1915 Reginald G Burgess, MA (Oxon), is appointed the seventeenth Headmaster. He is the first non-Trinity graduate to become Headmaster, having graduated from Edinburgh University and served on the staff of Merchiston Castle School, Edinburgh.

Portora Preparatory School formally opens as a separate department under Headteacher Miss E E Hunt.

1917 Burgess is drowned trying to rescue a friend during a holiday in Castleknock. W N Tetley, BA (Cantab), becomes acting Headmaster.

The Reverend E G Seale, MA, is appointed the eighteenth Headmaster, arriving with a number of pupils from Cork Grammar School. He consolidates the gains made by Burgess, after the falling numbers under McDonnell.

1918 The House system is introduced.

1921 World War I Memorial Tablet in the Steele Hall is consecrated and the new Tercentenary Sanatorium opened by The Primate.

The Old Portora Union (OPU) is officially formed in Dublin.

1923 The Officer Training Corps (OTC) is established.

Portora joins the Headmasters Conference (HMC) as the leading Irish Public School.

1925 The School purchases 15 acres of land beside Castle Lane to create the Lower Rugby Pitches.

1929 The cricket pavilion is built on the Upper Playing Fields.

1930 New science laboratories are constructed in the courtyard area opposite the gymnasium.

1935	Construction of Gloucester House commences.
	Ian M B Stuart, MA, is appointed nineteenth Headmaster, following Seale's retirement.
1936	Gloucester House is opened by the fifth Lord Erne.
1939	World War II commences and several members of Portora Staff leave to join HM Forces.
1940	Portora wins the Ulster Schools Rugby Cup.
1941	Portora wins the Ulster Schools Rugby Cup.
1942	Portora draws in the Ulster Schools Rugby Cup and is allowed to keep the trophy.
1945	Stuart resigns and writes an open letter to all parents explaining his actions.
	The Reverend Douglas L Graham, MA appointed the twentieth Headmaster. In his first term, starched collars, tail-coats and top hats are abolished as the school uniform for Sunday Church, in favour of soft white shirts, herringbone suits and caps.
1947	The Education Act 1947 (Northern Ireland) is passed and Portora reorganises to accept the new form of entry for 11+ dayboys.
1948	The construction of the Reay Memorial Gates commences.
	The Henry Francis Lyte Memorial Concert is broadcast from the Steele Hall.
1949	The Reay Memorial Gates are dedicated.
1951	The rowing eight travels to Henley Royal Regatta, and the shooting team to Bisley, both for the first time.
1953	Graham resigns to become Headmaster of Dean Close School, Cheltenham. A T M Murfet becomes acting Headmaster.
1954	**The Reverend Percival (Val) Rogers, MBE, MA, DipEd**, becomes the twenty-first Headmaster. Extensive changes are made to the range of subjects taught within the School's curriculum.
1956	Rogers commences an ambitious new building and renovation programme, which lasts for the next ten to fifteen years.
	Portora Housing Association Ltd is formed to provide convenient and affordable accommodation for married staff.
1957	The Erne Head of River race, first organised by Portora Boat Club, takes place during March.
1962	A new and very much larger Gloucester House School is opened on the Lakeview site, and by late 1966 the combined numbers for both Upper and Lower Schools rises to 306 dayboys and 232 boarders.
1962	Construction of six staff houses is completed in Castle Lane.
1973	**Thomas Garrett, BA (QUB)**, becomes twenty-second Headmaster, the first Ulsterman and Queen's University graduate to be appointed.
1975	Girls are accepted as boarders in the Upper School.
1977	The School celebrates 200 years on the Portora Hill site, with a pageant written by Headmaster Garrett and set to music and directed by Robert Hort, entitled 'Two Hundred Years at the Top'.
1978	**Dr Alan R Acheson, BA, PhD**, is appointed the twenty-third Headmaster, when his predecessor, Garrett, accepts the Headmastership of his old School, the Royal Belfast Academical Institution (RBAI).
1982	Dr Acheson leaves Portora after only four years for a post in Australia.
1983	**Richard L Bennett, MA, Dip Ed**, is appointed the twenty-fourth Headmaster of the School and takes up his duties in early January 1984.
1985	Jayne McCartney and Leigh Cordiner become Irish Twin Pairs rowing champions.
1987	The Beckett Joyce Award is inaugurated.
	8 November: the Enniskillen Remembrance Sunday bomb.
1988	Malaysian students are recruited.
1991	Girls no longer admitted.
1992	The Kincade Report is published, recommending amalgamation with the Collegiate School.
1995	Boarding ceases.
2002	**J Neill Morton, BA, BSSc, DASE, MA(Ed), MA, PQH(NI)**, is appointed twenty-fifth Headmaster.
2003	The Old Portora Union (London Branch) hosts its 50th Anniversary Dinner and decides to publish this history of Portora Royal School in time for the quatercentenary celebrations.
2007	Portora prepares for quatercentenary celebrations in 2008 to mark 400 years since foundation.
	The President of Ireland, Dr Mary McAleese, visits Portora in October.
2008	The Queen visits Armagh Cathedral in March for the traditional Maundy Thursday service, to which the Headmasters of the five Royal Schools are invited.
	Quatercentenary Dinner and Ball are held over a weekend in mid-September at Lough Erne Golf Resort.

One

Foundation, masterships and outline history

Portora Royal School, Enniskillen is the popular name for one of the five Royal Schools established by King James I of England (James VI of Scotland) during the early 1600s, as part of his government's vision for the Ulster Plantation. For several hundred years the School has been called the 'Free School' or 'Royal School' of Fermanagh, or Enniskillen. The School has also been designated unofficially the 'Classical School', the 'Great School', or the 'Grammar School' at Enniskillen. For those who prefer the Classical touch, the School has also been referred to as 'Scholam regiam, Juxta Enniskillen'. However, the official name of the School in legal documents, since the formation of the Fermanagh Protestant Board of Education in 1891, has been and remains 'Enniskillen Royal School'.

The current name of Portora was initially used by the inhabitants of Enniskillen to describe the School's new location within the Townland of Portora, when the foundations of the main buildings were first laid out on Portora Hill in 1777. During the mid- to late Victorian era, the incumbent Master, the **Reverend Dr William Steele** (S, 1857-91), made the name Portora so popular that the establishment became routinely known as Portora Royal School, and for most Portorans it has always remained as such. The foundation of all the Royal Schools, and in particular that of Portora, is best understood by those who have some background knowledge of pre-Plantation Ulster, particularly west Ulster, and the unique circumstances

Left: This portrait of King James I of England (King James VI of Scotland) hangs in the main dining hall and was presented to the School in 1951 by the Old Portora Union. It shows a likeness of King James, c1621, after a painting by the Dutch portrait artist, Daniel Mytens.

Portrait of Sir Arthur Chichester (1563-1625), who, together with his Attorney General, Sir John Davies, was the architect of the Plantation. Chichester was himself a Grantee, with substantial holdings in Counties Down and Tyrone.

O'Doherty's castle in Burt on the Inishowen peninsula, whose lands were seized by Sir Arthur Chichester after the former's execution in 1608.

prevailing in Fermanagh during the early 1600s. There are three interesting questions to be answered:

- Why were only five Royal Schools established for the original nine or ten counties of Ulster?
- Why did the Commissioners take ten years to establish the Free School for Fermanagh?
- Why did the Free School open at Castle Balfour and not within the Shire town of Enniskillen?

Irish politics and pre-Plantation Ulster

The impetus for the Plantation of the western parts of Ulster originated during 1607 with the 'Flight of the Earls'. Hugh O'Neill, Earl of Tyrone, and Rory O'Donnell, Earl of Tyrconnel, fled to the continent with a large following of local chiefs and native Irish clansmen, under what the British establishment considered to be suspicious circumstances. Convinced that some form of treason had been planned with the Spanish, the Crown authorities took steps to confiscate the lands of O'Neill and O'Donnell, and all other holdings of their attendants and associates. Initially, guided by the Lord Deputy of Ireland, Sir Arthur Chichester (1563-1625) and his Attorney General, Sir John Davies, a relatively small-scale import of mainly Protestant colonists was planned. They would supplement the local inhabitants and 'the deserving Irish' in order to populate the new settlements scheduled for creation within the escheated (confiscated) lands. These escheated lands comprised some half million acres of west Ulster countryside.

Changes in the offing

However, in 1608, following a further rebellion by another Ulster chieftain, Sir Cahir O'Doherty from Donegal, who felt cheated by what he considered a slight to his loyal support for the Crown, this earlier low-key concept was quickly abandoned. O'Doherty was captured, tried and executed for his alleged crimes, and therefore a further large swathe of escheated lands became available to the Dublin authorities as additional areas for settlements.

The Plantation now increased in scope and magnitude. The native inhabitants of the affected areas now found that their proposed stake in the revised settlement had been greatly reduced, thus provoking considerable and lasting discontent. The main beneficiaries of this revised Plantation plan were new and future English and Scottish Lowland settlers., who, along with other trusted official organisations, such as Church foundations and Trinity College, Dublin (established in 1592), were the recipients of nearly three quarters of all confiscated lands.

The Royal Proclamation and Order in Council of 1608

The foundation of the new County Schools was enshrined in a Privy Council decree of 1608, which outlined the Crown's wish to provide free schools for the inhabitants as well as for future waves of Plantation children. It was expressed as follows: '*That in every one of the said Counties there shall*

*be a convenient Number of Market towns and Corporacions erected for the
Habitation and settling of Tradesmen and Artificers; and that there shall be
one free school at least appointed in every County for the education of youth in
Learning and Religion'.*

The Plantation of Ulster

Although entitled the Plantation of Ulster, the scheme drawn up during the
years 1609-10 involved only six (later reduced to five) of the nine counties
in the Province: Armagh, Cavan, Coleraine/Derry (amalgamated to become
known as Londonderry, although Derry was never strictly classed as a county),
Donegal, Fermanagh and Tyrone. The Plantation within the five counties was
supervised by the Plantation Commissioners. However, the settlement of the
newest county of Londonderry was financed and managed by a committee
known as the Honourable Irish Society (the Irish Society), whose membership
was drawn from many of the major and minor mercantile guilds within the
City of London. The settlers administered by the Irish Society were drawn
mainly from surviving campaigners of Chichester's army who had fought
during the previous Nine Years War in the Province.

The Irish Society operated within government guidelines, but acted as
a separate administration outside direct government channels (perhaps an
early example of the government employing contractors as in the modern
Private Finance Initiative (PFI) scheme). Although Londonderry was the
recipient of a Free School in 1617 (now known as Foyle and Londonderry
College), it was specifically sponsored through the Irish Society by the Master
of the Merchant Taylors' Company of London. It was never deemed to be one
of the original Free Schools, which were officially listed as Armagh, Cavan,
Donegal, Fermanagh and Tyrone. The schools in these five counties were later
confirmed and defined as Royal School Foundations by Charles I, and were
later mentioned in a written review of 1640 by the Irish House of Lords and
Parliament.

Exceptions to the Ulster Plantation

The remaining three counties of Ulster – Antrim, Down and Monaghan – were
never part of the scheme that was implemented in 1610-11.

The first two counties, Antrim and Down, had been designated for land
distribution just before James's accession in 1603. McDonnell, the Earl of
Antrim, was confirmed in the ownership of a massive area (about a third of
a million acres) in Antrim, stretching from just north of Carrickfergus to
Dunluce. The ownership of Clandeboye, an O'Neill stronghold, was radically
changed at this time, because several English landowners, including the
incumbent Lord Deputy himself (Chichester), later acquired estates here in
this more northern part of the province. In the southern part of Clandeboye,
which included Bangor and Newtownards, two lowland Scots – Sir James
Hamilton and Sir Hugh Montgomery, both courtiers to King James – also
received massive estates. The Irish Chieftain of Clandeboye and all his
followers of the O'Neill clan were also restored to about a third of this area at
the same time.

The seal of the Honourable Irish Society,
whose members financed and supervised the
settlement of the newly created County of
Londonderry. Membership for this Society
was recruited from twelve Livery Companies
in the City of London. The Society then
sought to ensure '*rising generations be
trayned up in useful industrie and civilitie,
learning, religion and loyalties'.*

County Monaghan was also deliberately excluded from this latest planning of the Plantation. Many years earlier, in 1591, land ownership throughout Monaghan and certain fringe holdings in the counties of Armagh and Tyrone had been reorganised and regulated mainly amongst the Irish themselves, albeit with the cooperative and voluntary import of a few new English and Scottish settlers. This early reorganisation was undertaken to diminish the autonomy of a dissident but reformed clan of Gaelic-speaking followers after the execution of their Chief, The MacMahon.

Government officials in Ireland, satisfied that at least three counties were relatively peaceful and stable, now concentrated their efforts on populating the escheated lands of the five remaining counties of Western Ulster with cooperative Irish natives, as well as imported English and Scottish settlers.

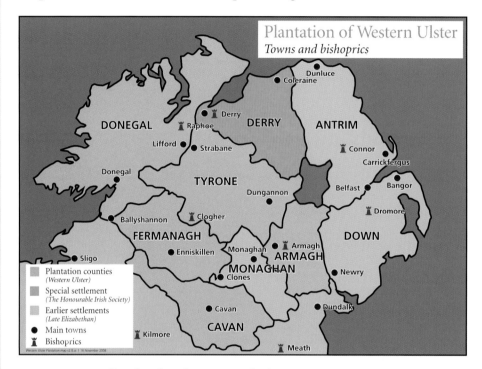

Government policy for the Plantation of Ulster
Current government administrators in both England and Ireland felt that previous settlement schemes for Ireland had foundered because the land grants were too large, allowing a vacuum to develop within the civil administration. This was particularly evident when major landowners took no interest in living locally and became absentee landlords. Government officials were determined not to make the same mistake with Western Ulster, so they created smaller, more numerous land grants: by maximising the number of settlers they prevented any individual from becoming too powerful locally. It was also deemed prudent to consider religious instruction, provision of education and the establishment of a system for training necessary craftsmen, artificers and tradesmen to create a successful infrastructure in both current and future needs.

Outline conditions for the Plantation
During the Plantation, the conditions for Undertakers (ie those who were granted proportions of escheated land), were set out in a book, called 'A Collection of Such Orders and Conditions, as are to be Observed by the

undertakers upon the distribution and Plantation of the Escheated Lands of Ulster'. Subsequently, this document listed the Ulster Counties with escheated lands as: Ardmagh, Tyrone, Colrane, Derry, Donegall, Fermanagh and Cabhan (note the old-fashioned spelling). These seven counties were later reduced to six when Colrane and Derry were amalgamated to become Londonderry, whose development was then transferred from the Commissioners to the Irish Society. The remaining five Counties were then handsomely rewarded with escheated lands for financing their Free Schools. Records show that the various county schools were initially granted the following acreages of cultivable lands, excluding lakes, woods and bog-land: Donegal (1,121 acres), Cavan (1,536 acres), Fermanagh (2,160 acres), Tyrone (2,735 acres) and Armagh (730 acres).

Concept for the West Ulster Plantation
To begin with, there were three standard measures and conditions for the grant or proportion of land that might be distributed to approved Undertakers:
1 Undertakers granted 1,000 English acres were required within two years of Letters Patent to build a strong Court or Bawne.
2 Undertakers granted 1,500 English acres were required within two years of Letters Patent to build a stone or brick House with a strong Court or Bawne about it.
3 Undertakers granted 2,000 English acres were required within two years of Letters Patent to build a Castle with a strong Court or Bawne about it.

The proportion and conditions for potential Undertakers were also designated to be of three distinct kinds:
1 English or Scottish Undertakers who were to plant their portions with English or inland Scottish tenants of their choice.
2 Servitors in the Kingdom of Ireland who might take Irish, English or inland Scottish tenants of their choice.
3 Natives of Ireland who were to be made freeholders.
(Servitors were military personnel or government officials, rewarded for their services to the Crown with appropriate land grants in Ulster, under similar conditions to Undertakers as outlined above.)

Distribution of the land
The King appointed Undertakers and Servitors and then declared in which county each should have his proportion. Yearly fees for the land were paid to the King. Severe conditions were placed on the Undertakers curtailing the sale of any of their lands to a third party, and an oath of Supremacy was required before Letters Patent could be issued. All English and inland Scottish tenants were encouraged to build settlers' housing near the castle, house or bawne for defence.

For seven years the Undertakers could transport and import commodities grown on their former lands without paying any dues or customs. For five years they could bring into Ireland utensils for their households, materials and tools for building and husbandry, and cattle to stock and manure the land, without paying customs.

A thematic land map of the Ulster Plantation showing the allocation of areas to the various categories of settlers. Note that Fermanagh was a fairly well-balanced mixture of settlements.

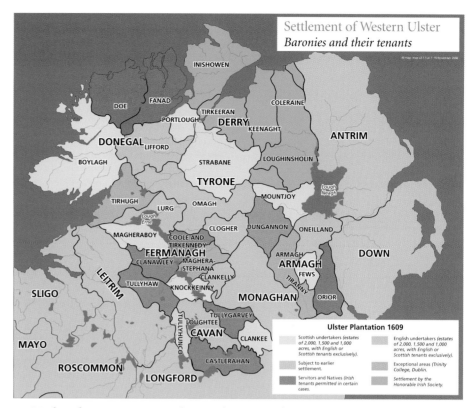

Undertakers were expected to settle twenty-four British males per thousand acres of land, and a high proportion of these settlers were to be married men with families. Building conditions were also stipulated, according to the size of the proportion granted. However, continuing political uncertainty in Ireland militated against large numbers of Protestant settlers arriving by the end of this initial period. Subsequent migration resulted in a population of only some 40,000 settlers in Ulster by 1640, instead of the initial estimate of 55,000.

The thematic map of Ulster shows the different categories of grantees across the six (later five on formation of Londonderry) counties involved in the formal plantation of Ulster in 1610-11. In these counties, the Undertakers and the Londoners received probably somewhat over 40% of the land acreage. The Servitors received about 15-20% of the acreage and the native Irish were restored to approximately 15-20% of the land. Church-owned land of varying amounts and form accounted for perhaps a further 15-20% of the acreage. Smaller areas of land, say 10%, were also provided for various cultural purposes – to endow the Free School proposed within each county, or to support the new university, Trinity College, Dublin, and certain other charitable uses.

The major Undertakers, during the first settlement, comprised some 60 persons of English origin, 60 Scots from the lowlands and about 60 Servitor grantees. The Irish grantees numbered almost 290, but many of these were granted or restored to just small or partial estates, with perhaps some 20 or 30 receiving larger holdings on a par with those granted to the English and Scottish Undertakers. In organisational terms, the individual grantees of both Scottish and English Undertakers were grouped together in sub-divisions of counties known as 'baronies', and this gave the Ulster plantation its unique cohesive regional character.

The Londonderry Plantation, conducted through the Irish Society, involved just that one county. The Society then allocated the available land in varying proportions to some twelve livery companies of the London mercantile organisation, such as the Grocers, Fishmongers, Tailors and a host of minor contributing guilds, all of which operated as corporate Undertakers.

However, ownership of land is often very different from occupation, and some areas of Ulster and certain selected estates were more highly colonised by tenants than others. Over time, many tenancies were not allocated exactly within the Plantation law, since the treatment of native Irish tenants was strictly defined. Undertakers exceeded their legal limits with Irish tenants because they could charge the Irish tenants more rent, safe in the knowledge they were unlikely to inform the authorities.

The civic development of Fermanagh

The preliminary pre-Plantation planning covering Fermanagh began in Autumn 1606, with an event known as '*the Visitation of Ulster*', when the Lord Deputy of Ireland, Sir Arthur Chichester, accompanied by his Attorney General, Sir John Davies, left Dublin and made a tour of Monaghan and the four western counties of Ulster to acquaint themselves with civic matters. In County Fermanagh they viewed two or three places for the possible creation of strategic towns and villages, and felt that Lisgoole, where there was an existing abbey, was a strong candidate. Another place under consideration was '*Inish-kellin, which was an island crossing site between the lakes of Lough Yearne*'. They reserved judgement on the final location for the Shire town, and also the location for the Free School, for further and later discussion with the newly appointed Bishop of Clogher.

The Church of Ireland in Fermanagh

The Right Reverend Dr George Montgomery, DD (1569/70-1621) arrived in Ulster, during the late autumn of 1606, as the new Bishop of Clogher, but retaining his position as the Dean of Norwich Cathedral. He was the younger brother of Sir Hugh Montgomery, who had been given several large and significant estates in the Ards peninsula prior to the Plantation. The See of Clogher had been vacant for decades, so Montgomery now embarked on a survey of his new diocese and its inhabitants. Almost immediately, he managed to obtain the bishopric of Derry and Raphoe, which he added to his appointment at Clogher. He later brought over his family from England to live in Derry.

The new Bishop then famously became involved in a blazing row with Hugh O'Neill, Earl of Tyrone, shortly before the Flight of the Earls. Tyrone challenged the Bishop by saying, '*My lord, you have two or three bishopricks, and yet you are not content with them, but seek the lands of my earldom*'. Montgomery replied, '*Your earldom is swollen so big with the lands of the church, that it will burst if it be not vented*'. The immediate problem was resolved by O'Neill himself, when he fled the country in 1607 and joined the Flight of the Earls.

When the very lucrative See of Meath became vacant in 1608, Chichester immediately recommended Montgomery for the post, clearly hoping to divert him from any further controversial work in Ulster. As it happened,

Bishop Montgomery, from a portrait in Clogher Cathedral (© Dean and Chapter of Clogher). Montgomery was a busy 'political cleric' with three bishoprics and was not a significant figure in helping to establish the Free School for Fermanagh. However, his successor Spottiswood was very active and ensured that escheated lands for both the School and the dioceses of Clogher were recorded legally. Spottiswood had several encounters with the civil administrators, Governor Cole and Lord Balfour – all of whom he suspected were trying to covet escheated lands improperly.

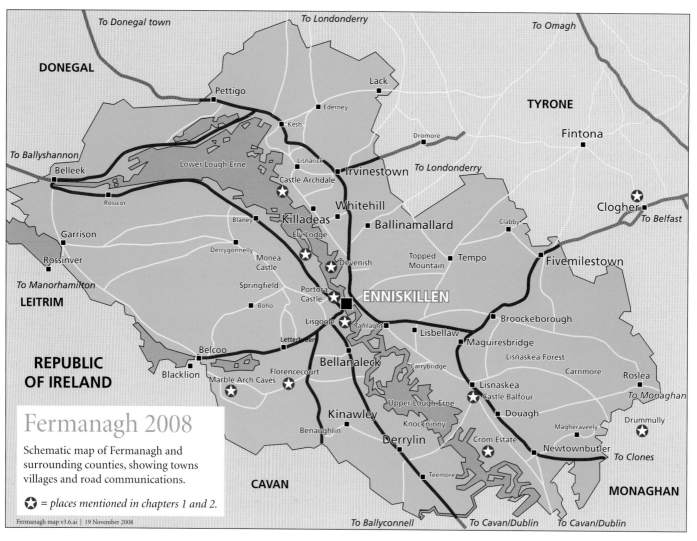

Fermanagh 2008

Schematic map of Fermanagh and
surrounding counties, showing towns
villages and road communications.

⊛ = *places mentioned in chapters 1 and 2.*

Fermanagh map v3.6.ai | 19 November 2008

**Map of County Fermanagh showing towns,
villages and locations mentioned in this
history.**

while Montgomery duly accepted the additional duties as Bishop of Meath,
he also managed to exert sufficient influence at Court to retain the diocese of
Clogher, even though he did not reside in either Tyrone or Fermanagh, and
continued to live at his residences in either Derry or in what he regarded as
the more socially acceptable town of Navan in County Meath. Montgomery
was much involved, throughout his various dioceses, with the introduction
of the new King James Bible (begun in 1604 and finally published about 1611),
along with the Church services associated with the revised Book of Common
Prayer. He was also a leading light in the search for, and administration and
management of, recusants throughout his various dioceses. It is not surprising
that with so many and varied Church, pastoral and social duties, Montgomery
never took much interest in progressing the establishment of the Free School
for Fermanagh. Until his death in 1621, Montgomery held on to most of his
appointments in all three dioceses, and retained the prestigious position of the
Dean of Norwich until 1614. Although buried in Navan, his official portrait as a
Church of Ireland Bishop has always been retained in Clogher Cathedral.

Iniskellin not Lisgoole is finally selected as the County town

Originally, it was intended that each Free School should be built at or
near the main county town within the selected counties. However, at the
time, Fermanagh had no township to which the description 'county' could
be applied. In fact, the county had no real settlement to which even the

description 'town' could apply. Several locations for the new shire town were discussed by the authorities in Dublin and Fermanagh, including the possibility of developing an area alongside the Abbey of Lisgoole. However, in late 1608, Sir Arthur Chichester put an end to all prevarication and informed his Attorney General, Sir John Davies, of his final decision for Fermanagh in a letter which read: '*as in this county there is neither town nor civil habitation, Iniskellin is the fittist place for a shire town and to be made a Corporacion*'.

An early map showing the three islands that make up the township of Enniskillen. This unusual view has the North point oriented towards the bottom edge of the map.

Cole is appointed Governor of Iniskellin (hereafter called Enniskillen)

By 1610 Chichester had received instructions from the Court in Hampton that a certain Captain William Cole (1576-1653) was the most suitable candidate to be put in possession of certain lands in and around the island of Enniskillen. Cole was a Devonshire-born soldier, who had served time in Munster during the early 1600s, and with the Provincial Governor had then moved north to Fermanagh (1607) in a new capacity as Captain of the Longboats and Barges at Ballyshannon and Lough Erne. By 1611 Cole was resident in the rebuilt Maguire Castle at Enniskillen, and was gradually developing Enniskillen and its military barracks as the new strategic town. Subsequently, Chichester entrusted Cole with the urgent and rapid development of Enniskillen as the shire town for Fermanagh, and in 1612 Captain William Cole was duly appointed the '*Town Constable of Iniskellin with an attendant Corporacion*'. Thus the original idea of establishing a shire town at Lisgoole was totally abandoned, along with any idea of siting the Free School beside the old Abbey.

Cole was an efficient administrator and prospered commercially as a landowner, and by 1614 he had purchased the townland of Portora and was building a further fortified dwelling and castle outside the township of Enniskillen, alongside Portora Narrows.

Portora Castle was constructed in 1614-16 both as a gentleman's residence and a military fortification, but it was soon leased to the Church of Ireland for use by the Reverend James Spottiswood, DD, pending his appointment as

The ruins of Portora Castle today, originally built between 1614-16. For a more detailed description of the Castle's use and history, see chapter two.

Bishop of Clogher, c1621, in succession to Montgomery. As the new Bishop of Clogher, Spottiswood was to become an important figure as the guardian of Church lands as well as the administrator of endowments for the Free School of Fermanagh. He occupied Portora Castle as his official Church residence until 1629, when the Cole family moved there after a fire which had destroyed part of their former living quarters at Enniskillen Castle. The Cole family eventually vacated Portora Castle, c1710, having by then finally decided to develop Florence Court as their permanent family seat.

A late start for all Royal Schools and the search for a new School site

Over several decades Cole was responsible for the total planning, layout and construction of civic facilities within Enniskillen, as the newly chosen township and administrative centre for Fermanagh. However, there seemed to be little urgency or positive action on his part in pursuing or establishing an alternative school site to replace Lisgoole (now firmly quashed by Chichester), so the establishment of the Free School for Fermanagh languished.

Indeed, King James was so angered by the delays in establishing any of the five Free Schools that he eventually sought and enlisted the help of the Archbishop of Armagh, local bishops and clergy to hasten the progress and construction of these schools. It is interesting to note that, while the original Royal Proclamation of 1608 emphasised learning and religion as the most important duties of the Free Schools, James, in an open letter c1614 to his Lord Deputy, now included the specific words '*furtherance of manners*' as an important function of the Free Schools. At that time, the word 'manners' entailed the introduction of an English lifestyle, and had not acquired its modern connotation of 'etiquette'.

Enniskillen as a rival location for the site for the Free School

While Cole was struggling with the design, layout and construction of several bridges on the complicated island site of Enniskillen, Sir James Balfour, Kt (1583-1634), a prominent Scottish Undertaker, was making great strides to complete his model township at Ballybalfour (the modern town of Lisnaskea).

An artist's impression of the Castle Balfour complex and bawne around 1624. Described by Pynnar as 'a completed two storey schoolhouse, and a gentleman's large residence currently in occupation by the immediate Balfour family'.
(© NI Environment Agency)

In early 1618 Captain Nicholas Pynnar, an Engineer Officer and an officially appointed Inspector of Fortifications & Works, was commissioned by London to conduct a visit to Ulster and report on the progress being made by several major Plantation Undertakers with substantial holdings in Fermanagh. He summarised the progress at Ballybalfour by listing some seventy men working on the near-completion of '*a bawne, a castle, a churchyard with a layout for the construction of a church, a completed two storey schoolhouse, and a gentleman's large residence currently in occupation by the immediate Balfour family*'.

By contrast Pynnar, slightly later in that same year, reported on Cole as making slow progress on the Island sites at Enniskillen, where there was '*a bawne of lime and stone sixty feet long sixty broad and twelve feet high with two flankers*'. Contrasting the progress at Enniskillen with the situation at Lisnaskea, Pynnar reported additionally that Balfour had built, alongside his fortified area, some forty timber and plaster dwellings, in a tidy street-lined manner, and all inhabited '*by true British hearts*'. With such a glowing report in hand, Balfour now used his family's influence with the English Court to secure the King's approval for the appointment of his friend and personal chaplain, the **Reverend Geoffrey Middleton, MA** (S, 1618-26) to become the Master of the Free School for Fermanagh. Balfour also offered the use of the fine schoolhouse that he had built within the fortifications of Castle Balfour as a first location for this Free School.

The Reverend Geoffrey Middleton becomes Master of the Free School
One early problem encountered by all the Free Schools was the identification, distribution and final allocation of endowment lands. Contemporary maps and documentation of all endowments were poorly defined, mainly owing to the interpretation of the descriptive boundaries and surveys for acreages, which constantly changed with the seasons and the flood waters of the Erne. However, during preliminary survey activities in the years 1616-18, Balfour established that much of the land provisionally assigned for endowment of the Free School in Fermanagh was conveniently adjacent to his own Plantation grant and other sundry freehold acquisitions belonging to the Balfour family. He further argued and suggested to officials that, siting the Free School at Ballybalfour, with Middleton as the appointed Master under a fee farm residency (akin to but not quite a freehold tenancy), would prevent trespass, and circumvent illegal development of any adjoining endowment lands set aside for funding the proposed Free School.

So, while Balfour waited for the bureaucrats to catch up with reality, he provisionally opened his schoolhouse as a going concern, and funded Middleton's initial Mastership from his own pocket to which he added additional fees from the attendant pupils. Eventually, records show Royal approval for the first Mastership in the name of '*Reverend Jefferey Middletoune, MA*'. At last, on 13 August 1618, we find Letters stating: '*Grant to Geoffrey Middleton to be public school-master, preceptor and rector of the free school in the county Fermanagh during good behaviour*'.

A year or so later, King James reconfirmed Balfour's holdings as an Undertaker, and Middleton's appointment as Master of the Free School

Castle Balfour ruins in 2007, after restoration and repair to comply with modern safety regulations. There is no sign of the original schoolhouse which must have been located in the foreground, in what is now part of the Parish Cemetery.

Reverend Geoffrey Middleton, MA
(s, 1618-1626)

- Graduate of Trinity College, Dublin.
- Appointed Chaplain and local adviser to Sir James Balfour, c1612.
- Appointed by Letters of King James I, dated 13 August 1618, to Mastership of Free School, in the name of Reverend Jefferey Middletoune, MA.
- Gifted the Rectorship of St Comans, Drummully, 7 December 1620.
- Wife Bridget and two children given assurances by King Charles I, 1626, of continuing financial support in the event of Middleton's death.

for Fermanagh, to which he also added the rectorship of Drummully, in the diocese of Clogher. Documents of the time record the first entry, dated 3 December 1619, reading: '*Grant to Geoffrey Middleton the office of public schoolmaster in Fermanagh, continuing to hold during good behavour*', and the second entry, of the same date, reading '*Presentation of Geoffrey Middleton, MA, to Drummully rect., Clogher diocese vacant by lapse or otherwise and in the gift of the Crown*'. Shortly afterwards, Balfour was justly rewarded for his civic efforts with ennoblement (at a price, no doubt), taking the title of Lord Balfour of Clanawaley.

A review of the first ten years

So, after some ten years of indecision, intrigue, prevarication and feuding following the initial Royal Proclamation of 1608, the Free School for County Fermanagh was finally established at Ballybalfour in 1618, and was not located at Lisgoole or Enniskillen, as had been variously considered. Most of the Free Schools in the other four counties were also established around this time, Dungannon Royal School claiming to be the first, with a documented start, albeit in a temporary location, around 1614.

The answers to the three opening questions would now appear to be relatively clear:

- Five Royal Schools were established under the Royal Proclamation of 1608. King Charles I later issued instructions, about 1629, for the foundation of two further Royal Grammar Schools (one for County Wicklow and one in King's County). There is further recognition of this initial figure of five in a memorandum in the Irish House of Lords about 1640, which names only five Royal Schools in Ireland (those that were established by the Proclamation of 1608) for Armagh, Cavan, Dungannon, Enniskillen and Raphoe.
- The delays and different conditions in establishing all the Free Schools were due to government bureaucracy and indifferent county and Church administration.
- Finally, the inhabitants of the county should be grateful to Balfour who, for whatever motives, was able to offer a substantial new school building for its citizens and the services of his personal chaplain to take up the Mastership of the Free School for Fermanagh within the fortified environs of Castle Balfour.

Some historians argue that none of the Schools should claim a royal foundation until after King James had died and was succeeded by his son, King Charles I. In about 1626, during the second year of his reign, King Charles issued Letters Patent, giving final directives to the Primate in Armagh for the allocation of all endowed lands scheduled for use by the five Free Schools and Trinity College, Dublin. In short, those historians will claim that it was King Charles that finally legitimised the 1608 Proclamation a legal entity.

A feud develops with the new Bishop of Clogher

When the Right Reverend James Spottiswood, DD (1567-1645) was appointed Bishop of Clogher in 1621, in succession to Montgomery, he was enraged to find that the Free School for Fermanagh had been established at Ballybalfour and not in the Shire town of Enniskillen, as originally planned. He immediately lodged a protest with the Privy Council in London.

He pointed out that Enniskillen had been officially incorporated as the county town for at least six to eight years before the approval for the Free School at Ballybalfour, and that the Letters Patent for the development of the Shire town included provisions for a site on which to build this Free School. He argued that the Free School for Fermanagh must be under the administration of the appointed Constable of Enniskillen, Sir William Cole, and should be located in the Shire town for Fermanagh. Furthermore, Spottiswood suggested that Balfour's scheme to give Middleton (scathingly called *'Balfour's creature'*) a fee farm lease of the School's endowed lands was merely a ruse by Balfour to acquire the School's proposed endowment lands by long-term stealth. He accused him with the cutting suggestion *'that perhaps his eyes were set upon to swallow them'*. There is no evidence to support the actual grant of a fee farm lease to Middleton, although his wife Bridget and two children did receive a King's letter, c1626, notifying them of financial assistance in the event of Middleton's death.

Fisticuffs and a murder charge

History indicates that Spottiswood and Balfour became engaged in a drawn-out feud on this and several other domestic matters, in which they came to fisticuffs on at least one occasion, when visiting the King in London.

Conflict developed also between their respective households and staff in Fermanagh, which eventually led to a raid on Portora Castle grounds by Balfour activists, to drive away cattle belonging to the Spottiswood family. During this fracas a local official was injured and subsequently died, so the incident developed into charge of murder against Spottiswood himself. Fortunately, the personal accusation of murder involving the Bishop was eventually dismissed by a Dublin Court. The detailed arguments between Spottiswood and Balfour, though historically interesting, are outside the scope of this narrative. However, they certainly set the scene and may account for the eventual removal of the first Free School in later years from the Ballybalfour site to its rightful location in the Shire town of Enniskillen.

Little else is known about the life of Middleton and his tenure as the first Master of the Free School, or his appointment, by Royal Assent, as the Rector of Drummully. Originally Drummully was the site of the old Celtic Church of St Coman, near Clones in County Monaghan; later, during the early Victorian era (c1844), the medieval Church was demolished and a new one built (c1864) and renamed the Church of St Mary.

Bishop James Spottiswood, from a portrait in Clogher Cathedral (© Dean and Chapter of Clogher). Spottiswood came from an influential Scottish family and was on intimate terms with the King James I, and succeeded Bishop Montgomery to the See of Clogher. He immediately rented Portora Castle, from Sir William Cole, and set about reorganising his dioceses. Clogher had suffered administratively under Montgomery, who had two additional large bishoprics in his tenure and paid little attention to matters in Fermanagh. Spottiswood, who was also a Privy Councillor immediately clashed with Sir William Cole and Lord Balfour over the distribution of escheated lands earmarked for funding the Clogher dioceses and those allocated for the Free School for Fermanagh. Spottiswood was a successful champion for the Free School and over the years ensured that all charitable funds were legally put in order. Spottiswood fled the county during the Irish Rebellion of 1641 and died in London 1643. He lies buried in Westminster beside his brother, a former Chancellor of Scotland and onetime Archbishop of Glasgow and latterly also St Andrews.

The Free School for Fermanagh
Develops initially at Castle Balfour

> ### Reverend Richard Bourke, BD, MA
> #### (s, 1626-1661)
>
> - Entered Trinity College as a scholar 1614 (thought to be listed as Richard Burgh in TCD Matriculation Book).
> - Graduated BD 1621 and (possibly) MA, c1624.
> - Appointed Rector of Clonnkyne, 1624.
> - Appointed to the Mastership of the Free School of Fermanagh by King Charles I on 28 September 1626.
> - By 1628, was known to have appointed Ushers (assistants) to undertake most of his official school duties, while he remained Rector of Clonnkyne.
> - Probably transferred the Free School from Ballybalfour to Schoolhouse Lane, Enniskillen, c1641-1643.
> - Interviewed by Commissioners, c1643, on events surrounding rebellion, at Ballybalfour, which was initiated by local chieftain - Ruari Maguire.
> - Longest serving Master of the School.

> ### Thomas Dunbar, MA (died 1694)
> #### (s, 1661-92)
>
> - Appointed under Commonwealth Rules, 23 May 1659, as Master of the Royal School, Raphoe.
> - Married the daughter of Dean Conyngham of Raphoe, Donegal.
> - Appointed on 15 or 16 July 1661 by Letters Patent, Charles II, to be Master of the Royal School at Enniskillen.
> - Dunbar's appointment to Enniskillen was subject to a bar on acceptance of any future ecclesiastical preferment.
> - Deemed to be an important county figure in opposition during the Williamite Wars, and attainted by the Irish Parliament, 1690.

The Rector of Clonnkyne succeeds Middleton as Master

The Reverend Richard Bourke, BD, MA (S, 1626-1661) succeeded Middleton as the second Master of the Free School in 1626. King James I had died the previous year, so both the patronage and Letters Patent for all the Royal Schools now rested in the hands of his son, King Charles I. When King Charles assigned the endowed lands for the Fermanagh Free School, for some strange reason the Letters described its location as being at Lisgoole, a location that had been rejected some 15 years earlier; this must surely be a good example of early government maladministration in the field of education. The mistake is thought to have raised again the whole question of why the Free School for Fermanagh was still not situated within the county town, and may have contributed to the eventual removal of the School from Ballybalfour to Enniskillen during Bourke's Mastership.

Bourke and his Ushers (assistants) were the subject of an official government inspection after he had been in post for some two or three years. They were reported in Fermanagh public records, c1629, as diligent in their duties at the Free School at Ballybalfour, with the following additional information: '*the number of schollers in the said schoole are now three score or there abouts, all except three being Irish natives*'. It is interesting to note that, after ten or more years at Ballybalfour, the Free School for Fermanagh was flourishing, and had not only encompassed and integrated with Plantation stock but also catered for the local native Irish. Bourke continued in his post as Master for thirty-five years, until 1661, when the **Reverend Thomas Dunbarre, MA** (S, 1661-1692; hereafter Dunbar) was appointed the third '*Master of the Free School for Fermanagh (Eniskillin)*'.

Dunbar had been appointed under Cromwell's Commonwealth as the Master at Raphoe, but he was now appointed to Fermanagh (Enniskillen) on 15 July 1661, by Letters Patent of Charles II, where his terms of engagement were expressed as: '*to enjoy the office as amply as Geoffrey Middleton or Richard Bourke or any previous master provided that if the said Thomas Dunbar did accept any ecclesiastical preferment, the grant of Master and custody of the school shall become void*'.

Castle Balfour torched during Irish Rebellion of 1641

There are no known surviving documents outlining the change of the School's location from Ballybalfour to Enniskillen, but logic requires that it must have been after 22 January 1629, when we read of the School's inspection at Castle Balfour, and before 15 July 1661, when Dunbar arrived on the scene at Enniskillen.

However, it was well recorded that the town of Lisnaskea and Castle Balfour, were spectacularly torched during the Insurrection of 1641, under orders from the displaced local Irish chieftain, Ruari Maguire. The living quarters of Castle Balfour were sufficiently damaged for the garrison inhabitants to move out of the precincts, but there is no information on the fate of the remaining fortified facilities. Furthermore, since Balfour and his two surviving sons had all died without male issue in the two or three years before 1636, the Balfour dynasty and the Clanawaley title had become extinct. The Balfour name was no longer of any influence in the future development of the Free School.

A further clue emerges in 1643, when a Commission was appointed to establish the causes of the Irish Rebellion of 1641. It is officially recorded in the Manuscript Depositions of Trinity College, Dublin, that evidence was obtained from a '*Richard Bourke of Enniskillen, C. of Fermanagh, Bachelor in Divinity, Minister of God's word*' about the incident. Most historians have assumed this Bourke to be the incumbent Master of the Free School, and have deduced it was most likely that, by 1643, both he and his pupils had already moved from the Castle Balfour site to Enniskillen, some time before the date of this inquiry. However, alternative opinion suggests that the move may have been much later, taking place just before the appointment of Dunbar as Master.

To complete the record, Castle Balfour was repaired in 1653 and then occupied and used by General Ludlow of the Parliamentary Forces during the Cromwell purge of Ireland. The strategic importance of the area led to the town changing hands many times over the years before 1821, when it finally came under the control of the Earls of Erne, by purchase. Castle Balfour was inhabited right up to the early nineteenth century, when it again caught fire and was finally abandoned.

Castle Balfour, a fine example of an historic Plantation castle, has been undergoing a sensitive programme to restore it as a landmark and focal point in Lisnaskea. The original Schoolhouse site is no longer visible and was probably demolished, and the foundations cleared, before its footprint was incorporated into the layout of the present cemetery.

The Enniskillen Free School
Starts as Enniskillen Free School and becomes Enniskillen Royal School

The move to Enniskillen
Enniskillen had grown considerably under the Governorship of Cole, whose administrative services had been recognised by the Crown, in 1617, with a baronetcy. Cole had a long and distinguished career as Town Governor, and by the early 1640s, in spite of his age, was also a serving Colonel with the local militia. He also found time to become a Member for the Borough of Enniskillen in the Irish Parliament. Right from the early days, a site and sufficient space had been allocated by Cole for building the Free School and its associated recreational gardens; it just lay dormant in Enniskillen town until the School moved from Castle Balfour.

The School's location in Enniskillen was described some years later by the Dean of Clogher, the Very Reverend William Henry, as occupying grounds in the town '*on the northern side of the church by the Lough*'.

Further, a manuscript held in the British Museum (Sloane, No. 202), gives an account of 'Publique Schooles for the Province of Ulster, 1673', as recorded in writing by the incumbent Protestant Primate in Armagh, Dr James

Margetson. It states: '*In the Diosese of Clogher there is a free schoole at Eniskillen, endowed to the yearly value* 120 *pound¸ per annum, whereof a Mr Thomas Dunbarre is Master*'.

The move to Enniskillen, the end of the Commonwealth and the restoration of the Monarchy in 1660 now started a trend of referring to the school as the Enniskillen Royal School. It is interesting to note that the endowments for Fermanagh were £120 per annum, two to three times the value of the other Royal Schools: Cavan £40, Raphoe £45, Armagh £30 and Dungannon £60. Dunbar's final years were turbulent, owing to the political and civil disturbances of the Williamite Wars (1688-91). The Protestant population of Enniskillen raised a volunteer force to defend the town and defeated the approaching Jacobite army. Dunbar, as a prominent Enniskillen citizen, was attainted (outlawed) by the King James II Parliament in Dublin.

Enniskillen town map showing Schoolhouse Lane and the site of the Free School (73). The map unfortunately contradicts the description given by the Dean of Clogher, who stated 'the school occupied a site on the northern side of the church'. The use of Castle Balfour during the Cromwell era suggests that the move of the Free School to Enniskillen was more likely to have been undertaken in 1643 than the alternative suggestion of 1661.

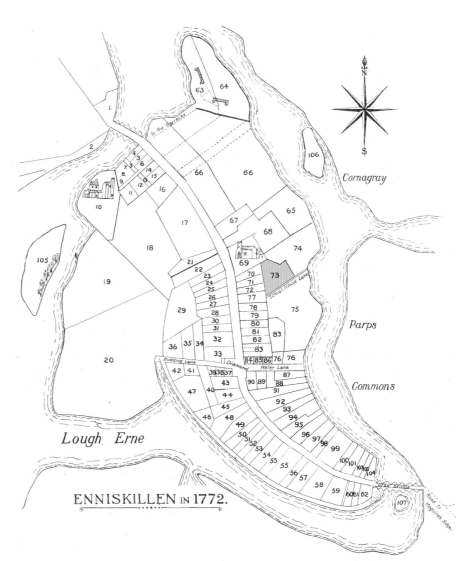

ENNISKILLEN in 1772.

GEORGE BENNIS, MA, MD

(S, 1692-1700)

- George Bennis was born in County Clare.
- Entered TCD at the age of 22, and graduated BA in 1688.
- Obtained his MA and graduated with the degree of MB in 1691.
- Appointed to the Mastership, 16 March 1692.
- Continued the active study of medicine and was awarded an MD in 1699, a year before his retirement.

A Doctor at the School

Following Dunbar, **George Bennis, MA, MD** (S, 1692-1700) was appointed as the new Master of the Enniskillen Royal School on 16 March 1692. A native of County Clare, he entered Trinity College, Dublin as a mature scholar (aged 22) in 1685. He graduated initially in Arts and then continued his graduate studies in the Arts coupled with a further degree in Medicine. In the Summer of 1691 he was simultaneously awarded an MA in Arts and an MB in Medicine. During his appointment and tenure as Master, he eventually obtained his Doctorate in Medicine in 1699; the following year he resigned from the Mastership to pursue a medical career.

Another medical Master

The fifth Master to be appointed to the School, in 1700, was **John Dennis, DD, FTCD** (1700-1714). He was a youthful entry to Trinity College as a scholar (aged 16), and graduated initially in Arts. He accepted a Fellowship, before he, like his predecessor, changed to Medicine. Dennis was eclectic and soon diverted to Theology, receiving his doctorate in 1711. However, his main interest lay in parochial duties, and during 1712 he was collated to the parish of Cleenish, whereupon he resigned his Mastership. He was later appointed as the Rector of St Patrick's Church, Monaghan (1715-25) and was the incumbent at Magheraculmony (1725-45). Before his death in 1745 Dennis was appointed the Vicar General of Clogher.

A review of the first 100 years

The Free School for Fermanagh had been established at Ballybalfour. After some 30 years it had moved to Enniskillen town, where it was known as the Enniskillen Free School and latterly the Enniskillen Royal School. The first two Masters had been clerical scholars, followed by Thomas Dunbar, a schoolmaster/administrator. He in turn was followed by two Arts graduates, Bennis and Dennis, both of whom later embraced the medical profession. These two Masters must have been very early students of the sciences associated with medicine, since Trinity College, Dublin did not formally establish its Medical School and Chair of Medicine until 1711.

There is no doubt that the Mastership of Fermanagh and its generous supporting endowment were able to attract high-class academics from Trinity College, but this also raises the question: what was the relevance of its highly scholastic curriculum to the preparation of local inhabitants for work and employment in the emerging community of County Fermanagh?

One can see from the Plantation map that County Fermanagh was an interesting and highly diverse Plantation. It was one of the few areas in Ulster with a well-balanced allocation of English and Scottish Undertakers, Servitors, native Irish and deserving Irish making up the new range of landowners and tenants, many of whom eventually received Letters Patent from the Crown for their land grants. Of the five Royal Schools, the Free School for Fermanagh enjoyed the wealthiest foundation and largest endowments.

The Mastership of the School has always been considered a prestigious appointment throughout academic circles in Ireland. From the very outset, the Free School for Fermanagh (or Portora, as we now call it) was well-connected to both Trinity College, Dublin and the established Church of Ireland, but it has never discriminated on religious grounds in its intake of pupils. Indeed, over the centuries, Jews, Muslims and Christians have all been accepted and educated within its walls.

Among the more interesting students of those early years was **Charles Leslie** (OP, 1660-64), second son of Robert Leslie, Bishop of Clogher (known

REV. JOHN DENNIS, D.D. 1700-14

JOHN DENNIS, MD, FTCD
(s, 1700-1714)

- Dennis was the son of a Waterford merchant and entered Trinity in 1691 at the age of 16.
- Graduated BA in 1696, then changed to Medicine and was admitted to a Fellowship 1697.
- Appointed to Mastership of Enniskillen on 17 May 1700.
- Resigned his Fellowship 17 June 1700 having accepted the position of Master at Enniskillen.
- Finally diverted to Theology when he obtained the degrees of BD 1709 and DD 1711.

CHARLES GRATTAN, MA, FTCD

(s, 1714-1745)

- One of seven sons of Dr Patrick Grattan, Senior Fellow of Trinity College, Dublin and a family friend of Dean Jonathan Swift.
- Entered Trinity College, 1701, at age 13. Graduated BA 1706 and MA 1710.
- Took a Fellowship, but was removed on 26 May 1713, having refused Holy Orders.
- Appointed to Mastership of Free School of Enniskillen on 5 May 1714.
- Died in Fermanagh, 13 June 1746, and was buried in Enniskillen churchyard.
- His wife subsequently died at Belturbet, 1756.

REV. WILLIAM DUNKIN, D.D. 1746-63

REVEREND WILLIAM DUNKIN, DD

(1709-65)

(s, 1746-63)

- Entered Trinity College, thanks to a substantial bequest from an aunt.
- Graduated BA in 1729 and MA in 1732.
- Ordained in 1735.
- Was awarded a DD in 1744.
- As a young man had a reputation for foolish acts and clever poetry.
- His appointment to the Mastership, by the Earl of Chesterfield, Lord Deputy of Ireland, on 6 August 1746, was described as to 'The Great School of Enniskillen'.

as the 'fighting bishop'). After his schooldays in Enniskillen, Charles went on to Trinity College, Dublin, took Holy Orders and became an Anglican clergyman. However, while Chancellor of Connor he refused to take the oath of allegiance to William and Mary, on the grounds that their accession broke the principle of the Divine Right of Succession. Leslie left Ireland and eventually became the Protestant chaplain to the exiled Stuart court in Europe, and wrote extensively on religious matters.

The Classical School
A term used by Dean Swift to enhance the Mastership of Grattan

A long mastership begins with Grattan
The strong link and ties with Trinity College, Dublin continued when **Charles Grattan, MA, FTCD** (S, 1714-46) was appointed the sixth Master of the Royal School at Enniskillen. Grattan (1688-1746) was the son of a Senior Fellow at Trinity College, and entered the College at the very youthful age of thirteen, graduating BA at the age of only eighteen in 1706. He then obtained a Fellowship, but was forced to relinquish the position three years later when he refused to take Holy Orders. Dean Jonathan Swift was a long-standing friend of the Grattan family and later, when on more familiar personal terms, he wrote a poem to Grattan, in which the following lines appear:

'But that the world might think I played the fool,
I'd change with Charlie Grattan for his school,
What fine cascades, what vistas might I make,
Fix'd in the centre of the Iernian lake'.

During the Grattan Mastership, a young **John Cole** (OP, 1720-26), a direct decendant of the first Constable of Enniskillen, Sir William Cole, received his early education at the School. Cole was later to become Baron Mount-Florence of Florence Court. **Margetson Armar** (OP, 1716), who eventually owned the Castle Coole estate, in addition to the Blessington properties at Fivemiletown, was a fellow pupil a few years earlier. Grattan had a long Mastership of the School, over thirty-two years, and died on 13 June 1746. He is buried at Enniskillen. He was responsible for initiating the strong classical tradition at the School, which was to last for nearly 200 years, until the Education Act 1947 (NI) permitted entry to the Upper School at Portora without the taking of a written or viva voce Latin examination.

The Great School of Enniskillen
Reference by the Lord Deputy in Dublin describing Enniskillen Royal School

A further link with Dean Jonathan Swift
Grattan was succeeded as Master by the **Reverend Dr William Dunkin, DD** (S, 1746-1763). Dunkin was officially appointed by Lord Chesterfield, Lord Deputy of Ireland, in 1746 to 'the great school of Enniskillen', and retained the Mastership until 1763. As a young student in Dublin, Dunkin (1709-

1765) had gained a reputation for foolish acts and clever poetry. Thanks to a bequest from an aunt, Dunkin had been soundly educated in classics at Trinity College, Dublin, where he was a brilliant scholar and quickly came to the notice of Dean Jonathan Swift of St Patrick's Cathedral. Prior to his Mastership at Enniskillen, Dunkin had been the Master of the Cathedral School, Dublin, and was also a former Latin Master at St Patrick's School, Dublin. Swift had already remarked of him: '*A gentleman of much wit and the best English as well as Latin Poet in this kingdom*'.

On his death, Dunkin was further described by Swift as a gentleman of genius, learning, friendship and hospitality. His burlesque, *The Parson's Revels* (published posthumously in 1770), was highly regarded and describes a series of characters representing different levels of contemporary Irish society. Seamus Deane, a twentieth-century Irish literary critic, called him 'probably the most underrated poet of eighteenth-century Ireland'.

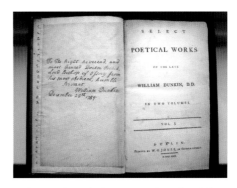

Title page from 'Select poetical works of the late William Dunkin DD', published in 1796.

Developing an all-Ireland reputation

The growing popularity of the Enniskillen Royal School, as a place of both social and academic excellence, increased considerably during the Masterships of Grattan and Dunkin. The School generally attracted an all-Ireland mix of pupils, because it had developed a sound reputation for academic excellence, classical scholarship and a highly successful stream of entrants to Trinity College, Dublin, by means of both tied scholarships and open exhibitions.

In Georgian times, university students generally preferred to study the Classics, Law, Divinity and Philosophy. The advent of Medicine at Trinity had only just begun by about 1711, and Science and Engineering did not develop into popular subjects leading to a professional career until Victorian times. During the era of Grattan and Dunkin, the Enniskillen Royal School could be justly proud of its alternative names, when it was regularly described in both conversation and text as 'The Classical School of Enniskillen' and 'The Great School of Enniskillen'.

George III's Charter appoints Noble

The next Master, the **Reverend Mark Noble, MA** (S, 1763-1795), was appointed by the Earl of Hertford as the eighth Master of the School. Noble (1725-94) had entered Trinity College, Dublin as a sizar in 1745, securing his MA in 1754. However, he found on taking up his appointment in Enniskillen that his predecessor had engineered a lease of the lands endowed to the School, and had placed them in trust for the Dunkin family, reserving only a nominal rent of £310 per annum for the personal use of the Master.

Noble also found that the accommodation in the Schoolhouse Lane site, now well over a hundred years old, was dingy and cramped for both staff and pupils. This was disappointing for such a well-known academic establishment. In spite of its previous academic success under the Masterships of Grattan and Dunkin, the numbers enrolled had gradually fallen to just five boarders and nineteen dayboys, of whom fifteen were free scholars. This fall in numbers was attributed to the poor physical state of the school buildings and the general lack of decent domestic facilities for both the staff and student bodies.

REVEREND MARK NOBLE, MA

(1725 -94)

(s, 1763-1795)

- Entered Trinity College, Dublin as a sizar in 1745. Graduated BA in 1749 and secured an MA in 1754.

- Appointed to the Mastership of Enniskillen Royal School by the Marquis of Hertford, 1761, on the death of Dunkin.

- Found that Dunkin had effected a lease of the School lands in trust for his family.

- Arranged with Lord Mount-Florence (Enniskillen) to vacate the Schoolhouse Lane site and build a larger new school on Portora Hill to accommodate 90 boys. Estimated cost was £3,000.

- For this transaction Lord Enniskillen exchanged more than 30 acres of his Portora townland for a much greater area of escheated lands owned by the School near Florence Court.

JOSEPH STOCK D.D., F.T.C.D. HEADMASTER 1795-98 BISHOP OF KILLALA 1798., WATERFORD 1810-13

REVEREND DR JOSEPH STOCK, DD
(1741-1813)

(S, 1795-98)

- Gained an entrance scholarship to TCD in 1759 and obtained his BA in 1761 followed by an MA in 1764.

- Took a Fellowship 1763 and then studied at Divinity School where he obtained BD in 1771 and DD in 1776.

- Appointed to Royal School Enniskillen 1795, and after only three years in post he succeeded Dr John Porter as Bishop of Killala and Achonry.

- At Portora he managed to transfer the rentals and leases for the School's endowment lands to his brother and other family members.

- Stock was a well-known author of scholastic editions of Tacitus and Demosthenes, which were in regular use by a number of schools.

- Captured during 1798 uprising in the West of Ireland, he was made a prisoner in his own Bishop's palace by General Humbert of the French invasion force.

- Wrote a controversial account of his time in captivity, which conflicted with the views of the British Government.

- Finally translated to the Bishopric of Lismore (Waterford), where he died in 1813.

The move up the hill

During the Schoolhouse Lane years, the School's endowed lands comprised 2,537 acres of profitable farmland and a further assortment of 801 acres of bog and slob (water-logged) land. This generated an income for the Master of about £1,270 per annum. In 1777 proposals and funding for the design and construction of new buildings were presented by Noble to the Education Commissioners, and after approval by the School Board, work on the foundations commenced. Over the next few years a substantial new building complex and an imaginative landscaped area for Enniskillen Royal School appeared on the crest of Portora Hill, and still dominate the northern skyline of Enniskillen town.

The land at Portora (33 acres) had been acquired by Noble from the Earl of Enniskillen, in exchange for an area of the School's endowed land, which was four times larger but of lesser value, adjoining the Florence Court estate. Having successfully completed this transaction, Noble now challenged other leases on the School's endowed lands which had been assigned to the family of his predecessor. Although he was successful in reversing the terms, he found himself out of pocket by £1,400 when the courts refused to award his legal costs. In total, Noble spent nearly £3,000 of his personal money to complete the new school on Portora Hill. This was more or less confirmed after his death in 1794, when his successor was instructed to pay the sum of £2,600 to his legal representatives, as partial compensation for the benefits provided by Noble. It should be noted that Noble also had an additional stipend from his curacy of Aghalurcher Parish Church (c1765), which pre-dated his appointment as Master of the Free School.

The School's geographical setting on Portora Hill, overlooking the River Erne and the nearby town, set it apart from most other educational establishments. When the Portora site first opened for business, during 1779, an advertisement in the *Belfast Newsletter* read: '*The Free School of Enniskillen will be opened on 25 inst in the House built by Mr Noble for the reception of 100 boarders. Prices are 5 guineas for boarders per quarter and 1 guinea for day scholars*'. It was quite some years before these ambitious figures were eventually attained, and they probably had to wait until the Mastership of Greham in the late 1830s before they were exceeded.

The main entrance to the School was embellished with wrought-iron gates, and the former right of way, which ran up and over the hill, was closed after a new road was constructed to Ballyshannon around the bottom of Portora Hill.

A Bishop in the making

The long-established and by now almost perpetual link with Trinity College, Dublin was reinforced, when the **Reverend Dr Joseph Stock, DD, FTCD** (S, 1795-98) was appointed to succeed Noble. As a youth, Stock (1740-1813) had been educated in Dublin, where his family were well-known hosier traders in one of the more fashionable areas of the capital, No. 1 Dame Street. Stock had already been appointed a Fellow of Trinity College, before attending the Divinity School, after which he obtained a Church preferment (1779) in the diocese of Raphoe. He was subsequently appointed to the Mastership

of Enniskillen Royal School in early 1795. Stock was deemed to be a very accomplished classical scholar, an excellent linguist (French) and a man of much culture. He published scholarly editions of Demosthenes and Tacitus, which were in standard use for schools over many years.

A report by a French visitor (M de Latocnaye) to Portora, while touring Ireland during 1796-7, is translated as follows: '*the place of schoolmaster at Enniskillen has become a sort of bishopric; it brings in about two thousand pounds sterling per annum. However the person who occupies the situation at present, Dr Stock (with whom I passed the two days I spent at Enniskillen) is a very highly educated man and besides having twelve or fifteen children of his own, has five or six nieces or nephews that he brings up himself and seven or eight boarders at one hundred guineas per annum. I have seen very few houses in which there were so many children, where such order reigned; but, on the other hand I never saw such a schoolmaster*'.

Stock's Mastership was short, however, since after only three years in post he was appointed Bishop of Killala and Achonry. He was barely in post at Killala when the French invaded County Mayo in 1798, and he was held prisoner in his own Bishop's palace by General Humbert. As a fluent French speaker, Stock was a genial asset for liaison with the French troops deployed in the area. The report on events was believed to have caused considerable embarrassment to the government authorities in both Dublin and London.

The architects for the original design of Portora House are not known, but Lord Enniskillen and Noble had clearly agreed that the building should be significant, gracious and befitting the site.

REVEREND ROBERT BURROWES, DD

(1759-1841)

(s, 1798-1819)

- Entered Trinity in 1772, aged 13 years, graduating with a BA in 1777.
- He took a Fellowship in 1782 and his MA in 1783.
- Joining the Divinity School he obtained BD, 1790, and DD, 1792.
- Appointed Rector of Cappagh 1796, and later exchanged for Drumragh (Omagh) 1807.
- Appointed Master, by Letters Patent, dated 24 January 1798.
- Befriended Henry Francis Lyte as an orphaned schoolboy, and paid for his education at Portora and Trinity College, Dublin.
- Conditions of his appointment stipulated residency at Portora and no more than 30 days' absence from the School in any one year.
- Was appointed Provost of Enniskillen.
- Resigned the Mastership and retired from teaching to become Dean of Cork, 1819.
- Died 13 September 1841, aged 82.

Burrowes is appointed

Stock resigned his Mastership on 24 January 1798 and was succeeded by the **Reverend Dr Robert Burrowes, DD, FTCD** (S, 1798-1820), who guided the School, by now one of the leading boys' educational establishments in Ireland, from its second to its third century.

Burrowes' first task was to void the £800 lease on the School's endowed land, which had been assigned in about 1795 to Steven Stock Esq, Dublin (the previous Master's brother), at a favourable amount of £1,473 from under-tenants, and then transferred to his brother, the Right Reverend Bishop Joseph Stock, the previous Master. This funding was now due for reassignment as compensation to Burrowes. The original change of lease for the School's endowed lands had been approved by the previous Protestant Primate (Newcomen), although the new Primate (the Hon William Stuart) considered the transaction to be somewhat tawdry, if not fraudulent.

Burrowes – the educationist

The Burrowes era at the School provides an interesting insight into education of that period. He was an efficient administrator and fortunately committed many of his thoughts to paper, so there are factual records of his ideas on education. These he laid out in a series of learned papers that he formulated for *Transactions*, the Society journal for the newly established Royal Irish Academy. He advocated the introduction of more science into Irish education, and campaigned against the growing tendency of the Irish aristocracy and aspiring landed gentry to send their sons for schooling in England. Burrowes was no doubt encouraged by correspondence and recommendations from two of his friends, Judge Robert Day and the Earl of Glandore (a kinsman), on the subject of educating a mutual male relative currently resident in Ireland: '*My scheme of education for one intended for Irish residence would be to send him to Austin, Carpendale [Armagh] or Burrowes [Portora] from thence to Trinity College, Dublin, till he took his degree, from thence to Oxford for a few years, and from thence as long as he liked to the Continent. His earliest and fondest prepossessions would thus be Irish while as his understanding was unfolded and ripened he would form in England useful and respectable acquaintance perhaps a matrimonial connexion and some such scheme as mine is become the more necessary to counteract the physical act of Union*'.

Burrowes – the humanitarian

Henry Francis Lyte (OP, 1803-1809) and his elder brother were both pupils at the School under Burrowes. When Henry was only nine, his father (a marine officer serving in the West of Ireland) deserted the family, and very shortly afterwards both his mother and elder brother died in tragic circumstances.

Burrowes recognised the young boy's talent, took Henry into his home and paid for the rest of his schooling and education. This was a truly compassionate act for someone already engaged in educating five children of his own. A tablet to Lyte has been erected in the School Chapel. After study at Portora and Trinity College, Dublin, he went on to write the words of 80 to 90 hymns, including the two well-known favourites, 'Praise, My Soul, the King

of Heaven' and 'Abide with Me'. The tablet in the chapel states that the latter
was the favourite hymn of King George V. One story behind this dates back
to 1927, when the newly formed BBC decided to broadcast the FA Cup Final
for the first time. In those days, pre-match entertainment comprised popular
songs and community hymn-singing, led by a conductor in a white tail-coat.
King George himself was to be present at this first BBC broadcast and protocol
naturally dictated that the King should give final approval of the arrangements
for the pre-match entertainment. He requested that the final item on the music
programme before kick-off should be his favourite hymn, 'Abide with Me'.

Burrowes – financial administrator

Around 1807, it was recorded that the enrolment at the School was sixty-five
boarders and between twelve and sixteen day boys. Fees for boarding were set
at 32 guineas per annum and an entrance fee of 6 guineas; day scholars were
charged 6 guineas per annum with an entrance fee of one and a half guineas.
The 1807 report on the School by the Commissioners of Education stated '*that
the (current) endowment of this School is unquestionably too large to be enjoyed
by the Master alone; when the lands are let (as it appears to us they ought to be)
there is little doubt of their producing two thousand per annum and upwards*'.

The final section of this report goes on to say: '*a quarter of this sum would in
our opinion be a sufficient allowance to the Head Master. Another quarter would,
we think, be advantageously applied to the foundation of the Second and Third
Masterships, at three hundred and two hundred pounds per annum. A great
part of the remainder should, in our opinion, be employed in the maintenance of
scholars on the foundation agreeably to the original intention in the establishment
of these Institutions, which are expressly denominated "FREE SCHOOLS"*'.

The question of the School's endowments and those of all the Royal Schools
rumbled on for many years until finally, in 1813, an Act was passed in Dublin
providing for '*the appointment of Commissioners for the Regulation of the several
endowed schools of public and private foundation in Ireland*'.

Fees, funding and discontent from Burrowes

In 1813 this new Commission met, and immediately put into practice the
final paragraphs of the 1807 report, which instituted a system of foundation
scholarships for the Enniskillen Royal School. The Commissioners also
arranged for a survey of the School lands, and instructed the Master to let and/
or grant leases over a twenty-one-year period to the best and most solvent
tenants.

This arrangement of scholarships financed from the endowed land holdings
of the School greatly reduced the income previously enjoyed by Burrowes.
He concluded that his financial position was best served by getting rid of
all boarders, and the associated rising costs for their food and lodgings, and
concentrating on applying any spare funds to day scholars. Burrowes entered
into a long correspondence with the Commissioners, outlining his scheme
for reducing the number of boarders and providing free places for up to fifty
more day scholars. However, they declined to endorse any of his proposals.
Frustrated by his inability to convert the School into a day school, and slighted

by the aspersions contained in the final report issued by the Commissioners of Education, Burrowes decided to leave the field of education.

He used his considerable influence in clerical circles to secure for himself the appointment of the Dean of Cork. Burrowes was an astute man, so, before his formal resignation, he procured an undertaking from the Commissioners to refund him the substantial costs that he had incurred for improvements and alterations to the School during his tenure as Master. He finally resigned his Mastership in 1819, and was succeeded in the following year by the **Reverend Dr Andrew O'Beirne, DD** (S, 1820-1836).

An early map of Portora House and lands, c1820, showing the original area of the Portora townland that was obtained from the Cole family. Unfortunately, the significance of the numbers on the map has been lost, but the plan shows very clearly the layout of the main School and surrounding outbuildings. It is interesting to note that the Reverend Dr Burrowes is listed as the occupant of the nearby Drumlyon, site of the modern Lower Rugby Pitches.

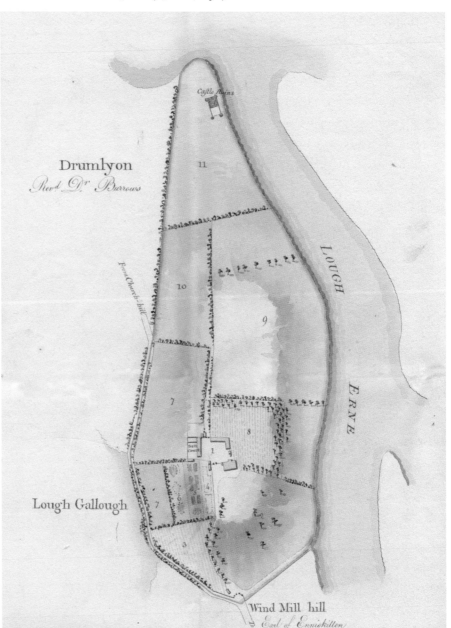

A review of education in Fermanagh

In the 1820s, the Commissioners of Irish Education listed 240 schools in County Fermanagh, of which eight were strictly Roman Catholic and ten solely Protestant: the remainder were non-sectarian in their intake, including the Enniskillen Royal School. Standards varied enormously, from Devenish School, built by a Major Dunbar for the sum of £22 0s 0d and staffed by just one schoolmaster, to the Ely Lodge School, built by the Marquis of Ely, for the sum of £100 0s 0d, its Master receiving a salary of £15 10s 0d per annum.

By contrast, Enniskillen Royal School was known to have cost over £3,000 to build; the final figure to complete the works to the standards of the time approached £4,000. The School also had annual endowments exceeding £2,000 for running the establishment. At the other end of the scale, Glencart School, in nearby Inishmacsaint parish, had been modified from a cow-shed for the total recorded sum of six shillings, and employed Mister James Timoney, a well-respected and very popular teacher, who enjoyed an official salary of £3 10s 0d per annum.

Here we may detour briefly to comment on the role and type of education available at Enniskillen Royal School, for by 1820 the Irish Education Commissioners had completed their review, and Burrowes had resigned the Mastership.

In some ways the academic situation is best illustrated by a publication of Burrowes containing Latin quotations, entitled '*indice verborum omnium que occurrant*', which can be translated as '*an index of all words (quotations) which occur (are known)*', assembled by '*Robertus Burrowes, DD, Magister Scholae Enniskillensis*'. In his preface to the student he states: '*the first of these will teach them the natural analogies which are the sources universally of metaphorical expression and the second will teach them an habitual reference to a radical word, by which alone the significance of derivation can be accurately obtained.*'

As this shows, the Master and staff employed at the Enniskillen Royal School were capable of providing a very high standard of classical education, yet such an argument could be assimilated only by highly intelligent scholars and potential university candidates. Was this the sort of education envisaged by the original Proclamation for the Free School for Fermanagh? Many of the town's inhabitants were beginning to express their doubts through the local press; they suggested that the Free School's education programme was not suited to the needs of Fermanagh boys.

O'Beirne starts with a new contract

O'Beirne (1771-1836) was a noted Hebrew scholar. When he was appointed as Master, the endowed lands and their rental income were firmly in the hands of the Commissioners of Education. From these funds the Commissioners gave O'Beirne £500 per annum as his personal salary, and then made the provision of a further sum of £500 for the payment of his assistant masters as follows:

- The Reverend C Weir, paid £250 per annum
- The Reverend J H Muller, paid £100 per annum
- The Reverend J Collins, probably a similar sum, and J Starmer and Wm Galbraith (employed respectively as English and Writing Masters) were paid from boarding fees.

O'Beirne died during the Easter term of 1836 and was buried in Rossorry Churchyard, where his gravestone has the following Latin text of his own composition, a translation being: '*Beneath are buried the mortal remains of the Rev ANDREW O'BEIRNE LL.D lately Principal (Rector) of the Royal School near Enniskillen – who when now spending his sixteenth year at Portora, died on 29 April 1836, aged 65 years, most humbly hoping that being partaker of Christ through the Holy Spirit of promise, he shall at the last day, together with those*

REVEREND DR ANDREW O'BEIRNE, MA,
LLD (1771-1836)
(s, 1820-1836)

- Entered Trinity College, Dublin, graduating MA 1818, LLD 1819.
- Appointed to the Mastership in 1820.
- Noted Hebrew Scholar; continued the scholastic excellence of the School.
- Died in tenure and was buried at Rossorry Parish Church, 29 April 1836.

Infra conditur quod mortale est,
Rev Andreae O'Beirne, LLD
Nuperrime Scoholae Regiae
juxta Enniskillen
Rectoris
die XXIX Aprilis
AD MDCCCXXXVI,
aetate LXV,
Humillime sperans ut,
Christi particeps per Spiritum
promissionis sanctum
effectus, in Die illa Ultima
una cum iis quos heic amavit
inter hos recensebitur
quibus
timentibus Dominum et
cognitantibus nomen ejus
coram Eo scriptus est liber
monumenti

Text from O'Beirne's gravestone in Rossorry Churchyard, written by him before his death.

he loved here, be enrolled with those for whom, as they feared the LORD, and thought upon his name, a book of remembrance was written before him.'

REVEREND DR JOHN GREHAM, MA, LLD
(died 1873)
(s, 1836- 1857)

- Attended Trinity College, Dublin.
- Graduated BA, 1813, completed his MA, 1818, and LLD, 1827.
- Headmaster Waterford.
- Appointed to Mastership in 1836 on death of O'Beirne.
- Constructed north and south wings to Portora House and modernised domestic washing and heating system.
- Resigned June 1857.
- Died Kingstown February 1873.

A continuing syllabus of Classics for education

O'Beirne's successor was the **Reverend John Greham, LLD** (S, 1836-57), who had been a very successful Master of the Waterford Corporation Free School. When Greham started at Enniskillen, he brought with him a number of boys who had been boarders at his old Waterford School. He was soon given the nickname 'Silver' by the boys in Enniskillen, as it was rumoured that a silver plate had been internally inserted during a surgical operation. Greham was a clergyman schoolmaster and Classical scholar steeped in Latin and Greek grammar.

An interesting picture of this Master, the School and indeed the educational practice of the period is provided by **Lombe Atthill** (OP, 1841-43), a contemporary pupil at the School. Atthill was later to become a distinguished Master of the Rotunda Hospital and President of the Royal College of Surgeons, Ireland. In his autobiography, published posthumously in 1911, and entitled 'Recollections of an Irish Doctor', he wrote of his schooldays at Portora as follows: *'The headmaster certainly was a remarkable, if narrow-minded man; he did his duty to the best of his judgement, and lived for his school. His one object in life was to see his pupils' names in the honour lists, and to attain this he never spared himself. He was in the schoolroom (and there was but one room for the 180 boys) from 7.30 am, summer and winter, till 3.00 pm when school was over, except, of course, the interval of an hour and a half, between nine and ten-thirty o'clock for breakfast and washing, which latter was not expected to be done by the boys before breakfast. Out of school hours we never saw him; his only recreation was a constitutional walk.'*

The fact that Atthill had transferred to Portora from Maidstone Grammar School gives added credence to the fine academic reputation and excellence of Portora, which he described as: *'An Irish school, supposed to be the best in the country, a reputation resting wholly on the fact that pupils from it obtained very frequently first place at the entrance examinations for Trinity College, Dublin. For this they were carefully prepared – indeed crammed.'*

In spite of its unique rural setting, there were few recreational facilities at the school, although there are some historic references to the existence of a fives court and some ball-alleys; nor were there any other extra-curricular activities. Pupils were made to concentrate on their academic and religious studies, with scant attention to leisure pursuits. However, Atthill makes a reference to having successfully organised an internal cricket match, during the early 1840s, which was played on the upper fields at Portora Hill.

Greham proved to be a good businessman

Greham was the second Master to have his salary funded directly by the Commissioners of Education; this had been fixed on his arrival at the School at £500 per annum. The Commissioners then allowed a further sum to finance the following assistant masters: the Reverend Jas C Weir, £250 per annum; Jas Cooper, £150 per annum; John Halpin, £150 per annum; Wm Wood, £100 per annum. An additional teacher, James McLean, was paid personally by the Headmaster.

The Commissioners also reported to the Lord Lieutenant that Greham, only a year after his appointment, had by judicious management created a flourishing financial and intake situation. Now the Commissioners were obliged to expand the Enniskillen Royal School with the erection of additional buildings. They also increased the accommodation for boarders, and created a collection of Classical books in a library designed to be even larger and better than that which had been previously established at Armagh Royal School. Under Greham extra wings were constructed, in 1838, on each side of the central main building. The north wing was initially designated for use as the School's infirmary, while the south wing afforded further classroom accommodation and dormitories for staff and students. The enrolments over the next several years showed a healthy situation, with pupils wishing to travel from most parts of Ireland. Tables for enrolment after the latest building construction were:

Year	Boarders	Dayboys	Free	Total
1839	108	30	Not known	138
1841	100	38	12	150
1842	112	38	16	166

The two additional wings added by Greham were originally labelled 'east' and 'west' wings by W Copeland Trimble in his Tercentenary Pamphlet (1918). Since the School faces east, nowadays, they are more correctly known as 'north' and 'south' wings.

The large drop in numbers attending the School during the period 1843-1845 (below) was due to an epidemic of scarlatina amongst the boarders, when the whole question of school sanitation was thoroughly examined and brought to the attention of the Commissioners. The result was that during 1844, and in the aftermath of the epidemic, the Commissioners of Education authorised '*an additional sum of £400 to be spent on an extensive washing room for personal cleanliness, especially amongst the younger boys*'.

Year	Boarders	Dayboys	Free	Total
1843	87	12	Not known	99
1845	57	0	Not known	57

Health was not the only problem for Greham; the school population was greatly affected by distressed conditions throughout the country, and there was also a drop in the number of dayboy entries from the local Fermanagh area, owing to poor economic conditions brought about by the Famine. In addition, and because of the Famine, the Education Commissioners now faced falling School endowments, as the tenancy holdings plummeted from 331 in 1846 to 271 in 1849, leaving a shortfall of funds for maintenance.

Signs of discontent from Enniskillen and Fermanagh residents

As if these problems were not enough, Greham also faced complaints from the townspeople of Enniskillen in the shape of a subtle press campaign led by William Trimble, the proprietor of the *Fermanagh (Impartial) Reporter*, who in 1855, in evidence to the Commissioners under the Chairmanship of the Marquis of Kildare, given in Enniskillen, stated: '*it is an universal complaint as regards the inhabitants of Enniskillen that the education received at Portora is chiefly, if not altogether classical, and of comparatively little or no utility to men of business and those who wish to push their children forward... the idea of being a free scholar at Portora is looked upon as. a sort of stand by, thou art not as we are,... and the more aristocratic take liberties, using their knives, and they cut and hew a coat or hat that costs a parent money to procure'.*

No doubt this campaign was highly successful in increasing sales of the *Impartial Reporter*, but it was not conducive to an amicable relationship between 'town' and 'gown'. During 1855 a public inquiry was held by the Endowed Schools Commissioners, and the School was inspected the following year by a Dr Ferguson, Assistant Commissioner. Both events had an adverse effect on Greham. He was not accustomed to criticism, and to be fair to him, the Commissioners had never even visited the School for any form of discussion during the previous twenty years.

Greham became very unsettled and before any official report or recommendation could be made by the Commissioners, he decided to resign his Mastership. The eventual report issued by the Endowed Schools (Ireland) Commissioners, c1858, reads: '*Enniskillen School is the most richly endowed of all the Royal Schools... it has not only exhibitions attached to it in connection with Trinity College, but also four scholarships of £20 pa... Dr Greham aided by an efficient staff paid from endowments... attained a high state of efficiency... It was inspected by one of our Assistant Commissioners, who reports favourably of the school, but notices the English instruction as weak and not successful... We are of the opinion that the inhabitants of Enniskillen are entitled to require that a complete course of English and commercial education should be provided in some department of the school...'*

By the time the report had been issued, Greham had already retired and had gone to live in Kingstown (Dun Laoghaire), Co. Dublin, where he died many years later in 1873; he is buried in Mount Jerome Cemetery, Dublin.

Portora Royal School
A name made popular by Steele, but never sanctioned for official documents

Portora Royal School, Enniskillen, becomes the popular name
In 1857, the **Reverend Dr William Steele, DD** (S, 1857-91) was appointed Master, in succession to Greham. Steele (1820-1898) was the choice of the Lord Lieutenant, George Howard, the seventh Earl of Carlisle, who had appointed him two years previously to the Mastership of Raphoe Royal School, Donegal.

It was Steele who popularised the name 'Portora Royal School' as the generally accepted name for the School, although the townspeople of Enniskillen had been using the name Portora and not Enniskillen Royal School for a considerable period.

After ten years in post at Enniskillen, Steele was hailed as the epitome of the great Victorian educator. His Mastership at Portora was compared in style to that of Dr Arnold at Rugby School, and Portora was considered the social Eton of Ireland within many circles of Anglo-Irish society.

This success was also aided by the development of Ireland's railway network. Enniskillen became the hub of several railway branches that were constructed to the north, east and west of the country between 1849 and 1858.

Pupils flocked to the School from all four corners of Ireland. It is to Steele that we owe much of the School's international and all-Ireland reputation which was to continue into the late nineteenth and early twentieth centuries.

In addition to his duties as Master, Steele had been given the living, in 1873, of St Molaise, on Devenish Island, by the Primate in Armagh. However, he installed his son, the **Reverend John Houghton Steele** (OP, 1858-68), as his curate and preached in the parish during school holidays only. A man with an immense sense of public duty, Steele was also Honorary Chaplain to the Duke of Marlborough, Lord Lieutenant of Ireland, and before his death in 1898 had also served a further six Deputies. He held the appointment as Provost (Mayor) of Enniskillen several times, and his son John Houghton was to become the personal chaplain to the fourth Lord Erne.

A prospectus for the School

In 1856, Steele, being the efficient administrator that he was, issued his first formal school prospectus, which remained much the same for many years to come. During 1865 we catch another interesting glimpse of an early era, when, at the behest of the Commissioners, a ban on smoking was introduced throughout the School. Every boy was made to sign a pledge.

Steele concluded that there were only six non-smokers in the School and that it would be very difficult to police a smoking ban, particularly as smoking was considered manly, and so many boys saw it practised by their elders and family members in the army. Nevertheless, the smoking ban was eventually incorporated into the published School Rules, a copy of which was displayed in every classroom.

Building expansion and alterations

A report by the Commissioners of Education for the period 1857-58 to the new Lord Deputy in Dublin, the Earl of Eglinton, records that, following '*the appointment of Steele as the new Master, the numbers of pupils (both boarders and day pupils) increased considerably*'. Their report continues that Steele had been obliged to rent premises in Enniskillen to accommodate pupils and to pay for extra staff from his own pocket. The Commissioners then informed the Lord Deputy that, from the surplus funds arising from the School's endowments, they '*had caused an advertisement in the newspapers for plans and estimates to undertake a major reconstruction of parts of the School and the building of a new Hall*'.

Between 1858 and 1862 Steele expanded the School and its accommodation with several major internal and external improvements. In 1859, the outer wings were connected to the main building with infill additions. The major external constructions, one of which Steele funded out of his own pocket, were situated to the west of the main School façade. One of these consisted of three classrooms on the ground floor, with a spacious room above, to be used by Lower School pupils. Today, this building perpetuates his name as the Steele Hall. The other major construction, for which he obtained official funding and started slightly earlier, was a new infirmary, later known to many Portorans as Liberty Hall. All these buildings are described in greater depth in chapter two.

REVEREND DR WILLIAM STEELE, MA, DD
(1820-1898)
(s, 1857-1891)

- Graduated BA in 1844, MA in 1856, BD and DD in 1874.
- Started life as Curate of Cottismore in Peterborough, 1844-52. Was Assistant Master at Foyle College, 1852-54, and Master of Raphoe Royal School, 1854-57.
- Headhunted by the Lord Deputy in Ireland, Lord Carlisle, to fill the Mastership of Portora following the sudden resignation of the Reverend Dr John Greham in 1856.
- Appointed to the living of St Molaise on Devenish Island by the Primate in Armagh (1873-98), but effectively handed over the duties to his son, Reverend John Houghton Steele, who was also the personal Chaplain to Lord Erne.
- Supervised and partly financed substantial building programmes on the site, including Liberty Hall, and the infills between the main building and the north and south wings. The Steele Hall building was initially financed by Steele himself.
- Presided over the halcyon days for Portora, achieving considerable access to Trinity for the Classics and Sciences and to both RMA Woolwich and RMC Sandhurst for military cadetships.
- Last years of his Mastership were difficult and Steele was permitted to resign on a full pension in 1891.

'No smoking pledge', introduced by Steele following adverse comment from the Commissioners of Education.

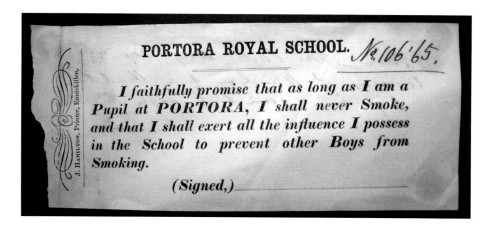

The new teaching and accommodation facilities introduced by Steele, together with the improved travel facilities afforded by the spreading Irish railway network (which reached Enniskillen in the mid-1850s), continued to attract more pupils to the School from all over Ireland, and even a few from England. The number of pupils continued to rise, at one time reaching 50 dayboys and 150 boarders, which necessitated the accommodation of some of them in housing at the foot of the hill in Willoughby Place.

And now – how about a separate school for dayboys?

Early in his Mastership, Steele was made aware by the Town Commissioners that they were not satisfied with the administration of the School's endowments, and that their citizens had been greatly inconvenienced by its move from Schoolhouse Lane to Portora Hill. He was also made aware of their dislike of the unequal treatment of boarders and day pupils, particularly the social stigma associated with free scholars. Steele then conceived the idea of opening a separate school for dayboys in the town of Enniskillen, leaving the Portora complex on the hill for an ever-increasing number of boarders.

A fine house was acquired in Wellington Place, regarded by many as a rather select area of Enniskillen; a dedicated Master was placed in charge of this venture. However, the arrangement did not meet with the approval of the townspeople who, at a specially convened meeting, pointed out that in their view the School existed for the citizens of Enniskillen. Its boys had the right to a free education in the school that was specifically endowed for them, and if any pupils had to go outside the buildings on Portora Hill, then these should be the boarders, who were there as a matter of courtesy and not of right. This meeting totally killed off the new venture and any continuation of a separate school for dayboys; the Wellington Place establishment was closed soon afterwards.

An article in the *Impartial Reporter and Fermanagh Advertiser*, c1864, sums up the events and situation as follows: '*In fact Portora, having become a fashionable school, to which the sons of gentry crowded in large numbers, with a considerable flushness of cash, the official position of the Head Master – he could not well overlook the matter, as the fees came to him – rendered it necessary that he should see how room could be made for pupils of "gentle blood" and, in the agonies of reflection Mr Steele gave birth to the bright idea of excluding the Enniskillen day-boys altogether*'.

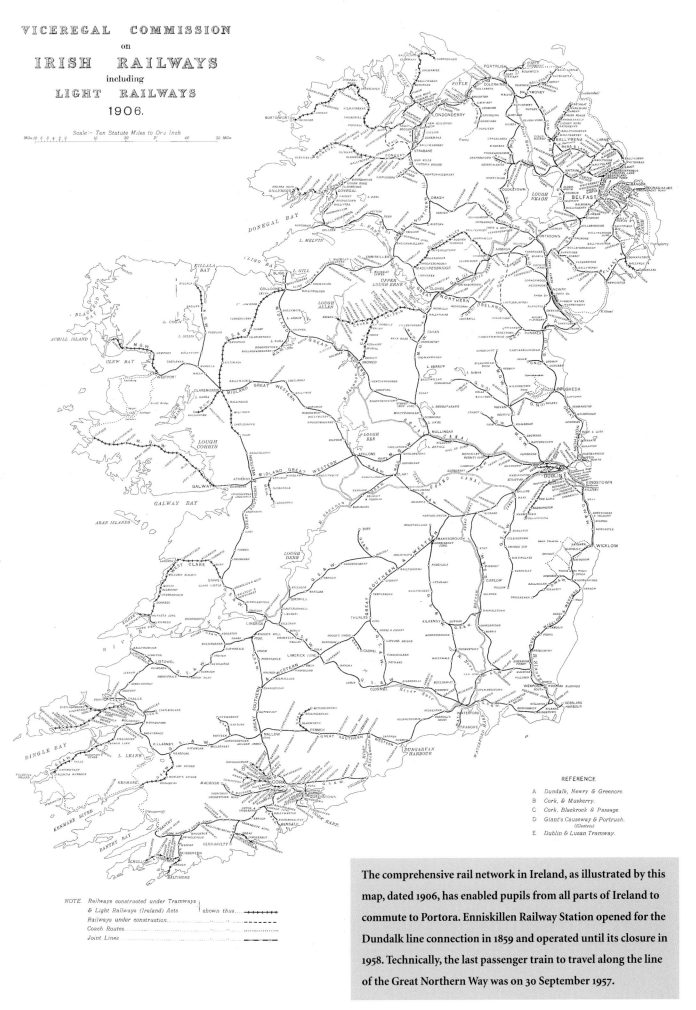

VICEREGAL COMMISSION
on
IRISH RAILWAYS
including
LIGHT RAILWAYS
1906.

Scale:- Ten Statute Miles to One Inch

REFERENCE

A Dundalk, Newry & Greenore.
B Cork, & Muskerry.
C Cork, Blackrock & Passage.
D Giant's Causeway & Portrush.
   (Electric)
E Dublin & Lucan Tramway.

NOTE. Railways constructed under Tramways
& Light Railways (Ireland) Acts   shown thus
Railways under construction
Coach Routes
Joint Lines

The comprehensive rail network in Ireland, as illustrated by this map, dated 1906, has enabled pupils from all parts of Ireland to commute to Portora. Enniskillen Railway Station opened for the Dundalk line connection in 1859 and operated until its closure in 1958. Technically, the last passenger train to travel along the line of the Great Northern Way was on 30 September 1957.

A photograph of the Junior School, 1858, taken on the front steps. It is interesting to note the different styles of headgear worn by the pupils in those days.

The townspeople then decided to force the issue with Steele, and formed a Committee which selected 'a lad' from Enniskillen for whom an education could be demanded under the Charter. The boy was duly interviewed by Steele and willingly accepted for a full and free education at Portora. He rose through his various classes, winning the School medal for English Literature in 1863 and 1867, and entering the Civil Service in the latter year. Forty years later, 'the lad' became one of only two servants of the Crown in Ireland to receive the Imperial Service Order from the Sovereign himself. He finally became the Acting Registrar of Deeds in Ireland, and retired to become a Justice of the Peace for the County of Dublin.

Towards the end of 1864, Steele encountered further signs of discontent from the Enniskillen Town Commissioners. In an attempt to influence the Commissioners of Education, Trimble published complaints in the columns of his newspaper, regarding the increase in fees and charges for dayboys. In the early 1800s, the fees for dayboys had been one and a half guineas a term; during the period 1820-1857, covering the Masterships of O'Beirne and Greham, they had risen to four guineas, and by 1865 Steele had increased them to twelve guineas a term.

A set-back for Steele

On 20 June 1865, in celebration of completing the half year, four boys from the Upper School proceeded down the Lake in a boat belonging to two of the Seniors. Encountering rough weather, the boat capsized and two of the boys were drowned. The subsequent inquiry absolved Steele because of his published rules on boating, and the jury declared him 'wholly blameless'. However, the following year a personal tragedy struck Steele himself, when, in 1866, his eldest son, **Frederick Steele** (OP, 1858-66), was drowned in a boating accident on the river between Devenish Island and the Derryargon shore.

In 1865, the School enrolment showed:

Year	Boarders	Dayboys	Free	Total
1865	112	63	27	202

Within this grand total (not including free pupils), the breakdown by denomination was: Church of Ireland 169; Presbyterian 3; Roman Catholic 3. Again the townspeople complained about the excessive endowments enjoyed directly by the Royal School and not realistically applied for the benefit of the local inhabitants as determined by the founding Proclamation. It is interesting to note that there were as many Roman Catholics at the School as Plantation Presbyterian stock.

A few years later a young **John Sullivan** (OP, 1873-79) arrived at Portora. He was the son of the Lord Chancellor of Ireland, Sir Edward Sullivan, and became a firm friend and colleague of the Reverend John Houghton Steele, the Master's eldest son, who later, after taking Holy Orders, acted for his father as his curate for Devenish. Both Steele (junior) and Sullivan converted to the Roman Catholic faith in later life, Sullivan becoming a Jesuit priest at Clongowes Wood College.

Although Steele's personal life was badly affected by the loss of his son, compounded by the nagging issues raised by local residents, the School continued to prosper until 1880. In recognition of his successful academic management of Portora, his Alma Mater, Trinity College, awarded him the degrees of LLB and LLD in 1878, even though he already held the higher degree of DD, which he had obtained in 1874. (It should be noted that, for a short period, the Board of Trinity College, Dublin passed a Grace which accorded all High Masters of important Irish Schools a higher degree or a doctorate, stip. con, after a period of successful Mastership.)

During their visit, the Commissioners appointed under the Educational Endowment Act, 1885, discovered that Steele had ceased to be in residence at the School, and was no longer taking an entry of pupils as boarders. By 1889-90, the number of pupils, both dayboys and boarders, had seriously declined, until it reached rock bottom with only 18 dayboys and no boarders. The Education Commissioners' Report of 1890 said: '*We have confined our expenditure on the buildings to what was absolutely necessary to prevent grave permanent injury*'. The immediate future looked extremely bleak.

The discipline of the boys also deteriorated, and the internal structure of the school started to show signs of extreme neglect. In effect, the School and its administrative system had totally collapsed. The annual allowance for Assistant Masters was reduced because of reduced numbers, yet this took place against

Frederick Steele. The Steele Memorial Prize was established in honour of Frederick Steele after his untimely death in 1866.

A group of staff and pupils on the front terrace during the Steele Mastership. This photograph, which accompanied an article in *The Daily Telegraph* in 2007, is reputed to include a young Oscar Wilde, who attended the School between 1864-71.

the background of increased income from endowments, which now reached £2,682 2s 5d a year. The difficulties of the 1880s were not wholly centred on falling numbers, but were also characterised by a perception that the endowments and objectives of the School were not sufficiently enjoyed by the Roman Catholic community. The local Catholic community, having only a few facilities in preparing for Intermediate education, pointed out the low usage of facilities at several of the Royal Schools, and suggested to the Commissioners that some of them, including Portora, should be closed and their endowments used for the benefit of educating Catholic children.

This threat to the lucrative Mastership at Portora induced Steele to take immediate remedial action. He imported the Reverend William Lindesay, a former Master of Tipperary Grammar School, to become Assistant Headmaster for Portora. At a stroke, the Commissioners noted rapid improvements for 1890-91 compared to the previous year: numbers rose to 59 boarders and 29 dayboys, giving a total of 88 for 1890, and rising to 98 the following year. Steele attributed this great improvement to the recent appointment of Lindesay, who on the move from Tipperary had brought many of his boarding pupils with him. This explained the remarkable and rapid revival of school numbers to nearly one hundred.

Fluctuating numbers

The following tables show the sudden and dramatic enrolment problems of the last decade of Steele's tenure:

Year	Boarders	Dayboys	Free	Total
1880	45	30	Not known	75
1881	0	18	Not known	18
1889	0	18	6	24

Lindesay's arrival in 1890 improved the situation considerably, and the situation was again revitalised by Biggs and further consolidated under Seale:

Year	Boarders	Dayboys	Free	Total
1891	59	39	Not known	98
1893	81	35	Not known	116
1894	71	31	Not known	102

It is interesting to see that some ten years later a similar situation developed during the latter days of McDonnell. No doubt this was exacerbated by problems associated with World War I, when the overall total went as low as 40 boarders.

Year	Boarders	Dayboys	Free	Total
1915	40	14	Not known	54
1917	58	17	Not known	75
1920	105	37	Not known	142

Deliberation by the Commissioners and two Education Boards are formed

For a number of years, the Endowed Schools Commissioners wrestled with several problems that affected the education of the Roman Catholic community, including their desire to obtain the Intermediate Certificate and other higher standards of education. In 1891, after much deliberation, the Commissioners framed a new scheme under the old Act of 1885, with two main principles:

1 The distribution of the existing Ulster Royal School endowments in equal shares to Catholic and Protestant communities of the district to which the endowments pertained.

2 The transfer of funds from the Commissioners set up under the Act of 1813 to a locally appointed Board, which would directly manage and control these funds for the benefit of schools entitled to receive aid from these bodies.

On 22 May 1891, the Commissioners for Education signed up in Dublin Castle to the creation of two new Education Boards, 'The Fermanagh Catholic Board of Education' and 'The Fermanagh Protestant Board of Education'. The latter remains today the trustee of the current Governing Body of the Enniskillen Royal School (Portora). The scheme also provided for the payment of a superannuation to incumbent Masters of the Royal Schools, whereby they would receive a pension for life equal to their current salaries.

Transfer of lands, property and cash adjustments

The Fermanagh Protestant Board of Education then accepted the premises and attendant real estate of the School, at an estimated value of £7,000 pounds, and placed a moiety of £3,500 with the Roman Catholic Board of Education for their building fund. These monies initially lay dormant for many years, but were used later to provide a secondary school for Roman Catholic pupils. Further financial adjustments were then made from the endowed lands, whereby 50% of the unexpired rental income for several former years was paid to the Roman Catholic School Board for their use.

The Deputy succeeds and continues progress

Steele retired as Master in 1891 and was immediately succeeded by his lately appointed assistant, the **Reverend Dr Walter Borcas Lindesay, LLD** (S, 1891-94), following ratification by the new Fermanagh Protestant Board of Education. Regrettably for all concerned, Lindesay's tenure was short, and after three very successful years he decided that his true calling lay in Holy Orders

REVEREND DR WILLIAM BORCAS LINDESAY, MA, LLD

(s, 1891-94)

- Graduated from Trinity College, Dublin.
- Well-known Headmaster of Tipperary Grammar School, 1874-90.
- Headhunted by Steele as his assistant to bolster failing enrolments at Portora, 1890.
- The first appointment by Fermanagh Protestant Board of Education to the Headmastership after the retirement of Dr Steele on 8 July 1891.
- Resigned in 1894 to undertake a series of parochial duties.
- Appointed Vicar of Holy Trinity Church, Tooting, London, 1906. (In November 2007, the former vicarage and grounds belonging to Holy Trinity Church, Tooting, were advertised for sale in *The Sunday Times* for £8.75m.)

and parochial duties. He resigned his Mastership in 1894, and after a number of junior church positions in Ireland and England he was subsequently inducted as Vicar of Holy Trinity Church, Tooting, London.

Consolidation after the changes

Lindesay was succeeded by **Dr Richard Biggs, LLD** (S, 1894-1904), Headmaster of Galway Grammar School, who, as seems customary for the era, brought several of his Assistant Masters and a number of pupils from his old school. The arrival at Portora of several Galway masters meant that the Protestant Board now had to retire or sack Messrs W J Valentine and W L Scott, the former having been a long-standing and faithful servant of the School for many years. Biggs already knew his predecessor Lindesay, since both had been candidates for the Headmastership of Tipperary Grammar School some years previously, a post for which Lindesay had been the successful candidate. Biggs, as we know, eventually obtained the Mastership of Galway Grammar School, which was part of the well-known Erasmus Smith Group of Schools.

Biggs made a good start at Portora, and the School's revival continued under the guidance of this new, genial, energetic and popular Master. He brought efficient management, created a happy atmosphere and increased total attendance figures at the School.

DR RICHARD BIGGS, LLD

(s, 1894-1904)

- Graduated from Trinity College, Dublin.
- Former Master of Galway Grammar School.
- Appointed by Fermanagh Protestant Education Board to Headmastership on 29 October 1894.
- He brought several key staff and boarding students to Portora from Galway, resulting in dismissal of some faithful Portora staff.
- Raised the level of sports at Portora, including success with several appearances in Ulster Schools Cup finals.
- Responsible for constructing the gymnasium c1897-98.
- Died in post after suffering a major heart attack while rowing a skiff on Lough Erne.
- Buried at Rossorry Parish Church.

Year	Boarders	Dayboys	Free	Totals
1894	71	31	Not known	102
1904	Not known	Not known	Not known	120

The first report on Portora by the Commissioners, shortly after the Biggs succession, reads: '*The efficiency and success of Portora Royal School continues under the present Head Master (Biggs) and his excellent staff; and the numbers at 26 June 1894 – 71 boarders and 31 day boys – indicate the esteem in which this old and famous institution is held by the public.*'

Biggs was responsible for building the School gymnasium on the site of some rather primitive washing and dry latrines, which had previously existed alongside and to the rear of the Steele Hall. He encouraged an increasing interest in organised sport and recreation. Portora managed to feature prominently in the Ulster Schools Cup, reaching the finals in 1899, 1902 and 1904, but were beaten on all three occasions by Methodist College Belfast.

Old Portora dinners and presenting portraits

Although the Old Portora Union was not officially formed until 1921, during the late Victorian era Portora undergraduates at Trinity College, Dublin had usually organised and hosted an annual dinner for former pupils at some suitable venue in Dublin. A rather smart silver gilt menu for such a dinner has been found for a date as early as 1879, priced 8s 6d at the Bilton Hotel, Dublin. It would appear that there were two tables, one for undergraduates and students, and a high table for the more mature and successful old boys. On one particular occasion there were no fewer than three Irish High Court Judges, all Old Portorans, at the top table.

It was during the Biggs regime that the practice of hanging portraits of previous Masters in the dining room was started. Biggs himself presented a number of engravings and paintings of earlier Masters. The portrait of Steele (painted by Miss Emily Steele) was unveiled on Speech Day in December 1898. The ceremony was conducted by the **Right Honourable Justice Gibson** (OP, 1857-63), who together with **W Copeland Trimble, JP** (OP, 1861), then owner of the *Impartial Reporter*, made a speech relating to the Steele era, on behalf of former boarding and dayboy pupils respectively.

Biggs saw the century out, unfortunately dying unexpectedly of a heart attack on 23 June 1904, while rowing a skiff up the lake. His passing was sadly noted in the local press as a great loss, not only to the School, but also to the local Parish and Enniskillen town itself. He was laid to rest in Rossorry Churchyard, where several of his predecessors were buried. Biggs managed to maintain School numbers in excess of 100, and at the date of his untimely death they stood at 120 pupils. His memory has been kept alive by the 'old boys' of the four schools where he had been a Headmaster: Mountmellick, Portarlington, Galway and Portora. Assisted by colleagues, they instituted a fund for a prize in his name at Trinity College, Dublin; known as the Biggs Memorial Prize, it is awarded to a candidate from any of the four schools.

Rugby, and a legend is born

Biggs was succeeded as Master by **Alaster McDonnell, MA** (S, 1904-1915), who had previously been Headmaster for six years at Armagh Royal School. On his appointment to Portora, McDonnell brought with him several other rugby-playing staff and pupils, including the legendary Ulster schoolboy and future Irish international **'Dickie' Lloyd** (OP, 1904-09).

McDonnell seems to have kept the game of rugby rather more to the fore than any other aspect of school life. The School's 1st XV, under the captaincy of 'Dickie' Lloyd, was invincible during the period 1905-09, and no fewer than seven of the team went on to play international rugby for Ireland. At the time it was rumoured (and 1st XV members used to boast to rival teams) that it was harder to gain your Portora colours than to be awarded an Ulster Inter-provincial Schoolboys cap.

McDonnell was described as a tall, well-built, athletic individual, who, having played rugby for Ireland himself, then turned his attention to training techniques and developed a talent for coaching sport, concentrating on both rugby and rowing. This attention to sporting activities appears to have been to the detriment of most academic subjects. The School received an unfavourable report from members of the Intermediate Education Board, following their visit in 1910, including the following comments: '*we found in each form a sediment of idlers, who have no intention of working. These boys are drawn from a social class which is becoming smaller in Ireland*'. One cynic dryly added that they were probably destined for a life in the British army.

Following this criticism, commercial subjects were introduced into the School's curriculum, and McDonnell engaged an additional master, S R Meeks, BA, to head up a new Commercial Department. Success was more or less instant, and in 1911 two boys passed first in all Ireland in the direct Bank Entry Examinations for both the Bank of Ireland and the Northern Bank. A third student took second place for the Northern Bank. This was, perhaps,

ALASTER C MCDONNELL, MA
(S, 1904-1915)

- Graduated from Trinity College, Dublin.
- Former Headmaster at Armagh Royal School.
- Appointed to Portora on 8 July 1904.
- Former Irish Rugby International noted for his prowess in coaching sport, specialising in rugby and rowing.
- Heavily criticised by Commissioners of Education, c1910, for the School's lack of academic performance in Classics and general education, all at the expense of games, particularly the pursuit of rugby and rowing honours
- Introduced Commercial Studies to the curriculum, after which the School gained considerable success in commerce and banking c1910/11.
- Resigned his Mastership in 1915 and went to teach at Eton College, Windsor.

the first stage of meeting that criticism of some fifty years before, during the Steele era, when Mr William Trimble and Mr William Auchinlake Dane made representations from the townsfolk of Enniskillen seeking a more enlightened syllabus than the traditional Classics.

Masters and pupils on the front terrace, Portora, 1909.

REGINALD G BURGESS, MA (OXON)
(S, 1915-1917)

- Graduated, BA, Edinburgh University.
- Classical Exhibitioner, MA, Queen's College, Oxford.
- First non-Trinity Master of Portora, having come from Merchiston Castle School, Edinburgh.
- On his arrival, 5 May 1915, immediately founded the Junior Department, the predecessor of Gloucester House.
- Coped with deaths of students during World War I.
- Drowned during summer holiday at Castlerock, 1917.
- Early death considered a great loss to School, the town and the parish.
- Interregnum filled by W N Tetley.

MASTERS & STUDENTS, PORTORA, 1909.

Again, this was a period of fluctuating numbers at Portora; by 1915 there were only about fifty boys at the School, comprising 40 boarders and 14 dayboys. McDonnell decided to leave Portora and Ireland altogether, and settled to a new life in England. He went on to become a master at Eton College, Windsor, where he had family connections.

The approach of World War I

McDonnell's successor was **Reginald G Burgess, MA** (S, 1915-17), initially an Edinburgh graduate, who had then become a Classical Exhibitioner at Queen's College, Oxford. Formerly on the staff at Merchiston Castle School, Edinburgh, he increased the number of pupils at Portora to 75 in his first year. In his second year, the number rose to 98, of whom 78 were boarders.

It was Burgess who started the Preparatory department at Portora in 1915. First known as the Junior School, it was established as a feeder for the Upper School. He engaged the redoubtable **Miss E E Hunt** (S, 1915-47) as Headteacher. Many of her former students recalled that her hallmark was a very flamboyant monogram, always written as E (dash) E (dash) H. For the next 99 terms Miss Hunt taught Latin, English and manners to successive generations of Preparatory schoolboys (referred to as 'maggots') at Portora.

A year later Burgess recruited another legendary member of staff, **A T M Murfet, MA** (S, 1916-57), who was later to become one of the first Housemasters. During a career of over forty years, Murfet was Head of Classics and deputy Headmaster and supervised rugby and rowing. In retirement, he carried on teaching Classics part-time for a further four years. His contribution to the School is remembered by the name of the Murfet Cloister.

For all his energetic work in raising numbers and improving the School, life for Burgess came to a tragic end. On holiday in Castlerock, during the summer of 1917, he drowned trying to rescue a family friend who got into difficulties while swimming.

Portora 1916. The Headmaster, Burgess, with Miss E E Hunt seated three away on his left and her ten 'maggots' seated in the front row.

The senior Mathematics and Science Master, **W N Tetley, BA** (S, 1891-1925), took over as an interregnum Headmaster until the Board of Governors met and appointed the **Reverend Edward G Seale, MA** (S, 1917-36), to be the new Headmaster. Seale arrived more or less in time to organise the celebrations for the tercentenary of the School's foundation.

World War I

World War I took its toll on Portora's sons: some 400 names are listed as having served, and the School's War Shrine records the names of 71 who were killed in action or died of wounds sustained during the conflict. These figures are remarkable when one considers that total numbers at the School rarely exceeded 100 pupils in any one year, and that they were at a low point of only 54 during 1915.

As might be expected, most Old Portorans served in the commissioned ranks, and many were highly decorated. In total, nine received the Distinguished Service Order (DSO), and no fewer than 35 were awarded the Military Cross (MC). The most highly decorated, **Fredrick M W Harvey** (OP, 1902-1906), a cavalry officer with Lord Strathcona's Horse, was awarded the Victoria Cross (VC), having earlier been awarded the Distinguished Service Order (DSO) and Military Cross (MC). He also received the Croix de Guerre (CdeG) from the French allies. At School, Harvey played rugby during the early 'Dickie' Lloyd era and went on to play for Trinity College, Dublin, and Wanderers. He was later called out as a full international for Ireland against Wales in 1907 and France in 1911. Two of his nephews, the Tarrant brothers from County Cork, attended Portora during the 1940s.

A return to excellence

With the appointment of Seale we enter a period when the School was to flourish again. In 1918, a School War Memorial Committee collected over £800, mainly as a tribute to those who had served and died in World War I, but also to mark the tercentenary of the School's foundation. The Committee decided

REVEREND EDWARD G SEALE, MA
(1871-1936)
(s, 1917-1936)

- Educated at Wesley College, Dublin.
- Trinity graduate who gained a reputation as a very successful Headmaster at Kilkenny and Cork Grammar Schools before his appointment as Headmaster at Portora.
- Introduced the House system for boarders in 1919.
- Instrumental in the foundation of Old Portora Union (OPU), 1921.
- Introduced the Officer Training Corps as a significant activity in 1923.
- Purchased the lower rugby fields in 1925 to increase scope of second teams for representative sports.
- Built the Preparatory School, Gloucester House, in 1936.

to present the School with a new modern Sanatorium or Cottage Hospital, which was duly opened in the early 1920s.

In 1919 the boarding department was divided, for pastoral purposes, into four Houses named Ulster, Munster, Leinster and Connacht (Connaught, the alternate Anglicised spelling adopted by the first Housemaster, A T M Murfet), into which boys were placed irrespective of their county of origin. The House system, modelled on the English Public School concept of boarding houses, was designed to improve the esprit de corps of pupils by bringing teamwork to a whole new range of activities that were suited, or could be adapted, to House competition.

The Provisional Committee of the Old Portora Union (OPU) held its first meeting in Dublin, on 9 March 1921, with the **Right Honourable J G Gibson, PC** (OP, 1857-63) as President.

Seale started the Officer Training Corps (OTC) at Portora in 1923, with some 57 boys enrolled for military training, and an OTC Pipe Band was later formed to enhance interest in parade ground drill. The OTC was initially parented by the Royal Inniskilling Fusiliers, and for many years cadets were privileged to wear the cap badge and buttons of this distinguished Irish Regiment. Seale also joined the Headmasters' and Headmistresses' Conference (HMC), which, together with the OTC, enabled him to make nominations for cadetships at the Royal Military Academy, Woolwich (Artillery and Engineers), and the Royal Military College, Sandhurst (Cavalry and Infantry).

By 1928 the number of pupils in the Upper School had risen to about 100 boarders and 50 dayboys, with 15 boarders in the Junior School. However, during the 1920s and 1930s, with the greatly increased numbers of boarders from all over Ireland, the social differences between boarders and dayboys were again becoming an issue. As **Vivian Mercier** (OP, 1928-36), who became Professor of English at the University of Colorado, USA, noted in his tract 'The Old School Tie', published in 1946, '*Boarders were largely the sons of Church of Ireland clergy, Anglo-Irish land owners, country gentlemen, the traditional professions, bank managers and the like; however the aristocracy, senior clergy, the titled and the wealthy still tended to send their sons to school in England. By contrast the Portora dayboys were from an altogether different social group. They were the sons of local town shopkeepers, policemen, small farmers, in effect members of what was considered at that time and to use Marxist jargon, the petit bourgeois class. The dress, manners, local accent and vocabulary of most day boys marked them off from the more urbane and sophisticated Anglo-Irish boarders.*'

The school authorities did little to discourage the aloof attitudes of the boarders towards the local dayboys The facilities provided for dayboys were inferior to those enjoyed by the boarders, and many staff felt that the School could do without the dayboys. Despite his antipathy towards the dayboys, Seale must rank among one of the great Headmasters, his name being perpetuated at the School by the Seale Room in the main building, formerly used as the Seniors' Library and by Upper School prefects as a place for study and evening prep.

A vivid pen-portrait and sketch of Seale is also given in 'The Old School Tie', by Mercier: '*Which brings us to the Headmaster – the most important thing of all in a school. Seale was headmaster during all my time except the last two terms, and had been there for ten years when I arrived [1928]. He was a headmaster of the old sort, a clergyman, a classicist, a disciplinarian – but first and foremost a gentleman.'*

Seale revitalised Portora as a successful Irish Public School. He also laid the foundations for Gloucester House, to house the junior department, but did not live to see its completion as an independent Preparatory School located in a new building at the foot of Portora Hill.

The Stuart era

Seale was succeeded by **Ian M B Stuart, MA** (S, 1936-45), who had previously taught in England at St Paul's School, London, and Harrow. He had also been the Headmaster of Beaminster, a co-educational Grammar School in Dorset, and seemed to be the ideal candidate for the Headmastership of Portora.

Like most of his predecessors he was a graduate of Trinity College, Dublin. However, his degree was in History, Politics and Economics, so he possessed a background totally different from that of the previous twenty incumbents, who had either a Classical or clerical background. Stuart, a former Irish Rugby international, inherited an Upper School with 173 pupils, of whom about 100 were boarders. He inherited also the Preparatory School, Gloucester House, which was soon to be completed, and which had been initially designed to accommodate some 30 boarders.

Up to this time the Upper School had no chapel, and when such a facility was required, improvisations were made in the main school dining hall. It was Stuart, a layman, who converted the gymnasium into a place of worship, and furnished it with a second-hand pulpit and a harmonium; prayers were said and hymns sung there every day.

The war years in Fermanagh

In 1939, before the outbreak of World War II, several members of the Portora OTC stayed on at School during the summer holidays to construct an air-raid shelter under the direction of their Commander, **Major G V Butler,** (S, 1926-49). This shelter is a long-forgotten piece of history. No longer visible, it was described as being in the area where the line of trees separates the parade ground from the upper playing fields.

During the war a Royal Air Force station was established at St Angelo. This was used for ferried Fortresses and Liberators that ran short of fuel in the neighbourhood. It was also used by both the RAF and Fleet Air Arm for testing newly developed and usually secret modifications to rockets. Two flying-boat stations were also established in Fermanagh, one at Killadeas (training and repairs) and the other at Castle Archdale (operations over the Atlantic). Large swathes of the Fermanagh hinterland and several local stately homes were requisitioned by the War Office, and used as accommodation and training grounds for the American Army ground forces in preparation for the combined Allied operations leading up to D-Day. Stuart forged considerable social and sporting links between the School and members of the Allied Forces stationed throughout the area.

IAN STUART, MA
(s, 1936-1945)

- Graduated from Trinity College Dublin.
- Irish International Rugby player.
- Assistant Master at St Paul's School, London, and Harrow on the Hill.
- Headmaster of co-educational Grammar School in Dorset.
- Appointed as Headmaster following retirement of Seale.
- Shortly after appointment, Stuart broadcast a history of the School on the BBC, which was later published as a supplement to a very comprehensive set of Rules and Regulations he wrote for pupils attending the School.
- Organised and coached a successful return to Ulster Schools Rugby for three years during World War II.
- Resigned by writing an open letter to all parents, claiming that the School's Board had ignored his position as the appointed Headmaster and Chief Executive for all school staff.

Last of the topper brigade. Seniors assemble for Sunday service at the Cathedral. This Sunday dress was abolished during the Headmastership of the Reverend Douglas Graham, in favour of grey herringbone suits.

An iconic 'box-brownie' photograph of General 'Ike' Eisenhower, as Supreme Allied Commander, reviewing the American Forces on the Lower Rugby Pitches during his wartime visit to Portora, prior to the commencement of D-Day operations.

I hope you will see to it that your son maintains regular attendance at Portora until the Term ends on July ....

In the past there has been a tendency for some Day Boys to cease attending when the Certificate Examinations are over.

The last three weeks of the Term are most important.

IAN STUART.

Attendance-card from the Stuart era.

Some time before D-Day, General 'Ike' Eisenhower came to the School to review American troops at a parade on the Lower Rugby Pitches. His visit was of course kept secret, much to the astonishment of **Captain Henry Scales** (S, 1924-60) and his OTC contingent, who had chosen that very day to mount a field-day and exercise on the hill above the lower fields. The US Army had placed sentries along the hedge, and on seeing soldiers apparently creeping up on them, they immediately demanded to know who and what they were. Fortunately Scales was able to explain, and the incident passed without an exchange of fire. This visit was recorded in writing by Headmaster Stuart, who stated he received a personal letter of thanks from 'Ike'.

The Americans stationed in Fermanagh were very popular, and at their peak outnumbered the local town inhabitants two to one. By and large, they were made most welcome, especially by the younger ladies of the town. There were additional contacts with the School, some of which are outlined in more detail in chapter nine, when American bulldozer crews attempted to level the upper playing fields as a training project in the run-up to D-Day operations.

At the end of the War, the School inherited a fine fleet of whalers for use by the Royal Navy Section of the newly formed Junior Training Corps (JTC), which replaced the old OTC; the JTC was later rechristened the Combined Cadet Force (CCF), which incorporated the Air Training Corps (ATC) formed in the early part of World War II.

Rugby success returns to Portora

Success at rugby, in particular in the Ulster Schools Cup, had evaded Portora for many years, but wartime spirits were lifted during the Stuart regime, when the School's 1st XV peaked for three years at Ravenshill. Portora won the Ulster Schools Cup in 1940 and 1941 by beating Coleraine, and drew in 1942 against Royal Belfast Academical Institution (RBAI). Because of wartime conditions, a replay was not possible and, as a gesture of goodwill, the Headmaster of RBAI suggested sportingly that Portora should continue to keep the Cup, as the reigning holders. Further details of these successes will be found in chapter five.

Stuart decides to resign

In 1945 Stuart sent an open letter of resignation to all parents outlining his reasons for leaving Portora. In it he referred to parents complaining of the food and the medical treatment of their sons. He explained that, while the Royal Schools Act recognised the Master as the School Board's Chief Executive, the present Portora Board had effectively cut him out of most decision-making by not advising him of their meetings, their agenda, or even when such meetings were likely to take place. In spite of his allegations concerning the Board's management style, he offered to resign and it seems they needed no further encouragement to accept.

He left at the end of the Summer Term, 1945. Before his departure, he had a comprehensive clean-out of fixtures, fittings and old archives from the Master's House. It was said that, in a fit of pique, he burnt a considerable amount of School memorabilia and associated historical records.

It is only fair to note that Stuart had been the Master throughout the War, when shortages of food, staff and transport were at their worst. Nevertheless, his laissez-faire attitude to discipline resulted in the boys doing much as they liked, and the staff, comprising not only some long-term faithful members but also many temporary 'wartime' people, were at a loss to know how to cope with his ways.

Stuart had, however, modernised the daily routine at Portora, and published a set of rules and regulations in a pamphlet of somewhat intimidating military style and detail. He planned to open a preparatory school in the Belfast area after his resignation. However, this project never materialised and he went to America, to become the Director of Students' Guidance at Mercersburg Academy, Pennsylvania.

Post-war revival

Stuart's departure made way for the **Reverend Douglas L Graham, MA** (OP, 1919-27 and S, 1945-53) as Headmaster of the School. Graham (1909-90) was an Old Portoran, a former Exhibitioner in Classics at Trinity College, Dublin, and in Holy Orders. All of this made for a traditional Master of Portora, and continued the connection between the School, the Church of Ireland and Trinity College, Dublin. Graham arrived back as Master in time for the Michaelmas Term of 1945, twenty years after being a pupil himself. Consequently, there were no fewer than three Housemasters and several other members of the teaching staff who had taught him, and remembered him as just 'young Graham – the schoolboy'.

In the intervening years he had become a well-known undergraduate at Trinity, a university boxing champion, a trialist for the Irish rugby team and an Assistant Master at Eton College. He had also completed his wartime service as an energetic Naval Chaplain with the RNVR. In maturity he was an imposing man, with a very commanding presence, and he took over a school with 147 boarders and 116 dayboys.

REVEREND DOUGLAS L GRAHAM MA
(1909-90)

(S, 1945-53)

- Pupil at Portora, 1919-27.
- Graduated as Classical Scholar from Trinity College, Dublin, 1930.
- British University champion boxer (light heavyweight).
- Irish trialist, rugby football.
- Former Assistant Master at Eton College.
- Followed his father into Holy Orders 1937.
- Served as RNVR chaplain with HMS Trinidad, which was finally sunk in Arctic waters by two JU88 bombers.
- Restructured the School to take in the 11+ entry of day pupils following the 1947 Education Act (NI).
- Started sending crews to row at Henley and teams to shoot at Bisley.
- Resigned in 1953 to become Headmaster of Dean Close School, Cheltenham.

The Public School atmosphere

Graham rapidly reorganised the teaching side of the School, drawing on his experience as a Master at Eton College and service as a chaplain with the Royal Navy. One of his early reforms for School dress was to abolish the black jacket, striped trousers and Eton collar, which had been the traditional Sunday uniform for nearly a hundred years. Boys had also been expected to wear top hats to Church on Sunday. Much to everyone's surprise, on the first Sunday of the Winter Term after the arrival of Graham, the boarders were informed at breakfast time that top hats were no longer required. The School and House prefects had a quick conference and told all boys to wear their toppers to Church, but to throw them into the river at the West Bridge. A pupil of the time recalls that it was quite a sight to see scores of toppers floating down the Erne towards the boat houses. The prefects had apparently discussed and organised this rather drastic solution to ensure that the Headmaster could not change his mind. Graham then introduced the grey herringbone suit as the formal replacement for Sundays. In Winter, a tweed sports jacket and grey flannels became the normal everyday wear for Upper School pupils; in Summer, the striking yellow and black blazer was worn.

Graham immediately embarked on a programme of marketing Portora as the leading all-Ireland Public School, on both the UK and international scene, by embracing a number of bilateral exchange programmes with American, French and Swiss schools. He fostered trans-Atlantic relations with New England preparatory schools in America, by offering exchange scholarships to and from Portora through the English Speaking Union. One of the more interesting early trans-Atlantic exchanges featured our own **Samuel McGredy,** (OP, 1942-48), who attended Tabor Academy, Marion, Massachusetts. His family had developed McGredy Roses of Portadown to international fame, and the young Sam, in later business life, exported the whole enterprise from Portadown to New Zealand (see also chapter eight). Graham attached great importance to the recruitment and retention of high-calibre teaching staff, and chose some interesting personalities to replace retiring personnel. One of the most notable was **Jack Wheeler** (S, 1948-94), who was to become an institution at the School for nearly fifty years.

To raise the School's profile, Graham entered Portora for prestige events more generally associated with the larger English Public Schools, such as rowing at Henley Royal Regatta, and shooting for the Ashburton Shield at Bisley. Moreover, as an Old Portoran himself, he naturally attracted a high proportion of pupils who were themselves the sons of Old Portorans or had family connections with the School. Graham also used his Trinity and service connections to recruit pupils, being highly successful in attracting pupils with OPU connections from mainland UK.

Through his wife, Graham was well connected socially with many leading professional and business personalities in Dublin, and from his own clerical background he had many contacts throughout Ireland. In a dull, post-war Enniskillen, he quickly became a well-known figure, with his powerful cathedral sermons and his driving around the Fermanagh countryside in his distinctive black Ford V8 Pilot car.

Ashburton Shield, 1950s. A young Captain Jack Wheeler with his Bisley Shooting Team. Third from the left standing is a young Charles Jones (later General Sir Charles Jones) and left front row a young Walton Empey (later Archbishop of Dublin). It will interest people to know that the team used to cycle from Portora to the ranges at Letterbreen with their Lee Enfield rifles slung over their shoulders. Their ammunition was carried in their front baskets or rear panniers. Tranquil days in the 1950s.

The regional Grammar School

An Enniskillen Grammar School for dayboys

The introduction of the Education Act (NI) 1947 meant that Portora now enjoyed a government-financed stream of 11+ pupils, selected from the most able and academic boys in the local area. Consequently, many Fermanagh boys, after primary school, had the opportunity to proceed to Portora for a free secondary education. This opened up the possibility of gaining entry to a university or other higher education establishment, without their parents facing undue problems of finance.

This 11+ entry also shifted the balance of teaching towards the more numerate and clever dayboys, away from the Classically grounded boarders, most of whom came via the Gloucester House entrance examination, or from one of the English or Irish Preparatory Schools. The traditional rivalry and antagonism between the boarders and 'day-dogs' was still noticeable, but it diminished as the number of dayboys increased. There was a gradual integration of the student body, as more and more dayboys participated in games, joined the CCF and generally displayed an interest in sharing School leisure and extra-curricular activities.

During 1948, construction commenced to erect new elaborate memorial gates at the main entrance to the School. The Reay Gates, as they are called, formed a fitting memorial for two brothers, **Derek Reay** (OP, 1931-39), and **Geoffrey Reay** (OP, 1932-43), who had been killed in action while serving with the Royal Air Force during World War II. The four Corinthian pillars, supporting the gates and side railings, were dedicated to the memory of **Captain William E Irwin, RA** (OP, 1927-29), of the Indian Army. The memorial gates were formally opened in a colourful ceremony during the Summer Term 1949, attended by members of the Reay family, important county families and many local townspeople, all in the presence of the Governor of Northern Ireland, the fourth Earl Granville; see chapter two.

Henry Francis Lyte Memorial Concert for BBC Radio (Northern Ireland)

The Winter Term of 1948 saw several months of rehearsal for the Centenary and Anniversary celebration of the life of Henry Francis Lyte. This was broadcast live from the Steele Hall by the BBC (NI) Orchestra under their newly appointed Conductor, Dr Havelock Nelson, who had been a junior contemporary of Graham and his younger brother at Trinity College, Dublin; the descant choir was formed from the treble voices of Gloucester House boys.

Trinity College, Dublin, the favourite university

During Graham's time, the established connections with Trinity College, Dublin were greatly enhanced by a regular supply of undergraduates from Portora. The Trinity correspondent for the Old Portora Union (OPU) letter, writing in November 1953, stated that, on one recent morning, he had counted over forty OPs passing through the Front Square of Trinity. He was aware also of a further twenty OPs attending various activities within the College. It is little wonder that in 1954, one English undergraduate, totally surrounded by

Old Portorans during Commons in the Trinity Dining Hall, was heard to say: '*Are there any other schools in Ireland besides Portora?*'

Graham left Portora at the end of the Winter Term of 1953 to become Headmaster of Dean Close School, Cheltenham, a move that surprised many members of the staff, Old Portorans and current pupils alike. Graham never lost touch with the School, however, and following his move to England, and for many years afterwards, he corresponded with his old Housemaster, Mickey Murfet, and contributed many articles to the annual OPU letter. Having been instrumental in the formation of the London Branch of the Old Portora Union during his Mastership in 1953, he continued to attend annual dinners in London, and was President of the OPU (London Branch) during 1984-85.

A second Oxford Man becomes the new Master

Graham was followed in the summer term of 1954 by the **Reverend Percival (Val) H Rogers, MA, MBE** (1954-73), an Oxford graduate and former Head of English and Senior Chaplain at Haileybury and Imperial Service College, Hertford. Rogers (1912-2001) was the first Headmaster who was English by birth and education. However, being in Holy Orders, he maintained the traditional clerical link. He was also fortunate that his wife, Mary, whom he had met as a student at Oxford, had been brought up in Belfast and had other Irish connections. After some years, Mrs Rogers joined the staff and her literary and community contributions had a considerable influence on Portora and County Fermanagh.

The Rogers era brings us from the realms of past history into those of current affairs; several recent and current members of staff and some Governors were themselves pupils at the School during his Headmastership. Rogers was a man of phenomenal physical and intellectual energy. He guided the School out of the period of post-war austerity and into one of government-sponsored prosperity. Under Rogers, life at Portora became hectic for both staff and pupils.

Ambitious building programme commences

Change and an ambitious building construction plan, costing upwards of £400,000, continued unabated over the next ten to fifteen years. Finance was a mixture of government grants, capital fees and a generously supported appeal fund of over £100,000, subscribed mainly by Old Portorans. Funds accelerated in 1963 with the arrival of **Robert W L Hort** (S, 1963-83), a Cambridge graduate who masterminded much of the necessary funding, before he joined the academic staff. Sporting and recreational facilities were likewise developed and improved. The numbers of pupils attending the School continued to rise, and in 1964 the boarding accommodation was further extended and many other facilities renovated. During this period Portora reached its highest ever total number of pupils: by 1967 the numbers had risen to 306 dayboys and 232 boarders.

In 1964 a totally new Gloucester House was opened by the 6th Earl of Erne, on a site across the Ballyshannon Road at Lakeview, in a repeat of the ceremony performed by his father, the 5th Earl of Erne, in 1936 when the first

REVEREND P H ROGERS, MBE, MA (OXON)
(1912-2001)
(s, 1954-1973)

- Graduated from St Edmunds Hall, Oxford University, MA English.

- Chaplain and Master at Haileybury and Imperial Service College, Hertford.

- Served in Europe and completed WWII with rank of Major, RA. Mentioned in despatches (Twice) and awarded MBE (Military) for services rendered.

- Ordained, St Albans, 1947.

- Appointed as the Headmaster of Portora 1954, in succession to the Reverend Douglas L Graham.

- Responsible for a major building and renovation programme, 1956-70, including the building of the new Gloucester House on the Lakeview site.

- On his retirement from Portora he took up several ecclesiastical appointments in USA, Ireland and England.

- Finally went to live in Oxford, where he and his wife were active in the Bodleian Library on programmes involving reading for the blind.

Gloucester House was opened. The curriculum of the new Gloucester House and the Upper School was totally modernised. Portora was one of the first schools in Northern Ireland to offer a scientific mix of Computer Studies, Business Studies and Engineering. Drama became the flagship of the arts in the School, with the inauguration of the Beckett Joyce Award, and subsequently the formal twinning of Portora with Clongowes Wood College.

The finance for all these changes was a continuing problem, and Rogers was first and foremost an educator, not an engineer or an accountant. He was obliged to rely on his Appeal Fund managers and a succession of Bursars, to track the income and expenditure required for his ambitious expansion plans. Finding and generating funding was a constant worry, and cash-flow remained a problem.

Rogers retired from his Mastership at Portora in 1973, after nineteen years of service and presiding over a considerable number of changes to the School and its syllabus. Despite the relative smallness of the School, compared to most English Public Schools, he built up a really ambitious curriculum which introduced Russian, Engineering, General Studies, Business Studies and IT. It was he who ended Portora's commitment to the Northern Ireland Junior and Senior Certificates in favour of a switch to English-style O- and A- level educational qualifications. Rogers also encouraged pupils to enter mainland universities instead of taking the traditional routes to Queen's in Belfast and Trinity in Dublin.

As a Headmaster he was probably the last Portora will see of what may be thought of as the traditional cleric. Rogers had both fans and critics, but he was always respected by staff, boys and parents. His staff continued to observe old-fashioned proprieties; they still wore gowns, and at no point would any of them consider addressing him as Val, certainly not in front of other staff or boys.

Rogers took a great interest in Irish politics, and in retirement became President of the Fermanagh Alliance Association. He once summed up his political commitment by saying, '*I am aware of the Border, but I do not feel threatened by it*'.

When Rogers and his wife Mary retired from Portora, he initially went to the United States as an assistant priest at Trinity Church, New Orleans. He then returned to Fermanagh as Director of Ordinands in Clogher Diocese before settling in Oxford, where they both took an active interest in the Bodleian Library and recording texts for the blind. He was a regular dining member of the OPU (London Branch) and was President for the period 1992-1993. His funeral at Basingstoke in Hampshire attracted a large attendance of family, friends, former staff and OPU members living in England; the service was conducted by the **Right Reverend Henry Richmond, MA** (OP, 1949-54), a former Bishop of Repton, who had also conducted Mary Rogers' funeral service a year earlier.

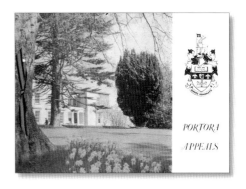

During the 1960s and 1970s the School organised an appeals system to help finance an ambitious building programme. Prior to moving across onto the teaching staff, Robert Hort was appointed to be the Appeal Co-ordinator. Two of the publicity brochures produced during these years and sent to parents and interested parties are shown above.

THOMAS J GARRETT, BA (QUB)

(s, 1973-1978)

- First graduate of Queen's University Belfast to be Headmaster at Portora.

- Wrote a pageant entitled 'Two Hundred Years at the Top' to celebrate the School's 1777 move to Portora Hill.

- Warned the Governors, c1977, that the traditions and success of many boarding schools were unlikely to last as a feature of modern education and that boarding was fast becoming an outdated concept throughout Ireland.

- Introduced the twinning of Portora with Clongowes Wood College.

- Resigned to become the Headmaster of his old school, Royal Belfast Academical Institution (RBAI).

DR ALAN R ACHESON BA (QUB), PHD

(s, 1978-1982)

- Graduate of Queen's University, Belfast.

- Former Head of History at Campbell College, Belfast.

- Lay Reader in Church of Ireland.

- IRFU referee.

- Introduced girls as boarders to Upper School and initiated the closure of Gloucester House.

- Resigned to become Headmaster of The King's School, Parramatta, Australia.

The Campbells are coming

Rogers was succeeded by **Thomas J Garrett, BA** (S, 1973-1978). Garrett arrived at Portora from Campbell College, Belfast, where he had been a Housemaster and Head of German. He was also the first Ulsterman and Queen's University graduate to become the Headmaster at Portora. His tenure was one of consolidation after the tremendous growth of students, building and reconstruction that had taken place during the Rogers era.

During Garrett's time the School's finances were stabilised, and they partially recovered from the somewhat frenetic cashflow problems of the past. In 1977 Portora celebrated the 200th anniversary of its move to its present site with a pageant written by Garrett himself, entitled 'Two Hundred Years at the Top', which was directed by Robert Hort. During Garrett's tenure, **Richard Elliot** (OP, 1973-78) was the first student from Northern Ireland to win the Young Scientist of the Year Award (1974).

As early as 1975, Garrett warned the Portora Board that he thought that boarding was a diminishing method of education in a modern Irish society. This decline applied equally both north and south of the border as more local and regional education facilities improved. Garrett left Portora in 1978, after only five years in post, to return as the Headmaster of his old school, the Royal Belfast Academical Institution (RBAI).

He was followed by another colleague from Belfast, **Dr Alan R Acheson, BA, PhD** (S, 1978-82). Acheson, like his predecessor, came from Campbell College, where he had been Head of the History Department for five years. He came from Hollywood in County Down, and was educated at Queen's University, Belfast, where he took an honours degree in Modern History and then a PhD in Theology. After graduation he spent seven years in the Royal Army Education Corps. He was a Lay Reader in the Church of Ireland and an Irish Rugby Football Union (IRFU) referee. He brought a flamboyant management style to Portora, and was an enthusiastic advocate of delegation. When the Masonic School in Dublin was closed, Acheson was quick to offer a welcome at Portora to many of its boarding pupils.

Girls might be an answer to the problem of numbers

The year 1979 saw a break with the tradition of the previous 361 years, when Portora became co-educational. A number of girls were accepted as boarders and the pastoral House system was revised to include a new girls' boarding facility based on the Old Sanatorium. The first official two girls in the Upper School at Portora were **Janet Osborne** (OP, 1975-1982) from Belfast and **Linda Watson** (OP, 1976-1984) from Killybegs, both of whom had brothers boarding at the School. Initially they were assigned to Leinster House, before the foundation of a Head's House specifically for girls. The number of girls steadily increased from the original nine boarders and two daygirls of 1979, to a maximum of 31 girls in 1984, of whom 14 were boarders. After this the number of girls slowly decreased until 1991, when there were only four girl boarders; by 1992 just one solitary daygirl remained. Acheson left Portora at the completion of the Christmas Term 1982, to become the Headmaster of The King's School, Parramatta, New South Wales, Australia.

Girls might be the answer – a class reunion from the late 1980s.

The difficult years

In January 1983, **Richard L Bennett, MA, DipEd** (S, 1983-2002) arrived at Enniskillen to become the twenty-fourth Headmaster. When Bennett was appointed, he restored the traditional link with Trinity College, Dublin, where he had graduated with an honours degree in History and Political Science. He had the additional advantage of possessing a DipEd from Queen's University, Belfast: as he said, 'he had a foot in both camps'. Bennett was appointed to Portora after many years of academic experience as Head of History, Politics and Economics, and Senior Boarding Master at Coleraine Academical Institution (CAI).

Before the appointment of Bennett, the Portora Board, under the chairmanship of the Right Reverend Dr Gordon McMullan, Bishop of Clogher, had already decided to concentrate all school activity on Portora Hill and to close down Gloucester House at Lakeview. On Bennett's arrival, the amalgamation of the two Schools was to be the first of the many challenges that he would face over the next nineteen years.

As a preliminary to any move from Gloucester House, essential improvements had to be carried out to the buildings on the Portora site, and the most pressing requirements were living quarters and private study facilities for Sixth Form boarders. This was achieved on the upper floor of the main building by providing bed-sit facilities, together with a common room, kitchen, shower and wash-room. This accommodation, which was undertaken during the years 1983-84, was similar to that being provided in university halls of residence, and at the time was regarded as second to none. At the same time the few remaining girl boarders were moved from the old Tercentenary Sanatorium to the upper floor of the Headmaster's House as temporary accommodation, prior to a final move into the vacated Munster House (the original Gloucester House).

Janet Osborne (OP, 1975-1982) and **Linda Watson** (OP, 1976-1984) were not the first girl students to grace Portora. That distinction officially belongs to Miss **Joan McCutcheon** (OP, 1922-24), who was a niece of Mrs Margaret Seale, wife of the Headmaster. She lived in the Headmaster's house, while attending classes at Portora for over a year. According to McCutcheon history, Joan had a marvellous time as the only girl at the School; her brother **Oliver McCutcheon** (OP, 1918-23) was a direct contemporary of **Samuel Beckett** (OP, 1920-23), both at Portora and later at Trinity College, Dublin.

Joan, unable to participate in School sport, was given the task of stable girl and general supervisor of the yard area and outbuildings. She also managed the farming interests carried out at the School, which at that time were quite extensive. Some thirty years later, Joan was the proud mother of the Headboy, **G W (Bill) Strahan** (OP, 1950-55), who won a State Exhibition to Oxford University, to read Law.

Another unusual girl who lived at Portora was Miss E F Valentine, daughter of William J Valentine, who was the Senior Classics Master during the Steele era and who practically ran the School from 1883 to 1891, in his capacity as the Second Master. Later, during the early 1950s, Miss Valentine, now an elderly Mrs Galway, corresponded with Headmaster Douglas Graham on various aspects of School life for his series of reminiscences published in his OP newsletters.

She told him that she played rugby while living at Portora. She was enlisted on the wing, along with her brothers during the late 1800s, when they were *'short of a man'*, thus completing a back line of Valentines for most rugby training! She wrote, *'Portora had a vigorous rugby team and played the town and various other schools in my father's time.'*

RICHARD L BENNETT, MA, DipEd
(s, 1983-2002)

- Educated at Coleraine Academical Institute (CAI).
- Graduated from Trinity College, Dublin and continued in education with a Dip Ed From Queen's University, Belfast.
- Returned to the staff of CAI and became Head of History, Politics and Economics as well as Senior Boarding Master.
- On appointment, he was immediately given the task of resolving many pressing administrative and financial problems inherited from the past. In addition, he had to find financial solutions to falling numbers of boarders attributed to community troubles in Ulster and Fermanagh. Housing, real estate and buildings were sold. Boarding facilities were closed and the situation was eventually stabilised.
- Many buildings were sympathetically restored and major improvements made to the School's portfolio of real estate and associated facilities.
- The School achieved high standards in the national examination league tables.

Boarding

The first ten years of Bennett's regime were very challenging. Boarding was rapidly becoming a thing of the past, and the decline in the number of UK and Irish boarders was improved only slightly by small numbers of pupils coming from Hong Kong and Singapore. Boarders had declined steadily in number from a peak of 245 in 1966 to 112 in 1982. However, this latter number had been artificially boosted by an influx of 21 and 28 boarders in 1980 and 1981 respectively, following the closure of the Masonic School in Dublin. On the other hand, the number of dayboys had increased from 291 to 387 during this period of decline in boarding. Bennett had come from Coleraine, where he was responsible for the day-to-day coordination of the boarding department, comprising 300 boys and twelve resident masters. He was therefore well aware of what was required for a successful boarding unit. An immediate marketing initiative was launched involving the retired **George C Andrews** (S, 1933-76), who had been the Ulster Housemaster for many years. In 1983, four boarding scholarships, worth £1,000 each, were offered in the hope that at least one pupil from each province of Ireland would be attracted. However, of the seven applications in the first year, only one came forward from the Republic of Ireland. This was very significant, as it illustrated the increasing lack of any interest from the South, which had always been the major area for recruitment of boarders. In the second year, only two applications were received for scholarships, neither of which was from the South. Despite the excellence of the accommodation and the marketing initiatives that had been introduced, the number of boarders, including four girls, declined to 61 by September 1985. This decline in boarding fortunes was attributed mainly to the 'Troubles'; but it was due also to the ever-increasing competition from good and improving local schools near major centres of population throughout Ireland. It may be noted that, during the later years of the Rogers era, there were early signs that the increase in community strife in the Six Counties was having a detrimental effect on the recruitment of boarding pupils from the Republic, the United Kingdom and overseas.

Marketing the School to students from overseas

In 1985 the Portora Board contributed £500 towards a publication entitled 'Boarding in Ulster', which featured all boarding schools in the Province. This booklet had wide distribution throughout Ireland, the United Kingdom and further afield. Other initiatives were also undertaken with the aim of increasing the numbers of boarders at Portora to around 100. By September 1987, despite these marketing efforts, the number had declined to 32, including nine weekly boarders. In 1988 there was a further major marketing exercise by all Northern Ireland boarding schools in Hong Kong and Malaysia, in which Portora was represented by the Headmaster himself, who went on tour to the Far East to interview potential candidates. This met with limited success.

The introduction of Malaysian pupils to the School brought a welcome breadth of cultural and religious diversity to the Portora community, as well as a high standard of academic study and ambition. However, the overseas market was difficult to maintain, and after several successful years the numbers started to tail off. At this stage the whole viability of boarding at Portora was again being questioned by the Board of Governors. This was nothing new, for it will be recalled that a previous Headmaster (Garrett) had expressed doubts as early as 1975 about the continued viability of boarding.

Amalgamation with the girl's Collegiate School a possibility

With the passing of the 1947 Education Act (NI), Grammar Schools could admit pupils who passed the transfer test, commonly known as the 11+. The proportion of the total transfer population admitted to Grammar Schools was normally around 27%; for Portora, this meant an intake of around forty day pupils. With the decline and closure of boarding, Portora was destined to become a very small selective school, which could seriously limit the breadth of the curriculum and the range of extra-curricular activities. The number of pupils at Portora in 1990 was 343, including 26 boarders. The 'sister school', Enniskillen Collegiate Grammar School, was having similar problems with falling numbers. In October 1988 the Boards of Governors of Portora and the Collegiate, facilitated by the Western Education and Library Board, agreed terms of reference for a study into educational provision in County Fermanagh. The terms of reference for this study, which was to be undertaken by Dr James Kincade, a former Headmaster of Methodist College, Belfast, were as follows: '*to prepare a report reviewing existing grammar school provision at present provided by the Collegiate and Portora Grammar Schools, taking cognisance of falling rolls and educational changes in Northern Ireland. The report should consider all the options in order to optimise the resources available and to ensure the best possible post primary school system for the Controlled and Voluntary Protestant sectors*'.

The Kincade Report

The outcome of the Kincade Report was a recommendation to amalgamate the Collegiate and Portora on the Portora Hill site, and to form one co-educational Grammar School taking one third of the transfer pupils. This proposal led to a very heated debate. The Portora Governors were broadly in favour of the proposals, but they had some reservations regarding both the loss of the Portora ethos, and also the long-term status of the new school as either a 'voluntary' or a 'controlled' establishment. Portora was traditionally a 'voluntary' Grammar School, which had its own financial budget directly from the Department of Education. The Collegiate, however, was 'controlled,' which meant that it was accountable to the Western Education and Library Board, rather than directly to the Department. The majority of teaching staff at Portora favoured the status quo, with the prospect of increasing the intake of boys to the school. The Collegiate governors, staff, pupils and parents launched a very vigorous campaign opposing the amalgamation. Despite this strong opposition from the Collegiate, the Western Education and Library Board recommended acceptance of the Kincade Report and amalgamation on the Portora site. After detailed consideration, Lord Belsted (Minister with Responsibility for Education) announced in January 1992 that amalgamation would not proceed. The Minister also confirmed that Portora could no longer

Headmaster Bennett with a group of Malaysian students on the main terrace outside the Stone Hall. The pupils were an equal mix of Malay and Chinese Malay, who together brought Buddist and Muslim diversity to the School.

accept girls as day pupils. Girls were first admitted to Portora in 1972, and over the years they made a valuable contribution to School life.

New opportunities

The three years between the commissioning of the Kincade Report and the Minister's final decision were frustrating for Portora staff because of the uncertainties they created. After the Minister's announcement, the Headmaster, with the Governors' approval, announced a progressive ten-year development programme for Portora. It stated that *'the school would provide education which is broad and balanced in the best senses, combining high academic standards with breadth of opportunity for all its pupils, maintaining the traditions of excellence which the school has been privileged to provide for so long to the young people of County Fermanagh and from further afield'.*

During this period, the Department of Education was also preparing new arrangements for admissions to schools. The new rules meant that the traditional 27% intake of transfer pupils to Grammar Schools would disappear, to be replaced by open enrolment. Schools would now be obliged to publish admission criteria and admit pupils up to the School's physical capacity. This development had a big impact on Portora, because the previous limited intake of about 40 would now have to increase to about 80. This might be good for pupil numbers, but it would have a grave diluting effect on the overall academic quality of the School: it would create new challenges for teaching and learning. However, over the years 1990-95 a compromise was reached, and the Portora intake, at the School's request, was reduced from 80 to 70, so that numbers could increase steadily to a maximum figure approaching 500 from the former 1990 figure of 343.

The Governors decide to close all boarding facilities

In September 1994 the Board of Governors decided that the Boarding School would have to close at the end of the academic year. There were now only 15 boarders, a unit which was considered to be no longer a viable social community. This was a sad occasion for the Board of Governors and the Headmaster. Despite the excellent accommodation and the extensive marketing initiatives, viable boarding numbers could not be sustained. Furthermore, from 1982 until the boarding facility was closed, the Governors had subsidised boarding from School funds to an amount in excess of £150,000. The demise of boarding was attributed mainly to community troubles, and for Portora in particular, the Enniskillen bomb in 1987 was a grave disincentive to even the strongest supporter of the boarding ethos. Almost immediately after the Enniskillen bomb, pupils from the South of Ireland ceased to enrol. Further reasons included: travelling time and distance of Fermanagh from main centres of population; a tendency throughout the UK for parents to send their children to the nearest day school in the interests of easy accessibility; rising standards of education at other locally available schools; boarding no longer seen as necessarily a good thing; easier access to other Grammar Schools as a result of lower transfer numbers; and, finally, a boarding education was no longer seen as essential family expenditure.

Furthermore, increasing affluence in the Republic after the Irish Government had embraced the Eurozone for finance and business meant that many Anglo-Irish families living south of the border now considered a working future in Ireland and Europe desirable, rather than seeking fame and fortune by emigrating to foreign parts, or by 'crossing the water' to England. In 1993, the boarding department was closed and Portora became a day school.

It must be emphasised however that Bennett's achievements were many. With strong support from **Mark Scott** (OP, 1948-55; S, 1985-2001) as his Estates Manager, he made a substantial number of major improvements to the fabric and facilities of the School, including landscaping and a considerable programme of tree planting throughout the grounds. On his retirement, Bennett left the fabric of Portora and its sporting facilities in excellent condition, the School's finances were healthy, the management structures robust, and its academic standing extremely high.

The twenty-fifth Master

At the beginning of the academic year 2002, **J Neill Morton BA, BSSc, DASE, MA(Ed), MA, PQH(NI)** (S, 2002) was appointed as the successor to Bennett and became Headmaster of a school with 480 pupils, all dayboys. Morton was the third person from Campbell College, Belfast to be appointed Headmaster at Portora. He was at Campbell for some twenty-five years, having served as Senior Teacher in Charge of the Sixth Form, Head of Department, Housemaster and Head of Drama. He was also involved in athletics, coaching and managing Northern Ireland teams at international level, including the Commonwealth Games in Edmonton in 1978.

Immediate changes were made to the system of pastoral care for boys during the academic year 2004-05. A pastoral House for boys in Year 9 was established and given the name Belmore House, pupils then moving to Ulster, Munster, Leinster or Connacht in Year 10. For administrative reasons, each pupil is usually assigned to his eventual House on entry to Year 8. They are normally assigned to Houses on a random basis, with the provision that any preference for a particular House is respected, and brothers can expect to be placed in the same House. Parents and grandparents can also make a choice for a relative to be allocated to a specific House.

J Neill Morton, BA, BSSc, DASE, MA(Ed), MA, PQH(NI)

(s, 2002-)

- Born in Belfast in 1949, educated at Annadale Grammar School.
- Graduated from Queen's University, Belfast in English, Psychology and Sociology.
- Returned to Annadale for five years, after completing a second degree.
- Moved to Campbell College in 1977, to teach English. Remained for 25 years in various roles: Head of Department, Housemaster, Teacher in Charge of Drama, Teacher Governor, Senior Teacher and Head of Sixth Form.
- Appointed Headmaster of Portora Royal School in 2002.

Events for the Quatercentenary – 2007-08

Visit to Portora by the President of Ireland, October 2007

The last two years, leading up to the School's Quatercentenary, now form part of its most recent history. In the autumn of 2007, the School was honoured to receive the President of Ireland, Dr Mary McAleese, on the afternoon of 23 October 2007. The President was greeted on arrival to Portora Royal School by **Samuel B Morrow, OBE** (OP, 1949-54), Vice-Chairman of the Board of Governors, who in turn introduced the President to the Headmaster. The President received a copy of the book, 'The 1608 Royal Schools', to which, together with Her Majesty Queen Elizabeth II, they had penned the preface.

The President of Ireland, Dr Mary McAleese, and Headmaster Neill Morton on the steps of the north wing entrance of the School on 23 October 2007.

Maundy Service at Armagh Cathedral, March 2008

On 20 March 2008, history was made when Her Majesty, Queen Elizabeth II, accompanied by His Royal Highness, The Duke of Edinburgh, attended the Royal Maundy Service in St Patrick's Church of Ireland Cathedral, Armagh. This is the first occasion that the annual Maundy service has been held in Northern Ireland. Over 400 people made up the congregation and saw Her Majesty distribute Maundy money to 82 men and 82 women representing the years of the Sovereign's life. Both Primates participated in the Order of Service, which was led by the Dean of St Patrick's Cathedral.

Her Majesty meeting representative pupils from all the Royal Schools and seen here talking Neil Cody, Headboy 2007, Portora Royal School.

Earlier on the Thursday, Her Majesty had been the guest of honour at a reception, held in the Royal School Armagh to celebrate the 400th Anniversary of the five Royal Schools of Ulster. Her Majesty met the headmasters and chairmen of all five Royal Schools and about 130 guests, including selected pupils and the Head Boy of Portora Royal School – Neil Cody.

Quatercentenary Dinner and Ball, September 2008

The main School event for the year was a weekend gathering held over the weekend of 13-14 September 2008 and organised by **Robert Northridge** (OP, 1955-62; S, 1973-), Deputy Headmaster of the School. After various activities on the Friday night and Saturday morning, the highlight was the Quatercentenary Dinner and Ball, held at the Loch Erne Golf Resort on the Saturday evening.

There was a very credible turnout from members of the OPU (London Branch) who, with wives and partners, travelled from many parts of the UK and occupied several large tables for the evening. After the dinner, various formal toasts and speeches, Robert Northridge was inducted as the new President of the Old Portora Union (2008-2010). As a fitting gesture the toast to the OPU was proposed by Dr Raymond Murphy, President elect of the Clongowes Union, representing our twin school in the Republic of Ireland.

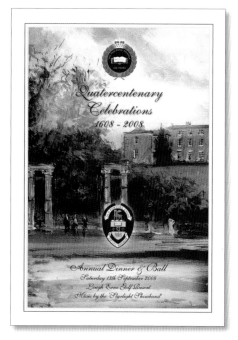

Cover of the dinner menu from the Quatercentenary Dinner and Ball, 13 September 2007.

A group of guests attending the Quatercentenary Dinner and Ball, held at the Loch Erne Golf Resort, enjoying pre-dinner drinks on the terrace.

A summary of four centuries and the future

The Headmaster now has the tremendous challenge of taking a former famous Irish boarding school into the next millennium as a local Grammar School for dayboys. In 1608 James I, as a part of his vision for the Ulster Plantation, decreed that a Free School should be provided in each of the planted counties for the benefit of the children of the county. Portora is Fermanagh's Free School, with the stated purpose of 'the education of youth in Learning and Religion'. It could be said that today Portora is finally achieving in the most admirable fashion the aims envisaged by the 1608 Proclamation. Recent years have marked a return to serving the people of County Fermanagh, the stated purpose of the original foundation. Today, visitors to Portora can see parts of the School built during the eighteenth, nineteenth and twentieth centuries, reflecting its long and varied history.

But history does not stand still. In November 2008 the Ministry of Education (NI) announced that it was terminating the 11+ examination as the method of entry to Grammar School education throughout Northern Ireland. For well over 100 years Portora has maintained an entrance examination to ensure high academic standards. The Ministry has not yet announced its future plans for the re-organisation of secondary education within the province. However, it is clear that the next 400 years could be just as eventful for the School as the previous 400.

Some members of the Old Portora Union may be moved to paraphrase and alter the familiar words of our famous School hymn ('Abide with Me') to read, *'Change, not decay, in all around I see'*. It may be appropriate to conclude with a phrase made popular by Headmaster Douglas Graham: *'Floreat Portora'*, and allow their imagination to envisage what the twenty-first century may bring to the School.

Governors and governance

Introduction

The informal photograph above was taken during 2007 and shows most of the Governors gathering for a Board meeting on the steps of the north entrance of the School. The current Board totals twenty-seven members and there is some considerable history behind this figure.

For many years the governance of the Royal School Enniskillen functioned according to the whims of the incumbent Master, who had more or less unfettered access to the rents and endowments available from the escheated lands. Several Masters also had the personal wealth or sufficient commercial acumen to build and improve the School's facilities during their tenure of office.

Most Royal Schools were pretty independent and their scholastic reputation rested with the incumbent Master. There was little or no interference from the Government-appointed Commissioners for Irish Education, who merely inspected schools on request or in a rather haphazard manner. At Portora, Greham, when he was Master, had his first visit from the Commissioners after some twenty years in post, and he greatly resented their interference. In fact, he resigned as a direct result of their inspection and was critical of their findings, feeling they did not reflect the current successful state of the School.

Lord Justice Fitzgibbon's Commission

In 1885, Lord Justice Fitzgibbon was appointed by the Dublin Government to adjudicate on claims by certain sections of the local communities throughout Ulster that the endowments enjoyed by the Royal Schools were not sufficiently available to Roman Catholic pupils. In the case of Fermanagh and to be fair to Portora, the archive

Board of Governors 2006-07. Back row: J Styles, S Balmer; Second row: J Kerr, Reverend Precentor B Courtney, J Dickie, P Little, J Mullan, I Crawford; Third row: G McNeill, M Coalter, Mrs M Cooper, Mrs B Johnston, Mrs S McElroy, R Toner, N McClements, N Baxter; Front row: Ms N Heap, Mrs D Frazer, H Logan, J N Morton (Headmaster), Right Reverend Dr Michael Jackson, Bishop of Clogher (Chairman), S Morrow, T Smith, Mrs A Stronge (Bursar); missing: Sir Anthony Hart, I Kennedy, G Moore.

records show that several Masters actively encouraged the attendance of Roman Catholics. The School records show there were always several Roman Catholic boarders and dayboys at the School, although they were nearly always fee-paying and not free placements from the town.

The findings and recommendations of the Fitzgibbon Commission are now well known and as a result the lands and buildings of the Enniskillen Royal School were assessed and capitalised at a value of £7,000. This amount was then divided equally between the two new local Fermanagh Education Boards, one chosen and acting for the Protestant population and the other catering for the Roman Catholic community. The Protestant community in Enniskillen, because of their long and traditional associations with the Church of Ireland and Trinity College, Dublin, were given the opportunity to retain the buildings on Portora Hill for their continued use as a school. This offer was subject to the payment and distribution of their moiety (£3,500) to the newly formed Catholic Board. This was duly achieved to the satisfaction of both communities.

As a result the new Protestant Board of Education for the County of Fermanagh, appointed under this scheme on 21 May 1891, was as follows:

Representing the Diocesan Council of Clogher The **Right Reverend Charles Stack, DD** (OP, 1853), Bishop of Clogher; the **Reverend Charles T Ovenden, DD** (OP, 1865), Incumbent of Enniskillen and latter Dean of St Patrick's Cathedral, Dublin; the Reverend Arthur Haire-Forster, Rector of Ballynure, Clones; William R Cooney, Enniskillen; **Edward Smyth** (OP, 1863), Enniskillen. (Both Haire-Foster and Cooney sent their sons to Portora.)

Representing the General Assembly The Reverend S Cuthbert Mitchel; the Reverend J A Allison, Monaghan; William Carson, Enniskillen.

Representing the Methodist Conference **William Gault** (OP, 1852).

Nothing changed in basic structure for 80 years, except the formal nomination of a Chairman, Vice Chairman and Honorary Secretary. Naturally personalities changed and there were co-opted members selected from local personalities of note such as the incumbent Lord Erne rotating with the Earl of Belmore. In more recent times the Duke of Westminster joined the Board. For many years the position of Honorary Secretary was occupied by a member of the Trimble family (proprietors of *The Impartial Reporter*). The first Secretary appointed to the Board being **W Copeland Trimble** (OP, 1861); he was later followed by his son **W Egbert Trimble** (OP, 1892-1900).

Copeland Trimble wrote the first comprehensive history of Enniskillen town with a supplement covering Portora Royal School for its Tercentenary of 1918. Above left: W Copeland Trimble, JP and right: W Egbert Trimble.

New governance requirements

Following the publication of the Education Act (1984) there were significant changes made to the Board of Governors. The new Act called for the inclusion of elected teacher and parent governors to any school board.

In the case of Portora, the Board would now comprise ten members representing the Fermanagh Protestant Board of Education (five appointed by the Church of Ireland, three by the Presbyterian Church, one by the Methodist Church and one co-opted member); four appointed by the Department of Education; two elected parents and two elected teachers making a total of 18 members.

This development ushered in a new era of accountability for the governors and certain aspects of school life. In November 1992 the Department of Education announced it was introducing a new category of Voluntary Grammar School, which would qualify for 100% grant aid on approved capital projects. This proved to be a tempting offer for the governors as major capital works were still to be carried out at the School. To qualify for this new status the School trustees (the Fermanagh Protestant Board of Education) could no longer hold a majority on the Portora Board of Governors.

A debate and a decision to alter the Board

A debate ensued, some Board members fearing that this loss of control could in time erode the ethos of the School. However, this proved to be a minority view and the Board of Governors applied for the new status in June 1993. The newly constituted Board now has twenty-seven members – twelve representing the Fermanagh Protestant Board of Education (nine plus three co-opted); nine appointed by the Department of Education; three elected parents and three elected teachers. The new arrangement meant that the School would not have to raise 15% of the cost for any new capital projects.

Changes to the Chairmanship

Traditionally, the Bishop of Clogher was elected Chairman since the Church of Ireland membership was the major element in the make-up of the Fermanagh Protestant Board of Education. When the Right Reverend Brian Hannon retired from his Church office and also from the chairmanship of the Portora Board in 2002, the Board decided that any governor could be elected as chairman. It is perhaps appropriate, as the School celebrates its quatercentenary, that the current Chairman of the Board of Governors is the Bishop of Clogher, the **Right Reverend Dr Michael Jackson, MA, PhD, DPhil** (OP, 1967-75).

Two

Buildings, real estate, landmarks and countryside

Buildings and places can have just as strong an influence on the memory as people and events, and the buildings, real estate and countryside associated with Portora are no exception. This chapter will chronicle the main buildings on the Portora hillside, and describe the various landmark buildings around the town such as Willoughby Place, the Redoubt and St Macartin's Cathedral, all of which have been used to enhance the School and its activities over several centuries. There are also various scenic places in Fermanagh, such as Devenish Island, Castle Archdale, St Angelo and Marble Arch, that were often used for educational field trips, scout camps and Combined Cadet Force (CCF) exercises. These landmark places in Fermanagh may also bring back memories to those boarders, from Gloucester House and Portora, who were taken out for picnics by parents and friends during term or, when old enough, enjoyed simple weekend outings with their bicycles.

'Location, Location, Location', a common twenty-first century phrase – might seem a somewhat inappropriate expression to apply to a very traditional seventeenth-century institution, but for Portora it is apt, because the School has occupied three different locations since its foundation four hundred years ago:

- Castle Balfour, Lisnaskea   1618–c1643
- Schoolhouse Lane, Enniskillen   c1643–1777
- Portora Hill, Derrygonnelly Road   1777–present day

Left: Aerial photograph of Portora from the 1980s, with the Tercentenary Sanatorium and Liberty Hall still visible.

The first location

Ballybalfour within the Carrowshee Estate

Castle Balfour, after repair and safety restoration, stands guard over the modern town of Lisnaskea.

Castle Balfour, Lisnaskea

After ten years of ecclesiastical, political and administrative lassitude, dating from the original Proclamation of 1608, the Free School for Fermanagh was eventually established, around mid-Summer 1618, within the fortified area of Castle Balfour, by courtesy of Sir James Balfour. His father, Lord Burleigh, was an influential Scotsman in the Court of King James, and the family was granted proportions in County Fermanagh during the Plantation scheme for Ulster. Sir Michael, the elder son, was given what is now known as the old Crom Castle site, and Sir James, the younger brother, took title c1610-11 to the Carrowshee Estate of 1,000 acres, as part of the original Plantation. Sir James Balfour and his immediate family then came over from Scotland and took up permanent residence, c1616, in Fermanagh to develop the Castle Balfour site. Between 1616 and 1618, Sir James, who was the more enterprising member of the Balfour family, had made great strides with the construction and completion of a castle, a family residence and the new model township at Ballybalfour (the modern town of Lisnaskea).

Subsequently, Balfour offered the use of his two-storey school building, now nearing completion within the castle fortification, together with the services of his personal chaplain, the Reverend Geoffrey Middleton, MA, who became the appointed Master, thus providing a complete package of a Free School for Fermanagh to the Government authorities. The authorities, who were under considerable pressure from the Primate and, indeed, the King himself to implement the Free School for Fermanagh, raised no objections to this proposition. The transaction was subsequently confirmed, by a King's letter dated 13 August 1618, effectively establishing the first Free School for Fermanagh at Castle Balfour.

A brief description of the Balfour schoolhouse site may be found in a report compiled during 1618-19, by Captain Nicholas Pynnar, who, in his capacity as the Government Inspector of Fortifications and Works, wrote a series of progress reports covering several Plantation castles around the Lough Erne area, including the Balfour lands at Carrowshee. The report describes the first site of the School as follows: '*there is also a school, which is now 64 feet long, and 24 feet broad and two stories high. This is of good Stone and Lime, strongly built; the Roof is ready framed and shall be presently set up.*'

During 1626-27, the Archbishop of Armagh, James Ussher, was entrusted by the King and authorities in Dublin with the distribution of the lands earmarked for the endowment of the Free School of County Fermanagh. These escheated lands comprised some 39 Townlands totalling around 2,777 Irish acres, which when fully let later during the eighteenth century produced an income in excess of £2,000 per annum for disbursement by the Master. The original Letters Patent, dated 1626, inexplicably described the Fermanagh Free School's location as Lisgoole, a location that had been rejected some fifteen years before, and yet again draws attention to government maladministration. However, this mistake or confusion may have set the wheels in motion for the authorities to orchestrate the eventual move of the School from Ballybalfour to Enniskillen during the Bourke Mastership.

The School grows to over sixty pupils within ten years

The next clue to the early history of the School comes from the Inquisitions of County Fermanagh, in a report dated 22 January 1629, which states: '*Richard Boorke, Master of the Free Schoole of the County Fermanagh, by himselfe and his ushers [assistants], hathe diligently executed and discharged the place or office of a schoolmaster at Ballibalfour… The number of schollers in the said schoole are now three score or thereabouts, all except three being Irish natives.*' It is encouraging to find that, after ten or more years, the Free School for Fermanagh, although still at Ballybalfour, was flourishing and catered not only for the local native Irish but also encompassed the new Plantation stock living at Carrowshee. Bourke, as we know, continued in his post as Master of the Free School for thirty-five years, until the Reverend Thomas Dunbarre, MA (hereinafter Dunbar) was appointed by Letters Patent to become the third 'Master of the Free School for Fermanagh (Eniskillin)'.

During the Rebellion of 1641, Castle Balfour was the subject of a local insurrection, and we next find a report that in 1643 evidence was taken from '*Richard Bourke of Enniskillen, C. of Fermanagh, Bachelor in Divinity Minister of Gods word*', covering the whole incident. The wording suggests that the Free School for Fermanagh had already moved from the Carrowshee estate (Lisnaskea) to Enniskillen by this date.

The escheated lands assigned to the Free School for Fermanagh all fell within the Barony of Clanawaley, which was the domain from which Sir James Balfour took his title on ennoblement. Their proximity to his own lands no doubt contributed to the 1622 report by the new Bishop of Clogher (Spottiswood) to the Privy Council that Balfour had 'his eyes set upon them'.

The second location

Schoolhouse Lane, Enniskillen

A move into the shire town

The date when the School moved from Castle Balfour to Enniskillen has remained uncertain, but the majority opinion has usually favoured the early 1640s. At last, the Free School for County Fermanagh became firmly established in the shire town, which was of course the original intention, as envisaged by Chichester. After this move the School began to be known as the Enniskillen Free School. Whatever the facts, 1661 is the date recorded on the current Mastership Board hanging in the School's Dining Room over many decades. During the latter part of the Bourke Mastership and the early days of the Dunbar regime, the country was still governed by the Commonwealth Parliament, so it was some years before Enniskillen Royal School came into regular use as the official title.

Schoolhouse Lane

The site of the Enniskillen Free School was described by the Right Reverend William Henry, an early eighteenth-century Dean of Clogher, as '*on the northern side of the Church by the Lough*'. The School was accessed from a lane running east, at right angles to the main street, and was commonly known as Schoolhouse Lane; see maquette overleaf. Thereafter the School settled

This enlargement of an early twentieth-century photograph of the Masters' Board for Fermanagh Royal School shows the location of the School as being in Enniskillen from the start of the Dunbar Mastership in 1661. This contradicts the 1643 date favoured by many historians.

down for the next hundred years or more with a succession of lay and clerical Masters, who were all graduates of Trinity College, Dublin. The Enniskillen Free School in turn gained a national reputation for fine Classical scholarship, and sent many of its students to Trinity for matriculation and further education. In the eighteenth century, under the guidance successively of both Grattan (S, 1714-46) and Dunkin (S, 1746-63), *'the Great School of Enniskillen'* became so popular throughout all Ireland that the facilities and buildings in Schoolhouse Lane rapidly became insufficient for the requirements of its staff and pupils.

Under the original Town Charter (1612), the first Constable, Captain William Cole, had been obliged to provide a location for the Free School at Enniskillen, and from the outset had earmarked the Schoolhouse Lane site, until it was finally occupied in the 1640s. Well over a hundred years later, the continuing need for further facilities on the crowded Schoolhouse Lane site was voiced by the Master, the Reverend Mark Noble, who described the site as *'in a close and dirty lane, with no proper accommodation for scholars'.*

Map of Enniskillen by James Leonard, a philomath, 'a seeker of facts'. It shows the Free School located at 'G'. This positions the school east of the church, and not north, as described by the Dean of Clogher.

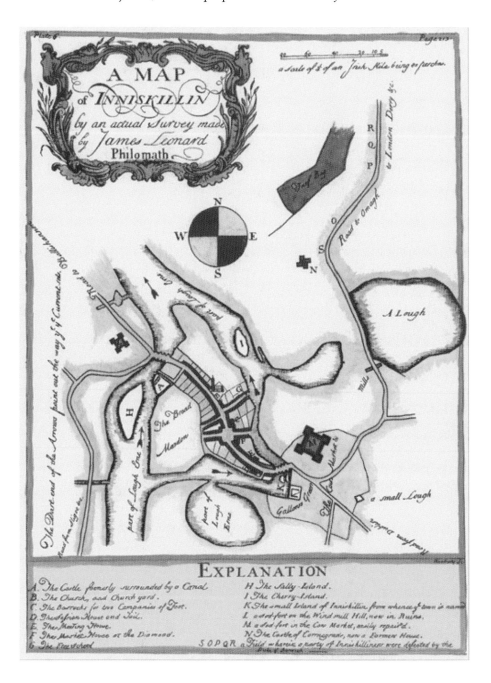

Photograph of a 3-dimensional maquette depicting the town with the Enniskillen Royal School area circled. In later years the incumbent Master complained that he was '*obliged to clear wandering sheep, cattle and goats from the premises, instead of parsing Latin*'.

Once again, therefore, it fell to a Cole successor, the Right Honourable Lord Mount Florence, to provide a solution, and find a new location that suited the immediate academic needs and long-term future requirements for the Enniskillen Royal School. Portora Hill seemed to be the most desirable site, and after mutual negotiation between the interested parties, the Free School parted with 120 acres of indifferent land from its endowments at Doohat Glebe, near Florence Court, in exchange for 33 acres of high-quality Cole land at Portora Hill.

The third location
The School on the Hill

Portora, a townland and a place of tears

From earliest times, the site of the Narrows within the Portora townland was of the utmost importance as a fording place. For many years, before the redefinition of land into counties, the Narrows of the Erne River marked part of the boundary between the provinces of Connacht and Ulster. This explains the necessity of building a fortress to guard this vital point downstream from Enniskillen. The Portora townland was included in the 1,000 acres of the Dromskeagh Estate acquired by a Scottish grantee, Jeremy Lindsay, under the original Plantation scheme. In October 1612, Sir William Cole, now Constable of Enniskillen, purchased the Portora townland from Lindsay, thus adding this new holding to his growing estate, which included land on nearby Enniskillen Island and other substantial acquisitions along the nearby shorelines.

One meaning of the word 'Portora' is said to be 'a place of tears', because during the time of Celtic Christianity, the departed left the shores of south Fermanagh by the ford or quayside situated by the Portora Narrows, on their final journey to Devenish Island and several other holy islands in upper Lough Erne, which were used for Christian burials. Other interpretations or folklore versions range from 'crock of gold' to 'muddy waters'. However the true origin is probably a linguistic derivation of the port of the Toora. The 'tuath' (settlement) of Toora dates back to early Celtic times, when the O'Flanagan tribe, of the Ui Neill stock from Leinster, became one of the first families to settle in what is now called Fermanagh. The Latin-inscribed stone inside the ruins of St Mary's Abbey, Devenish, tells us that an O'Flanagan was a Prior there in 1449, and an O'Flanagan presence was still there at the time of the Dissolution of the Monasteries.

Portora Castle seen from the Narrows, a watercolour by William Wakeman (S, 1862-1890). Wakeman was a personal friend of the Wilde family, and a well-known antiquarian, artist and drawing master at Portora during the Steele era.

The Castle was further ruined when a group of schoolboys from Portora tried excavating the foundations with a view to conducting experiments with home-made gunpowder. During the Summer of 1879, one unfortunate pupil, Robert Purser, was killed in this incident. His brother, Claude Purser (OP 1868-71), was one of the best-known Latin scholars in Europe, and eventually became Vice Provost of Trinity College, Dublin. The Castle in now in the hands of the State.

Portora Castle

The castle built by Cole alongside the Portora Narrows, c1614, has the residential house built across one side of the fortified enclosure, which was a common Scottish style employed by most Plantation grantees. The original entrance was probably in the south-east wall, and may still be among the ruins. A stone which was known to be in existence over the entrance in 1900 carried the initials 'J.S.' (James Spottiswood) inscribed on both sides.

In 1619 Captain Nicholas Pynnar described Portora Castle as being '*a bawn of lime and stone, with four flankers and a stone house or castle three storeys high, strongly wrought*'. Three of the flankers remain, including the two on the west flanking walls of the castle. These round towers, about three metres in diameter, have several gun-loops. Inside the castle can be seen proper fireplace chimneys in both the north and west walls.

Shortly after its completion, the castle was rented by the Reverend Dr James Spottiswood, from Sir William Cole, as the Diocesan Palace for the See of Clogher. Soon after his appointment as Bishop of Clogher, he suggested to the Privy Council that a substantial portion of the Free School's endowment lands were '*convenient and neighbourly*' to the Balfour holdings. Spottiswood also drew attention to the scheme suggested by Balfour for these endowment lands to be held in fee farm terms by Middleton, who was disparagingly referred to as 'Balfour's creature', following his appointment as Master of the Free School. (A fee farm grant out of a freehold folio is treated in much the same way as the complete freehold transfer, but also in perpetuity.) Since none of the endowment land ever changed hands, however, the Spottiswood stewardship of the School's assets proved effective. Spottiswood stayed in residence at Portora Narrows until c1628. He was a great champion of the Fermanagh Free School and of the scheme to relocate the establishment from the original Castle Balfour site to the shire town of Enniskillen.

Following Spottiswood's departure from Portora Castle, it was occupied by several different members of the Cole family, until Sir Michael Cole and his family moved there permanently after their former residence, Enniskillen Castle, was partially destroyed by fire in 1710. The family remained at Portora Castle until about 1716, when Sir Michael's son, Sir John Cole (1680-1726), a former pupil at the Royal School, Enniskillen, started building Florence Court as the long-term Irish seat of the recently ennobled Cole family.

The ford and quay by Portora Castle have always been an important strategic feature of the Erne waterways, and the riverside path from the West Bridge in Enniskillen to the Portora River and Narrows was a public right of way. It was also a popular walk for Enniskillen townspeople until c1856, when the Master (Steele) and his neighbour Edward Irwin, Esquire, JP, of Derrygore House, managed jointly to obtain a legal closure of the route.

Reclamation works along the Narrows in the late Victorian era (c1880), and latterly during the Erne drainage scheme (1951-60), revealed numerous artefacts, including Bronze Age weapons, stone axes and a fine bronze dirk, which were recovered from the riverbed.

A move up the Hill from the Town

The photograph of the main buildings on Portora Hill shows that the external view has not greatly changed over the last one hundred and fifty years.

Main frontage of the School showing the central block with additional north and south wings and later infills.

The complete façade reflects construction over three distinct phases. The first phase of the main school building, which dates from about 1777, was authorised by the School Board, and consisted of the central portion of an impressive three-storey building, incorporating a lower semi-basement facility for domestic staff. The construction was financed personally by the new Master, the **Reverend Mark Noble** (S, 1763-94), to the tune of £3,000, and was initially known as Portora House. In accordance with the practice of the time, the building provided a single large schoolroom for all pupils, with a number of additional rooms for the accommodation and feeding of up to seventy boarders. There was also provision of domestic facilities for Junior and Assistant Masters, who, if single, were expected to sleep in staff cubicles in the dormitories. The domestic staff, kitchen quarters, food-preparation areas and the primitive washing facilities of the time were all housed in the semi-basement. Although the façade of Portora may look today like a classic neo-Palladian Georgian country house, it was not, and never has been, a stately home converted for use as a school.

First phase – Portora House [**1** ; *numbers refer to plan on page 80*]

An early etching of the school (detail below) shows the result of this first phase of construction. During the latter part of the eighteenth century, Fermanagh was distinguished by continuing high-quality construction projects, as local

…continued on page 82

Portora Royal School
buildings and real estate c1960

1. Original Portora House.
2. School yard.
3. North wing – infirmary (1838-40).
4. South wing – classrooms, dormitory (1838-40).
5. Infill – Stone Hall (1860s).
6. Infill – Master's Hall (1860s).
7. Pump Yard/slope.
8. Liberty Hall (c1860s, now demolished).
9. Steele Hall (c1860s).
10. Gymnasium (c1900).
11. Sanatorium (c1920, now demolished).
12. Boathouse and jetties (1860s onwards).
13. Sergeant Major's house (1925, now demolished).
14. Cricket Pavilion (1929).
15. Chemistry laboratory (1930s).
16. Stepaside (1936).
17. Gloucester House (1936).
18. Reay Gates (1949).
19. Swimming Pool (1950s).
20. Teaching block (1958).
21. Portora housing (1960).
22. Scales Physics Laboratory (1960).
A. Early recreational areas (1800s).
B. Cricket Pitch.
C. Upper Playing Fields (1944-49).
D. Lower Playing Fields (1925).
E. Tennis courts.

Detail from the engraving in chapter one showing the original 1777 central block, which had a handsome porch and was known as Portora House. The yard and outbuildings to the rear also date from this time.

gentry, landowners and the townspeople concentrated on the building of Erne Castle, Castlecoole, Belmore, Florence Court, Ely Lodge and large residential areas of Enniskillen town, all of which employed many skilled local and imported tradesmen.

The architects for the original school building are not known, and unlike some of the country houses listed above, the internal finish is not particularly ornate. Even today, one can appreciate the lasting quality of the basic stonework and construction techniques undertaken by those long-forgotten craftsmen. This first phase of the new school building was designed to provide accommodation for fifty to seventy boarders and twenty local dayboys or free scholars. The dramatic geographical setting of the School, overlooking the River Erne and the nearby town of Enniskillen, set the Portora site apart from all the other Royal Schools. When Portora House opened during 1779, an advertisement in the *Belfast Newsletter* stated: '*The Free School of Enniskillen will be opened on 25 inst in the House built by Mr Noble for the reception of 100 boarders. Prices are 5 guineas for boarders per quarter and 1 guinea for day scholars*'. It was some years before the figure of 100 was eventually attained, and it was probably not until the Mastership of Greham, in the late 1830s, that it was exceeded. It is interesting to note the discrepancy between the design figures and the advertised ones, probably an early example of marketing and advertising creeping into education.

The schoolyard and stabling [❷]

As the main building progressed, the 'L'-shaped block of yard buildings was developed to the rear of the grand façade. A central feature was a hand-pump and well in the courtyard. During the nineteenth century this two-storey stone block housed the haylofts, stabling, fodder and pens for domestic animals including cattle, sheep and pigs that were kept on site to supplement bought rations. The stabling also provided single quarters to accommodate male servants, who were kept apart from the female domestic staff, whose accommodation was in the basement of the main building.

Over the years the yard buildings have been variously used as workshops, laundry, carpentry classrooms, dayboys locker room and study areas and latterly (c1990s) the hayloft was converted into the School Chapel. After the demise of boarding, the old school bell was taken out of the tower and placed in the yard. The last bell-ringer was **Albert (Bert) Cranston** (S, 1935-85), a faithful servant for over fifty years. In his final bequest, Bert left a legacy to the School, which has been used to provide a series of name-boards in the main school building, recording the details of past Presidents of the Old Portora Union and former Captains or Head Boys of the School.

Second phase – the need for more space

Just as the old Schoolhouse Lane site had become too small for the staff and pupils, by the early 1800s even the new and enhanced school buildings on Portora Hill required expansion. This was due to the growing popularity of the School, which was a direct result of its academic success and the expansion of Ireland's transport network. By 1838 an extension had been planned by the Master, Greham, to cater for a total of 120 boarders and 60 dayboys. This second phase of construction was executed by the School Board and its own architects.

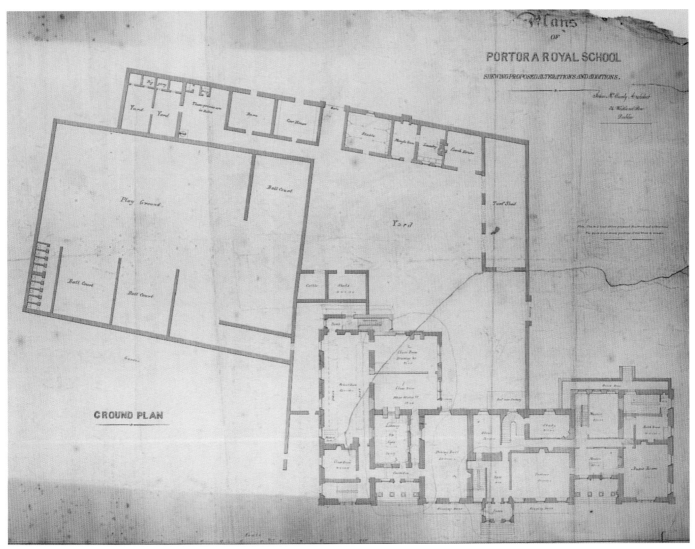

The sanitary arrangements for boarders at that time were far from salubrious. This is how they are described by **Lombe Atthill** (OP, 1840-43) in his autobiography: *'No basins or jugs were allowed in the dormitories, and the lavatory, such as it was, was situated below the level of the ground, being virtually a flagged cellar. Along its sides were benches, in which were cut circular spaces holding wooden bowls to be used as basins. On the floor in front of them lay a thick plank on which we stood, and which was always saturated with moisture. In*

Architect's drawings from the 1800s showing proposed alterations to the School frontage, including the retention of a central entrance. These proposals were not implemented. The drawings clearly show the layout of buildings behind the main block, including the schoolyard, ball court and turf shed.

The North Wing was constructed for use as an infirmary, and the South Wing was used for additional classrooms and dormitory accommodation. Note that the wings were not yet connected to the central block.

the centre of the floor were tubs full of water. When a boy wanted to wash his face or hands, he took one of the wooden bowls, as likely as not full of dirty water left by the last user.

'This he emptied on the floor, which sloped towards a large opening under the one window which lighted the place; then, stepping off the plank, he filled the basin by dipping it into the tub, and proceeded with his ablutions. No light was allowed in the lavatory in winter and for the first two winters I was there I regularly washed in the dark, feeling along till I got to an empty basin and filling it as best I could, in the dark winter mornings, out of a tub. In general, I was alone, even when the mornings were brighter, for only some five or six boys out of the whole school washed before breakfast; they were not expected to do so.

'During my last winter at this school this vile arrangement was altered, a proper lavatory erected, water laid on and light supplied during the dark winter mornings.'

Third phase – infill of the two wings [③ and ④]

Records show that with these newly enlarged facilities, the School was capable of housing the planned number of boarders and day pupils. Several years later, a serious and unspecified illness broke out amongst the boys. This was the era of the Irish Potato Famine; the general health of the nation was very poor and the Commissioners of Education immediately sanctioned an additional capital sum of £400 to undertake a major refurbishment of the sanitary and washing facilities at the School.

Improvements were made ten to fifteen years later, when the **Reverend Dr Steele** (S, 1857-91), at his own expense, commissioned John McCurdy, Architects, Dublin, to complete the infill between the central block and the new wings. This provides the familiar external frontage of the two rows of four stone Doric columns linking both ends of the main School. The south portico now carries a plaque commemorating **Oscar Wilde** (OP, 1864-71), and provides

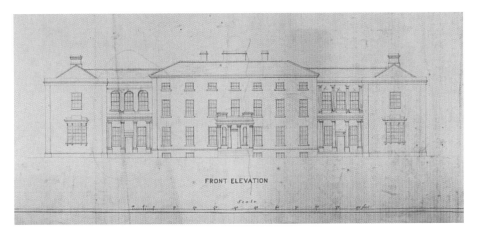

FRONT ELEVATION

Architect's elevation drawing of the frontage of the building showing a central entrance. The central block of seven windows was commissioned in 1777, with additional north and south wings added c1838. The completion of the Portora façade and infill behind the Doric pillars was commenced c1856, along with the initial construction phases of the Steele Hall and Liberty Hall.

a suitable entrance to a fine tiled hallway, commonly referred to as the Stone Hall. This has a splendid mosaic of the Royal Seal incorporated in the centre of the floor. The north portico has a similar commemorative plaque dedicated to that other literary giant of the School, **Samuel Beckett** (OP, 1920-22). This has now become the entrance to the Headmaster's domestic quarters, and the Governors' access to the Seale Library and the boardroom facilities.

The Pump Yard [7]

Along the south wing there was a steep slope downwards, which contained a well and pump. This area was situated between the School and the newly proposed Examination Hall (later known as the Steele Hall).

Liberty Hall [8]

Liberty Hall was built in the late 1850s as the isolation ward and infirmary for boarders. It was initially designed to replace the north wing of Portora House, which was the first isolation and sick-bay facility at the School. It had numerous changes of use during its existence. After the opening of the Sanatorium in 1922, Liberty Hall was converted to dormitory facilities for Leinster House boarders, with domestic and office accommodation for the Housemaster of Leinster, **Major G V Butler, TD** (S, 1924-49). Butler had been a World War I Sapper, and he also undertook the duties of School Bursar, including the supervision of domestic, financial and property interests.

When boarding was at its height, Liberty Hall was used also as a hotel during half-term breaks and holidays, to provide for those pupils who could not leave the School because their parents or guardians lived too far away. More recently, it had been used for teaching modern languages and geometrical drawing, and for technical stores. Eventually, the building had deteriorated too far to attract funding from the Department of Education (NI) to refurbish it to current standards. It was finally demolished in the 1990s to make way for Phase III of the new technical buildings.

The Steele Hall [9]

In about 1859, and at his own expense, Dr Steele financed and built a new set of low-level classrooms with a large schoolroom on the storey above. This upper storey is now known as the Steele Hall, in memory of one of the more notable Masters of the School. Like the infills joining the east and west wings to the main school, the new building was designed by John McCurdy, Architects,

The Royal Seal, as a mosaic, in the centre of the Stone Hall. This version depicts the arms of King James 1 and the date of 1618, which was the date when the Free School was first established at Ballybalfour. (See also Chapter 10, Appendix B, for the full story on the various crests used by the School).

Liberty Hall began as the infirmary. It was purposely built well away from the School so that it could be used as an isolation hospital.

Dublin, and ran parallel to the west side of the main School building. In 1899, a wide sloping access was constructed to provide entry to the upper level from the main school, and a steep flagged and grassy bank, with two sets of steps, provided access to the classrooms below. Different generations of pupils will have memories of differing functions within the Steele Hall. As already stated, the upper storey was originally designed to be a single large classroom for boys in the Lower School, but over the years the facility has been called the 'Lower School Room', the 'Examination Hall', the 'School House' and 'Big School'. Later it took on the functions of an assembly hall, a theatre for drama, and a chapel for boarders' Sunday evening services. It was even rumoured that, during the Mastership of McDonnell, 'Dickie' Lloyd (of the famous 1907 rugby team) was allowed to practise his drop-kicking techniques in the hall during bad weather.

House classrooms underneath the Steele Hall [9]

There were originally three classrooms and a lavatory with washroom facilities on the lower level beneath the Steele Hall. In 1892, however, the structure was found to be shifting downhill, so an architect from the Education Commissioners recommended the construction of three external buttresses on the south side, and the insertion of an additional wall on the lower floors, to give stability to the floor above, thus increasing the number of classrooms to four. The first science laboratory at Portora was opened, in about 1900, in one of these lower classrooms. Later, during the 1920s, these classrooms were modified to provide four Houserooms for Junior boarding pupils of Ulster, Munster, Leinster and Connacht. They were also used as Junior study rooms for evening prep, which was traditionally supervised by the duty master in one classroom, and three duty House Prefects in the remaining classrooms.

During the 1920s, a stage was added to one end of the Steele Hall, with three piano music rooms constructed beneath the stage area on the lower floor, where there had been washrooms and lavatories. In general, the Steele Hall remained unaltered until the mid-1960s, when Val Rogers began his second phase of improvements and new construction throughout the School.

The Steele Hall laid out for Morning Assembly and Sunday Evening Services before the mid-1960s. The photograph was taken c1948, from the stage end of the building. Anyone keen enough to count the number of chairs may be interested to know that there are exactly 222. Initially, chairs were allocated for naming to families whose sons had fallen in World War I, and then to school leavers who subscribed ten shillings. The custom ceased when the numbers reached the Hall's capacity.

A gallery is added and the stage is improved [9]

Increasing numbers of day and boarding pupils meant that the Steele Hall was no longer adequate for seating students and their guests on public occasions. Rather than demolish and build anew, the Hall was extensively renovated and modified during the early 1960s, with a gallery that could accommodate a hundred or more extra seats. At the same time, the stage area was redesigned and a new proscenium arch was built. Total renovation of the electric wiring was implemented, and, in a two-phase programme, a three-manual Makin organ was purchased and installed to provide a first-class venue for any event that the School might wish to organise. **A E (Tony) Smith** (S, 1952-65), for twelve years Head of the Music Department, helped to raise funds for the organ during his early retirement, and the organ is dedicated to his memory. The chairs have now been transferred to the School Chapel for congregational use.

The Memorial Boards and tributes to the fallen of the Boer War and World Wars I and II, which were originally installed inside the main hall, have now been relocated to the vestibule and entrance area of the Steele Hall. The latest boards recording School Exhibitioners are displayed in the entrance corridors, leaving only the original boards listing former Royal Scholars and Exhibitioners in their traditional setting of the Steele Hall.

The former House classrooms on the lower level were redesigned and renovated as language laboratories during the Bennett Headmastership, and a balancing fourth buttress was added to secure the south wall of the main Steele Hall. Outside, the old greenhouses and propagating sheds for garden produce in the Master's Garden have been demolished.

The Steele Hall as it is in 2008, after the addition of a gallery. Although the facilities and capacity of the hall have been improved immensely, it lacks the atmosphere and grandeur of the original building.

Wellington Place – an unsuccessful experiment

In about 1860, Steele decided to establish separate classroom facilities, outside the main School grounds, for dayboys. He rented several adjoining houses in Wellington Place, a smart area of central Enniskillen, engaged a dedicated Master in Charge and transferred all dayboys and free scholars to this location, thus leaving the Portora buildings exclusively for the use of boarders. As we know, there was great hostility to this course of action, and within the year Steele was forced to abandon his concept of separate education for day pupils. The Wellington Place location was closed and pupils returned to accommodation on the Portora Hill site.

Playing fields receive attention from the Governors [A]

We learn from **Lombe Atthill** (OP 1841-44) that no games were taught or encouraged during his time as a pupil at Portora, except the casual use of a ball court alley. During the summer of 1842, however, Atthill and Shaw (the son of Sir Fredrick Shaw, Recorder of Dublin) managed to organise, teach and train two cricket teams for a local match of Senior versus Junior boys on the fields at Portora, described as *'a rough field, all hills and hollows'*. As in a true schoolboy story, the Juniors, led by Atthill, triumphed over the Seniors, led by Shaw. Historically, cricket was the first formal team game to be introduced to Portora, probably some time in the 1850s, by the Carson brothers from Armagh, who surprisingly were encouraged by the Headmaster of Armagh Royal School to attend Portora Royal School. At the time, Armagh was the foremost school for cricket in Ireland. The elder of the two brothers, **J J H Carson** (OP, 1853), was later to become a Director of the Bank of Ireland.

Fortunately, the Lord Deputy and the Commissioners of Education realised during the 1860s that exercise and competitive sport were an important part of all-round education, and voted the necessary funds to improve the playing fields and associated facilities at Portora. In their Annual Report to the Earl of Carlisle, the Lord Lieutenant, dated 1863-64, the Commissioners of Education wrote: *'in consequence of your Excellency's recommendations to us... we caused a cricket ground to be to be formed at Portora... the expense of which exceeded what was first expected, which was due to the hilly nature of the ground ...it gives great satisfaction to the numerous pupils who avail themselves of it.'* The same report contains an early notification of the impending completion of Liberty Hall, as well as preliminary schemes for the design and construction of a large schoolroom, which later became the Steele Hall.

It is worth recording that, although the grass surfaces of the Upper Playing Fields were improved considerably by this early nineteenth-century renovation, it would be at least another eighty years before the whole area became a level playing field. This was eventually achieved with the help of the US Forces during World War II, 1944-46, when US construction units used the Portora playing fields to train bulldozer operators prior to the invasion of Normandy and subsequent Allied occupation of Germany. An eyewitness has written: *'As I recall, there was a considerable height difference then between the upper and lower grassed areas – five or six feet maybe more and the upper area had a marked transverse incline. The Headmaster let the US bulldozer drivers practise there before embarking for the D-Day invasion. There were several gantry 'dozers employed on training... each of which was operated with a rear drum lifting the blade by a hawser cable, which was then supported by an overhead gantry, that ran the whole length of the 'dozer. The 'dozer trainees extended the main cricket area and levelled the higher area by dint of pushing masses of spoil down the hill towards the lower football fields. They eventually reduced the height difference between the two areas to under three feet!'*

Most members of the Portora staff were furious that Stuart had allowed the US 'doughboys' to bulldoze their hallowed turf in an attempt to create a single playing field. The army crews tried to achieve this by pushing everything from the centre outwards and down the slopes, without any separation or segregation of the various sub-soil levels. In practical terms, this resulted in all valuable topsoil being systematically covered by tons of underlying earth and rock. It was never finished, and later attempts to grow grass where it had been partially finished failed miserably. After the war, in 1946-48, a team of civil engineering contractors was engaged, at considerable expense, to lay a new drainage scheme, backfill the surface with decent topsoil and re-turf the whole upper area. This was then quickly transformed into a quarter-mile running track, with central straights for sprints and hurdles and an off-set safe area for field events. All of this was achieved in time for use on Sports Day, at the end of the Summer Term, 1949.

The gymnasium [10]

Construction of the gymnasium started about the turn of the century (c1898-1900), during the Mastership of Biggs, when games and sporting activities became popular, and representative teams could travel more easily on the expanded rail networks to and from Enniskillen. Its introduction as a school facility also coincided with the rising popularity of Swedish drill, physical jerks and boxing training, all of which had became popular activities in the army and navy and throughout the English Public School system. The gymnasium and its sporting functions were nearly always supervised by retired

The gymnasium was built on the site of the old dry trench latrines, on the fringes of the School yard and ball courts. In this photograph we see Corporal Gore and his pupils with Indian clubs for Swedish drill. The pupil in the foreground is wearing old leather boxing gloves.

non-commissioned officers of HM Forces, who in later years also doubled as permanent staff instructors for the Officer Training Corps (OTC), when it was formally established with War Office approval in 1923.

Physical Training becomes Physical Education

In later years the gymnasium facility was given a great boost with the arrival of **Jack Wheeler** (S, 1948-1994) on the teaching staff. After demobilisation from the Rifle Brigade, as one of the youngest ever Warrant Officers in the British Army, Wheeler completed a diploma course in Physical Education at Loughborough College, England. He was one of the first batch of post-war civilian Physical Training Instructors (PTI) working in English educational establishments; he specialised in teaching Physical Education (PE) as well as coaching and training sporting teams. Wheeler, almost single-handed, refurbished the gymnasium with war-surplus gym equipment, and brought a professional expertise to the coaching of all School teams. His musical PT display on the School Sports Day in 1949, performed on the Parade Ground with over 60 participants, was something of a show stopper.

Preparations for the physical education display at the 1949 Sports Day with Jack Wheeler on the left hand side of the lower photograph.

The Tercentenary Memorial – Sanatorium and Cottage Hospital [ ]

In former times, when the School had a large boarding department, those pupils who were taken ill during the School term were isolated in this building, lest they infect those in the regular dormitories. The Sanatorium stood to the immediate right of the main School building, along a short access road which joined the track and steps leading down to the boathouse. The wooden bungalow was commissioned in 1918 as a combined Tercentenary and Great War Memorial, made possible by a subscription of £800 from Old Boys and local friends of Portora. It was designed as a cottage hospital to replace the medical and sick-bay facilities at Liberty Hall, which were shortly to be used for the boarders of Leinster House. The sloping site, complete with a wide, cantilevered veranda, gave it an air reminiscent of the Indian Raj, or some other far-flung part of the Empire. The central A-frame wood and plaster structure housed the medical examination room and sick-bay. There was also a small combined scullery/kitchen, bathrooms and toilets, as well as domestic accommodation for the Sister in Charge, and a spare staff-room for a possible assistant in times of need. The two sick-bays were typical army-type wards, with eight or ten beds in each wing and a long wooden table down the middle of each central aisle. While convalescing and allowed out of bed in their dressing-gowns, patients used the tables for dining at meal times, or for playing board games and constructing jigsaws.

During the infamous freezing Easter Term of 1947, both Gloucester House and Portora suffered a double bout of whooping cough and measles. Both wards of the Sanatorium were full, one with Portora boys, the other with Gloucester House pupils. Naturally, competition developed between the two sick-bays, especially on those afternoons when the Sister in Charge, **Miss E E Hall SRN**, (S), took a few hours off to go shopping in Enniskillen. Competitive activities were soon stopped, since the prime contest in question, to see who could leap the farthest, involved two boys, one from each ward,

running barefoot down the outside veranda in their pyjamas, vaulting over the balcony and diving into the huge bank of snow below. Fortunately, Miss Hall, who must have had a sense of humour, banned the game by saying that she didn't have a third dormitory for pneumonia cases.

During the 1990s, thoughts were given to the renovation of the building and its conversion to a Sixth Form Centre after it had served as a dormitory for girls. However, the Sanatorium was an early do-it-yourself project, undertaken originally by the Portora maintenance staff. The building specification of a timber and plaster construction was not best suited to the damp Fermanagh climate, and over seventy years it had gradually deteriorated. A further problem, which led to its eventual demise, was that asbestos tiles, deemed at the outset to be one of the latest and best materials, were used in the construction and insulation of the roof.

This unusual building was finally demolished during the early 1990s. Appropriately, the old Tercentenary Memorial nameplate has been preserved and placed inside the main School building, outside the entrance to the School Archive Office.

The boathouse and jetty area [12]

Various facilities and structures have come and gone on this site since the mid-1800s. At the end of World War II, there was a need to replace a cattle barn, which had been used to house the School livestock during the winter months. The existing facilities were now well beyond repair. The McNeill family – notably **D B McNeill** (OP, 1923-30) – financed the construction of a new facility, which doubled as a cattle shed during the Winter and a boathouse for the Spring and Summer. The boats were hoisted to the roof during the winter, and when the cattle were turned out to pasture in the Spring, the floor was hosed out, the boats brought down and the space used as a very passable boathouse for the duration of the rowing season.

The boathouse, 2007.

The boathouse and jetty in 1915, with an eight out on the water.

The Lower Rugby Pitches [D]

The Lower Rugby pitches and Castle Road connecting them to the Narrows were purchased in 1925 for the sum of £1,500, and in total added an additional area of 15 acres. This acquisition, made during Seale's Headmastership, at last provided alternative playing fields for an increasing number of official School teams. By the mid-1920s these included a regular second fifteen for rugby, as well as a soccer facility for the boys in the Junior School. The new Lower Pitches, although frequently flooded, were at least level. Depending on the rainfall, the river levels of the Erne were never entirely predictable, and for home matches the visiting players usually complained that if it was dry they were playing in thick mud, or if it was wet they were swimming. The Erne drainage scheme, c1952-66, improved the situation considerably.

Sergeant Major's cottage [13]

At the entrance to Castle Road, on the left, there was a two-storey farm cottage and garden, which for many years served as tied quarters for the Corps Sergeant Major and his family.

The Cricket Pavilion [14]

The Cricket Pavilion on the Upper Playing Fields was commissioned in 1929, and comprised a separate dressing room for each of two teams, a score-board facility and a long lean-to facility to the rear, which was used for storing tools, mowers and a heavy roller for the wicket. During the 1930s, shortly after the facility was commissioned, a group of boys, led by **Jasper Wolfe** (OP, 1925-31) from West Cork, organised a mock chariot race around the pitch with the heavy roller. The event got totally out of hand and the inevitable occurred, the roller finding its way at an ever-increasing speed down the steep slope to the Narrows and into the River Erne. It has never been found, in spite of an extensive search at the time by the miscreants themselves, and considerable engineering works and dredging of the area in later years for the Erne Hydro-electric Scheme. Wolfe, or probably his father, was asked to contribute a hefty compensation for its loss, a sum equal to half the fees for a term.

Cricket Pavilion. By early tradition, the only spectators allowed to use the seats in the pavilion were visitors, members of staff and any holder of a School team sports colour.

Chemistry and Physics Labs in the gymnasium courtyard [⑮]

The old Chemistry and Physics building was a classic of early laboratory design. Its lofty ceiling with its skylights harked back to an era before there were fume cabinets and fluorescent lighting; back to a time when the almost traditional chemistry smell of hydrogen sulphide (rotten eggs) would have been removed by that natural ventilation we now call draughts. From the beginning the Laboratory was the domain of **Henry Scales** (S, 1924-60), the first Senior Chemistry Master, Housemaster of Munster and later Deputy Master of the School. **James 'Jasper' Malone** (S, 1934-50) presided over the other laboratory, which was equipped for the teaching of Physics, until he left Portora to become the County Education Officer.

Above: ground view of the 1930s Chemistry and Physics laboratory, built in the 1930s. High in the background are the windows of the former Connacht Dormitory (now the Galbraith Library) and immediately above the labs is the roof of the old changing rooms for games and sport.

Left: Henry Scales with a class of pupils. The photograph is believed to have been taken some time during the 1930s and may well have been posed, because of the wide range of ages of the boys and the fact that one of them is wearing short trousers.

For generations of Portorans, lessons in the laboratories were probably all that they would remember of Physics and Chemistry. Time was to take its toll. Some may recall that during periods of high winds and rain the skylights, which formed an integral part of the natural ventilation system, had a distinct tendency to leak and shed the odd pane or two of glass on to the classrooms below. The time eventually came when the new laboratories had been built, and the old construction was due for demolition. The School assembled and stood and watched as a mechanical digger went to work on the old walls. Demolition revealed that the structure had in part incorporated substantial stonework from some previous age. The fine ashlars (cut stone blocks) were carefully marked and numbered, picked out from the rubble and set aside by the contractors as a possible feature for some future building project. The site was finally levelled and resurfaced as a car park, leaving no remnants of that period in the history of Portora, apart from a photograph as evidence of the inevitable need to provide for the increasing number of cars now parked within the School grounds.

The Seale Room during the period it was used as the Junior Classroom.

The Seale Room during the period it was the Sixth Form library.

The Seale Room 2008, now used as the Governors' Conference Room. Historic photographs from various eras decorate the walls. The World War I Roll of Honour and a portrait of Seale are clearly visible.

The Seale Room

The Seale Room was the drawing room in the Master's quarters when Portora House was built in 1777. It later become the 'Junior Classroom' for Miss E E Hunt when she was appointed Head of the Junior School in 1915. When Gloucester House opened in 1936, the Juniors had their own facilities and the Headmaster, Stuart, refurbished the room as a Senior Study and Library which became known as the Seale Memorial Library. Today the Seale Room is used as the Governors' Conference Room with chairs bearing the names and dates of former Governors. It is also used for staff meetings and as a minor examination room.

Roll of Honour

An important corner of the Seale Room is dedicated to the Roll of Honour for World War I and an illuminated book of participating service personnel. The cabinet for the war shrine is made from teak recovered from the sixth HMS Britannia, when the ship was broken up in 1916 and its materials dispersed throughout the Kingdom as mementoes of World War I. It now records the names of over seventy pupils who were killed or died of wounds during the war. Beneath the shrine is a vellum book recording the names of all Portorans who served during World War I.

The first Gloucester House and Stepaside [16 and 17]

The first Gloucester House building and its accompanying staff house, Stepaside, were both completed in 1936, on the lower south side of Portora Hill. The style of the building is reminiscent of a Mediterranean villa in the art nouveau style, with brilliant white walls, wooden-shuttered windows and a green tiled roof, all very daring for the Enniskillen of those days. The surplus earth from the excavations for the new building was used to create the Upper School Parade Ground, which also provided a suite of hard tennis courts on top of the hill. The building was designed to accommodate thirty boys as

Gloucester House, 2007 from the
Ballyshannon/Bundoran Road.

boarders, and had three classrooms, a dining room and a cloakroom on the
ground floor. Initially, the first floor comprised three dormitories of different
sizes, washrooms and staff accommodation; the attic area was used to house
several music rooms.

Outside, on the west side of Gloucester House, there was a large wooden
hut known as the 'Rec Room'. It served as a recreation space where assembly,
cubs, table tennis and other indoor activities could take place during inclement
weather. A grass playground below Stepaside completed the Preparatory
School complex, which could also count on the full use of all the sporting
facilities of the Upper School. This included the twice-weekly trip up the hill
through the Master's garden to the gymnasium for PT and boxing lessons.

Stepaside was originally designed as accommodation for the Headmaster
of Gloucester House. During World War II it was used by Stuart as an annex
to his quarters at Portora, when it housed his mother. It was further retained
by Stuart to house members of his family for several years after he left Portora
on assignment to the United States. When Lakeside Gloucester House was
commissioned in the 1960s, the old Gloucester House had a succession of uses
as classrooms, boarding accommodation for Munster House, and finally as
boarding accommodation for girls.

Later, during the 1980s, Stepaside was occupied for a time by the
Headmaster, Richard Bennett, when the main Portora buildings were being
converted to accommodate female boarders. This explains the name of the
House for girls, Head's House. Both the old Gloucester House building and
Stepaside still form part of the Portora estate today. However, they are not used
by the School, but are rented out to Government-sponsored institutions.

Front entrance to Gloucester House, from
the entrance driveway.

Reay Gates [18]

The Portora gates at the bottom of the hill are now perhaps as much a symbol of the School as the original eighteenth-century building on top of the hill. The gates were crafted by Musgrave & Co Ltd, Belfast, and erected in 1948, in memory of **Flight Lieutenant Derek Reay, RAF** (OP, 1931-39), and his brother, **Flying Officer Geoffrey Reay, RAF** (OP, 1932-43), who perished while on active service with the RAF during World War II. The four Corinthian pillars were from Inishmore Hall, and were erected in memory of the late **Captain W E C Irwin, RA** (OP, 1927-29), of the Indian Army, who died at Imphal during the Burma Campaign in World War II.

Reay Gates, 2006.

The opening ceremony was performed in 1949 by the Governor of Northern Ireland, Earl Granville, whose somewhat casual dress, a tweed suit, caused considerable local umbrage. Most of the Portora Staff wore their academic robes, while members of Enniskillen society turned out in morning coats or dark suits and bowler hats. There were muttered comments that the Queen Elizabeth's brother-in-law should have known that a dark suit would have been the more appropriate dress for this formal occasion.

Reay Gates the day before the official opening in 1949.

The Redoubt – temporary boarding accommodation for Juniors

After World War II, expanding numbers meant that classroom and dormitory accommodation was becoming difficult to find on the Portora Hill site. In 1948, junior boarders at the Upper School were moved off the main School site to occupy 'The Redoubt' (see later in this chapter under Landmarks).

Rogers' extensive building programme

The 1950s and 1960s witnessed the most extensive building and renovation programme since the School was built. The ambitious plans attracted the attention of that famous old magazine *The Illustrated London News*, when a series of drawings was published in 1958. The main addition was a new two-storey block of classrooms, which was opened in 1959 and extended later, with an Engineering workshop and a Physics laboratory on stilts.

New classroom block opened in 1958, with the Observatory on the left-hand side.

A new Biology lab, dining hall, gym extension and changing rooms, tennis courts, fives courts and six staff houses were built in Castle Lane. A small Chapel area was created above the stables, with room made to house some of the existing memorial tablets that commemorated individuals.

Swimming pool [19]

For many years, swimming at Portora had taken place in the River Erne at various locations, ranging from rafts and a stage in the Frying Pan during the early 1900s, to several ad hoc facilities at Portora Castle and the Narrows. For a time during the late 1940s, Jack Wheeler made temporary arrangements near the Killeyhevlin Hotel to stage inter-House competitions. Finally, in 1958, with the substantial support of a £10,000 grant from the Old Portora Union, a purpose-built open-air swimming pool and changing facility was completed within the School grounds near the Reay Gates. For over fifty years this pool has now been an attraction to generations of Portorans, as well as to the residents of Enniskillen who were allowed to become season members of the Portora Swimming Club. This was an initiative founded by Major Jack Wheeler and his wife to give swimming lessons to the Enniskillen Community – over 30,000 people participated in the programme.

Post World War II building programme

Graham era

1945-50
Boathouse.
Upper playing fields levelled.

1951-54
Upper playing fields improved.
Parade ground resurfaced.

Rogers era

1955-60
Swimming pool (phase 1).
New classroom block (phase 1).
Engineering workshop.
Physics labs on stilts.
Changing rooms and boiler.
Dining Hall, Servery.
Biology Department.
Portora Housing Incorporated.
Rugby Pitches.

1961-65
Rifle ranges.
Six staff houses opened.
Kitchen remodelled.
Gymnasium enlarged.
Gloucester House, Lakeview.

1965-70
Small Chapel.
New fives courts.
Steele Hall gallery.
Cloisters.
Dayboys' house-rooms.
Playground.
Re-housing of boarders.

The OPU Memorial Swimming Pool.

New Gloucester House at Lakeview.

Photograph of the boarders' Dining Hall from the late 1940s, laid out for a festive occasion – floral table decorations were not an everyday feature!

A view of the Dining Hall during 1980s refurbishment.

The Old Dining Hall, as it is known today, following a major refurbishment during the 1980s.

Gloucester House – Lakeview site 1960

The initial success of Gloucester House as a 'feeder' school for Portora enabled the Preparatory Department to expand. By 1964, it was necessary to move to a new and larger complex at Lakeview, on the far side of the Derrygonnelly Road. The building on the Portora side of the road was vacated, and the whole of the former Preparatory School facility was converted into accommodation for Munster House boarders.

'*At long last the New Prep. is finished, perfected, named, and formally opened. As everyone knows, the School has been honoured by permission to name the new buildings after His Royal Highness the Duke of Gloucester*'.

These were the opening words of his speech on 25 March 1936, when the 5th Lord Erne opened the original Gloucester House. On 30 October 1964, the 6th Lord Erne came to Lakeview to open formally the new buildings, and to pass on the name of Gloucester House to the new Lakeview facility. The Assembly Hall at the new Junior School was designed to hold 350 people, but a great many more were able to witness the opening ceremony with the aid of Gloucester House staff, who, no doubt, found their experience of rugger-scrum training of great value.

Upper School developments

During the early 1900s, and over a period of time in the basement area, a number of improvements and modifications were made to the original eighteenth-century fabric of the main building. These included the installation of a boiler for central heating to the dormitories, a boot room, a strong-room for ammunition and weapons used by the OTC, and an electric service lift providing access from the back kitchens to the third floor. This last facility enabled bulk laundry and linen to be collected and then easily distributed to the various dormitories via the Linen Room, as well as transporting food, afternoon tea and refreshments from the kitchens for use in the Seale Library and the Staff Common Room on the first floor.

The Old Dining Hall

In the main building, the Old Dining Hall has remained much the same for many years, with its fine collection of portraits depicting numerous Headmasters, and silver sporting trophies displayed in cabinets; all were a familiar sight to many generations of boarders. Alongside, there is an assembly area, which was and still is known as the Stone Hall.

Along one wall of the old Stone Hall were House notice boards, and a School notice board for posting School Teams and match results. By the staircase down to the basement there were reading benches for newspapers and selected magazines. Old drawings show that the Stone Hall first served as the School library.

Willoughby Place houses, which provided Ulster and Leinster Houses with boarding accommodation during the 1960s.

Willoughby Place

Some houses in Willoughby Place were used by Steele in the late 1860s as overflow accommodation for his boarders. In the 1960s, three houses in Willoughby Place were purchased by the School and were again used as off-campus accommodation, housing at different times Ulster and Leinster House boarders.

The new Chemistry block

Chemistry and Biology, those essential elements of the sciences, are now studied in new laboratory surroundings, which run along the path of the old 'Covered Way'. As yet, there are few marks on the still shining and polished benches; the porcelain and stainless steel still gleam. The current classes of young scientists have not yet dared to carve their names in the polished woodwork in an attempt to gain immortality. They know that until true recognition is rightfully achieved, their current actions can attract only immediate and extreme displeasure. Only when some future honour is

New Science laboratories. The name 'Henry Scales Memorial Laboratories', used for previous laboratories, has been retained for these new facilities.

…continued on page 102

99

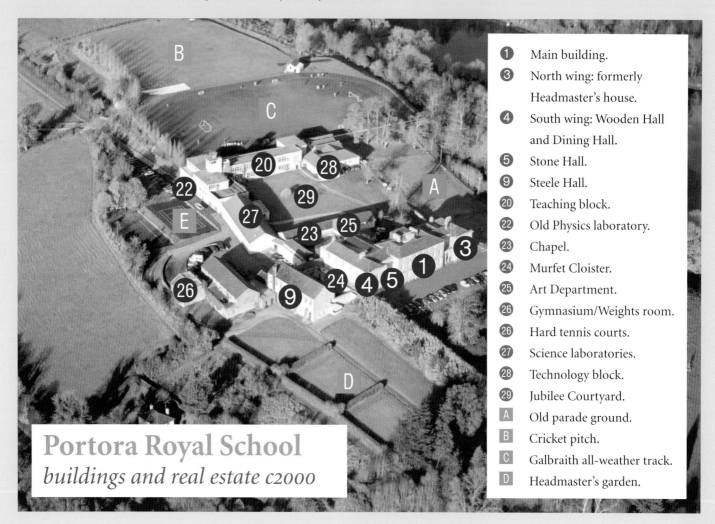

1. Main building.
3. North wing: formerly Headmaster's house.
4. South wing: Wooden Hall and Dining Hall.
5. Stone Hall.
9. Steele Hall.
20. Teaching block.
22. Old Physics laboratory.
23. Chapel.
24. Murfet Cloister.
25. Art Department.
26. Gymnasium/Weights room.
26. Hard tennis courts.
27. Science laboratories.
28. Technology block.
29. Jubilee Courtyard.
A. Old parade ground.
B. Cricket pitch.
C. Galbraith all-weather track.
D. Headmaster's garden.

Portora Royal School
buildings and real estate c2000

In 1983 **Richard Bennett** (S, 1983-2002), ably assisted by his Estates Manager, **Mark Scott** (OP, 1950-56; S, 1985-2001), commenced an extensive programme of renovation, improvement and extension, which lasted for nearly twenty years.

The central building (1777) and its north and south wings (1849) were restored, re-roofed and made ready for future generations of pupils. Some of the dilapidated buildings and outdated structures were demolished; others were upgraded to modern standards. The campus received professional landscaping, and a programme of planting trees and shrubs was implemented.

The present status of the Portora Estate can be fully appreciated only by a visit to the School. However, some idea of the restoration work that has been achieved over this period can be gained from the descriptions and photographic evidence in this chapter.

Starting in 1983
Two new classrooms constructed.
Supervised study facilities.
Upgrading toilets and showers.
Rebuild of the Murfet Cloister.
Careers Centre.
Upgrade of swimming pool.

1987
Refurbished science laboratories (Henry Scales).
New toilet blocks beside Steele Hall.
Upper Sixth Common Rooms.
Modern language centre.
Technology block.
Kitchens.

1994
New laboratories.
Henry Francis Lyte Music Rooms.
Upgraded offices.
Stone Hall refurbished.
Wooden Hall staircase refurbished.
Sanatorium demolished.

1996
New science laboratories started.
Murfet Cloister rebuilt.
Millennium Quad completed.
Old Physics laboratory on stilts demolished.

2000
North wing renovated.
Lower Rugby Fields re-laid.
Galbraith all-weather running track.

South wing renovations, 1990s

Completed in 1994, the renovation of the south wing included: upstairs, the new Galbraith Library, reading room, gallery, staff resource room, stores, and careers suite, and downstairs, the new or improved facilities of the Henry Francis Lyte Music Rooms, upgraded offices, refurbishment of the Stone Hall and Dining Hall, classroom and reprographics room.

Renovations to south wing: demolition.

Stone Hall, south side: entrance to Wooden Hall and Dining Room (before and after).

Stone Hall, north side: entrance to School Office (before and after).

recognised will a future Headmaster proudly declare: '*and this is the very place where that famous chemist sat as a young pupil.*'

The old Biology laboratories escaped the fate of the Chemistry site and were to enjoy a new future. Re-roofed, re-walled and refurbished, they were to rise phoenix-like as the new Art Studios and help develop a new generation of photographers, potters and artists.

The old Physics laboratory

The Physics laboratory was built during the 1960s on top of two pillars. By the 1980s it had to be replaced, for it was declared unstable and likely to fall down. There must have been some considerable error in the structural calculations, and it proved to be a most difficult building to demolish. The contractors were obliged to hire a special crane and advanced cutting equipment, and it was eventually removed piece by piece, so that nothing remained except more space for another car park. On completion of the site clearance, it was calculated that the demolition had cost more than the original construction.

The Murfet Cloister – a 1980 reconstruction of the old passageway

During the early 1900s, the area between the Dining Hall and the Steele Hall was called the 'Pump Yard' because of an old iron drinking fountain in the middle of the grassy slope leading down to the Lower Classrooms beneath the Steele Hall. Sometime in the 1920s, a lean-to roof was erected along the whole length and outside wall of the Dining Hall. The roof was supported by iron pipes, and the whole construction was designed as protection against the weather when walking to and from the Wooden Hall entrance of the main building to the Steele Hall ramp and the rear doors of the Dining Hall. Some wit, in a spirit of levity, nicknamed this new edifice 'The Cloisters', and the name stuck.

During the renovations of the 1980s the whole level area was covered in, and in 1987 it was formally re-named 'The Murfet Cloister'.

The Galbraith Library

In 1994 a new library was constructed where formerly there had been dormitories. The library was dedicated to the memory of **Dr Noel Galbraith** (OP, 1921-25), a generous benefactor who, throughout his lifetime, and in a later bequest in his will, gave substantial monies to Portora for amenities. The shelving and panelling units are all constructed of Irish Ash, which even now gives the appearance of being new, but should mellow with time and blend with the period character of the old School buildings.

The photograph on page 103 shows the old Connacht Dormitory, c1948, long before its conversion to the Galbraith Library. Several baths and additional lavatories were situated beyond the far door. Note the rather spartan conditions existing at Portora during the 1940s, and probably mirrored at most boarding schools throughout the United Kingdom during the war. It was doubtless conditions such as these which trained many a British Officer to consider himself to be in luxury when he was subsequently consigned, after capture, to a German Stalag camp.

Demolition of the original Henry S Scales Physics Laboratory, the infamous 'building on stilts'.

Above: Murfet Cloister; below: the plaque reads, 'This Cloister is dedicated to the memory of A T M MURFET, Classics Master, Housemaster of Connacht, Deputy Headmaster, 1916 PORTORA 1961'.

Above: old Connacht Dormitory, now the site of the Galbraith Library.

Left: The Galbraith Library – the old and the new. Traditionally printed books and pamphlets, in the background, sit alongside a bank of modern computers and on-line IT systems, located front left.

Round-up of the Technology Department building work

The new Technology Department buildings have been built in several phases. Liberty Hall was finally demolished in 1997. On the site, there now stands the third-phase extension and a new Information Technology and Computer Suite, which was opened in 2000. Today each pupil in an IT class has his own work station, and is allocated space on the main School server where he may save his work. In addition to the computers in the IT suite, each classroom has at least one networked computer.

The Millennium year saw also the opening of a new Physics Laboratory to replace the laboratory built in 1960, the original dedication to Henry S Scales being continued here.

Technology Department.

Round-up of building work

Extensive improvements to the basements in the main building were carried out in 1993, and the Henry Francis Lyte Music Rooms and Sixth Form Common Rooms were opened.

Further building and improvements were carried out, and in 1996 a new suite of laboratories for the Biology and Chemistry departments was opened. The Art Department was modernised and furnished with extensive facilities for photography, pottery and computer work. A whole new School computer network was established. The Rugby Pitches were re-laid, and an all-weather running-track and sports field were established.

The Jubilee Quadrangle

The Royal Jubilee of 2003 saw the construction of the Jubilee Quadrangle, a paved area bordered by the tuition block, the new science laboratories and the Art Department. At its centre is a white-stem birch, whose silver bark will be a future shining inspiration to pupils.

Before and after: the upper playing fields were transformed from all-grass to all-weather. From the 1950s to the 1980s, the top playing field was used for rugby in winter and athletics in summer. Eventually the grass was removed and the Galbraith all-weather athletics track laid out.

Jubilee Quadrangle.

Finances in the early Grammar School years

When Portora was a Voluntary Grammar School, the Board of Governors had to find all the capital necessary for the provision of boarding accommodation. Approved new or improved facilities for teaching attracted an 85% grant from the Department of Education. The remainder had to be found by the Board of Governors. In 1984 the School's indebtedness amounted to £103,000. In 1985, a Finance Committee representative of the Board of Governors reported the bank overdraft as 'serious'. By 1986 the Lakeview site had been sold to the Western Education and Library Board and to private developers. Unfortunately, the Department of Education was entitled to reclaim a proportion of the grant aid received by the Portora Board in respect of the building of Gloucester House. Nevertheless, the capital realised from this sale, and the cost savings achieved by concentrating all school activities on the Portora site, made a very significant contribution to Portora's finances. A further boost to finances came in 1987, when the Portora Housing Association decided to sell the six houses in Castle Lane and give the proceeds to the Fermanagh Protestant Board of Education, which was an integral part of the Portora Board. The Portora Housing Society (incorporated in 1958) had built the houses in 1960, with the aim of attracting teachers to the School by providing low-cost accommodation on the Portora estate. The sale of these houses realised just over £100,000.

Portora Chapel

Over the years, attempts were made to establish a Chapel in the grounds of Portora, but it was a lay Headmaster, Stuart, who gave the School its first Chapel. He purchased a second-hand harmonium and pulpit, and installed both on a semi-permanent basis in the gymnasium. Val Rogers constructed a small Chapel at one end of the old Hay Loft over the former stables in the School yard. In 1974, the School Chaplain, the **Reverend Canon J D G**

Door to Chapel.

Kingston (OP, 1952-59; S, 1970-2001), having extended the structure into the rest of the upper loft, launched an appeal to renovate the area completely, and finally established a permanent site worthy for worship.

Old Portorans, with considerable support from individuals, local businessmen and neighbouring parishes, contributed generously, and raised sufficient funds to undertake a tremendous and skilful conversion of the existing facilities. Inevitably, that stalwart of the time, Major Jack Wheeler, was the moving force behind the construction. Together with senior boarders, he supervised the installation of the electrical and heating systems; he then built the reredos in the Sanctuary, and designed and installed the two stained-glass windows of St Peter and St Paul, one on each side of the Communion Table.

Music was greatly enhanced with the presentation of a Gulbransen Pacemaker electronic organ, donated by Mr and Mrs Leach in memory of their son **Jonathan Leach** (OP, 1966-74) and his sister, who were tragically killed in a road accident on 14 July 1979. In the Chapel courtyard stands the old School bell, mounted on a miniature bell-tower, which was manufactured and presented, in November 1997, by Fisher Engineering of Ballinamallard. The bell is now tolled only for services. Many will recall **Albert 'Bert' Cranston** (S, 1935-85), whose task it was to ring that bell at appropriate and exact times to guide the School's routine before the days of electronic and computer technology. The bell came from the stable yard of Inishmore Hall, the Montgomery estate that supplied the pillars for the main gate.

Landmarks

Most pupils who attended the School, and certainly those who were boarders, cannot fail to have been impressed by the countryside around Portora.

The Free School for Fermanagh has always been closely associated with the Church of Ireland, and the first schoolhouse was located alongside the Church within the fortifications of Castle Balfour. Two local churches have become 'landmark sites' for generations of Portora boarders and the former Gloucester House Preparatory School. Over the years, a number of Old Portorans have returned to Enniskillen to become curates or rectors at both churches, and several have moved to other dioceses as canons, deans or bishops.

Enniskillen Parish Church and Cathedral

When the School moved from Ballybalfour to the County town of Enniskillen, during the 1640s, it re-located to Schoolhouse Lane, which more or less bounded the precincts of the old Parish Church. Boarding pupils from the Royal School became honorary parishioners. It was the custom at Enniskillen to set apart several pews for the 'young gentlemen', and an interesting Vestry note of 1776 records: *'the ground on the north side of the church where the Bishop's Court was formerly held should be given to the Reverend Mark Noble, the present Schoolmaster of Enniskillen (in case the Lord Bishop of Clogher shall give up his right to the same) for the purpose of building a seat for the use of the young gentlemen who shall be in his care…'* In a further Vestry note of 1801, mention is also made of setting apart pews for the use of the School of Enniskillen.

Interior of Chapel.

Silver chalice and paten.

Stained glass window of St Peter.

Originally called St Anne's Parish Church, Enniskillen, the Church was subsequently raised to the status of the Cathedral Church of St Macartin, c1920, thus giving the diocese of Clogher the rather unusual status of having two cathedrals, the other being in Clogher itself.

Rossorry Church

During the Masterships of both Greham and Steele, all boarders were marched to Rossorry Parish Church, in which the townland of Portora is situated. Later, Upper School pupils attended Enniskillen Cathedral on Sunday mornings. However, during Douglas Graham's Headmastership, they attended Rossorry on the first Sunday of the month, and sometimes on special occasions. Masters and boys from Gloucester House attended Rossorry regularly.

The Redoubt

'The Redoubt' is situated above the West Bridge, off the Sligo Road, on Windmill Hill, the site of a seventeenth-century, star-shaped artillery fort. The moat, rampart walls and remains of a swivel gun are still visible. During World War II, the buildings had been used as a hospital, and after the war it was commissioned as a dormitory for junior boarders of the Upper School. As a dormitory, without any heating it was freezing, but from its ramparts it afforded a superb panorama of Enniskillen, the River Erne and Portora. This was hardly sufficient motivation on a frosty morning to sustain a bunch of starving, post-war, twelve-year-old schoolboys wending their way to Portora for breakfast. During the early community unrest of the 1950s the Redoubt was occupied by unmarried and later by married members of staff from Portora. For a time a special section of the security forces was billeted in the upper barrack section, when passwords were required to gain access to the accommodation.

Two views of The Redoubt.

The countryside

Many Old Portorans will retain memories of specific places visited in pursuit of extra-curricular activities undertaken during their school-days. Mention may be made of the following places:

Castle Archdale

This was originally the family estate of the Archdale family, many of whom attended Portora during the twentieth century. Castle Archdale was a valuable RAF Station during World War II. It was a prime base for Coastal Command activities over the Atlantic, being the most westerly station in the UK and so able to protect Atlantic convoys further out than any other. Most members of the Portora Air Training Corps (ATC) gained valuable training experience there, and enjoyed being taken for flying trips during and after the war, until the base was finally de-commissioned. During the late 1940s and 1950s the area was used for CCF Field Day training, and the estate became the regular venue for the major annual 'Night Operation' exercise.

Older members of the OPU (London Branch) will recall that **Vice-Admiral Sir Nicholas Archdale, 2nd Bart, CBE** (OP, 1892-96) was our second President in 1954-55. The estate is now a large recreational area and country park with extensive activities centred on the waters of Lower Lough Erne.

Devenish Island

The Island, set in Lower Lough Erne, possesses the most spectacular ancient ecclesiastical remains in Fermanagh. Founded in the sixth century by St Molaise, the oldest remaining building is the little ruined church built in that early style described as cyclopean and known as Molaise's House. Although not the oldest feature, the most attractive is the iconic Round Tower. Used primarily as a belfry, and secondly as a storehouse, most round towers were constructed for the preservation of the monastic treasures during the Danish invasions. Many members of the Portora Boat Club will have memories of seeing the Devenish tower in the distance, as they strained on their oars during training.

Devenish round tower. Devenish Island will have many memories for former pupils. It was also a popular venue for the MV Kestrel boat-cruise which was organised for the Quatercentenary celebration weekend in September 2008.

The Island has several other links with Portora, the earliest being a Christian burial ground for the departed, who started on their final journey from the Portora Narrows. In Victorian times the Master, the **Reverend Dr Steele** (S, 1857-91), was appointed the rector of St Molaise, by the Primate in 1873; after taking Holy orders on graduation from Trinity College, Dublin, his son, the **Reverend John Houghton Steele** (OP, 1858-68), served as his curate.

Florence Court and Marble Arch

The Florence Court demesne was originally developed by John Cole, in the mid-1700s, after his ennoblement as the first Baron Mount Florence. It was then developed as a family seat for the future Earls of Enniskillen. Situated eight miles from Enniskillen, on the Sligo Road, it has views and spectacular scenery looking towards Benaughlin and the Cuilcagh Mountains. The limestone caves of Marble Arch lie only four miles away, and these features have provided practical geography and geology lessons to countless boys from Gloucester House and Portora during their early days as cubs and scouts.

Florence Court and the Cole family have many further connections with Portora and Gloucester House. To begin with, a number of acres of the escheated lands belonging to the School at Florence Court were exchanged in 1777 for 33 acres on Portora Hill. In early days several members of the Cole family were educated at the School, and more recent Earls have served on the Board of Governors.

Ely Lodge

Ely Lodge is located on the southern shore of Lower Lough Erne, four miles from Portora, and through marriage with the Hume family, has a long history as an original Fermanagh Plantation undertaking. The Earl of Ely married the daughter of Sir Gustavus Hume of nearby Hume Castle and they both went subsequently to reside in Ely Castle.

John Henry Loftus (OP, 1861), was the family and professional name of a local clergyman who later became the Marquis of Ely. In 1870 the original castle, thought to be in danger of collapsing, was blown up, but the stable block remained, and this was then extended to become Ely Lodge. During World War II, the lakeside facilities of Ely Lodge were used as a flying boat station for the American Forces, and from 1942 to 1944 the Lodge and grounds housed an extensive military training facility for the United States Army prior to the D-Day landings.

In 1948, Ely Lodge became the home of Colonel Robert Grosvenor, who was later to succeed as the 5th Duke of Westminster. The Ely Estate was then to become a popular venue for Portora's CCF field operations under **Colonel H G Halpin** (S,1936-76), and Colonel Grosvenor, at one time a School Governor, was a generous supporter of other outdoor activities on his estate. His foresters used to give impressive and exciting practical lessons on tree-felling to packs of cubs from Gloucester House, and scout groups from Portora.

Later, the estate became the summer retreat of the Westminster family, and the young Gerald Grosvenor, the 6th Duke of Westminster, received his early education in the Kindergarten of the Enniskillen Collegiate School and at Gloucester House. Ely Lodge remained part of the Westminster Estate until the 1980s, and is now the home of the Cathcart family.

The agricultural part of the estate has been transformed into the Castle Hume Golf Course; near by lies the new Lough Erne Golf Hotel and Spa where the Old Portora Union hosted their Quatercentenary Dinner and Ball in September 2008.

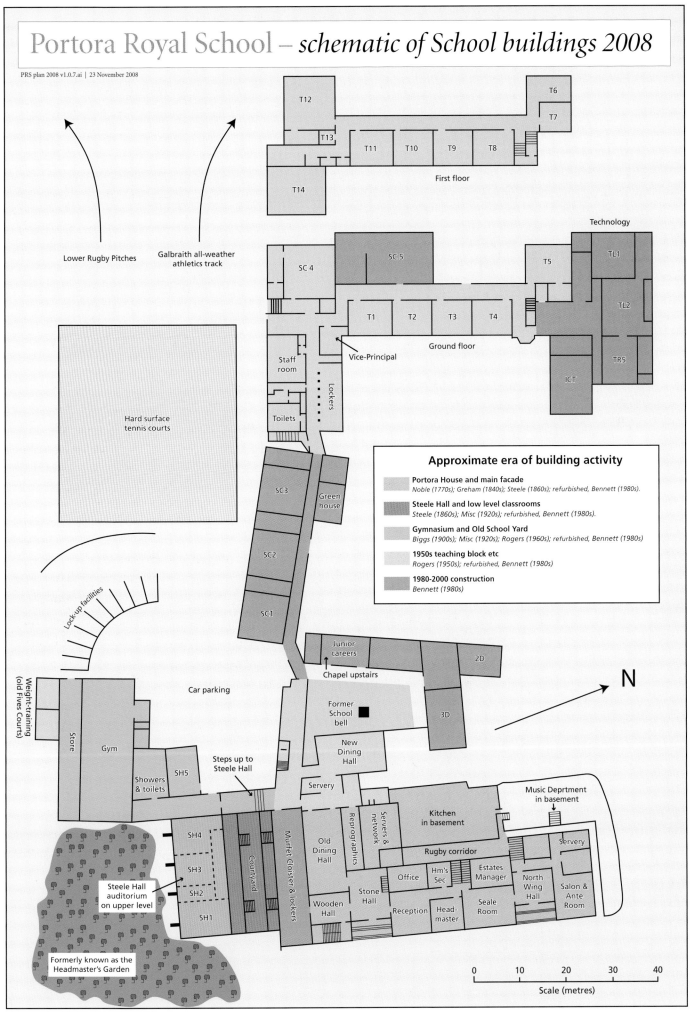

Portora Royal School – *schematic of School buildings 2008*

PRS plan 2008 v1.0.7.ai | 23 November 2008

T12

T6

T7

T13

T11 T10 T9 T8

First floor

T14

Lower Rugby Pitches

Galbraith all-weather athletics track

Technology

SC 5

SC 4

T5

TL1

TL2

T1 T2 T3 T4

Ground floor

TR5

Staff room

Vice-Principal

Lockers

ICT

Hard surface tennis courts

Toilets

Approximate era of building activity

Portora House and main facade
Noble (1770s); Greham (1840s); Steele (1860s); refurbished, Bennett (1980s).

Steele Hall and low level classrooms
Steele (1860s); Misc (1920s); refurbished, Bennett (1980s).

Gymnasium and Old School Yard
Biggs (1900s); Misc (1920s); Rogers (1960s); refurbished, Bennett (1980s)

1950s teaching block etc
Rogers (1950s); refurbished, Bennett (1980s)

1980-2000 construction
Bennett (1980s)

SC3

Green house

SC2

SC1

Lock-up facilities

Junior careers

2D

N

Chapel upstairs

Car parking

Former School bell

3D

Weight-training (old Fives Courts)

New Dining Hall

Store

Gym

Music Deprtment in basement

Servery

SH5

Showers & toilets

Steps up to Steele Hall

Servery

Kitchen in basement

Reprographics

Servers & network

Rugby corridor

SH4

Old Dining Hall

Office

Hm's Sec

Estates Manager

North Wing Hall

Salon & Ante Room

Murret Cloister & lockers

Courtyard

SH3

Steele Hall auditorium on upper level

SH2

Stone Hall

Reception

Head-master

Seale Room

Wooden Hall

SH1

Formerly known as the Headmaster's Garden

0   10   20   30   40

Scale (metres)

Three

The House system

This book is primarily concerned with the history and development of the School, but for many of us, it was through the House system that we lived on a day-to-day basis. Yet the House system was not introduced until relatively late, in 1918, and today in 2008 has already lost much of its importance. Thus, in less than a hundred years, the system that guided the experiences of many of us at Portora had been introduced and developed to a peak in the late 1960s and early 1970s, only to be largely superseded by a system of form tutors that followed the cessation of boarding in the 1990s.

It should be emphasised from the beginning that the House system was primarily connected with boarding and keeping boarders gainfully occupied; this led to an increase in sporting activity within the School and thus the House system and sport became closely linked.

One could perhaps say that at Portora the House system never quite achieved full maturity. By comparison, we can think of the fictional Hogwart's School with its four houses and how developed and self-contained they appear to be. Nevertheless, in terms of individual character, each House at Portora (Ulster, Munster, Leinster and Connacht) had a definite identity and each had a strong effect on the lives of boarders. This was due in large part to the characters and longevity of tenure of many of the Housemasters. Inevitably, there was less of an effect on dayboys, but their Housemaster and the playing of sport for the House nevertheless provided a focus of identity on their journey through the School.

Left: Gloucester House cricket team, 1951 (detail); see page 225 for full photograph.

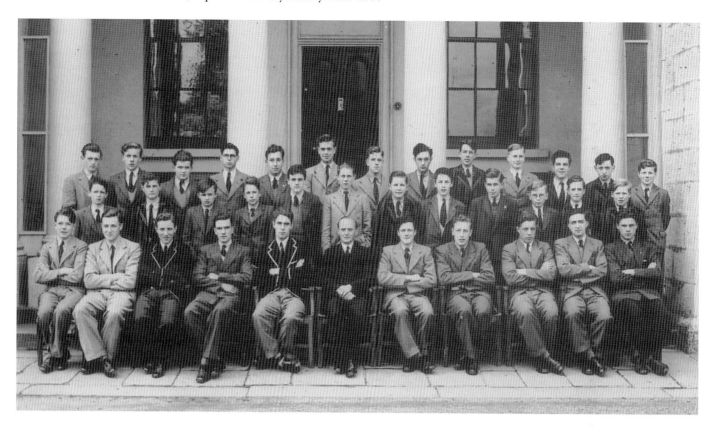

Ulster House, 1946. Housemaster, George Andrews, C de G (centre), having returned from distinguished wartime service with the Free French Navy, poses for a formal photograph of Ulster boarders. It does not include the younger boarders in Form 2, since these pupils (mainly ex-Gloucester House) were accommodated in a classroom dormitory in the Upper School for their first year, before moving into the main Ulster House accommodation. There were few, if any, dayboys since the 11+ intake from Fermanagh had not yet started. In the rear row (sixth from left) is Julian Kulski (see page 207).

Today, as is common in many other major day schools, 'pastoral care' is largely provided through a tutor-based system. In 2008 Houses, and terms related to the House system, remain part of a tradition rather than having a practical application.

The House system

In the second decade of the twentieth century, Headmaster Seale was determined to make Portora as much like an English Public School as possible. English Public Schools had a House system dating back over a hundred years, and Seale decided Portora should have the same. Thus in Autumn 1918 the four Houses we still know today were established. The Houses were simply named after the four provinces of Ireland and not after local eminent families or the like, as with other schools in the Province and elsewhere in Ireland and England. The allocation of House colours was: red for Ulster, yellow for Munster, blue for Leinster and green for Connacht.

No House had any preference, significance or meaning above any other House. Boys were allocated to Houses without any reference to social status or origin, although it was the practice to place all brothers in the same House. By 1922 all of the Housemasters (Messrs Tetley, Murfet, Stannard and Breul) were Cambridge graduates, and this seemed to set a precedent that continued for many years.

At the end of World War I dormitories were established on a House basis, and a House sports competition was initiated as part of the House Championships. This set a pattern for life in the School, which remained fundamentally the same for over fifty years with some progressive changes. This also coincided with a period of relative peace in the North of Ireland, and a time when numbers at the School were boosted by residents from the South sending their children to the North for their education, following partition.

During this period there was a succession of long-serving boarding Housemasters who followed in the footsteps of their predecessors. **Tetley** (S, 1891-1925), **Butler** (S, 1926-49), **Murfet** (S, 1916-56), **A W Barnes** (S, 1932-66), **G C Andrews** (S, 1933-76), **H G Halpin** (S, 1936-76), **H S Scales** (S, 1924-60), **F E Rowlette** (S, 1943-81), **A N Peterson** (S, 1945-63) and towards the end, **R W L Hort** (S, 1963-83), **D S Robertson** (S, 1967-83) and **J Pratt** (S, 1970-89) all made huge contributions to the life of the pupils in their Houses, and many kept in close contact, both with the School and past pupils, long after their retirement or departure from the School.

Boarding houses

For a boarder the House replaced his home. Indeed the first Houses in English Public Schools were exclusively boarding houses, and the word House simply described the separate building in which the boys lived, with the Housemaster and his wife, or if single, possibly a matron, taking the place of parents.

The development of discrete House buildings or areas at Portora is described in chapter two of this book. Boarding reached its peak in the early 1970s, by which time a boarder would wake up in a dormitory organised by age group in a building or area of the School dedicated to his House. He would have breakfast at a table with his Housemates and then gather his books and items from his Houseroom prior to Assembly (grouped by House) in the Steele Hall. As the day progressed, breaks from classes may have been taken in a Houseroom, meals and Junior prep were all by House until he finally returned to the House dormitory and the daily visit of the Housemaster at lights-out.

House identity was very strong from the beginning and remained strong all through the boarding period, whatever developments or refinements to the system there may have been. At one stage a boy's House could be determined by the tie he was wearing; however, by the 1960s the only remaining vestige of differentiation was the House colour of the button on his school cap.

Housemasters

Housemasters were a major influence on the lives of most Portorans. They took the principal role in dealing with parents, writing references for applications to universities and in providing guidance on where and what their pupils might do after leaving Portora. As one ex-Housemaster ruefully commented, this involved giving parents bad news. Interestingly, and strange as it may seem in our modern, regulated world, the role and responsibilities of the Housemaster were never formally documented.

Many Housemasters spent most of their teaching careers at Portora, frequently seeing several Headmasters come and go. One commentator on English Public Schools has written that *'it was easier to turn a Vicar out of his pulpit than to eject a Master from his House'*. Many Houses were imbued with characteristics determined by their Housemasters, some of whom acquired almost iconic status within the Portora ethos.

The archetypal Housemaster at Portora was, of course, 'Mickey' Murfet; one of the original four Housemasters, he ruled Connacht from 1918 to 1956. One imagines that he provided a template for many during his career. He

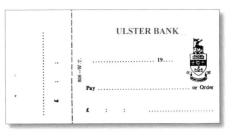

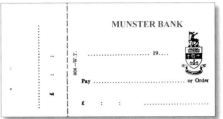

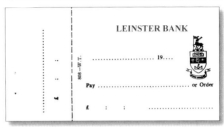

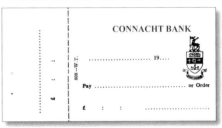

School life reflecting real life. Houses ran their own banking systems, complete with chequebooks. Boys would draw money from their account to purchase items from the School's tuck shop.

For many years, prior to inflation, several generations of boarding pupils in the Upper School were issued with a sixpenny piece (2.5p) each Thursday night. This weekly handout was to be used to purchase a stamp for the Sunday letter home to parents. Surplus change was used to pay-off any debts incurred and the excess was splurged on buns and chocolate goodies from the tuck-shop. The duty master on Sundays also dispensed a penny piece (0.5p) to each boy as a donation to the Church collection.

Boarding Housemasters

1918 – 1973

Ulster

W H Tetley, Mr Scott, Mr King,
A W Barnes, D George,
G C Andrews, D S Robertson.

Munster

Mr Tate, Mr Stannard, Mr Russell,
Mr Dickson, Mr Grant, H S Scales,
F E Rowlette.

Leinster

Mr Kennedy, Mr Breul,
Mr Bearder, Mr Cook, G V Butler,
L S Breadon, A N Peterson,
J V Tapley, R W L Hort.

Connacht

A T M Murfet, A W Barnes,
R E Bell, H G Halpin.

Dayboy Housemasters

1955 – 1973

Ulster

Mr Spence, J V Tapley,
M G Schrecker.

Munster

W P Barbour.

Leinster

D A R Chillingworth, T A Elliott,
J W A Mills, Revd J G D Kingston.

Connacht

H G Halpin, Mr Smith, J V Tapley,
B Morwood.

Gloucester House Headmasters

1936 – 1983

A W Barnes, Mr Pilkington,
J V Tapley, P L Rice, Mr Sheppard,
D E S Dearle, R P Broad,
J W A Mills.

Head's House

Mrs P Acheson, W P Barbour,
Ms Herdman-Grant; Dr Gilfillan
was Housemaster of the girls for
a year.

was also the first of many Housemasters who were Cambridge graduates. By tradition the School's Headmaster was a Trinity College, Dublin graduate, but the prevalence of Cambridge Housemasters lasted well into the 1960s, Andrews, **M G Schrecker** (S, 1953-75), **R E Bell** (S, 1956-63), and Hort being later examples.

Cambridge University

Some senior staff, including **Val Rogers** (S, 1954-73), **R P Broad** (1956-72) and Barnes were Oxford graduates, but it is perhaps no coincidence that the majority of candidates applying to Oxbridge went to Cambridge Colleges.

Under the guidance of George Andrews many boys, both boarders and dayboys from all Houses, went up to Sidney Sussex, but Bell (Pembroke) and Schrecker (Queens') also influenced applicants. Portorans were also successful with applications to St Catherine's, St John's, King's, Trinity, Clare, Christ's and Churchill.

Andrews followed in the footsteps of 'Mickey' Murfet and was Housemaster of Ulster from 1938 to 1968. He was a devoted Cambridge man; he had his own distinctive style, and the almost ritual playing of bagpipes by his charges in the Cloisters under his bedroom window on St Patrick's Day gives some idea of the character of Ulster House. Similarly, other Houses reflected the different personalities of their Housemasters.

By the 1960s the boarding House was physically separated: Connacht was in the Redoubt, some distance from the School; Munster was in the original Gloucester House building; Leinster was in Liberty Hall; and Ulster remained in the main School building. This seemed to accentuate the differences, strengths and identities of each House and, therefore, the importance and influence of the Housemaster.

The careers of many of these Housemasters are recorded in chapter seven. From the middle to the end period of the system, a prominent example of a long-serving Housemaster was 'Ed' Rowlette, who was in charge of Munster from 1951 to 1973. He was Irish as opposed to English, and from Trinity College, Dublin as opposed to Cambridge. During his career at Portora he served five Headmasters compared to Murfet's four and Andrews' three. He had a very different personality and was very well known throughout the School. His influence could be seen at the 50th OPU Dinner in London in 2003. When it became known that he would attend, a large number of ex-Munster boarders suddenly appeared at the event, flying in from around the globe. The same factors were obviously true in the English Public School system. A writer in 'Punch' magazine observed:

> He served three Heads with equal zeal
> An equal absence of ambition;
> He knew his power, and did not feel
> The least desire for recognition;
> But shrewd observers who could trace
> Back to the source results far-reaching,
> Saw the true Genius of the Place
> Embodied in his life and teaching.

In modern educational jargon the House system would be described as providing 'pastoral care'. As a new boarder, your dormitory Prefect was the person who made sure that you knew the form; what to do and when to do it. He was there to provide advice and guidance. The House system divided the School into manageable units, where many people provided all-round guidance and a degree of care. However, much of this was provided and administered by boys through the Prefect system, a practice that today might be considered unacceptable.

The end period

The end period, from the end of the 1960s to the early 1980s and into the early 1990s, saw some very prominent and influential Housemasters. The work of Robert Hort and David Robertson is recorded in chapter seven and the contributions of James Pratt and **Martin Todd** (S, 1979-2005) should also be mentioned.

The Prefect system

The Prefect system was introduced as early as 1905 and therefore precedes the House system. The first six prefects to be appointed were Flood, Malone, Bateman, Fetherstonhaugh, Harpur and Biggs.

Eventually the House and Prefect systems combined. To begin with, most Prefects were Captains of sport and Heads of societies. In fact, the School List from this period shows House Captains being listed beneath all other Captains. House Captains were frequently House Prefects as opposed to School Prefects during this time. However, during the 1940s, House Captains were elevated in the School List to follow the School Captain or Head Boy at the head of the School List. House Captains were also generally School Prefects.

We can deduce from the name that the position of House Prefect meant just that; with their more limited powers they operated only within their own House. They were largely concerned with the daily lives of the more junior boys in the House. They frequently acted as mentors, exercising fairly elementary discipline through their role as dormitory Prefect and showing new pupils 'the ropes' of life at Portora.

However, School Prefects continued to have wide-ranging powers over all pupils, which by the mid-1960s were (thankfully) seldom fully exercised. The Captains of the major school sports continued to be School Prefects, and as such were involved with boys from all Houses.

Connacht House Prefects' study, 1968-69. Left to right: J N Macauley, C W R Guy, S C Corry, R J Woodrow and F R S McMahon. (Photograph: J C S Earle)

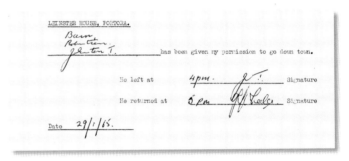

Pupils were not allowed to go into Enniskillen without permission. Houses ran a scheme where pupils had to get a leave pass signed out and back. Here is one from the 1960s for Leinster House, signed out by Victor Tapley and signed back by Jack Wheeler.

House cups

Football
Pratt Cup

Cricket
Hadoke Cup

Rowing
Henning Shield

Athletics
Lowndes Cup

Relay
17th Brigade Cup

Tug of War
13th Regiment USA Cup

Cross Country Run
Collum Shield

Swimming
West Cup

Swimming Relay
Butler Cup

Swimming Relay
Morton Cup

Football Junior
Sidebottom Cup

Cricket Junior
Barlow Cup

Shooting
Frith Cup

House Plays
E.A.D.S. Cup

Hockey
Enniskillen Cup

Sailing
Verscholye Cup

Basketball
Marrinan Cup
House Drill Cup

Singing
Dalzeill Cup

The Prefect system played a significant role in the running of the Houses. Housemasters played a prominent role in the selection of House Prefects and House Captains. For these reasons Houses had a significant involvement in the way the School was run.

Dayboys and the House system

Initially, dayboys were allocated to the same Houses as boarders, sharing the same Housemasters; it is worth noting that in other schools this was not always the case. In 1955 a separate and additional Housemaster for dayboys was appointed for each House.

The boarding Housemaster still chose the House Captains for the various sports, but dayboys and boarders combined together into common House teams as they did for School teams.

In Fermanagh, the underlying problem was that many dayboys lived some distance away and could have a journey of an hour or more to and from School. Transport would generally run to coincide with the end of lessons and not the end of the sporting day; a day pupil playing in a school team might have left home before 7.00 am and not return until after 7.00 pm. He would still require his evening meal and need time to complete his homework. Those day pupils who participated in sporting and other activities (for example, plays, cadets and societies) had to show great determination and resilience to succeed.

Dayboy Housemasters

Dayboy Housemasters followed the same pattern as boarding Housemasters. Many remained in post for long periods and all of them contributed greatly to the lives of both boarders and dayboys throughout the School. **W P Barbour** (S, 1952-83), **J V Tapley** (S, 1942-80), **D A R Chillingworth** (OP, 1934-41; S, 1949-66), **T A Elliott** (OP, 1948-55; S, 1959-2000) and Martin Schrecker all deserve a mention for their tenures as dayboy Housemasters, as well as all for their other contributions to the School life of both dayboys and boarders.

Overall contribution of Housemasters

Masters in the School were a unifying influence across the School for both dayboys and boarders. In particular, one should not assume that the contribution of a Housemaster (either day or boarding) was limited to his own House or area. One can think of 'Darcy' Chillingworth, who was Leinster dayboys Housemaster for many years, but also ran athletics with great enthusiasm and dedication; Bob Bell coached rowing and produced several highly successful school plays; Ed Rowlette was the mainstay of tennis and coached and refereed rugby; Barbour, who coached, umpired and selected the Junior cricket team and was also involved with rugby. George Andrews was almost fanatical about rowing; Robert Hort was prominent in school theatre. There were many examples. In this way the contribution of the Masters increased contact and awareness between dayboys and boarders.

Overall influences in the School

It can be seen that there were many Masters other than their own Housemaster who exerted influence and guidance on the boys. The diverse personalities of both staff and boys created an atmosphere of tolerance, which meant that there was always a healthy variety of opinion. There were many strong and influential characters beyond the confines of one's own House who were instrumental in providing advice and encouragement. One can also think of 'Doc' Simpson, Mrs Benson, Barnes (who in later years relinquished his House duties), Ainslie and Schrecker. Opinions and advice were never in short supply at Portora. But while other personalities in the School may have had a significant influence over a boy, the House and the Housemaster always provided the general backdrop to his existence and daily life.

The House system and sport

In England, the House system had been in place for many years and had a strong influence on sport. The early development of the House system in England coincided with, and perhaps even contributed to, the growth of many games such as rugby and cricket, which were codified during the Victorian era.

A selection of School colour caps for various sports. In the bottom left hand corner is a School cap which has been customised with a yellow bobble indicating Munster House. Colours for the other Houses were red (Ulster), blue (Leinster) and green (Connacht).

The development of sport in Public Schools was so strong that it changed the nature of sporting activity at the universities (principally Oxford and Cambridge) from horse racing, gambling and drinking to athleticism. This reached the point where there were articles in *The Spectator* around 1900 bemoaning the fact *'that the universities were more given over to sport than learning and the arts'*.

At Portora inter-House competitions in the major sports were introduced during the inter-war years and other sports were added over time. Although many sports were keenly contested at an inter-House level, not all of them contributed to House Championship points. Memory tells us that House matches at Portora were played with terrific intensity and produced more injuries than the average School match. This was not unusual in the English Public School system. A versifier at Marlborough College in 1895 wrote:

> *Our hearts are throbbing – as Homer would say*
> *They are kicking our bosoms, 'tis House match today,*
> *And an icy fear is ingested in our hearts*
> *For such are the tremors that a House match imparts.*

Another factor in inter-House sport was that, each House having to raise teams, many more boys were inducted into competitive sport.

Finally, the development of House competitions created constructive activity, which helped to avoid a hundred or more boys with time on their hands getting into some form of trouble.

House Championship

The House Championship was the culmination of all of the House competitions over the year; the major sports of rugby, rowing and cricket plus the minor sports such as swimming, tennis, shooting and rugby kicking all contributed and House points were awarded commensurate with the perceived importance of the sport. The climax of the House Championship was

House champions

1919	Munster
1920	Munster
1921	Ulster & Connacht
1922	Connacht
1923	Connacht
1924	Munster
1925	Connacht
1926	Ulster
1927	Connacht
1928	Ulster
1929	Munster
1930	Munster
1931	Munster
1932	Connacht
1933	Leinster
1934	Munster
1935	Leinster
1936	Leinster
1937	Connacht
1938	Leinster
1939	Leinster
1940	Connacht
1941	Leinster
1942	Connacht
1943	Leinster
1944	Connacht
1945	Connacht
1946	Connacht
1947	Connacht
1948	Connacht
1949	Ulster
1950	Leinster
1951	Munster
1952	Connacht & Leinster
1953	Leinster

normally Sports Day which took place on the last day of the Summer Term. On many occasions the winner of the House Championship was still in doubt until the last race of the day.

The original sports that contributed points to the House Championship in 1918-19 were: football (Michaelmas) 5 for the winners and 2 points for the runners-up; football (Lent) 5 for the winners and 2 points for the runners-up; cricket 5 for the winners and 2 points for the runners-up; sports (athletics) 3 points for the winners and 1 point for the runners-up.

By 1925 this list had grown to: football (Michaelmas) 5 points for the winners and 2 points for the runners-up; football (Lent) 5 points for the winners and 2 for the runners-up; boxing 2 points for the winners and 1 for the runners-up; House run 1 point for the winners; shooting 2 points for the winners and 1 for the runners-up; cricket 5 points for the winners and 2 for the runners-up; swimming 2 points for the winners and 1 for the runners-up; sports (athletics) 3 points for the winners and 1 for the runners-up.

In 1946 there was only one rugby (also known as football) competition and a rugby kicking competition (place, touch and drop) was introduced. Rowing was not added until 1949 and tennis until 1951. In 1958 junior rugby made a brief appearance and junior cricket in 1960, although fully reinstated by the 1970s. Boxing at the School ended in 1963 and sculling was added in 1964. Shooting was dropped for obvious reasons around 1973.

However, this was not the limit of inter-House competitions: the list of House Cups on page 116 gives a much fuller picture of the scale of the activities. Indeed, further sports such as badminton and table tennis were played in the School, as was rugby fives from the late 1960s until the 1980s. A more complete description of the sports played is given in chapter five.

House Championship winners

So, which House or Houses dominated the House Championship? Individuals will have different opinions based on their recollections of the period they were at the School. It may be a surprise to many that Connacht won the most times: at its weakest from the 1950s to the mid-1970s, Connacht had established a lead in the first thirty years of the competition that was never overtaken; it was particularly strong in the 1940s. On the other hand, the other three Houses each had decades when they did not win the Championship at all: Leinster in the 1920s and 1970s, Ulster in the 1930s and Munster in the 1940s. Leinster was top in the 1950s and Ulster in the 1960s, with Munster showing strongly in the 1970s. Overall, counting to the time when the boarding houses were combined in the early 1970s, Connacht had maintained its lead, being three or four wins ahead of Leinster and Munster, who were two or three ahead of Ulster. After this time and up to the end of the 1980s, the House Championship gradually lost its importance. Leinster, however, appears to have the distinction of being the only House to have scored zero points in a House Championship year (1927 and 1968).

Decline of the House Championship and the original House system

As a result of the Troubles and other difficulties, boarding entered a sharp decline in the early 1970s. Boarders gradually decreased in numbers until boarding ceased in 1993. As early as 1974 boarding Houses no longer had their own Housemaster. Munster and Ulster were combined under Robertson and Leinster and Connacht under Hort. This effectively marked the end of the House Championship as it was originally conceived, although it continued for a time and an increasing number of sports, sailing and squash was added during the 1970s. During this period Munster was the leading House, followed by Connacht, with Ulster and Leinster in the rear.

As boarding numbers continued to decline, there was eventually only a single Housemaster for all boarders. When boarding ceased altogether a new pastoral system, based on tutoring, was introduced.

In 2007 the traditional Houses were retained (Ulster, Munster, Leinster, Connacht, Belmore and Gloucester House) but performing more of an administrative role. All of the boys are still assigned to one of the four traditional Houses on their arrival at the School. Within each House there is a Formmaster for every year, Gloucester House and Belmore representing Year 1 and 2 pupils. This division of responsibilities for pastoral care across a greater number of staff ensures that sufficient time is available to look after the needs of individual boys.

The allocation of boys to Houses continues to provide a basis for intra-School sport and although various sports may be contested in any given year, the House Championship has lost much of its focus.

Sport in Portora today

It would be wrong to make any connection between the success of School sports teams and the House system. Today, School teams for many sports thrive and achieve great success. The increased availability of good transport facilities means that there are more competitions against teams outside of the School. Boys from all around Fermanagh are now able to participate fully in sport. If better transport facilities had been available to dayboys, the School might have achieved so much more during the 1950s and 1960s.

One knows from experience and reading the records that in the 1960s, for example, dayboys made great contributions to School teams. However, the percentage of dayboys representing the School in the major sports was perhaps about 20% at most, whereas it should have been around 50% based on overall numbers in the School. On the academic front, by contrast, the expected 50% split between dayboys and boarders was reflected in the numbers gaining places at Oxbridge. Today's School teams, made up entirely of dayboys, shows the extent of the talent that in the past went untapped.

Gloucester House

We should mention Gloucester House in this chapter. Gloucester House was the Preparatory School for Portora, taking both dayboys and boarders from the age of 5 or 6 up to 13, or two years after the 11+ examination.

House champions	
1954	Leinster
1955	Connacht
1956	Ulster
1957	Connacht
1958	Munster
1959	Munster
1960	Leinster
1961	Leinster
1962	Munster
1963	Ulster
1964	Leinster
1965	Ulster
1966	Ulster
1967	Ulster
1968	Connacht
1969	Munster
1970	Munster
1971	Munster
1972	Munster
1973	Munster
1974	Ulster
1975	Connacht
1976	Connacht
1977	Connacht
1978	Munster
1979	Munster
1980	Munster
1981	Munster
1982	Connacht
1983	Connacht
1984	Connacht
1985	Leinster
1986	Leinster
1987	Ulster
1988	Connacht
1989	Leinster

Staff, boarders and dayboys of Gloucester House in 1937. Staff are, left to right: Mrs Burns (Matron), James Malone (Teacher), Mrs Clarice Barnes (Headmaster's wife), A W Barnes (Headmaster), Miss E E Hunt (Headteacher), Grattan Halpin (Teacher).

Gloucester House visit to St Columb's Cathedral, Londonderry, for Ash Wednesday during the early 1960s. Headmaster R P Broad is on the right-hand side.

Gloucester House Lakeview site from 'Lovers Lane' during the 1960s. In the foreground are the new classrooms, while in the background is the original Lakeview house.

The separation of Junior boys predates the House system. The Junior (Preparatory) School was founded in 1915 for up to thirty boarders. For the first 21 years it was located in the main school buildings with its own dormitory, classroom and Headteacher, **Miss E E Hunt** (S, 1915-47). Known as 'Lizzie', she ruled her boys, called 'maggots' by the rest of the School, with a rod of iron.

The Junior School was such a success that a new home was needed and Gloucester House was built. With its own driveway at the bottom of Portora Hill it was a success from the start. Barnes was appointed Headmaster and Miss Hunt became the Headteacher; they were assisted by Mrs Barnes, a Matron and two teachers. Although formally opened by the Earl of Erne in 1936, it was named after the Duke of Gloucester, who happened to be visiting Fermanagh on his honeymoon at the time. Coincidentally, the current Duke of Gloucester was the representative of the Queen at the 400th anniversary commemoration service in Armagh Cathedral for the Five Schools in 2008.

Although primarily founded as a Preparatory School for Portora, Gloucester House nevertheless became an entity in its own right, providing suitable preparation for other public and private schools throughout Ireland and the United Kingdom. Gloucester House grew to the extent that it acquired Lakeview, which provided additional dormitories, football, rugby and cricket pitches, and a huge area that included two lakes for outdoor activities.

A House system was introduced. The Houses were originally named Picts and Scots but later changed to Devenish and Belmore (colours green and blue respectively). This division was related purely to sport and drama; dormitories and all general activities were organised on a school basis. However, as a curiosity, the School list of 1954 records the two Houses as 'Mr Haslett's House' and 'Mr Dibley's House'. When Gloucester House was extended to include all of the day population. two additional houses, Rossorry and Erne, were added.

In the 1960s Gloucester House under Broad's Headship moved completely to new buildings on the Lakeview site, and Munster boarders took over occupation of the original Gloucester House building. Finally, the original building was taken over by the girl students at Portora.

John Mills (S, 1962-85), a Queen's graduate and one of a number of Masters of Ulster origin who joined the staff in the 1960s, became Headmaster, having taught Physics and been a Housemaster of dayboys at the Upper School. Gloucester House was eventually closed in 1983.

Personal recollections from the early 1960s, when Richard Broad was the Headmaster, include an incident that occurred when one of the endless succession of inconsequential 'crazes' swept through the School. Mice of all shapes, sizes and colours were secretly kept in lockers and other hide-outs. All went well until someone decided to bring his pet over to the Lakeview dormitory. Unfortunately, but predictably, the mouse escaped and made its way upstairs to the Broads' flat. The screams of the Headmaster's wife marked the end of that particular craze.

Gloucester House had much more supervision than the main School and many activities such as games were compulsory. It also had a strong Scouts section directed by Senior boys from Portora and aided by the extensive grounds at Lakeview where various activities could be undertaken.

As a footnote, conditions at modern boarding schools are very different from the cold, draughty rooms with high, single-glazed windows and stone floors that existed in the old Lakeview building.

Head's House

The last House established at Portora was Head's House. In 1978 three girl boarders, **Janet Osborne** (OP, 1975-1982), **Linda Watson** (OP, 1976-1984) and **Amanda Maguire** (OP, 1978-82), were initially affiliated to Leinster House and accommodated in the old Sanatorium. The following year, when numbers rose to 11 (nine boarders and two daygirls), a new House, called Head's House, was formed, and the headmaster's wife, Mrs Prucilla Acheson, acted as temporary house mistress, until Bill Barber took over responsibility for the house. The numbers of girls ebbed and flowed and in 1986 there were six boarders and 16 daygirls. At one stage the number of girl boarders approached the same number as boys, and the peak of 16 daygirls shows a significant intake from Fermanagh that did not go unnoticed by the Collegiate School. By 1989, however, the numbers had dropped to single figures and in the early 1990s, when boarding ceased, there was only one daygirl.

A typical study bedroom for girls during the boarding era of Head's House.

Footnote

It is worth noting that former Headmasters and Housemasters are regular attendees at the annual Old Portora Union (London Branch) dinner. Rogers, Andrews and Barnes were all regular attendees and Graham, Barnes and Rogers served as Presidents. 'Ed' Rowlette has also attended on a number of occasions and Bell, despite having left the School in 1964, is a 'regular'. Schrecker was also present at a number of dinners while he was living in Hampton. Henry Scales was Master of Honour at the London dinner in 1960 when he tragically had a heart attack from which he subsequently died.

Conclusion

The House system has largely come and gone. Boarding and the House system became inseparable and when boarding ceased the system lost much of its importance. However, for many its influence and memory remain strong.

INTERMEDIATE EXHIBITIONERS
CERTIFICATE

1907	F. S. THOMAS,	MID.
1908	F. S. THOMAS,	SEN.
1911	L. S. JOHNSON,	JUN.
	N. TRIMBLE,	JUN.
1912	N. TRIMBLE,	MID.
	J. A. THOMPSON,	JUN.
1913	L. S. JOHNSON,	MID.
	J. A. THOMPSON,	MID.
	G. A. DEANE,	JUN.
1919	A. W. BAYNE,	SEN.
1920	O. W. McCUTCHEON,	JUN.
	C. R. F. MORTON,	JUN.
1921	R. L. McMORRIS,	SEN.
	O. W. McCUTCHEON,	MID.
	G. P. STEWART,	JUN.
	C. P. JONES,	JUN.
1922	O. W. McCUTCHEON,	SEN.
	T. R. F. COX, 1ST	MID.
	C. P. JONES, 1ST	MID.
	A. C. THOMPSON, 1ST	MID.
	C. P. STEWART,	MID.
	J. A. WALLACE,	JUN.
	H. S. CORSCADDEN,	JUN.
1923	T. R. F. COX,	SEN.
	C. P. JONES,	SEN.
	J. A. WALLACE,	MID.
1924	J. A. WALLACE,	SEN.
	D. L. GRAHAM,	MID.
	E. M. GRIFFITH,	JUN.

1925	J. A. WALLACE,	SEN.
	D. L. GRAHAM, 1ST	JUN.
	F. L. JACOB,	JUN.
1926	D. L. GRAHAM, 1ST	SEN.
1928	T. B. O'LOUGHLIN,	JUN.
	R. E. TAYLOR,	JUN.
1933	J. T. HANNA	JUN.
1934	J. W. H. McBRIEN	SEN.
1935	V. H. S. MERCIER, 2ND	SEN.

STATE EXHIBITION

1951	P. D. WARRINGTON
1952	JOHN R. CROCKETT
1954	G. W. STRAHAN 1ST
	M. T. KNIGHT
	R. A. LOANE
1960	T. D. KINGSTON

THE SYSTEM OF STATE EXHIBITIONS CEASED AFTER 1960.
UNIVERSITY AWARDS GAINED AT PORTORA SINCE 1957 ARE RECORDED ON THE HONOURS BOARD OUTSIDE THE NEW DINING HALL.

Four

Curricula

As we have seen in other chapters, much has changed at the School over the past 400 years and the curriculum is no exception. What is taught today differs significantly from what would have been taught in 1608; indeed, there would be very little in common between the two. However, the curriculum should not be looked at in isolation. Instead of starting with what was or is taught, one should start by asking: what was the purpose of this teaching and the curriculum and what was the School trying to achieve?

Here a word of caution must be introduced. Before the twentieth century, and the State's gradual involvement in education and the influx of public money, there were few requirements for schools to keep records of their activities. At times it has proved difficult to discover what the curriculum at the School actually was, particularly during the early years. In piecing the story together it has been necessary to draw on many sources, some from the School and others from elsewhere.

The early years

In chapter one we saw how Portora owed its existence to the 1608 decree of King James I's Privy Council, *'that there should be one free school, at least, appointed in every county, for the education of youths in learning and religion'.* In effect, this meant that the 'royal schools' were established to educate the sons of the English and Scots planters and their deserving Irish tenants, who were brave enough to settle on land forfeited after the Flight of the Earls in 1607. This early attempt at social engineering would have been unsuccessful without

Left: Intermediate Exhibitioners Board from the Steele Hall.

the promise of not only cheap land and personal security, but also education that would safeguard the religion and language of the new population. Rather like today's English-language schools abroad, the 'royal schools' were intended to provide an 'English' education in a 'foreign' land.

The sort of curriculum taught at Portora during these early years is very difficult to say; certainly, there was no such thing as a national curriculum. Unfortunately, the School's archives do not shed much light on this question. This is not unusual; Bill Bryson in his book, 'Shakespeare', has the same problem of a lack of original sources. He notes that *the life of a grammar school boy was spent almost entirely in reading, writing and reciting Latin, often in the most mind-numbingly repetitious manner*. Educational life at Portora was probably not very different from this.

However, early in the School's history, this aim of providing an 'English education' for planters' sons became diluted. The records for the inquisitions of County Fermanagh for 22 January 1629 note: *the number of scholars in the said schoole are now three score or thereabouts, all except three being Irish natives*. One possible explanation for this change might be that there were not enough local planters' children of school age to fill all the spaces, and native children (deserving Irish) were admitted to make up the numbers.

To judge by Strafford's letter to Archbishop Laud in January 1633, the Royal Schools seem hardly to have justified the educational hopes of their founders. He wrote: *The schools, which might be a Means to season the Youth in Virtue and Religion, are, either ill-provided, ill-governed in the most Part, or which is worse, applied sometimes underhand to the Maintenance of Popish School-masters; Lands given to these Charitable Uses, and that in bountiful Proportion, especially by King James, of ever blessed Memory, dissipated, leased forth for little or nothing, concealed contrary to all Conscience, and the excellent Purposes of the Founders*. It seems that the educational purpose of the schools had become of secondary importance to maximising the financial benefit of the endowed lands.

A Classical education

We have seen how the School broadened its role of educating local planters' sons to include educating local native Irish children as well. Later, this role expanded again, from providing education for the local inhabitants of Fermanagh to providing education for children from all over Ireland. For a school in a remote part of western Ireland to become an all-Ireland school is remarkable. How and why did it happen?

In Victorian times, improved communications resulting from the growth of the railways would encourage an all-Ireland intake, but Portora became an all-Ireland school earlier than this, back in the days of coach and horses. We must look elsewhere for the cause. One reason would have been the School's academic success. The curriculum would probably not have changed very much from the Latin education referred to by Bryson earlier, but the School was successful in building up a reputation for being both academically sound and very successful in getting pupils into Trinity College, Dublin.

Trinity College, Dublin

Portora and the other Royal Schools were not unique in providing a Classical education. However, secondary education in Ireland was generally poor. The majority of secondary schools provided some form of Classical education aimed at gaining entry to university. For example, there were a number of schools, known as the Classical Schools of Private Foundation, established in the seventeenth century, where the curriculum was mainly Classical, although it generally included other subjects as well. At Kilkenny College the boys were taught Classics, French, German, Arithmetic and Mathematics. At Middleton School the course of study was 'the usual classical one, preparatory to entrance into the University, with the addition of Euclid and Logic, and a good course of instruction in English'. But in Clonmel School, there was 'not much demand for classical instruction', as 'most of the Inhabitants' thought it better 'to educate their Children for Trade and Business'. By the beginning of the nineteenth century there were also a great number of small independent day schools in towns throughout the country offering a secondary education of a Classical style. In 1812 in Kilkenny, for example, Terry Doyle had a Classical School in Patrick Street; and some years earlier there existed Lawler's Classical School, Buchanan's 'English Academy' which taught French and Latin Grammar, and the school of Philip Fitzgibbon, who described himself as 'Classic Teacher and Professor of Book-keeping and Mathematics'; while Father Brophy and Father Brenan, an historian, had a school in Friary Lane in 1822.

Trinity College, Dublin, the ultimate academic goal for many generations of Portora scholars. From the 1960s onwards competition from other academic institutions increased; additionally, social, economic and other pressures reduced the appeal of Trinity to Portora students.

Free Schools
of Royal
Foundation.

It is necessary however to add, that from age and the decay of his memory, he is at present, and appears for some time to have been wholly inadequate to the conduct of such a Seminary; and we think it our duty to recommend that measures should be taken immediately for procuring a more efficient Master.

ENNISKILLEN SCHOOL.

The School Lands of Enniskillen School appear, by a survey taken in the year 1795, to contain about three thousand three hundred and sixty Acres English, of which two thousand five hundred and forty-eight are arable and pasture, and are situated about six or eight miles from the town; there is no Lease of them at present in existence, nor has been since the appointment of the present Master, the Reverend Robert Burrowes, D.D.; the Tenants pay their Rents according to a letting made by the late Master's brother, who held the Lands under a Trust Lease for his, the Master's benefit, granted by the then Primate (Newcome) at the reserved rent of eight hundred Pounds per annum, with a covenant for renewal fines, at the rate of one hundred per annum; they were then let to Undertenants for fourteen hundred and sixty-one Pounds per annum, which is the rent now paid; but the Trust Lease having being surrendered before the appointment of the present Master, the Leases to the undertenants of course became void, and no new ones have been since granted.

Doctor Burrowes states, that if they were now to be let, there would be a considerable rise of rent. His appointment is dated January the 24th, 1798, and is during pleasure. He receives the whole of the Rents, together with ten Pounds per annum for a house in Enniskillen, which was the old School-house; and 5 l. per annum paid by Lord Enniskillen.

The new School-house is a spacious building, capable of accommodating seventy Boarders, and is stated to be in good repair. There is a Demesne of thirty-three acres attached to the house, not included in the survey. There is a charge upon the Endowment for building, of thirteen hundred Pounds, being half of the original charge of two years income expended by the last Master but one (Mr. Noble.) The number of Boarders at the School in January last, was sixty-five, and of Day-scholars from twelve to sixteen. The terms for Boarders are thirty-two Guineas per annum, and six Guineas entrance; and for Day-scholars six Guineas, and one Guinea and a half entrance.

Doctor Burrowes states, that he has presented a Memorial to the Primate, for permission to build considerable additions to the House and Offices, which his Grace is disposed to grant, with leave to charge the usual proportion of the sum laid out on the succeeding masters.

Doctor Burrowes has three Classical Assistants (who all live in the School-house) and pays the first 100 l. per annum, and the other two 40 l. each. He has constantly attended in person to the duties of the School, which he appears to have discharged with equal diligence and ability, and the School is accordingly, and has been since his appointment, in considerable reputation. Doctor Burrowes had till lately the Living of Cappagh in the Diocese of Derry, which he has recently exchanged for that of Drumragh in the same Diocese (both in the presentation of Trinity College Dublin, of which he had formerly been Fellow). He resigned the Archdeaconry of Ferns, on his being appointed Master of the School of Enniskillen.

The Endowment of this School is unquestionably much too large to be enjoyed

Part of the entry for Enniskillen School from the 'Reports from the Commissioners of Education in Ireland 1809-1812'.

What was distinct about Portora was its academic success and standing. Part of this success was due to the links between the School, the established Church (Church of Ireland) and Trinity College, Dublin; forged at a very early stage, they served to influence the School's direction and curriculum. Almost from its foundation, there was a close relationship between the School, the Diocese of Clogher and Trinity. Part of the Plantation of Ulster allocated land to Trinity College, Dublin, and the links with the Church reinforced the relationship. It was the privilege of the Lord Lieutenant of Ireland to appoint the Master of Portora and he had close links with the Church of Ireland. Portora frequently drew its Masters from Trinity and the Church of Ireland. Gradually, a triangle formed: boys attended Portora and went on to Trinity; Masters of the School tended to be either graduates of Trinity or ordained clergymen, or both. The School attracted gifted staff. Two of the School's Masters from the 1700s have entries in the Oxford Dictionary of National Biography: **Reverend Dr W Dunkin** (S, 1746-63), and **Reverend Dr J Stock** (S, 1795-98). Quane remarks that Stock '*was an accomplished classical scholar, an excellent linguist and a man of much general culture. In addition to other learned works, he published school editions of Tacitus and Demosthenes, which were in general use in schools for many years.*' These often highly academic staff in turn succeeded in producing pupils who performed well at examinations. The accusation sometimes levelled at the School was that pupils were being 'crammed' for these examinations.

Trinity College, Dublin

As is becoming clear, any history of Portora's curriculum, its aims and goals, eventually includes Trinity College, Dublin. For many years, the aim of the Classical education provided by Portora was to gain entry to that university. Founded in 1592, 26 years before Portora, Trinity was for many years Ireland's only university. Taking its lead from universities elsewhere in the United Kingdom, especially Oxford and Cambridge, its syllabus for many years was highly academic. In a society where open examination to careers was unheard of, university education was vital. It can be said that it was the university of the ruling classes and the established Church. If one did not get a scholarship, one had to pay, and only the middle and upper middle classes could afford to pay. These strong links between Portora and Trinity College, formed early in the School's history, continued beyond partition and lessened only in the late 1940s with the arrival of 11+ pupils and the growth in demand for entry to English universities.

The early 1800s: the Burrowes era

Information about the School's curriculum remains sketchy until the nineteenth century. One of the first comprehensive accounts, 'Course of Instruction at Enniskillen School', was published by the Master, **Reverend Dr R Burrowes** (S, 1798-1819), in 1814.

He described a school where there were seven year-groups, of which two year-groups had two classes. The curriculum was noticeably biased towards the Classics. Indeed, for the first two years, it was not always thought necessary for the boys to have a daily lesson in English, reading and spelling. The curriculum started with Latin text. Even in the third year, the work was not written down but mainly learned by rote. Dr Burrowes, justifying this, said: '*nothing being found more injurious to boys' handwriting or productive of more irregularity and disturbance in a school-room, than the ordinary mode of writing exercises*'. History was introduced in the fourth year, but even then it was Greek and Roman rather than British history. Greek grammar was introduced in the fourth year, becoming the dominant subject by year six.

School hours were from 6:30am to 9:00am in Summer and from 7:00am to 9:00am in Winter; lessons resumed at 10:00am and continued until 3:00pm in the afternoon. In the evening there was study from 7:00pm to 8:30pm, preparing the following morning's lessons.

The school day appeared to be well planned and full. '*Prayers are read by the Master at nine before breakfast, and at nine before going to bed. The period from ten to three includes the attendance on the Writing Master, and on the French Master who teaches such as choose to learn French each day in the schoolroom; on Thursdays and Saturdays the School closes at one o'clock. Thursdays and Saturdays are in a great measure appropriated to extraneous business, the lessons in the Classics being on these days usually laid aside. Besides the Histories which have been already mentioned, and which after some time are reserved for these days, a portion of the time is laid out for mathematical knowledge. The boys from the beginning have attended the Writing master daily from one to two hours. It may therefore be assumed that they have acquired a sufficiency of information in Arithmetic when they have reached the division marked 7 to begin Euclid's Elements. They read the first and third and sometimes the sixth book, and are instructed afterwards in the elements of Algebra.*'

The religious instruction of the boys formed part of their education, even to the extent that it was usually made a part of the course of examination for scholarships. Sunday evening was appropriated for religious instruction and full prayers were read.

Burrowes noted that there were generally a number of boys at the School '*not intended for learned professions*'. These, while receiving a 'Classical education', also received a more conventional education, which included English grammar, written English exercises, Geography and British History.

A look at the teaching staff and their respective salaries also gives us an insight into the curriculum. As well as the Master, Burrowes, there were three Classical teachers on the staff (paid £100 0s 0d, £80 0s 0d and £50 0s 0d per annum), together with a French master (£70 0s 0d), a Writing master (£50 0s 0d), who also taught Arithmetic (and book-keeping for those intended for mercantile business), a Dancing master (£56 17s 6d) and a Drawing master (£79 12s 6d).

Burrowes would attend school each day, normally hearing the head class for at least one lesson a day, and one or two repetitions of each of the other classes in turn. He conducted the half-yearly examinations entirely by himself. '*The answering at repetitions for two months is noted down, and from this, with one examination in the whole portion gone through, the premiums are decided. The scholarship examination for entry to Trinity College, taken three months after the opening of school in January, is usually in Virgil, three or four Ovids, one of Sallust's War, and such a portion of Greek Testament as may give sufficient scope to try accurately the knowledge of the Greek grammar, plus a play of Terence, another book of Virgil or a larger portion of Greek Testament or Sallust. The number of scholars is eight – the emolument twenty pounds per annum to each.*'

The mid-1800s: Lombe Atthill's schooldays

By the mid-1800s we are fortunate to have another picture of educational life at Portora, from **Lombe Atthill** (OP, 1840-43). Written after he had retired in his seventies, and published posthumously in 1911, Atthill's autobiography describes his school days at Portora, thirty years after Burrowes' account. What he gives us is a remarkably detailed, although not entirely flattering, account of School life during the 1840s.

His parents sent him to Portora, '*supposed to be the best in the country, a reputation resting wholly on the fact that pupils from it obtained very frequently first place at the entrance examinations for Trinity College, Dublin. For this they were carefully prepared – indeed crammed.*

'*Having read the six books of Virgil, he went on to Horace, then to Juvenal and the Latin plays in succession. Our work was increased, that was all; and the same with Greek – Xenophon, Homer, Greek plays, etc., indeed every book named in the curriculum for the entrance examination of the University of Dublin. Having read these through, we began again. I went over most of them two or three times, so when I went up for the entrance examination I knew these books nearly off by heart; but my knowledge of the Greek and Latin languages was poor enough…*

'*One or two of the boys who were always at the top of the class gained high places at entrance, and classical Honours in the University course; but the rest of the class learned little. English was hardly taught at all, just a little history (and that ancient), and geography: indeed the latter was a mere form. Not a single boy learned French or German. Mathematics was relegated to a secondary place, and counted for little in school work; this was unfortunate for me, for Euclid and algebra gave me no trouble, while I never succeeded in learning Greek properly.*

'*Morning school lasted from 7.30 a.m., summer and winter, till nine o'clock; then we trooped to the dining-hall for breakfast. The boys reassembled for school at ten o'clock and remained in the classroom till three, except on Wednesdays and Saturdays, when we broke up at 2 p.m.*'

In the context of education of the early 1800s, Atthill's rather grim picture of school life was not untypical. Life at the major English Public Schools, such as Eton, Harrow, Westminster and Rugby, with which Portora was compared, was harsh. Indeed, what is surprising, when comparing Portora with them, is the high academic tradition that it achieved. Following a tour of Ireland in 1852, J Forbes, Fellow of the Royal Society and physician to Queen Victoria's household, summed up the purpose of the Royal Schools: '*They are in some respects similar to our endowed classical schools in England, and are intended to educate the children of the upper or middle classes destined for the University or otherwise.*'

The Steele era: a Victorian education

Queen Victoria came to the throne in 1837 and by the 1850s 'Victorian values' were filtering through into education. In 1864 the Clarendon Commission inquired into the administration, finance, studies, methods and extent of instruction at Eton, Winchester, Westminster, Harrow and Rugby. As well as having specific concerns about the regimes at some of these schools, society's general expectation of what a 'good education' should provide was changing.

RECOLLECTIONS OF
AN IRISH DOCTOR

BY THE LATE
LOMBE ATTHILL, M.D.
SOME TIME PRESIDENT OF THE ROYAL COLLEGE OF PHYSICIANS DUBLIN
PRESIDENT OF THE ROYAL ACADEMY OF MEDICINE IRELAND AND
MASTER OF THE ROTUNDA HOSPITAL

LONDON
THE RELIGIOUS TRACT SOCIETY
4 BOUVERIE ST AND 65 ST PAUL'S CHURCHYARD EC
1911

Title page from the 1911 edition of Lombe Atthill's book 'Recollections of an Irish Doctor'. It may be of interest to readers to know that the book was re-printed in 2008 as a limited edition by Ballinakella Press.

Life at Portora reflected these new ideas. Education was a competitive market, and schools like Portora were having to compete for pupils. The Rosse Report, issued in 1881, noted that the numbers attending the Royal Schools at the time were small, and with the exception of the Schools in Armagh and Enniskillen, showing a tendency to decrease. This was said to be due to the great prestige and popularity of certain English schools, better endowed and better staffed, to which many Irish boys were being sent; it was also attributed to the existence of successful private schools in Ulster.

Having built up a reputation as a Classical school of merit, the School was fortunate in the mid-1800s appointment of some highly dynamic Masters. These appointments coincided with social changes such as improvements in transport (rail transport in particular), resulting in a period during which the School was regarded as one of the premier academic schools in Ireland. On more than one occasion it was referred to as 'the Eton of Ireland'.

This 'golden era' reached a peak under the Mastership of **Reverend Dr W Steele** (S, 1857-91). An excellent appointee, Steele took over just at the time when new educational ideas were being discussed. Building on the already very high academic reputation of the School, he introduced many of the modern Victorian educational ideas coming into English Public Schools.

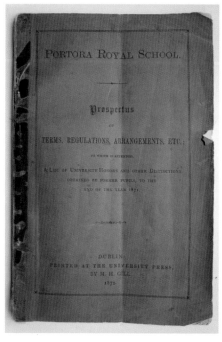

School prospectus from 1872, detailing terms, regulations and arrangements, together with a list of university honours and other distinctions obtained by former pupils to the end of 1871.

It was Steele who popularised printed prospectuses at Portora. One in the School archives, dated 1871, states: *'The School is divided into Upper and Lower. The three Lower Classes constitute the Lower School, to whose education the greatest possible attention is paid. Their School-room, Dormitories, hours for work and recreation, are distinct from those of the Upper School. The Upper School consists of the Three Senior Classes. Each Master in the Upper School has a separate Class-room, which is used as a Reading-room by his class out of School-hours. Boys are admitted into the School between the ages of 10 and 16 years. The course of Instruction embraces all that is implied in a sound and extensive English, Classical and Mathematical Education, including also French, German and Italian.'*

School numbers put pressure on space for teaching and accommodation and in about 1859 Steele built what became known as the Steele Hall. Now used as a hall to accommodate whole-school events, such as plays and assemblies, it was originally built as a classroom to relieve the overcrowded classrooms in the main building. An old boy, recalling the events, noted: *'Dr Steele transferred the Upper School to the new building, and if my memory serves me correctly, we of the Upper School attended in the Examination Hall for French, Drawing, Mathematics, and English, before the different masters, there, while we adjourned to the class rooms beneath for Latin and Greek.'*

Also during the late 1900s, the role and importance of sport grew. Portora's sporting successes are dealt with in greater depth in chapter five, but they owe their development and growth largely to the spread of sport as a curriculum topic in the late Victorian period. Prior to the 1840s there was little or no organised sport in schools and in this respect Portora was no different from the majority of Public Schools. Lombe Atthill notes this from his time at the School in the 1840s: *'…even more remarkable is the fact that no games were instituted. No doubt there was a fives court, but only one. Cricket was quite unknown, and neither football nor hockey were played. The senior boys deemed such games derogatory to their dignity, and no master took the least trouble to encourage games.'* Gradually, Public Schools saw the benefit of sport and developed it as part of the curriculum.

One pupil's recollections of the Steele era were recorded in the *Impartial Reporter* for 12 February 1891: '*Portora never turned out better men, and no school in Ireland shone more brilliantly with academic honours than Enniskillen Royal School at that time, when there were almost too many boys at school for the school accommodation and the number of masters. Portora's record was glorious, and we all felt proud of belonging to the foremost Irish school.'*

A useful source of information on the School for this period are the reports of the Commissioners of Education. Unfortunately, as with many original sources, they tend to concentrate on management issues, such as the numbers of pupils on roll, rather than academic ones. However, they give an overall view of the School at a time when it was very successful.

The late 1800s onwards – broadening the curriculum

Until well after the middle of the nineteenth century, secondary education was mostly in private hands and received no public assistance. The establishment of the National System of Education, and the great Famine of 1847, led to the decline and '*extinction of a great number of the rough middle class schools'*, the Hedge Schools in rural areas and the 'academies' in towns. Although the National System of Education was principally intended for primary

Junior pupils being taught technical drawing in what is now the Old Dining Room. Note the spheres, cones, cubes and squares. In this photograph, the panelling around the room is dark oak varnish; today, the restored panelling is a pale colour.

education, its introduction resulted in the closure of many private secondary schools, which had *'formerly enabled the middle classes, to a certain extent, to provide a suitable education for their children'.* The result was that the middle classes, Protestant as well as Catholic, were sadly in need of schools that gave instruction in Classics and Mathematics.

This decline in the number of secondary schools coincided with another change taking place during the late 1800s, namely the broadening of education beyond its upper- and middle-class heartland. Not all pupils were trying to enter Trinity College, Dublin. Secondary education also paved the way to openings in the Civil Service and the professions. The British Empire was expanding and required men to administer it and a traditional 'Classical education' was not always the best preparation for some of the new professions. Even the military were beginning to see the need for well-educated entrants.

This growth in demand from the professions for non-university-educated entrants coincided with demands from the middle classes for adequate secondary education for their children. Increasingly, civic leaders led the demand for schools to educate pupils for entrance examinations to the professions. From the 1850s onwards we see pressure applied on Portora from local inhabitants to implement a broader curriculum than the traditional one. Prior to this time the School's Classical curriculum had been unsuitable for the majority of local needs, and most of the School's intake came from elsewhere in Ireland. Increasingly the people of Enniskillen wanted to have a greater say in what Portora taught, to modify the curriculum to suit the educational needs of local children.

William Trimble, giving evidence to the Endowed Schools Commissioners on 15 October 1855, stated: *'It is an universal complaint as regards the inhabitants of Enniskillen, that the education received at Portora is chiefly, if not altogether classical, and of comparatively little or no utility to men of business and those who wish to push their children forward.'* The School had always had a number of 'free' places for local children; what was changing was the growth in demands for the curriculum to change to better suit the needs of these local children. Records show the difficulties on both sides as they moved towards change: Steele's plan to separate boarders entirely from dayboys, and letters and demands published in local papers. The *Impartial Reporter* noted in December, 1864: *'that the ample provision made by the State for the education of the children of the middle classes, is not enjoyed by these classes, but goes to support a splendid establishment for the education of sons of gentlemen from various parts of Ireland.'* Eventually, this local pressure was successful and in 1865 the Commissioners of Endowed Schools proposed changes that were introduced by the School.

Locally, Enniskillen townspeople and the School were trying to resolve the issue of how to provide a suitable secondary education. Nationally things were changing as well. The Kildare Commission of 1857-58 was appointed to report and make recommendations. They were very conscious of the need for secondary education, but, not surprisingly, hard put to know where suitable funding would come from. They proposed that secondary education, which

Royal Scholars board from the Steele Hall. Several scholars listed on this board are covered in greater detail in chapter 8: John G Gibson, James Bourchier, Oscar Wilde and John Sullivan.

they called 'intermediate', should, like primary education, be financed partly by local subscription and partly by a Government grant.

Their recommendations led to the Intermediate Education (Ireland) Act of 1878, which introduced into secondary education a system of 'payment by results', based on public examinations. A Board of Commissioners of Intermediate Education was set up. Public examinations were held annually, the examiners being chosen by the Board and approved by the Lord Lieutenant. This was a significant change. Hitherto, public examinations were rare; notable examples included those of the Science and Art Department, South Kensington, and examinations for appointments in the Civil Service, which had been thrown open to competition in the mid-nineteenth century.

The examination subjects included, among others, Latin, Greek, Modern Languages, History and Mathematics. There were three grades, Junior, Middle and Senior, with an examination for each grade. The Intermediate System was a godsend to both schools and pupils: the schools could now, if efficient, command a steady additional income, while intelligent pupils could by their own industry pay their way through a secondary school. Payments were made to schools based on the examination results, and a limited number of prizes and exhibitions were awarded to pupils of outstanding ability. Portora was very successful in these examinations. The School magazine of 1918 notes: *'At the intermediate examinations, 26 out of the school's 30 candidates passed. This represents a pass rate of 87%, when the average for all Ireland was 55%'.*

Scholarships

The School's ties with Trinity College, Dublin, were strengthened by the number of scholarships provided for students. In this respect, Portora had always been financially well endowed.

The School prospectus of 1871 notes that: *'There are ten exhibitions – five of £50, and five of £30 – attached to the School. Each exhibition is tenable for five years. No boy is eligible for an exhibition who has not been at a Royal School for three years at least, previous to his entrance into the University.'*

Free scholarships, of £20 per annum each, were conferred by the Commissioners of Education on those scholars who were most distinguished for proficiency in study and propriety of conduct, and were held during their stay at the School. In addition, the Commissioners of Education appropriated £400 per annum of the funds of the School for the endowment of five King's Scholarships of £50 each, and five of £30 each in Trinity College, Dublin, to be held for five years by scholars elected by the Board of Trinity out of those who had been three years at least in any of the Royal Schools of Enniskillen, Armagh or Dungannon.

Trimble, writing in the 1920s, itemises several scholarships: *'The Burke Prize was awarded to three Protestant boys from Enniskillen or Fermanagh who go to Trinity College; the annual sum of £7 for each boy, given by Revd William Burke, rector of Beragh, Co Tyrone, by his will dated 20 September 1818. The Steele Memorial, provided out of public subscriptions to perpetuate the memory of Frederick Steele, who perished in 1866; a yearly value of £12. The Quinton Memorial, balance of funds after providing a stained-glass window in*

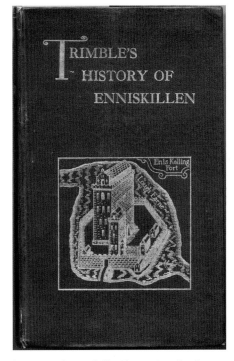

'History of Enniskillen' by W Copeland Trimble, published in 1919-20. Before the publication of this book, Trimble produced a pamphlet entitled 'Enniskillen Royal School at Portora', covering the history of the School to 1918. This was published by the Protestant Board of Education to part-fund the construction of the Sanatorium as a Tercentenary and War Memorial. The pamphlet contains a comprehensive account of the Scholarships and Exhibitions available to Trinity College, Dublin from all the Royal Schools and Portora in particular.

Enniskillen Church and brass tablet in the School Library, value about £1 5s per year, in memory of the Hon James Wallace Quinton, British resident, murdered at Manipur. The Biggs Memorial, in memory of Mr Richard Biggs, LLD, Headmaster 1894-1904, value for £5 13s. In addition to the foregoing permanent prizes, The Right Hon J G Gibson PC, one of the Justices of the High Court, has given a prize every year for a considerable time.'

The School's continuing academic success can best be illustrated by an item from the annual School magazine, 'Portora': *'H F Biggs has just capped a long series of College successes by obtaining the Mathematical Studentship for the year. We take the following extract from "The Irish Times": "Henry Francis Biggs entered Trinity College from the Royal School, Portora, in 1901, gaining the James Patrick Kidd Scholarship. He has obtained First Honors in Mathematics (6) and in Experimental Science (3), in addition to a Mathematical Scholarship in 1903, and a Lloyd Exhibition in Mathematics in 1904." We offer him our hearty congratulations.'* The magazine goes on: *'J E W Flood has obtained a divided first place in the examination for the James Patrick Kidd Scholarship with the magnificent total of 806. This is the fourth successive time that Portora has won this Scholarship. He also obtained First Prize in Latin Composition, First Prize in Greek Verse, First Prize in English Literature, Second Prize in Greek Composition, and Second Prize in Latin verse.'*

An intriguing photograph that poses more questions than it answers. Marked 'HB 1925' in the bottom right hand corner, it may date from the Edwardian era. Is that the Steele Hall visible through the folding glass partition behind the teacher? And who is the teacher?

The inter-war years – 1918-1939

This is a period characterised by national and world events whose impact on the School's curriculum and recruitment was delayed until after World War II. Politically, the major event was partition and the creation of the Irish Free State. Socially, the broadening of education beyond its traditional middle-class market had a significant effect on the School. From the 1870s onwards Portora faced increasing competition in attracting pupils. As a result of the Intermediate examination system, the number and quality of local secondary schools throughout Ireland increased, and Portora had to adapt to maintain its numbers. New curriculum subjects were introduced, and many changes of emphasis took place.

The establishment of the Irish Free State would have long-term effects on the School. Portora, located on the sparsely populated western edge of Ireland, had built itself up into an all-Ireland boarding school, drawing a significant part of its intake from the newly created 26 counties, and catering primarily for boys wishing either to continue on to university or enter the military or the Church, the emphasis here being the Church of Ireland. Significant numbers of these boarders came from the 26 counties, and many of those who went up to university chose Trinity College, Dublin. Initially, life continued as before: the sons of Old Portorans from the 26 counties continued to attend the School, and Portora continued to follow a curriculum geared towards the entrance requirements of Trinity College, Dublin. However, by the 1970s, the effects of the Troubles and Ireland's new-found prosperity from European Union membership impacted on boarding numbers. By the time boarding had ceased at Portora the curriculum was targeting universities, colleges and employers in the United Kingdom.

In describing the purpose of the School's curriculum, **Vivian Mercier** (OP, 1928-36), put it so well in his article 'The Old School Tie', in 'The Bell': *'What was the ultimate purpose of all this hymn-singing and football playing, this teaching of the Classics and how not to be cads? What was the object of the drilling in the Officers' Training Corps – which though not compulsory, numbered almost every boarder old enough to join, and a handful of day-boys as well – where boys of sixteen or seventeen became corporals and sergeants just as they became prefects in civilian life? This is not much more than a rhetorical question, because you all know the answer. The boarders, at any rate, irrespective of class background, were being educated to lead – to become empire builders, if you wish – just like their opposite numbers over in England. All sorts of minor pomposities used to come and tell us so, on Empire Day or Speech Day, and we laughed at them, but this war, like the previous one, has shown that they were right and we were wrong. My contemporaries, as well as my seniors and juniors at school, are officering the forces of the British Empire all over the world. I have a list of the Old Boys' Union here beside me, and at least half the names are marked with a dagger, meaning that they are 'On Service with the Forces'. Yet the majority of the boarders have, I think, always come from the Twenty-six Counties, and a true blue Orangeman would get a proper ragging at Portora. We used to organise, first an International Rugger match, then later an international swimming race, until the Enniskillen people finally objected to all such fixtures, because the Tricolour was almost certain to be brandished under their noses and the Soldier's Song sung. In the excitement, the Union Jack was liable to be quite literally trampled under foot, though honoured on every other day of the year.'*

The 1947 Education Act

Gradually after 1922, education in Ireland changed. It is estimated that in the early 1940s there were only 13,800 students in the few exclusive fee-paying secondary Grammar Schools in Northern Ireland. Like secondary education, tertiary education was also the preserve of the middle class. There were only 24 scholarships on offer from the local education authorities. This all changed with the Education Act (Northern Ireland) Act 1947, which was closely

During the Steele Mastership, both the Trimble and Dane families were strong supporters and critics of the School's Classical curriculum, expressing their views and those of the townspeople through the pages of the 'Impartial Reporter'.

Eventually a member of the Dane family presented a monetary prize for scholarship in the Sciences, which subsequently became the 'Dane Medal (for) Science'.

The medal illustrated above, ironically scripted in Latin, was presented to James E Wilson (London Branch President 2006-08), prior to him going up to St John's College, Cambridge.

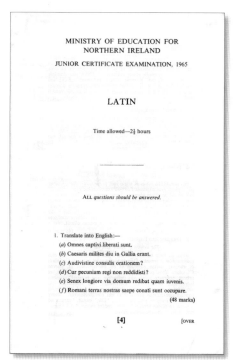

Northern Ireland Junior Certificate examination paper 1965.

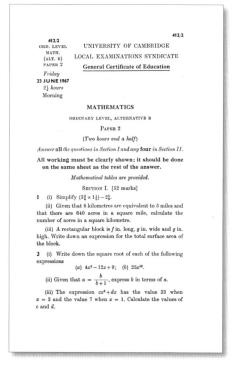

University of Cambridge General Certificate of Education examination paper 1967.

modelled on the Butler Education Act of 1944 which had been passed in the United Kingdom.

Reverend P H Rogers (S, 1954-73) reaped the rewards of the impact of Grammar School status and 11+ pupils, but in fact the major decision had been taken before he took office in 1954. It was during the era of his predecessor, **Reverend D L Graham** (OP, 1922-27; S, 1945-53), that the School took the important decision. The 1947 Act changed things dramatically. Prior to the 1947 Act the number of dayboys attending Portora had been small. This changed after 1947, when 30-50% of the pupils entering the School had now passed the 11+ examination. None of these new entrants had to learn Latin or Greek for the 11+; Portora's old heavily Classical education bias was broken and the School became the Protestant Grammar School for Fermanagh.

Portora's hands were tied. Almost overnight the academic structure of the School changed from a Classically-centred one targeted to the requirements of Trinity College, Dublin, into a boarding and day school with different, at the time rather uncertain, aims. Could the School have said 'no' to Grammar School status? Several English schools did, becoming fully private rather than have to take 11+ pupils. The effects of partition may have had an impact on the decision: the slow decline in the number of pupils from the 26 counties after 1922 was not matched by an increase in numbers of boarding pupils from Northern Ireland. The chances of success from 'going it alone' would not have been clear. Also, since the 1880s, financial control of the School had passed from the Headmaster to an Education Board, so technically Portora was controlled by the State and was not a Private/Public School in the true sense.

This dramatic influx of dayboys created major social and academic challenges for the School. Socially, the House structure was adapted to cope with dayboys in Houses with their own Housemasters, and an extensive building programme was undertaken to accommodate the new pupils. For many dayboys the distances they had to travel to school made it difficult to participate in sport and recreational activities, which usually took place after school or in the evening. For accounts of dayboys' life at Portora during the 1950s, see chapter nine.

The main academic challenge was the need to prepare these children for universities other than Trinity. Both Graham and Rogers saw the opportunities afforded by the 1947 Act and developed the school accordingly. New subjects were introduced, old ones declined (or even died completely), for example, Greek and Latin. New examinations were taken: Junior and Senior Certificates, set by the Northern Ireland Education Board were phased out to be replaced with A- and O-Levels set by the Cambridge Examining Board. New buildings were constructed (see chapter two). New universities and colleges were considered other than Trinity: Queen's, English universities, etc. Initially there was no noticeable change; throughout the 1950s a significant number of pupils were still going up to Trinity. However, as the 1960s progressed the change was noticeable. Leavers' destinations provide an interesting illustration of this. Of the 1967 'Summer of Love' leavers, 38 went to university: 14 went up to Trinity College, Dublin, 13 to Queen's University, Belfast, and the remainder to other British and overseas universities. By 1981, the destinations of leavers were far more widespread. Of the 31 pupils going up to university, 11 went to Queen's, only 2 to Trinity, and the rest to a wide range of mainly British universities. In 1988 the number going on to Queen's had declined to 5, the majority of pupils going to a evenly spread range of British and Irish universities.

Saturday Technology class.

2000 and the future

Over the centuries the School has had fluctuating fortunes, usually depending on the political and economic conditions of the time. That it has existed for so long in this turbulent place is in no small way due to its capacity to adapt. It was a product of Ireland's history and it has continued to reflect the trials and tribulations that have arisen, not only educational but also social and political. This is shown in the buildings, the students and the curriculum.

Now things have come almost full circle. The School was established in 1608 for the education of local boys within Fermanagh. With the closure of the boarding side of the School, it is primarily the local Grammar School for the county. Nothing stands still for long, and Portora must continue to evolve and adapt or it faces an uncertain future. It is fortunate that it has a long and illustrious history to recall and celebrate, but history has shown that in order to survive, the School and its curriculum must adapt and evolve rather than try and maintain the present or the past.

As we move into the next hundred years the School is still changing and adapting to new challenges that are presented to it: for example, attacks on academic integrity and falling birthrate. Today Portora is designated a Specialist School, with recently awarded Specialist Status in the Arts seeking *'to develop activities and contexts which will promote creativity and in which pupils are encouraged to take risks, to speculate, to perceive more broadly, to respond in different ways, to self-evaluate their attempts and to persevere'*. Clearly, while the School is proud of its past, it is also looking to the future and, through its curriculum, seeking to develop young people with intelligence, courage and leadership, who are able to manage, with support, their own learning and lives, and to contribute positively to society.

Biology class.

Five

Sport

Generations of Portorans have enjoyed the School's unrivalled site and environment. Its extensive estate of playing fields and woodland is lapped by the River Erne and the Lower Lough. In the early days only handball courts were provided, but over the past 150 years cricket, rugby and rowing have emerged as competitive sports. Gradually sailing, canoeing and fishing were enjoyed on the river and lake, and tennis, cross-country running and athletics were pursued in the grounds. Swimming took place, at first in the lake, then in the old steamship dock at Derrygore Point, and more recently in the open-air swimming pool, often under the watchful eye of the late Major Wheeler. For a time boxing and fencing were popular. Further afield, but still within easy reach, there was hill-walking, orienteering and camping with the Scouts, and more recently with the Duke of Edinburgh Award Scheme. The Officer Training Corps (OTC) and its successor, the Combined Cadet Force (CCF), have always provided a range of activities, which include marching, shooting and map-reading. In recent times, soccer, always a popular unofficial activity, has become a properly organised School sport.

Cricket

It is recorded that cricket was first brought to Portora in the early 1850s by **J J H Carson** (OP, 1853) and his brother, both from Armagh, with the support of the Headmaster of Armagh Royal School, then the foremost school for

Left: **Lagan Scullers' Head of the River 2006.**

Portorans enjoying a game of cricket on the upper playing fields. The prevailing weather conditions in Fermanagh, with its wind and rain, were always a problem for the Summer cricket season.

cricket in Ireland. Carson later became a director of the Bank of Ireland. According to another source, however, cricket was first played c1840: **Lombe Atthill** (OP, 1841-44), in his *Reminiscences of an Irish Doctor*, notes that he and some juniors challenged the Upper School. Atthill, born in Fermanagh, was a former student at Maidstone Grammar School before coming to Portora.

By the end of the nineteenth century the Portora cricket team was regularly playing about fifteen matches during the season against schools as far apart as Dungannon Royal School, Campbell College, St Columba's College and Raphoe Royal School, as well as locally stationed army teams and Fermanagh County Cricket Club. During the twentieth century, possibly only about half of all matches were played against school sides, and Portora regularly played town teams, for example Sion Mills, and privately organised teams.

In 1906 the tradition of presenting cricket caps was reintroduced, and inter-provincial matches between Ulster and Leinster schools were inaugurated. Portora regularly supplied one or two players to the Ulster side.

The wet Fermanagh weather and the odd outbreak of epidemics (mumps or measles) often interfered with play. In 1916 it was very wet and all matches were cancelled. In 1920 it was again very wet and there was an outbreak of mumps (blamed on Beckett senior).

During World War I travel was restricted, which dealt a severe blow to the game in School, as the team could not travel to many matches. In 1921 a change in the railway timetable made travel to matches or visits to Portora awkward. In the same year the School cattle were allowed to wander on to the cricket pitch, making it virtually unplayable.

Cricket also competed against rowing in school, and in 1918 it was noted that the *'team (was) weakened by the attraction of rowing or rather being in the Rowing Club'*.

Samuel Beckett (OP, 1920-23) was a key member of the Portora cricket team while at school. In 1920 his critique read: *'Can bat well at times but has an awkward habit of walking across the wicket to all balls. Good field.'* In 1925 he returned to captain the visitors in an Old Boys match.

In the 1920s and 1930s boys continued to be regularly selected to play for Ulster in the Ulster-Leinster schools matches.

During World War II Portora found plenty of competition among the forces stationed in the area (RAMC, Green Howards, Northamptons, Royal Artillery, 26th Troop Carrying Company, North Irish Horse), and played 17 RAF teams from Killadeas, St Angelo and Castle Archdale.

The cricket team benefited from the bulldozing by the American Army engineers of an area behind the school, which was converted into a rugby and cricket pitch, thus allowing two teams to practise simultaneously. Mr Barnes apparently tried to teach cricket to US Forces before they 'dozed the pitches.

During 1949-50 Headmaster **Douglas Graham** (OP, 1919-27; S, 1945-53) engaged a full-time Yorkshire professional cricketer, Christian Perfect, as coach; he amused us Irish by calling out, *'Uup and at 'im, lad!'* in a broad Yorkshire accent. It was said that many of the masters could not understand him when he joined them for staff dinner.

Monty Ainslie (S, 1959-72) came to Portora in 1959 and in 1966 was made 'Master in Charge of Cricket', a post he held until his departure in 1972. He is on recorded as saying: *'Cricket in Fermanagh is against the natural order of things.'* Despite this, his enthusiasm for the sport encouraged it to thrive at Portora and, although he was renowned for ignoring the rain, he too struggled with the wet Fermanagh weather: *'The misery of this bitter summer has been made tolerable only by the cheerfulness of the boys who have had to endure it, and the same attitude has survived the cancellation, owing to epidemics, of some of our already restricted number of matches.'*

In 1975 the Second XI entered the local Tyrone/Fermanagh league for the first time.

Cricket struggled with the timing of the state examination system and in the late 1980s it was commented that few Grammar Schools continued to play. This meant that Portora struggled to find competition at their level: *'It isn't very nice losing and we should know.'*

In recent years the School has competed in the Sherrygroom Trophy and the Stirling Trophy, and has played an annual fixture against Clongowes Wood College.

Rowing

Early rowing

With Portora's location by the River Erne it is not surprising to find mention of recreational rowing at Portora in the mid-nineteenth century. Rules and regulations displayed in every classroom during the tenure of **Reverend Dr William Steele** (S, 1857-91) as Headmaster included the following:

Sporting logos from 'Portora', the School magazine. They first appeared in the 1930s and were still being used during the 1960s.

Boating

9   *The Boating Season shall continue to be, as hitherto, from 1st April to the 1st October.*

10   *No boy shall ever be allowed the use of any boat, except those belonging to the School or a Master.*

11   *Two-oared Boats and Racing-gigs shall not go up the Lake higher than Killyhevlin, nor down the lake lower than Devenish.*

12   *No boy shall be permitted to go in any boat, unless (1) He has learned to swim; (2) And has received his Parents' written sanction; (3) And has had a paper setting forth his name, and names of the crew, and also the name of the boat, duly signed by the Head Master or Master-in-charge of the boats.*

13   *No crew shall have use of a boat for a period exceeding Two Hours.*

14   *Occasionally, on a holiday in fine weather, the Head Master may give special written permission to a Crew of Upper-school Boys wishing to go on an excursion up the Lake, to have the use of a boat for a period exceeding Two Hours.*

15   *The Boatman who has custody of the boats may, at any time, refuse to give a boat to any crew notwithstanding the Master's written order.*

There are many reasons for this attachment to rowing at Portora. The boys enjoyed much liberty in the midst of beautiful scenery, and especially attractive and never-to-be-forgotten were various excursions on the waters of Lough Erne. The School possessed several excellent four-oared boats, and sometimes the boys could remain out the whole day, camping on one of the many beautifully wooded islands of the Upper or Southern Lough, where they made a fire and cooked their meals.

The first record of competitive rowing at Portora appears in a *Belfast Newsletter* report of 25 August 1866, describing the City of Derry Boating Club Regatta of the previous day. Portora, in light blue and white, raced in a boat named 'Glimpse' and came fourth in a four-boat race over a course of two miles. They were beaten by Bann Rowing Club, City of Derry Boating Club and Belfast Amateur Rowing Club.

A picture of a Portora six rowing in front of Portora in the 1850s hangs in the Headmaster's Dining Room. In a 1937 edition of the School magazine, 'Portora', there is reference to the fact that the Boat Club would soon reach its centenary.

Pre-World War I

Although at the turn of the twentieth century there were in-School races, it was following the appointment of sports enthusiast **Alaster McDonnell** (S, 1904-15) as Headmaster that competitive rowing re-emerged with the appearance of Portora at Trinity and Derry Regattas in 1905. This was notable for the fact that not only were they the first schoolboys to enter open races, but also that they were good enough to win. In the pre-war years crews raced regularly at Boyne, Derry, Portadown and Trinity.

Formal racing was abandoned during World War I. In 1915, the same year as McDonnell left Portora, the roof of the boathouse fell in during a gale, destroying an eight and two fours. Following World War I and during the 1920s rowing struggled, especially as the short Summer Term was interrupted by a mid-term break, which restricted the rowing season to six or eight weeks.

At this time a Trinity Maiden four made an annual trip to Lough Erne to race a Portora four, and there were pairs races between Portora boys, although this was often restricted to only two crews. In 1923 a centre-seated boat was purchased from Jesus College, Cambridge, allowing School fours races, and in 1927 another evenly matched boat allowed the 'Groggy Fours' races to be initiated. This race later became the Henning Shield race and took place between the School Houses.

Schools rowing

In 1928 a challenge was received from Coleraine Academical Institution (CAI), but the race was postponed to the following year following the discovery that CAI rowed with sliding seats. In 1929 the race duly took place on Lough Erne, using both sliding seats and stake boats; Portora won.

By the late 1920s the Irish Amateur Rowing Union (IARU) was making a concentrated effort to encourage school rowing, and medals were produced for school races affiliated with regattas. Within a few years school rowing was flourishing in Belfast, Coleraine, Cork and Galway, and Portora was competing at annual fixtures with Dublin University Boat Club (DUBC), Royal Belfast Academical Institution (RBAI), Belvedere and CAI.

In 1933 **George Andrews** (S, 1933-79), a former cox at Sidney Sussex College, Cambridge, came to teach at Portora. As Master in Charge of Rowing until the early 1970s, he transformed the Boat Club, building steps down to the boathouse and slips, purchasing sectional eights, building a new boathouse, which was opened in 1950, and organising the first Erne Head of the River, the first Henley entry and the first Ulster Schools Regatta.

World War II weakened the Boat Club because there was a lack of fuel for the coaching launch. Also there were few trained staff available for training sessions, because of the 'call-up' for war duties and local demands for Air Raid Protection (ARP) duties during the evenings and weekends. Lastly George Andrews departed for the Navy.

By 1946, however, the Boat Club was active again with preliminary training during the Easter Term, followed by a 45-mile row around the lake on the first day of the Easter holidays. The same year saw the initiation of the Ulster Schools Regatta on the Lagan, with ten crews from

Rowing VIII 1907.

Nearly 50 years later, the 1st VIII preparing for Henley Royal Regatta.

**Passing the Watergate area of
Enniskillen Castle.**

Portora, Methodist College Belfast (MCB), CAI and RBAI racing for the Craig
Cup, which was won by Coleraine. In 1950 Portora won a record three events
at the Ulster Schools Regatta, and claimed to be the best-equipped school boat
club in Ireland.

Henley Royal Regatta

In 1951 Portora made their first trip to Henley Royal Regatta, becoming the first
Irish school to race there. They were knocked out by Monkton Combe in the
first round of the Princess Elizabeth Cup. However, this was the start of regular
trips to Henley, and in 1958 Portora progressed to the semi-finals, where they
were beaten by St Edward's School, Oxford. In 1964 Portora sent what was
possibly their strongest crew ever to Henley; unfortunately this was also the
year in which the event was, for the first time, opened up to American crews,
and Portora were beaten by Washington Lee, schoolboy champions in the US.
Without American crews it is possible they may have won. In 1980 Portora
reached the quarter-finals, to be beaten again by a US crew. Most unlucky
was the Henley crew in 1982, who broke an oar in the first stroke of their race
against Hampton School.

European racing

In 1954 Portora made their first trip further afield. Amsterdam Rowing Club,
who were hosting the European Rowing Championships, invited groups of
schoolboys from Ireland, England, Denmark, Switzerland and Belgium to the
event, and following the Championships they hosted an informal youth regatta
and a two-day recreational rowing trip.

In 2006 Portora travelled to Ghent Regatta in Belgium, the largest Junior
Regatta in Europe.

Irish champions

At the Metropolitan Regatta in 1955, Portora raced a Senior, Junior and Maiden eight, and although all performed well, only the Senior eight won. This was the first time a schoolboy eight had won at senior level in Ireland. Two years later, in 1957, Portora won the Senior four event at the Metropolitan Regatta, considered the 'Blue Riband of Irish Rowing'.

By the 1960s university and club crews had improved their coaching, and Portora could no longer compete at senior level. However, they came to dominate at junior level, winning the Schoolboy Championship in 1966 and 1967, and performing the double feat again in 1976 and 1977. Portora last won the eights event at the Championships in 1980; however, they have won many smaller boat categories since then.

Erne Head of the River

Erne Head of the River was initiated in 1957 as a practice event for Irish crews who were planning to race in England at Chester, Reading and Putney. It took place earlier in the season and was longer than other Irish Head races at that time. Dublin University Boat Club won the first race, with Queen's University in second place, and the two Portora crews, who had not had the benefit of Winter training, brought up the rear in third and fourth positions. In 1964 Portora won their own Head for the first time. Ten years later there were 15 crews competing, and within 25 years entries had reached 50 crews. The Head is now limited to 70 crews.

Portora Regatta

In 1967 Portora hosted the first Portora Regatta for Schools, an event deemed necessary by the number of schools entries at regattas, which that year had equalled the number of all other entries. Over the following decades the Regatta often included the Junior Irish Championships, until they were amalgamated with the Senior event.

International representation

The main feature of the first Portora Regatta was the Irish Amateur Rowing Union (IARU) Schoolboy Championship, which also decided representation for the new Home Countries Regatta (England, Ireland, Scotland and Wales) at Loch Lomond in mid-July. Portora was selected to represent Ireland in an eight and four, and went on to win both events.

The following year, 1968, Portora was again selected as the Irish four for the Home Countries Regatta and came second to England. The same crew was also selected by the IARU to race at the European Youth International Regatta at Amsterdam; Fédération Internationale des Sociétés d'Aviron (FISA) age restrictions, however, meant that they were too old to compete.

In 1982 two Portora boys were selected for the Irish four at the Junior World Championships in Rome.

Rowing IV 1946 with George Andrews centre and Julian Kulski standing on the right hand side.

Rowing Internationals 1995: Connor Kells, Stephen Jackson, Simon Janes and Andrew Jackson.

Henley memories – 1951

'There is nothing half so much worth doing as simply messing about in boats.' – Kenneth Graham

John Connor (OP, 1948-52) recalls his experiences as a member of the first crew from Portora to compete at Henley in 1951. The above photograph shows the 1980 crew racing past the Stewards' Enclosure.

There can be few places in the world as well situated for 'messing around in boats' as Portora on the shores of Lough Erne. Boating was clearly a natural pursuit and there are reports of A T M Murfet's interest from his early days at the School, notwithstanding his experience at Peterhouse, where he had contracted blood-poisoning as a consequence of rowing on the Cam. However, the premier sport was rugby. Rowing was a summer activity and the Boat Club was often a refuge for those lacking the patience for, or interest in, cricket. Until the late 1940s the investment in rowing facilities was modest: there were two antique tubs with fixed pins; two clinker fours, the 'Bann' and the 'Erne'; and a shell of indeterminate age, at

least two-plus feet at the beam, that had been acquired on the dissolution of the Newry Boat Club. These were accommodated in a low, open-sided structure.

At the end of the 1940s, (a) benefactor(s) provided the means for the construction of a new boathouse, though there was no immediate addition to the floating hardware, apart from an outboard motor for a coaching launch. Nevertheless, this was a sufficient boost to the recognised enthusiasm of George C Andrews (GCA) to seek greater challenge at Henley. While GCA was not always regarded as an endearing personality, there can be no doubt of his contribution to rowing in Ireland, and his drive in promoting the sport on the Erne waters. By 1950 it was decided that Portora would go to Henley Royal Regatta in 1951, entering for the Princess Elizabeth Cup, then restricted to schools crews from the United Kingdom.

Preparation got under way on occasional Sundays during the Christmas Term and early Easter Term. Until exit from the Schools Cup, thereafter, there were regular outings on Wednesdays and Sundays, come wind, rain, sleet, snow or dark of night. In about a hundred outings, close to five hundred miles were accumulated in deference to the rallying call, 'mileage makes champions'. At the Liffey and Lagan Heads the School won the clinker divisions, though the Junior Eights was lost to Trinity at Trinity Regatta – and then Henley.

By comparison with the routines of Enniskillen, the living was good. There was a visit to the Festival of Britain en route; the crew was accommodated in the Vicarage at Wargrave (now turned into several flats); the Headmaster's wife and her sister, Mrs Morris, replete with the Head's Ford V8 Pilot car, acted as breakfast cooks. Remember, food rationing was still in force. Although, for 'basics', rationing in Fermanagh was of little concern, when the car was being loaded (no ro-ro ferries in those days) and a case of eggs was observed in the vehicle, the question was raised how such a quantity came into the possession of the driver. Lunch was obtained at the Phyllis Court Country Club and its restored facilities, following wartime closure, enjoyed, and dinner taken every evening at the George and Dragon Hotel in Wargrave. One evening, rough cider was discovered, as was the fact that half a pint was more than enough to render the inexperienced legless.

Training for the race was under the supervision of a Mr Freebairn. A fine shell was borrowed from Merton College, and this boat could 'move' by comparison with the 'broad-beamed Newry eight', replete with its 'staggered seats'. The water seemed different, 'thicker' than the imperceptible flow of Lough Erne, and the Atlantic airs were replaced by the sticky humidity of the Thames Valley. The preparations went well. Creditable times were achieved to the Barrier and the whole course, albeit there was a remonstration for not understanding the obligation of a 'pacing crew' to stay behind and 'push', even if pacing Princeton's 150 pounders who would go on to win the Thames Cup, and then the race.

Portora were drawn against Monkton Combe School. PRS started well, and were up by a canvas at the Barrier, to build up a lead of about half a length by Remenham, breaking the established record for the event to enter the enclosure well up on Monkton by about a length. Alas, this must have been an intoxication, for as the enclosure roar rose, there was a 'crab': the rhythm was lost and Monkton Combe swept past to win by a length or more.

The week was finished out in Henley with a journey to Euston Station to catch the mail boat on the Sunday evening. The crew, while not despondent, felt less than fulfilled. As a last 'hurrah' on English soil they gathered on high stools round the soda fountain in the middle of the main dining room of the Tottenham Court Road Lyons Corner House. Each member was intent upon the consideration and consumption of a Knickerbocker Glory contained in a tall glass. Time was getting on for the boat-train's departure, a tube ride away. The sight of 'Tich' Andrews, seemingly on the verge of apoplexy, in the doorway, exhorting the crew to move, will probably never be forgotten or repeated.

Back in Ireland, the Junior Championship was won in Galway, after a horrendous journey in what must and ought to have been the Sligo, Leitrim and Northern Counties last bus.

Irish senior rowing in 1951 was not in the best of condition. Trinity, with great expectation following the achievements of 1950, disintegrated into what came to be known as the 'umbrage crew' following Trinity Regatta, so that a fit Portora crew might well have annihilated any crew at the Irish regattas: against adult or college crews the Junior Championship was little more than a routine exercise. Such is conjecture: for this was not to be, as the crew broke up after Galway. A foundation had been laid at Portora upon which much would be built in the coming decades. High hopes were held for the 1952 crew: there were four returned oars and therefore of Senior status in Ireland, having been successful as Juniors in the previous year. Portora did well in the Heads but lost in the first round of the Princess Elizabeth, and were unsuccessful in the Senior Championship at Portadown, though coming within three feet of Dublin University Boat Club (DUBC).

The Henley VIII, 1951

Bow	R F S Thornton
2	P R C Dowse
3	J C Fyffe
4	J F S Conlin
5	C H S Phipps
6	T J L McKinney
7	W D Seeds
Str	D W Orr
Cox	J Connor

(Reserve: M R Boyd)

Lost 1st round to Monkton Combe School; 0.5 length, time: 7m 06s

Jayne McCartney and Leigh Cordiner, Junior Pair, Irish Rowing Champions 1985.

In the mid-1980s **Patrick Armstrong** (OP, 1980-85) emerged as probably the most successful rower in the history of the Boat Club: over a two-year period he won almost 40 events, including five Irish Championships and two Home Countries Regattas, as well as racing at the Junior Worlds. In many events he raced with **Robert Storrs** (OP, 1978-85), who all but equalled Patrick's record.

Over the last twenty years Portora boys have continued to represent Ireland at the Home Countries, at the Coupe de la Jeunesse and at the Junior Worlds, winning several medals at the Homes, and medals at the Coupe in both 1995 and 2000.

Girls' rowing

When girls came to Portora, they too joined the Boat Club, and the first Portora girls' four raced at Portora Regatta in 1983. Two years later a girls' pair, **Jayne McCartney** (OP, 1980-86) and **Leigh Cordiner** (OP, 1983-87), won the Irish Junior Championships, and raced in the Home Countries Regatta where they were placed second.

Link with St Michael's School/College

Following the Enniskillen bombing in 1987 Portora invited third-form St Michael's boys to row at Portora, and ten boys took up the invitation. In 1995 two St Michael's boys won their international vests when they raced at the Home Countries Regatta.

Rugby

Rugby was first played at Portora in September 1884, by the few dayboys who remained after all the boarders had departed in the closing years of Steele's Headmastership. The initial proposal by the boys was not kindly received by the Master or other staff, and the use of the cricket pitch was at first refused. A prime mover behind the scheme was **W A Valentine** (OP, 1886), the eldest son of the Classics Master, supported by his own two brothers and his sister, brothers **John Davis** (OP, 1886) and **Arthur Davis** (OP, 1885-89), and J A Firth. From the beginning they played in the School colours of black and yellow and were nicknamed 'the Wasps'. They played matches against each other on Saturday afternoons, but lacked other clubs to play against until 1887, when Portora played their first matches with an external team and pitted themselves twice against Enniskillen Rugby Club.

By the turn of the century Portora were regularly playing between fifteen and twenty annual fixtures. Matches were primarily against other schools: Foyle College, Coleraine Academical Institution, Methodist College, Campbell College, Armagh Royal School, Dungannon Royal School, Sligo Grammar School, Raphoe Royal School, St Columba's College, as well as Trinity College, Dublin, Royal Inniskilling Fusiliers and an Old Boys team.

Portora mirrored developments in Irish rugby as a whole at this time: in 1883 there were 26 clubs affiliated to the Irish Rugby Football Union (IRFU), and by 1903 there were 60.

The Ulster Schools Cup is first referred to in 1899 when Portora were in the final, as they were also in 1902. In 1904 Portora defeated Armagh Royal School and Coleraine Academical Institution but lost to Methodist College in the final. Four boys were also selected to play for the inter-provincial side against Leinster.

Rugby team 1903-04.

Rugby was therefore in a healthy state before that former international and sports enthusiast, McDonnell, arrived as Headmaster in 1904. He developed the game significantly during his tenure. In 1905 Portora won the Schools Cup for the first time. The team was coached by McDonnell personally, and beat Foyle College and Dungannon Royal School to face Methodist College in the final. The whole school travelled by train to Belfast to watch the match at Ormeau, and Portora duly beat their Belfast rivals by three goals and one try to nil. Portora returned to Enniskillen on what had turned into a wet and dismal night, but despite this the station platform was thronged with people. A brake was found and the townsmen of Enniskillen yoked themselves to it and hauled the team right up to the school door.

'*The trophy has never before resided within our walls but, now that we have secured it, our hope is that it may often return.*'

The following year the team was noted for opening the season '*in a manner that can only be described as New Zealandish*' and again returned to Enniskillen with the Ulster Schools Cup.

In 1908 another strong team emerged under the tutelage of McDonnell. The Schools Cup was won in a final against Coleraine Academical Institution with a record score of eight goals and four tries (52 points) to nil. Many members of this team remained into the next season of 1908-09, which saw record scores being notched up. Five players on the team, **G H Wood** (OP, 1906-09), **C V MacIvor** (OP, 1895-1909), **R A V Jackson** (OP, 1904-09), **R A Lloyd** (OP, 1904-09) and **R B Burgess** (OP, 1905-09), went on to become Irish internationals.

Tragically, MacIvor was to die in 1913, at the age of 23, of injuries received during a practice match in College Park, Trinity College, Dublin. He was knocked on the head and, although dazed for a few moments, resumed play. Later he retired from the match and went to his rooms. That night medical advice was sought, and the following day he was moved to a nursing home

Rugby team 1906-07; Dickie Lloyd is seated front centre. The 1908 team had a remarkable run of successes: St Andrew's College were beaten 90-0, St Columba's College 54-0, Foyle College 77-0, Wanderers A 24-0, Campbell College 30-6, Armagh Royal School and Town 39-0, Coleraine Academical Institution 35-0, Lansdowne A 70-0 and Dungannon Royal School 37-0. With an unbeaten record throughout the season, the team won the Schools Cup, beating first, Campbell College 76-0, and then in the final, Coleraine, 42-0.

where he underwent an operation for a burst blood vessel in his head; he died shortly after the operation.

Lloyd was to keep in close contact with the School, and returned during the 1925-26 season to watch a 64-0 win over Dungannon Royal School. He returned again in 1947 to train the backs, and secured a half holiday for the School, when they won the first round of the Ulster Cup. Unfortunately, the team did not progress to the next round.

In 1911 Portora took the unprecedented step of withdrawing from the Ulster Schools Cup. The four finalists, Portora, Coleraine Academical Institution and two Belfast schools, were asked to arrange their matches between themselves. However, one Belfast school declared they would take no part unless it was arranged that *'Portora and Coleraine should travel to play all their matches, and that they themselves should not have to travel at all'*. In the semi-final Portora beat Methodist College but withdrew from the final.

Illness could sometimes lead to the cancellation of a fixture, and in 1917, although Portora defeated Armagh Royal School and Dungannon Royal School in the Schools Cup, they withdrew from the final against Coleraine Academical Institution owing to an outbreak of rubella. Two years later, during the 1919-20 season, another outbreak of measles prevented many regular fixtures.

In 1923 Portora again reached the Schools Cup final, played at Balmoral, but were beaten by Campbell College 23-0. In that year Samuel Beckett was Honorary Secretary of Rugby.

Practice matches against various English Public Schools were gradually introduced in the 1920s. House matches were first introduced in 1919, and during the 1924-1925 season Colours were instituted and proved an incentive to competition.

By the mid-1920s the Second XV appears to have been well established, with matches arranged independently of the First XV. The Seconds won all seven matches they played in 1924-25. Two years later, in 1926-27, there were three teams playing regularly: the team photo of 1924-25 shows all 30 players, including a young Douglas Graham, future Headmaster of the School.

During World War II many Belfast schools were evacuated, their rugby training interrupted, and Portora once more came to the fore. In 1940 the whole school travelled to Ravenhill to watch the team win the Schools Cup, beating Coleraine 6-3. It is recorded that 'in spite of the deluge an Enniskillen band had turned out to play the Cup to its rightful resting place', and the Cup was displayed in the Dining Hall. Portora were to beat Coleraine again in the Cup final in 1941, with an end of season score line of 13 wins out of 14 matches. In 1942 the Schools Cup final ended in a draw with RBAI. It should be added that the *Impartial Reporter* provided very good reports on all the matches, and on the problems with measles that spoilt the contest.

The impact of the war on the kind of opponents Portora were now playing is also obvious. Among the usual inter-school fixtures, matches against the Sherwood Foresters, the RAMC, the Royal Innsikillings Brigade HQ also feature, along with at least 13 matches against the RAF.

Later in the war American troops were stationed in Enniskillen, and General Eisenhower, Supreme Commander of the Allied Forces in Europe,

An unusual photograph of the 1st XV Rugby team in 1915. Someone must have had a sense of humour; one wonders who did the 'risk assessment' for it!

1924-25 Both 1st XV and 2nd XV rugby teams photographed together to celebrate a very good season for both teams. Second from the left standing is a young Douglas L Graham, future Headmaster of the School.

inspected American troops on the Portora rugby field. As mentioned earlier, American Army engineers also made an impact on the Portora landscape by flattening the area at the back of the school creating sports and games pitches.

A persistent problem was the state of the pitches at Portora, as they suffered from frequent flooding. In the 1954-55 season the pitches were under as much as six inches of water, and the team had to relocate to St Angelo for training. In the early 1960s two pitches were acquired at St Angelo, which, although useful for Saturday games, were unplayable during the week, for it was dark by the time the teams arrived. Finally, in 1966 a new lower pitch was built with a stone carpet, which is always playable and is regarded as one of the best pitches in the county.

The first Under-16 team emerged in the 1945-46 season, and in 1950-51 they competed in the Medallion Shield competition.

In 1961 the Portora rugby team went on tour for the first time, travelling to the Isle of Man to play King William's College. In 1965-66 the team made a three-match tour to England. Regular tours to Dublin and Cork were also organised. In 1973 a Rugby Fund to finance tours was suggested. More recently the School team has toured in Canada and Australia.

In the early 1960s Portora was invited to compete in the Rosslyn Park Seven-a-sides. This became an annual competition, attracting several strong rugby schools from Northern Ireland, and within a few years an Ulster Sevens competition was organised as a forerunner to the event. Portora returned again in 1980 after a break of six years.

Schools Cup memories – 1940s

Graham Little reports on the Schools Cup success that proved a welcome distraction to a town in time of war.

Sport has long been regarded as superb escapist entertainment, but when what you need to escape from is something as all-consuming as World War II, a very special kind of sporting event is required.

This Saturday, Portora are preparing to launch another quest for rugby glory in the Ulster Schools Cup, but there will be few supporters at that match who will remember how Enniskillen was captivated by the School's last run of victories in the second oldest rugby competition in the world, when a trip to Belfast provided temporary distraction from the activities of Mr A Hitler in Europe.

Throughout 1940-42, Portora remained undefeated in the Schools Cup, and such was the interest in attending the finals at Ravenhill, particularly the first win in 1940, that the Great Northern Railway put on a special train from Enniskillen to transport all the supporters.

The *Impartial Reporter* covered the 1940 final in great detail, reports of the day in Belfast filling the paper beside reports of battles in France and mainland Europe.

'There was an air of excitement in Enniskillen on Saturday morning that one could attribute to no really obvious cause,' ran the paper's editorial the following week. 'There did not seem to be as many people around as usual, and no wonder! For were not half the population in Belfast? Nothing else mattered, even Hitler and his confreres were for once forgotten.'

A large Enniskillen crowd mingled on the streets of Belfast with the supporters from Coleraine, Portora's opponents for the day, rousing Belfast out of her 'somewhat dull and sombre cloak of responsibility'. At Ravenhill, the appearance of Dickie Lloyd, the former Portora and Irish international out half, was an important boost for the Enniskillen school, as the 'Impartial' commented: 'Surely the presence of so great a player was half the battle to the boys!'

The sides were evenly matched, so evenly, in fact, that 20 minutes extra time had to be played to divide them. Eventually, 'one of the best forward packs seen in the competition for years' subdued their Coleraine counterparts, and Portora went into the lead, 6-3.

'At last the final whistle went and amidst terrific cheering, the excited crowd surged onto the field and chaired the day's heroes from the field in triumph,' enthused the 'Impartial'.

The victorious team stayed in Belfast for the weekend to find some release for the nervous energy built up over the past week, recorded the paper euphemistically, but the mass of supporters made for the train home.

'The journey home was one triumphant tour the whole way. The cheering and the singing never ceased. Mouth organs added their strain to the boys' voices. The momentary halts at stations gave the boys their best opportunity for creating a sensation.'

On arrival back at Enniskillen, the jubilant Portora supporters were received by a crowd from the town, headed by Mr George Whaley, JP, Chairman of the Urban Council. 'Not even an air raid could have dispersed the crowd gathered outside the station,' wrote the paper. 'People came from their homes to see what all the fuss was about. Surely it could only mean that the war was over and Hitler had committed suicide?'

At the School gates, the procession halted and the cup was raised for all to see, the silverware glinting in the light of the torches shining upon it. Greater cheers went up, the band played the entourage up the hill to the School, and the cup was borne into the building where it would reside for the next two and a half years.

The following year Portora retained the cup by beating Coleraine again, this time by a goal and two tries (11 points) to one penalty (three points). And in 1942 the Enniskillen boys made it three finals on the trot when they faced Belfast Inst, their opponents that Saturday at Ravenhill. The final was extremely tight: Portora and RBAI tied at five points each at the end of the game.

The Portora Headmaster, Mr Ian Stuart, himself a former Irish international, announced that his side would be unable to partake in a replay due to other School commitments, and despite a magnanimous offer from the RBAI Headmaster that Portora could keep the cup after remaining unbeaten in the competition for three years, it was eventually agreed that the trophy should be shared.

So ended one of the most glorious periods in Portora's sporting history, when tens of thousands of supporters packed Ravenhill for three consecutive cup finals. The brief, happy escape these days out at Ravenhill afforded the people of Enniskillen from the harsh reality of the World War II could not last forever, and a horrible testament to the time lies in the fact that, within a few years of their brilliant achievements, some of the stars of those Portora sides were dead.

Two of Portora's outstanding forwards in the 1940 cup win were selected to represent Ulster Schools that season, and the Portora captain, R N Parkinson-Cumine, was also elected captain of the provincial side. Oliver Duncan was awarded the first of three seasons of representative honours for Ulster, in the last of which he emulated Parkinson-Cumine by being selected as Captain.

Sadly, both Duncan and Parkinson-Cumine would later die in warfare. Lieutenant Olly Duncan was killed in action in Holland in October 1944, less than two years after leaving school, while Captain R N Parkinson-Cumine, who was awarded the Military Cross during World War II, was later killed in the Korean War. Geoff Reay, scorer of vital tries on Portora's way to the 1940 cup win and praised by a number of reports as 'the best forward on the field', was another sad casualty of the war. Flying Officer Reay was killed over France in November 1944 at the tender age of 21.

Portora's domination of the competition in the early 1940s has never been repeated. Unfortunately, in these days of increasing professionalism and competition at schools level, it is not likely to be. All the more reason, then, to celebrate the achievements of a country school sixty years ago who provided a day out in the city for the town's inhabitants, and showed the Belfast schools they couldn't always have things their own way.

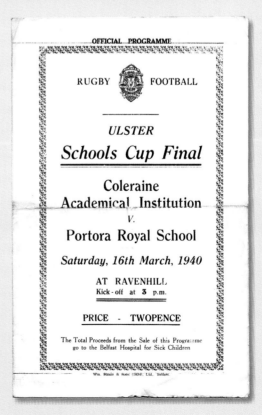

OFFICIAL PROGRAMME

RUGBY FOOTBALL

ULSTER

Schools Cup Final

Coleraine Academical Institution

v.

Portora Royal School

Saturday, 16th March, 1940

AT RAVENHILL
Kick - off at **3** p.m.

PRICE - TWOPENCE

The Total Proceeds from the Sale of this Programme
go to the Belfast Hospital for Sick Children

Wm. Strain & Sons (1934), Ltd., Belfast

James Harley (OP, 1982-87), Ulster Schools and Irish Schools International.

This Hockey team in its first season (1950-51) reached the finals of the Ulster Schools Cup and produced two outstanding Inter-provincial players – David Judge is seated on the left (see also chapter 9) and Bruce Dowling is seated on the right.

During the post-war era Portora found it increasingly difficult to compete on an equal footing with the much larger Belfast schools, for example Methodist College and RBAI. In 1972, after being beaten in the first round of the Schools Cup, Portora played in their first Schools Shield competition and reached the semi-final, to be beaten by Dungannon.

Even when the Portora team as a whole was not performing well, there were always key athletes who were regularly selected to play for Ulster Schools in inter-provincial matches, and for Ulster South County. In 1975 **James McCoy** (OP, 1969-75), was selected to play in the first-ever Irish Schoolboys XV, which was narrowly defeated by English Schoolboys at Lansdowne. In 1980 **Marcus Harvey** (OP, 1974-80), played the Irish Schoolboys and won full caps against Wales and England before going on tour to Australia.

In 2006 Portora reached the semi-finals of the Ulster Schools Cup for the first time since 1948.

Hockey

Hockey at Portora has always been considered a minority sport, and historically, most members of the Common Room considered it to be a girls' game. Nevertheless, Portora has contributed to Irish hockey in several significant ways. The first known Irish international hockey player was **Edward Percival Allman-Smith** (OP, 1901-04), who learnt his game mainly at Trinity College, Dublin. He then continued with the Army and had a distinguished military career, retiring as Brigadier General E P Allman-Smith OBE, MC.

However, **D N Coburn** (OP, 1915-20), from Banbridge, was a home-grown product, who played for Ireland and won 13 caps during the 1920s. In later years, his two sons, **G M Coburn** (OP, 1943) and **N B Coburn** (OP, 1945), proved to be equally adept at the game, and between them played first-class and inter-provincial Ulster hockey during the 1950s.

Another interesting player was **S H M Webb** (OP, 1921-23), who, in his final year at Oxford during the 1920s, was selected to play against Cambridge on the very day that he had been selected to play for Ireland v Wales. Webb decided that since this was his last chance for a Blue he should decline the invitation for an Irish cap, reasoning that he would have many future opportunities to play for Ireland. Unfortunately, the Irish selectors were so incensed with his decision that they never approached him to play again. In any case, Webb joined the Colonial Service, thereby limiting his availability for future selection. However, in the 1950s, his son **Peter M Webb** (OP, 1945-49) was a leading member of a series of four or five spectacular teams produced by Portora during the late 1940s and early 1950s, most of whose members went on to play for Trinity College, Dublin, and at least four of whom became Irish internationals.

This series of scratch hockey teams started when **J V Tapley** (S, 1942-80), observed a number of junior boys from the Upper School messing around with hockey sticks and a hurling ball on the tennis courts, one weekend afternoon. Most of the boys had been at Dublin prep schools that were well known for their prowess in hockey. Tapley, something of a hockey player himself, considered them rather good and suggested to the Headmaster, Douglas Graham, that a formal team should be started. Graham reluctantly agreed and the Portora team was formed, starting with a game against the RUC Depot. The team progressed and thrashed all the local opposition so soundly that they were entered for the Ulster Schools Cup. In their first season they reached the finals, but were narrowly beaten by Banbridge Academy, a school that has been, and still is, the premier hockey school in Ireland.

From those teams, three members, Judge, Dowling (both seated and wearing inter-provincial shirts in the photograph on page 154) and Shanks, provide an interesting end-piece to the story of Portora hockey.

David Judge (OP, 1949-54) is listed in the Hall of Fame as the longest and most capped Irish hockey player of his era, gaining 123 caps over twenty-one years (see also chapter eight).

After leaving Portora, **Bruce Dowling** (OP, 1947-51), played regularly for Ireland. He emigrated to Rhodesia in 1957 where he subsequently created another sort of record: he was first selected to play for a combined Rhodesia in the Currie Cup, and later represented both Southern Rhodesia and Northern Rhodesia in competitive international hockey. Then, following the break-up of the Federation and the demise of Sir Roy Welensky, he played for the newly formed Zambia (previously Northern Rhodesia) after independence.

Southern Rhodesia was in limbo and was agitating for independence when Ian Smith declared UDI on 11 November 1965 (Premier Ian Smith was one of 'the Few' from the Battle of Britain and chose the date carefully); the new Rhodesia was born. In all, Dowling played representative international hockey for five African countries and for Ireland, surely a unique record.

W D F 'Bill' Shanks (OP, 1942-50) was certainly one Captain of the Portora hockey team who provides another glimpse of sporting history. As a young boy at Gloucester House he had a terrible farming accident during one Summer holiday, when both his legs were almost severed by a belt-driven combine harvester. He was rushed to hospital, where his legs were saved. His shins and feet were pinned and stitched back together; after several terms' absence for recuperation and physiotherapy he returned to the Upper School wearing surgical boots and steel braces. His great achievement was to captain a most successful Portora hockey season as a very fine goalkeeper.

This series of teams from the 1950s was exceptionally lucky to have such a concentration of natural talent, and was further aided by the fact that two outstanding players were also nephews of the Master. Interest in hockey waned after the eventual departure of so many good players. Judge, Dowling and **Richard FitzSimons** (OP, 1949-53) went on to play for Ireland. Today, however, hockey at Portora has reverted to being a minor sport and House competition item.

An so to end with an amusing coincidence, in a recent match (2007) between Richmond and Teddington Hockey Clubs, marking their 125th anniversary, our current Old Portora Union (London Branch) President, **James Wilson** (OP, 1960-67), found himself playing for Richmond, when he spotted **Niall Keartland** (OP, 1966-71) turning out for Teddington.

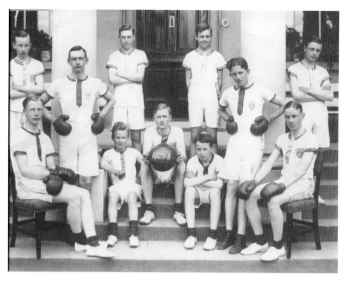

Boxing team 1927-28. The boxer standing by the right hand pillar is a young Douglas Graham, future Headmaster of the School.

Boxing team 1950-51. Back row: J Connor, D Ashfield, C G Turnbull; second row: W H Todd, P Ross-Todd, G P Murdock, W G V Mitchell; third row: R A Frazer, T H A Mitchell, J D Jessop (Captain), W J Slavin, R A Latham; fourth row: R F S Thornton and W S Gardner; front row: G A Clingen and L M Crawford.

Boxing

Introduction

Boxing, both amateur and professional, had become a very popular pastime with large sections of the British public from the 1860s onwards. The aristocracy, in the persons of the Marquis of Queensberry and the Earl of Lonsdale, took the lead in drawing up rules for the Amateur Boxing Association (ABA). The middle classes considered it a noble sport, and leading Public Schools such as St Paul's, Harrow, Highgate and Eton College engaged professors of boxing to teach the art of self-defence prior to university and the forces. It also appealed to the working classes as a gladiatorial event on which they could gamble; the working-class boy saw it as a chance to turn professional, to become rich and to escape the squalor of the urban slums.

In Ireland, the Irish Amateur Boxing Association was founded in Dublin in 1911, with a distinguished Irish-born British Army soldier, Major-General W R E Murphy, DSO, MC, as its first President. He later became the first Deputy Commissioner of the newly formed Irish Free State Police Service (later the Garda Siochana), and continued as President for many years, bridging the gap between the North and South of Ireland.

Boxing at Portora

Few members of the current staff and certainly no present-day pupils at Portora have any experience of schoolboy boxing. House competitions were last held in the late 1960s, and inter-school matches ceased some time before that. In fact, the last English Public School to list boxing as a sport was Winchester College, where the sport ceased to be taught around 1988. Yet boxing was a very important and popular sport in schools, colleges and universities for nearly 80 years.

The teaching of boxing began at Portora around 1900, after the construction of the gymnasium. When the House system was introduced in 1919, football, cricket and athletics were the only games that were contested for the House Championship. Boxing was added for the 1922-23 season; thereafter it was contested every year until 1962-63 when it was replaced by cricket after a ten-year gap. In all, boxing was considered a major school and university sport for some forty years, and certainly in its heyday the Captain of Boxing at Portora or Trinity was second only in respect and prestige to the Captain of Rugby Football.

Milling

For historical reasons, it may be useful to describe how boxing was conducted and competitively contested within the School. Essentially the sport was taught and supervised by the Company Sergeant Major (CSM) or NCO in charge of the gymnasium; all students had to participate. After elementary moves had been practised for several weeks, classes had to take part in the Easter Term 'milling'. This involved lining up each PT class in the School and sizing up each boy so that he had a near-counterpart in height and weight.

A ring was formed in the centre of the gym; two boys entered this ring and boxed for one minute. A winner was declared by the CSM, following which the next two contestants entered the ring for their one-minute contest.

From these milling contests the best exponents within the ABA weight categories were picked for the House teams, and then pitted, weight by weight and House by House, to decide the winner of the House Championship. House contests were fought over three one-minute rounds, and winners gained points for their House total.

Athletics and cross-country

Athletics and cross-country at Portora, like many facets of Irish sport, owe their origin to Trinity College, Dublin, when Headmaster **McDonnell** (S, 1904-1915) introduced them to assist in training the School's rugby teams. However, it was the foundation of the House system in 1918 that gave the real impetus to the promotion of the first annual School Championships and subsequent programmes of athletic matches.

Mickey Murfet, (S, 1916-45), was the early organiser of the House Athletics Championships, which were held on the Annual Sports Day (usually the last day of the Summer Term). He was solely responsible for this event for many years until he was joined in 1948 by **Jack Wheeler** (S, 1948-94), and **'Darcy' Chillingworth** (OP, 1934-41; S 1949-66/67) on his return to the Portora staff the following year. Chillingworth had been a good athlete as a pupil and also at Trinity College, Dublin. Together they provided enthusiastic direction for both cross-country and a well-run Sports Day until the late 1900s.

A notable athlete from the School was **I R Mowat** (OP, 1958-66), who became a member of the Senior Irish Athletics team while still at Portora.

Athletics photograph: 1946 sports day (l to r) B E Kendall, (OP, 1942-46), J R Haslett, (OP, 1941-47), J W W Dickson (1st), (OP, 1937-46), D Chapman, (OP, 1942-47), R J Graham, (OP), R Thompson, (OP); (in the background) A T M Murfet, S A Dore, R W W Tamplin, J M Pollard, (OP, 1945-48).

Cross Country team 1968-69. Standing (left to right) P D Robinson, T R Trinick, R M Swain; seated (left to right) A Allister, I J P Burn, R Downes (Captain), J W Mills and R H T N Hill.

Swimming

Swimming at Portora is a natural activity, close as the site is to so much water. The Portora Narrows is the first recorded location for the House swimming competition. Initially this was restricted to an 80-yard dash across the Narrows, but it was not really a success. The prevailing currents demanded a strong swimmer, and of course it was a restricted distance, favouring the sprint swimmers. In the early 1920s, the annual House swimming contest was relocated and held across from the boathouse, in the Frying Pan, where a fixed jetty plus a floating stage provided the means to have races of varying lengths. There was also a long-distance swim around the Frying Pan for the strongest swimmers.

Swimming matches were always somewhat ad hoc until the arrival of Jack Wheeler, who as usual brought a professional touch to the sport. Swimming was Jack Wheeler, and vice versa, and the construction of the present swimming pool complex, in 1958, owes a great deal to Wheeler and the OPU, which financed the project as one of the first programmes organised under the recently arrived Headmaster, the **Reverend P (Val) H Rogers** (S, 1954-73).

Swimming at Portora subsequently became a local phenomenon when Jack Wheeler and his wife Kay, over 32 summers, organised the Portora Holiday Swimming Club at the site and trained over 40,000 children in swimming and life-saving. The children came from all communities in Enniskillen and the surrounding Fermanagh countryside.

Other minor sports

Lawn tennis

Lawn tennis may seem a rather odd title for a game played on the former OTC parade ground, but for many years the game prospered under the guidance of **'Ed' Rowlette** (S, 1943-81).

Archive records show that School Tennis Colours were a long-established award dating from the early 1920s, but the game was not included in the House Championships until 1951. This late inclusion was probably encouraged by Ed Rowlette, who managed to engage a tennis professional for several weeks during the Trinity (Summer) Term in the late 1940s and early 1950s. This encouraged both boys and local Portora families to participate in the game and certainly made the activity a popular pastime. There are no records of any outstanding players other than the occasional inter-provincial schoolboy.

Association football (soccer)

During the late nineteenth century there are some references in the archives to a first XV football team winning a game 1-0. However, we are fairly certain that this must be an error, because there is no other evidence of team soccer being played at Portora until the late 1900s. Today soccer has become a very popular and successful activity at Portora.

In August 2006 there was an historical moment in the School's history. Andrew Little was offered the opportunity to become a professional footballer

with the Glasgow Rangers. Previously, in 2005, he had impressed selectors, and his form in the Under-17 European Championships alerted several professional clubs to his talent.

Portora Football team. Portora won 1-nil. However the team captain appears to be holding a soccer ball, in spite of posing with a 15 man team. Early Rugby or Soccer team? We shall never know.

Table tennis

Table tennis was popular with both dayboys and boarders. It was a sport played quite widely in Fermanagh, probably because it could be played indoors, avoiding the wet conditions so prevalent in the county. There was a hotly contested ladder that ran throughout the year. Matches for places on the ladder were generally played during breaks in the school day in order to involve both boarders and dayboys. There were also individual and doubles competitions during the year, and a School team on occasion (as in 1965) would compete in the Ulster Schools Cup.

In August 2007, Stephen Slater, a Year 9 pupil, was selected by the Irish Table Tennis Association to represent Ulster at the UK School Games.

Basketball

Basketball was a gymnasium game and so came under the jurisdiction of Jack Wheeler. Being an indoor game it was always a useful sport for coping with the Fermanagh weather, and from time to time the School produced some very good players. The most successful season was 1971-72, when the team had a record of six wins from six games. The star player was **PD Mowat** (OP, 1964-72), a younger brother of **IR Mowat**, who played for the Irish Schoolboys.

Six

Extra-curricular activities

Extra-curricular activities, like sport, did not form a significant part of education or School life at Portora until late in the Victorian era. During the 1800s, the old adage 'All work and no play makes Jack a dull boy' seemed to have rung a bell with the newly appointed Master, the **Reverend Dr William Steele** (S, 1857-91), who rapidly devised a set of rules and regulations covering leisure and water activities on the nearby River Erne. These rules applied to boating, fishing and sailing, and provided guidelines on safety measures as well as boundaries and distances permitted for all pupils and staff taking local outings or generally 'messing about in boats'.

Early in the 1900s, and long before the formation of the Portora Officer Training Corps (OTC) in 1923, we find that pupils were keen on musketry, and that as early as 1902 the School had formed a Shooting Team that won a national shooting trophy at Kinnagar Camp c1909.

Before World War II, a local clergyman, who was an enthusiastic supporter of hunting, actively encouraged Portora boys to follow the local hunt. Several boys did bring hunters back to School for local stabling and participated with the Enniskillen Hunt. And then there was the Portora schoolboy, **Arthur March** (OP, 1891), who won the Amateur Billiard Championship of Ireland in the early 1900s. One wonders if he was able to practise and what facilities were available at the School to enable him to develop his skills.

Left: The front cover of the play programme of the December 1965 production of Richard II, designed by A B Babington (OP, 1956-66).

2001 World Championship for Elephant Amateur Polo, Nepal: (top photograph) scene from the game (bottom photograph), the Ramada Ireland team holding highest scorer, Graham Little, aloft as they celebrate their victory.

Fast forward nearly a hundred years and we find that four members of the Ramada Ireland team – **Graham Little** (OP, 1989-96), his brother **Warren**, (OP, 1991-98), **Justin Woods** (OP, 1989-96) and **Graham Smith** (OP, 1994-96) – were a major force in winning the 2001 World Championship for Elephant Amateur Polo in Nepal. All had learnt their basic sporting skills on the playing fields of Portora (minus the elephants of course).

The range of extra-curricular activities is enormous

Over the years, leisure activities and pastimes outside the three major sports of rugby, rowing and cricket and the four traditional minor sports of hockey, swimming, athletics and boxing have been legion. Not all have survived, so for interest's sake a list has been compiled of a number of those clubs and societies that have been active, or mentioned in editions of the School magazines published since the end of World War II; the list appears at the end of this chapter. Naturally, the emphasis on sport and leisure activities has altered considerably as fashions and tastes have changed, but one major activity that has continued in more or less the same form over the last eighty years has been the Cadet Corps.

The Cadet Corps

The Corps and its spin-off activities such as the pipe band, shooting and the annual camp have had a considerable influence on countless pupils, whether or not they have been attracted to a professional service life. Two World Wars, National Service and numerous other military operations, all involving call-up, have made time with the Corps at Portora a valuable experience. Participation in Corps activities and training has often paved the way for many individuals to early promotion in the ranks, or to a commission during times of conscription and subsequent military service.

Portora's war record

The memorial tablets and numerous plaques throughout the School covering the Boer Wars, World War I and World War II record the names of nearly one hundred and fifty Old Portorans, who over the decades made the final sacrifice from the initial intake of nearly nine hundred boys, all from a fairly small School. A high proportion of pupils were resident in the South of Ireland. Most were commissioned and many were to be highly decorated, but not all; for many years one lowly sapper, who survived his wartime service, insisted that his regimental number as an Other Rank (OR) be added to his name on the Old Portora list.

The Officer Training Corps in schools and universities

The Officer Training Corps (OTC) and its modern successor, the Combined Cadet Force (CCF), can trace their history to the Haldane reforms of 1908, when the British Army sought to improve the officer structure, which had suffered badly from the effects of the Boer War. The OTC was introduced as part of the Territorial Army and Reserve, with a Senior Division (aged 17 plus) serving some eight universities in the United Kingdom, and a Junior Division (aged 13 plus), which was implemented for training officers from English Public Schools.

In Ireland, Trinity College, Dublin, was an early starter, the foundation of its OTC dating from 1910. Many English Public Schools and also some Grammar Schools (eventually some 180 in number) established their OTC contingents around 1912. Trinity College, Dublin, was particularly active in providing graduates for medical, veterinary and engineering duties during World War I and its OTC was mobilised during the Easter Uprising of 1916.

Portora OTC (1923-45)

The introduction of the OTC to Irish schools was complicated by the fact that suitable schools were smaller than those in England, and by the political situation resulting from the Easter Uprising and the eventual partition of Ireland in 1922. There was also the question of sponsorship by the Regular Army, with the disbandment of a number of famous Irish Regiments whose depots had been based in towns within the new Irish Republic.

Nevertheless, Seale decided to introduce the OTC to Portora in 1923, with an initial contingent of some 57 boys; two masters, Messrs Barlow and Cook, took charge. A year or two later, in order to prepare Portora candidates for the Army, Seale engaged the services of **Major Butler** (S, 1926-49), a former World War I Sapper, as their new Commander, with the support of **Captain Henry Scales** (S, 1924-60), late Royal Dublin Fusiliers, as his Second-in-Command. Butler arrived from King Alfred's School, Wantage, in 1926, where several years previously he had successfully established a thriving OTC. The Portora unit was initially sponsored by one of the local Fermanagh regiments, the Royal Inniskilling Fusiliers (the Skins), and henceforth the Portora OTC sported the Skins' regalia for their uniforms.

By 1928 the Portora OTC had grown sufficiently to support a pipe band, which performed regularly on public occasions such as the opening of the Fermanagh Assizes and providing the Guard of Honour at the Town Cenotaph

OTC pipe band 1929. Twenty years later the CCF pipe band was able to boast some twelve pipers and the Portora CCF contingent was in excess of 120 members.

on Armistice Sunday. The photograph on page 163 shows the embryo pipe band with a young **Cadet Sergeant Teddy Jones** (OP, 1925-31), who was later to become Lord Justice of Appeal for Northern Ireland.

The War Office usually provided additional funds for the employment of a retired Warrant Officer (WO) or Senior Non-Commissioned Officer (SNCO) to act as the Company Sergeant Major (CSM) for the contingent. The CSM usually performed other School duties such as running the gymnasium and taking physical training classes, boxing, fencing and sports training in general. For many years these duties were undertaken by CSM Ingham, MM (late Royal Marines), seen here in a 1935 photograph of the Corps at Strensil Camp, England.

The Corps is best remembered for exercising the 3 Ms – marching, musketry and manoeuvres. It produced many successful regimental officers for the British army, as well as a number of distinguished senior officers in various foreign armies, including generals in the armies of the United States, Turkey and India. The most notable came from the Jones family, from Dublin, which in the 1920s produced **General Sir Charles Jones** (OP, 1919-26), a brother of Teddy Jones. Sir Charles became Master General of the Ordinance and President of the Royal British Legion; his elder brother, **Colonel Hume Jones** (OP, 1918), was killed in action leading the Indian Frontier Force Rifles during the Italian campaign in World War II. (See also chapter eight.)

A junior contemporary of Charles Jones in the OTC was one of several Harris brothers from Tipperary, who later as **Lieutenant General Sir Ian Harris** (OP, 1925-29) was appointed GOC of Northern Ireland during the 1960s. (See also chapter eight.)

The Jones family appeared again in the late 1940s, when **Edward Jones** (OP, 1949-54), elder son of Sir Charles Jones (above), and his younger brother both attended Portora. Edward Jones, like his father, pursued an Army career and reached the rank of four-star general, when he was appointed the Senior UK Representative to SHAPE, Brussels. Thus, uniquely, a father and son overlapped as serving generals and as members of the Army Board.

On the outbreak of World War II, the Corps was expanded to cater for volunteers and those who, having received their call-up papers at school, left directly for wartime service. Several of the younger staff also left to join the forces. In 1941, the Air Training Corps (ATC) was added, under **A W Barnes** (S, 1932-66), then Headmaster of Gloucester House, as an alternative activity for older pupils who had completed their Certificate A, Part 1, in the Army Section. Cadet service with the ATC provided enhanced opportunities for those who wished to serve with the Royal Air Force. In total, for World War II, nearly five hundred OPs joined the Army, about one in ten being killed in action; about 100 joined the Royal Air Force, of whom one in five was killed.

Junior Training Corps (JTC) and Combined Cadet Force (CCF) (1945-80)
Most things connected with the Army will change and names are no exception. After World War II, the Corps became successively the Junior Training Corps, and then the Combined Cadet Corps, with little change to its role and

OTC at Boer War Memorial 1935.

Portora OTC contingent at Strensil Camp during 1936. The three permanent staff in the centre of the photograph are Captain Henry Scales, Major G V Butler, TD and CSM J G Ingham, MM (late RM).

activities. Portora then had three branches: a Naval Section, an Army Section (the largest) and an Air Force Section, hence the name Combined Cadet Force.

The Royal Navy Section, to give it its proper title, was commanded by **George Andrews** (S, 1933-76), who had now been demobbed from his RNVR duties with the Free French Navy. After the war the Navy Section was re-equipped with several 'whalers' donated as items left over from wartime use at the various RAF stations and flying boat bases scattered along the Erne. Whaling boats were great workhorses since they could be rowed, sailed or equipped with an outboard engine and were excellent for teaching basic seamanship.

Whalers in full sail with Enniskillen town in the background.

The Army Section was by far the largest, since one could not join the Navy or Air Force sections until completion of basic military training and the gaining of the basic cadet qualification of Certificate A. The pipe band was also popular. It was resurrected and re-equipped after the war with Irish pipes, having been started again from scratch during the late 1940s, under Pipe Major Bob Thompson from Lisnaskea. By 1955 the band had peaked at 12 pipers, when they were led by **Cadet Pipe-Major Mark Scott** (OP, 1949-56; S, 1985-2001), who later became a regular officer and on retirement was appointed the School's Estate Manager.

On reorganisation of the OTC, **Major Grattan Halpin** (S, 1936-76), late Royal Irish Fusiliers, who had returned to the School after a distinguished war record, commanded the new post-war CCF. He had been badly wounded during the Italian campaign and mentioned in despatches. In due course he was assisted by other returning staff, **P L 'Paddy' Rice** (OP, 1932-35; S, 1940-52), newly appointed Headmaster of Gloucester House, and **Leslie Breadon** (S, 1937-52), Housemaster-designate of Leinster. A further new arrival was of course the legendary **Jack Wheeler** (S, 1948-94), who, having joined the School in 1948 as the Physical Education Instructor, became a newly commissioned lieutenant with the post-war CCF.

The CCF permanent staff also changed, a new Sergeant Major in the form of Mr Pogue arriving to replace the retiring Company Sergeant Major (CSM)

CCF march past at the Annual General Inspection (AGI) of 1947.

J G Ingham, MM. Pogue was a small man with a very loud parade-ground voice. He had originally enlisted in the famous Royal Dublin Fusiliers (The Dubs), but on disbandment of the Fusiliers in 1922 had re-enlisted with the Royal Irish Fusiliers (The Faughs). Pogue and the newly promoted Captain Wheeler were keen on shooting, and together they raised the standards of marksmanship throughout the CCF with small-bore shooting sessions on the miniature range. When Major Halpin was promoted to Lieutenant Colonel, Pogue was quick to organise his own promotion from CSM to Regimental Sergeant Major (RSM). He then managed to obtain a pre-war army uniform issued only to RSMs in the Regular Army, complete with Sam Brown belt and pace stick. In this attire, he was a unique figure at most Summer camps and very much the talk of all sergeant majors from other school contingents.

RSM Pogue had several useful military connections, including a son-in-law who was a drill sergeant stationed with 'the Skins' at Omagh. He regularly came down to smarten up the Portora honour guards and band for important occasions. In later life Pogue's son, Jimmy, became a very distinguished RSM with the Royal Irish Rangers. RSM Pogue was succeeded by **RSM H Wills** (S, 1959-69), whose son William won the Infantry Sword at Sandhurst and on graduation joined the Inniskillings.

The junior and most recent section of the Corps, but also probably the most glamorous for a schoolboy, was the Air Training Corps (ATC). Formed in 1941, under Flying Officer Barnes and **Pilot Officer James 'Jasper' Malone** (S, 1936- 50), it enabled the ATC cadets to access training facilities and classes at most of the wartime RAF stations in the area. The stations housed both UK and USA contingents, whose various personnel operated flying boats and fixed-wing aircraft throughout World War II. Both flying trips and excellent food were to be prime features of life with the ATC. Post-war ATC training was unusual compared with that of the mainstream Army contingent: it included holiday employment as cabin staff on RAF transport aircraft and visits to Germany to view the sites of RAF wartime action. One such was a visit to the Ruhr Valley to see the post-war reconstruction of the famous sites of the Mohne, Sorpe and Eder Dams, which had been so effectively neutralised by the famous 617 Squadron RAF (the 'Dambusters'). (See also chapter nine.)

RAF bus. This was the type of transport used by ATC cadets to visit various sites in post-war Europe.

In general, the CCF's heyday was probably the period from the late 1940s to the 1960s, when all three service elements were still active and the Army Section alone was over a hundred strong with four House platoons and a band.

In the summer of 1959 at the end of the Annual CCF Camp, held at Cultybraggan, Perth, Scotland, Lieutenant Colonel Halpin handed over the command of the Portora CCF to Major Wheeler in a formal parade. The event was somewhat interrupted by a wholesale security alert, when another school's contingent declared that weapons were missing from their armoury. Like most such alerts, it proved to be a false alarm.

For several years the CCF received considerable support from Lieutenant Colonel Mark Scott, when he commanded the 4th (Volunteer) Battalion the Royal Irish Rangers. He ensured Regular Army training support for Portora cadets following the retirement of older members of the teaching staff and their replacement by a newer generation of teachers lacking military service experience.

During the late 1960s, military problems throughout the Province, in particular the community problems in Fermanagh, made for difficulties. Storage of arms and ammunition, coupled with an ageing staff lacking the necessary wartime or National Service experience for training the CCF Cadets, led to a decision to disband the CCF in 1980.

However, it ended on a high note: the CCF's last act was to enter the Northern Ireland Cadet Championship at which the Portora teams, led by Sean Fawcett of Derrygore House, came first and second. Fawcett went on to Sandhurst to become a regular officer in the Corps of Royal Engineers.

The Irish Guards come to the rescue

In 2004, the Force revived its activities as the Portora Detachment Army Cadet Force (ACF) under the command of Warrant Officer Class II (WOII) **Newall Hicks**, taking the badge of the Royal Irish Rangers. Unfortunately WOII Hicks died suddenly and command has now passed to **Graham Wilkie** (S, 2005-), an ex-WOI from the Royal Irish Regiment and Scots Guards.

The Detachment started with some 16 cadets and is gaining in popularity under the command of Wilkie, who hopes that it will soon grow to platoon strength. The Lords Lieutenant of Tyrone and Fermanagh have reached an agreement that in future Portora cadets will proudly carry the badge of the Irish Guards.

In the Summer of 2006, the ACF annual camp was held in Devon when the Portora Detachment became part of the First Battalion Army Cadet Force (1st Bn ACF) from Northern Ireland.

The Regimental Mascot of the Irish Guards visits Portora. The Portora ACF detachment is now cap-badged to the Irish Guards. Was this an early recruiting drive?

Cast of the School play, Christmas 1918.
Standing: G Morton, C F Allen, S Killingley,
W C Wilson, A O Babington, H R Jones;
seated: W Taylor, G T Bor (Max Adrian),
F E Beckett, G Warrington, V St G Vaughan,
H G Graham.

Drama

Drama, and in particular the School play, has been a major and long-established extra-curricular activity at Portora. During the Seale Headmastership, **A T M 'Mickey' Murfet** (S, 1916-56) produced the first School play, to coincide with activities on Speech Day. 'Mickey' subsequently continued this tradition, and by the time of his retirement had been responsible for the production of 38 consecutive School plays – an extraordinary achievement. The introduction and popularity of the School play led to the establishment of the House play competition, traditionally performed during the Easter Term.

Early productions were predictably selected from the traditional works of Shakespeare, Shaw, Wilde and other well-established playwrights. For obvious reasons, there has been some concentration on the works of Irish dramatists, in particular Oscar Wilde and, in recent years, Samuel Beckett.

The School staged a production of Wilde's 'The Importance of Being Earnest' on 30 November 2000, the 100th anniversary of the writer's death; girls from the Collegiate School took the female parts. In 2002 the School's association with Wilde led to the establishment of the annual Oscar Wilde Festival; this brings together writers, academics, artists, critics, musicians and actors in celebration of the seven years Wilde spent at Portora. At the 2003 Festival, Parliamentary Under-Secretary of State, Angela Smith, MP, unveiled an Ulster Historical Society blue plaque dedicated to Wilde; Professor Terry Eagleton gave an address entitled 'Saint Oscar'. At the 2004 Festival the School put on another performance of 'The Importance of Being Earnest'.

The producer and cast of the 1961 production of 'Waiting for Godot' (left to right): Mr Robert Bell (producer), Paddy McClintock (Lucky), Bill Murtagh (Gogo), Mark Benson (Pozzo), Ken Aberdein (Didi) and Michael Waller (the Boy).

Scene from the 1961 production of 'Waiting for Godot'.

Of Beckett's works, 'Waiting For Godot' has been the most frequently staged. The 1961 performance, produced by **Robert Bell** (S, 1956-62) was perhaps the most memorable: **Billy Murtagh** (OP, 1956-63), who subsequently joined the RUC and was, tragically, killed during the Troubles, and **J K Aberdein** (OP, 1952-62) took the parts of Gogo and Didi respectively. As the review in the School magazine 'Portora' put it: *'The roles of Gogo and Didi have a depth of significance demanding a high level of sustained vigour, with an underlying awkward pathos, which might well have taxed very much older actors.'* Later, in the summer of 1962, the production transferred to Dublin as part of the Dublin Festival; *The Guardian* gave it a very favourable review. In 1997 Leinster House won the House plays competition with their production of 'Waiting for Godot'; and in November 2006, in the guise of 'The Portora Players', the School performed the play as part of the Fermanagh Winter Arts Festival, in commemoration of the 100th anniversary of Beckett's birth.

Particularly relevant to the subject matter of this book, '200 Years At The Top', a pageant or, more accurately, a dramatised history of the School was performed in 1977 as part of the School's bicentenary celebrations, 1777 being the year in which the School moved from Schoolhouse Lane to Portora Hill. The then Headmaster, **Tom Garrett** (S, 1973-78), wrote the script; the producer was **Robert Hort** (S, 1963-83). The pageant was very successful: it was meticulously researched and had to overcome many technical problems, spanning as it did a history of 350 years and having 120 speaking parts.

In 2006 the School mounted an ambitious production of Frank McGuinness's 'Observe the Sons of Ulster Marching Towards The Somme'. Over the years other notable productions have included: Shaw's 'Arms and the Man'; O'Casey's 'Shadow Of A Gunman', 'The Plough And The Stars' and 'Juno and the Paycock'; Shakespeare's 'Richard II', 'Julius Caesar', 'A Midsummer Night's Dream' (a joint production with the Collegiate School), 'Much Ado About Nothing' and 'Twelfth Night'; Yevgeny Schwartz's 'The Dragon'; Max Frisch's 'The Fire Raisers'; Christopher Fry's 'The Boy with a Cart'; Goldsmith's 'She Stoops to Conquer'; André Obey's 'Noah' (produced by Neville Peterson); 'A Crack in the Ice' (based on a story by Nikolai Leskov); Stoppard's 'Enter a

Two scenes from the play 'Observe the Sons of Ulster Marching Towards the Somme', produced 26-27 January 2006.

Beckett Joyce Award Ceremony, 1997, the 10th anniversary. Maurice Walker, Seamus Heaney, Mark Elliott, Lisa Hulme (Head of English), Nathaniel Adams and Robert Barr (President, Clongowes Union). Mark's winning entry was called 'Music Matters'; Nathaniel's runner-up entry was called 'Trapped in Thought'.

Free Man'; Joan Littlewood's 'Oh What a Lovely War!'; W B Yeats' 'Purgatory'; Lady Gregory's 'The Rising of the Moon'; and Patrick Kavanagh's 'Tarry Flynn'.

Beckett Joyce Award

The School's connection with Samuel Beckett led to the inauguration of the annual Beckett Joyce Award, a creative writing competition between the School and its twin, Clongowes Wood College, Naas. The Award aims to nurture the talents of a new generation of writers and is, of course, named after illustrious past pupils of the two Schools, Samuel Beckett and James Joyce. In its inaugural year, 1987, the winner of the competition was Brian Judge of Clongowes. Over the years, many famous literary figures, for example, Seamus Heaney, Jennifer Johnston and Brian Keenan (author of *An Evil Cradling*), have adjudicated the competition.

2007 marked the 20th anniversary of the Award. On this occasion the competition was adjudicated by Merlin Holland, the grandson of that other famous literary Portoran, Oscar Wilde; the first prize went to Michael O'Donohoe of Portora for his short story 'Parallel Lives'.

Gilbert and Sullivan

Innovation and the arrival of **Mrs Rene Benson** (S, 1957-78) led to ambitious musical entertainment in the form of Gilbert and Sullivan Operettas. 'The Pirates of Penzance' was first performed in 1958, followed by 'HMS Pinafore' in 1962. In producing 'The Pirates', Rene Benson did not lack heavyweight assistance: according to the School magazine, 'Portora', she was *supported throughout by Mr Smith, Director of Music, Mrs Rogers, Mistress of the Chorus, and Mr Bell, Director of the Spoken Word*'. Robert Hort produced 'Cox and Box' in 1964 (in fact, only half a Gilbert and Sullivan operetta, the libretto being the work of F C Drummond). This production featured **Christopher Johnstone** (OP, 1961-67) ('Johnston with an "e"', as he was known), the nephew of Moura Lympany, the concert pianist, as Sergeant Bouncer.

Cast of the 1958 production of 'The Pirates of Penzance'.

This marriage of drama and music continued to be a feature of life at the School. In 1984 **Billy McBride** (OP, 1958-65; S, 1972-2006) decided to re-stage 'The Pirates of Penzance' in the newly enlarged Steele Hall. The producers were **Fidelma Boyd** (S, 1981-88), and **Geraldine Herdman-Grant** (S, 1977-2007). This production benefited from an orchestral accompaniment, and from having **Richard Pierce** in the role of the Pirate King. On the final night, an Edwardian supper of fish and chips was served to the 400-strong audience, many of whom took the trouble to dress in period costume. In 1986 'HMS Pinafore' was performed again; this time Fidelma Boyd was the producer and Billy McBride the musical director. **Neil Hannon** (OP, 1982-85) and **Bryan Mills** (OP, 1979-86), both members of Divine Comedy, and **Zara Turner** (OP, 1977-85) were members of the cast.

Chorus from the 1984 production of 'The Pirates of Penzance'.

Music

Following a tradition going back as far as the nineteenth century, when organists from the old St Ann's Parish Church taught music at the School, the post of Director of Music at Portora has for many years been held in tandem with that of the Organist and Choirmaster of St Macartin's Cathedral. However, the latest unbroken link with the Cathedral begins in the 1930s with **E Lloyd Simon** (S, 1934-55). It continued through **Tony Smith** (S, 1956-66) and **Philip Tyack** (S, 1968-74) and was followed by the return of Billy McBride from London in 1972. Billy remained on the Portora staff, until his retirement in 2006, when he had become its longest serving Director of Music.

Between 1956 and 1966, Portora became a major musical force in its own right under the direction of Tony Smith. It was during his time that the School Orchestra was born. As this was long before the establishment of the Western Area Board Music Service (WABMS), local musicians were drafted in to help with tutoring. The brass instruments were taught by Mr Watson (father of Joan Wilson), who also trained the Ballyreagh Brass Band; thus a link between the School and the local community was firmly established. Tony Smith also took over the annual School carol service, converting it from a low-key event held in the Steele Hall at the end of each Christmas Term to a major Enniskillen performance at St Macartin's Cathedral.

School choir and musicians in St Macartin's Cathedral.

Education and progressive enlightenment in music
Tony Smith also arranged regular trips to Derry for Portorans to hear the BBC Symphony Orchestra on the occasion of their annual visit to the Province. At one of these visits the Portora musicians met the conductor Sir Colin Davis himself, thanks to **Martin Schrecker** (S, 1953-75), who knew him personally from their London days. In addition, Tony Smith taught a number of Portorans to sing in the Cathedral Choir. For some, this became the highlight of their music-making; they included a young Billy McBride, Richard Pierce, and Robert Pierce and **Leslie Ternan**, (OP, 1961-67). The WABMS came into the School in the late 1970s and provided tutors in brass, woodwind and

Drama publicity

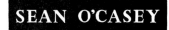

From its very early history the School play has been an event involving the whole School. As well as acting, there were roles for pupils who could participate in activities such as lighting, scenery design, production and publicity. Over the years there has been a strong tradition of innovative and eye-catching programmes, posters and associated drama publicity. The selection here is but the tip of the iceberg. Regarded by many as ephemera, much of this publicity has been destroyed, but some has been preserved and it is hoped that this small collection will prompt others to look out anything they may have and donate it to the School Archives.

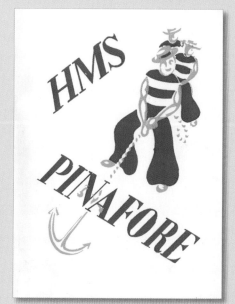

A selection of School play programme covers from the 1950s and 1960s. 'The Shadow of the Gunman', designer unknown; 'The Importance of Being Earnest' (1966), designed by John Macauley (OP, 1964-67); Christmas Plays (1968), designed by John Humphreys (OP, 1960-69); 'The Pirates of Penzance' (1958), designer unknown; HMS Pinafore' (1962), designer unknown; 'Waiting for Godot' (1961), designer unknown.

A poster for 'The Dragon' (1967), designed by John Humphreys.

Paris, Easter 1936

'As prognosticated last term, two parties, a senior and a junior, visited Paris during the Easter vacation. Both had a thoroughly enjoyable time. We crossed on the last night of term, and spent a day in London; the morning, watching the annual procession of the Cambridge and Oxford boats on the Thames, and the afternoon at the Ideal Homes Exhibition at Olympia. Thence we proceeded via Newhaven-Dieppe, arriving in Paris in the early hours of Sunday morning. Here the parties separated, the seniors going to the Cité Universitaire, the junior party to very comfortable quarters in the rue Vaugirard. We were very fortunate as regards weather, food and health, and the senior party in finding plenty of congenial society. The usual places were visited, and both parties found plenty to appeal to their respective interests. To say that all who went returned speaking fluent French would perhaps be an exaggeration, but it is beyond dispute that everyone learned something. The only mishaps were that a member of the junior party, on the rough crossing to Dieppe, found it too much to hold on to his supper and his ticket at the same time, and lost both. (The ticket was recovered afterwards.) And one of the seniors had a nasty jolt when he discovered the amount of duty payable on about a gallon-and-a-half of perfume.

It is hoped that similar visits may be arranged in future years, and many of those who went to Paris have expressed their intention of taking part in them if they can possibly do so.'

Names of the boys who went on the 1936 Paris trip with George Andrews included: J N Blood-Smyth, R D G Creery, J C Hosie, N A Magrath, W H McComb, A G MacMullen, J B Neill, D E Reay, G N Reay, W H Ritchie, N J Sloan, A W J Tanner, P D Warren.

strings, the result being that more and more pupils were able to master an instrument to a high level.

When girls arrived as boarders in the late 1970s the School had a permanent top line in the choir (no more breaking voices!). This led to the formation of the Portora Singers, a chamber choir specialising in unaccompanied singing. They initially performed once a week at assembly, and they later undertook outside engagements at various venues in the County.

The Cathedral Carol service

Over the years the Cathedral Carol service has developed beyond recognition, with over a third of the School taking part each year. The choir regularly numbers more than 100 voices along with brass and percussion, handbells and Northumberland pipes (but not necessarily all at the same service!). Each year a special carol is composed for the choir; it features processional drummers, as well as pupil organists. The School has recorded a CD of the carol service music called 'Stopping by Woods' and more recently a DVD was produced; both are still available from the School. It may interest readers to know that for the DVD recording the choir exceeded 190 voices, while the band and orchestra numbered 45 members.

Ardhowen concerts

These concerts ran annually for 18 years and were always sold out immediately tickets went on sale. They were staged in aid of the Fermanagh branch of 'Riding for the Disabled', and over the years raised thousands of pounds for the charity. Special guests such as the Strabane Concert Brass and the Cathedral Choir were invited to perform; even the Bishop of Clogher featured in a piano duet! In the interval, **Robert Northridge** (OP, 1955-62; S, 1973-) organised an enormous raffle (in which it seems that Rene Benson always won a prize). For one of the concerts Billy McBride borrowed a set of music handbells from the Cathedral, which led to the birth of the Portora handbell team. Eventually the team played on local BBC radio and later progressed to a television performance for a Christmas special. Not to be outdone, members of staff formed a second handbell team, which performed on special occasions and eventually took part in the Ardhowen concerts. Alas, it was quickly noticed that Robert Northridge had little sense of musical rhythm, but he always got a great laugh from an appreciative audience.

Performers and successful career musicians

Many Portora pupils have excelled at their musical activities and have achieved high grades on their chosen instruments. Several have gone on to successful professional careers in music.

- **Dr Keith Acheson**, (OP), now a Director of Music, was an excellent flautist during his time at the School and is now teaching composition at the University of Ulster.
- **Gareth Knox** (OP, 1969-72) has won numerous prizes for the piano, including recognition for his performances at the Dublin Feis. He went on to study at the Royal Academy of Music in London, where he formed his Piano Trio which now performs worldwide.
- A current pupil, **John Sheridan**, in his 4th form year passed Grade 8 on piano with distinction and in the 5th form gained a diploma (Dip LCM) in piano, one of the youngest students ever to achieve this standard.
- **Neil Hannon** (OP, 1982-89), **Bryan Mills** (OP, 1976-86), and **Ivor Talbot** (OP, 1980-85), were all members of the well-known group, 'Divine Comedy'.
- **Glenn Moore** (OP, 1979-86) is an organist in Clogher diocese.

Many of today's Portora students, who initially started their musical careers as a hobby or a leisure activity, gained their first exposure to an audience by performing as soloists during School assembly. As Director of Music, Billy McBride ensured that solo performances were treated as far as possible as formal events, complete with advance advertising and poster publicity (courtesy of the digital camera), and that they covered most instruments from piano to the orange flute. Students later progressed to performances at the Cathedral Harvest or Christmas services; many became guest performers in other churches throughout the diocese.

The Pipe Band and the Brass Band

In 2003, the Portora Pipe Band was revived and made its first appearance on the terrace after the School Remembrance Service. Since then it has performed at the theatre and in concert and has even appeared on television.

The School now boasts a fully-fledged Brass Band under the direction of Stephen Magee, a Western Education and Library Board brass tutor, who has also taken on responsibility for conducting the annual carol service. Billy McBride reverted to playing the organ and together they made a formidable team which gave much pride and pleasure to the townsfolk of Enniskillen.

St Macartin's Cathedral

The School's association with St Macartin's Cathedral was reinforced in 2006 when the Bishop of Clogher, the **Right Reverend Michael Jackson** (OP, 1967-75), asked Billy McBride to take charge of music for the commemoration of the 1,500th anniversary of St Macartan's evangelising in what is now the Diocese of Clogher. He also commissioned him to compose a special piece for the choir and to act as organist. Soloists selected from the School's choristers sang at the commemorative service in Clogher Cathedral to which the Archbishop of York was invited as a special guest.

A musical item from the School magazine, 'Portora', 1908
A phonograph made its appearance this term and for a month you might have heard 'Go Away Little Crocodile' or 'Cheyenne' any time of the day, but now the strains are hushed, for a football put an end to most of the records and finally to the instrument.

100 years later, Portora musicians provide live music.

Scout camp with George Andrews on the right hand side at the rear.

A group at the Scout camp in Brittany, 1939.

Other activities

Scouting

Scouting at Portora owes its foundation to **George Andrews** (S, 1933-76), who, shortly after his arrival in 1933, organised most of the scouting and camping activities for the 1st Portora Troop, until he joined the Royal Navy during the early part of the War. His first King's Scout from the Troop was **J F Q Switzer** (OP, 1934-41), who went on to Cambridge and subsequently became a Fellow of Sidney Sussex College (Andrews' old College) many years later.

During the early part of World War II Andrews took the Troop camping up and down Lough Erne each summer, usually to a wooded island but also to Mullaghmore, where they camped in the grounds of Classiebawn, Lord Mountbatten's castle, and fished for mackerel in boats from the harbour. The Easter holidays were marked by a camp near Marble Arch, high in the mountains, beside a bitterly cold river taking melted snow down to Lough Melvin. Andrews organised trips to the underground caves there; these are now famous, but in those days nobody took much notice of these wonders, so it was left to the likes of Portora Scouts to explore and map them, crawling along dark tunnels by the light of a candle.

When Andrews left for naval duties, the mantle for Scouts and Cubs fell on **J V Tapley** (S, 1942-80), who ran the organisation for many years and continued the success of the Portora Troop by producing another King's Scout during the late 1940s, **N C Haire** (OP, 1946-50), whose nickname was 'Bunny' – what other nickname could he have?

Unfortunately the added attractions offered by the OTC (later the CCF) meant that many pupils gave up scouting as soon as they were eligible to join the cadets. However, the Portora Scouts and Cubs continued to thrive at Gloucester House, and in later days Senior boys from the Upper School assisted in the running of both organisations.

Duke of Edinburgh Award Scheme

The Duke of Edinburgh Award Scheme has remained a popular activity at the School. This was particularly evident after the CCF was disbanded. The present scheme is supervised by **Graham Wilkie** (S, 2005-). The Award takes approximately one year to complete and involves four main parts, namely, the Expedition Section, Service Section, Skills Section and Physical Recreation Section.

Currently, the Expedition Section trains locally in the countryside of Fermanagh and Tyrone. The Skills Section is covered by the school syllabus for Technology, Art and Music. Physical Recreation can be covered by participation in rugby, rowing, football and cricket within the School.

With regard to the Service Section, it is the responsibility of the candidate himself to obtain experience with assisting pensioners or working with voluntary groups such as St John's Ambulance, the Army Cadet Force or the National Trust. On average, there are some eight to ten candidates participating for Silver and up to a dozen completing the Bronze Award.

Clubs and societies

The School has always encouraged extra-curricular activities. Some of the official clubs and societies that have occupied and entertained pupils over the years are: Aero-modelling Club, Art Club, Astronomical Society, Chess Club, Christian Education Movement, Computer Club, Darts Club, Debating Society, Drama, Field Club (an amalgamation in 1965 of the former Natural History, Agricultural and Ornithological Clubs), Film Society, Folk and Jazz Society, Geographical Society, Gramophone Society, Historical Society, Modern Languages Society, Motor Club, Music Society, Photographic Society, Portora Singers, Portora Union of Foresters, Radio Society, Record Club, Scientific Society, Social Services Group, Student Christian Movement (SCM), Tiddlywinks Club, and Wireless Society.

Space permits us to describe the activities of only a few of these societies. The driving force behind the Historical Society was **David Robertson** (S, 1967-83). Over the years it attracted such speakers as: Enoch Powell (Ulster Unionist MP for South Down); Conor Cruise O'Brien (author, diplomat, politician); Garret Fitzgerald (Taoiseach of Ireland and Fine Gael Party Leader); Prof Vivian Mercier (OP, 1928-36) (scholar, critic on Beckett); Lord Lowrie (Lord Chief Justice of Northern Ireland and a Lord of Appeal In Ordinary); Hugh Leonard (Irish writer); Henry Kelly (Classic FM broadcaster); John Parker (Chairman of Harland and Wolff); Graham Reid (Belfast playwright); Adrian Dunbar (actor); Adam Butler (Minister of State for Northern Ireland); Dr Michael Loftus (President of the Gaelic Athletic Association); John Hume (MP, Leader of the SDLP and MEP); and Patrick Sandford (Director of the Lyric Theatre, Belfast). The Society made such an impression on other schools, and they became so interested in taking an active role in it, that it was decided, in the academic year 1985-86, to re-form the Society as 'The Fermanagh Sixth Form Forum' and to encourage all schools in the area to participate in its activities.

After a lapse of several years the Debating Society was revived in 1978 under the guidance of David Robertson, the subject of the first debate being 'This House believes that Portora should become fully co-educational'. A member of the Society, **Neville Armstrong** (OP, 1972-79), provided the high spot of the year by advancing to the final of the Queen's University Individual Debating Contest.

The Chess Club enjoyed some success over the years. In 1971 **W T Ramsay** (OP, 1969-72) was a joint winner of the Ulster Schoolboys Championship and, as a result, was chosen one of the official Ulster representatives at the Irish Schoolboys Championship. In 1976 the Portora team won the O'Sullivan Cup for the tenth year in succession, in competition with schools from Fermanagh, Derry and Tyrone.

E. M. Seale
1934

Seven

Some School personalities – past and present

In the history of any school the nature and policies of its Headmaster must inevitably be dominant features, but the nature of his assistants could also have a great influence on the way the school developed.

The first recorded assistant staff member was called **George Annand** (S, c1627). Very little is known about him except for a reference in the 'Memoriall of the Lyfe and Death of Dr James Spottiswood', where he is recorded as a schoolmaster of *'Balfours place and towne'*, who conducted messages and business between the Balfour and Spottiswood families, when they were feuding over the status of the Free School and other sundry domestic matters. Annand seems to have been one of two 'Ushers' employed as assistants by the **Reverend Richard Bourke** (S, 1626-61), who was appointed to the second Mastership of the School under Letters Patent from Charles I. Bourke combined his position as Master of the Free School for Fermanagh with that of the Rector of Clonnkyne, and therefore felt the need to employ additional staff for educating the *'three score or thereabouts'* of known pupils mentioned in the Fermanagh public records of 1629.

Assistant teachers in Irish schools were very varied in quality and dedication, however. It was traditional for those who weren't doing well in their chosen profession, or who had even failed at university, to turn to teaching. The relics of such a tradition could still be discerned even in the mid-1900s. They cut sad figures, and are commonly to be found as stock characters in the novels of Dickens, Trollope and Evelyn Waugh. But the Public School reforms of the late nineteenth and early twentieth centuries meant that those

Left: Headmaster Reverend Edward G Seale (S, 1917-36).

seeking an appointment on the staff of a celebrated school, such as Portora, required a respectable degree and good references.

In later years, it became common to hire as Master someone who had been a successful Headmaster elsewhere. A new Master was often accompanied to Portora with staff and boys from his previous post.

The curriculum expanded considerably, a greater emphasis being placed on high scholastic standards and success at games, both of which could enhance a school's national reputation. This meant that the size of the School increased considerably, and the standards required became more demanding. A varied array of colourful staff members begins to figure prominently in Portora's history, figures vividly remembered by Old Portorans. They were not all teachers. Some were members of the domestic staff and others were school officials. All of them left their mark and contributed to the Portora experience.

From the Steele era we have a tablet in the Chapel dedicated to Guilelimi Johannis Valentine, who, as **W J Valentine** (S, 1883-1904), was the Senior Classics Master at Portora, and father of the Valentine brothers, **William** (OP, 1886) and **John** (OP, 1892). Together with their sister, Miss E R Valentine, the brothers were reputed to have been responsible for some of the first organised rugby at Portora (see chapter one). Guilelimi (William), as Second Master, also acted as Headmaster during the last difficult years of the Steele Mastership.

Selecting individuals has proved difficult, because archive material before the Steele era is scarce. However, the following personalities should register as living legends or current memories with many Old Portorans. Accounts have been chronicled in date order of their arrival at the School; we have not included any staff who are very recent retirees or currently in post.

W N Tetley

W N Tetley (S, 1891-1925) had been a 'Wrangler' (a Cambridge student who has achieved first class honours in the Mathematics Tripos; the term ceased to be used in 1909), but at Portora he taught Physics and Chemistry. He was also widely known throughout Ireland as a botanist, being especially noted as an expert on mosses, the search for which was particularly fruitful in a damp county like Fermanagh. On one of his expeditions into the wilds during World War I he was even arrested as a suspected spy.

Tetley was a *'burly figure with a heavy moustache and gold-rimmed spectacles'*. Unfortunately, he had a pronounced speech impediment, which meant that, despite his academic record and his prowess at cricket and rowing, Headmaster Seale felt justified in paying him no more than what another former Headmaster, **Douglas Graham** (OP, 1919-27), later called 'a peppercorn' salary. Even so, he made his mark and remained at the School for 35 years. He was eventually appointed Second Master and in 1917 actually became acting Headmaster for a term. In 1923 he became the first Treasurer of the Old Portora Union. Even so, he was never universally popular. He antagonised **Samuel Beckett** (OP, 1920-23) and his friends in particular. Beckett was never interested in science and once annoyed Tetley by pouring expensive sulphuric acid down the lab sink, apparently thinking (or pretending to think) that it was water.

W N TETLEY

(s, 1891-1925)

- Graduate of St Catharine's College, Cambridge.
- Joined Portora as Senior Science Master.
- An early and proficient rowing and cricket Master.
- Acting Headmaster for a term after Headmaster Burgess was drowned, 1917.
- First Housemaster of Ulster, 1918/19.
- Elected as Honorary Treasurer of OPU, 1923.
- International and national botany expert (particularly mosses) and had several academic credits for discoveries.
- Remained Treasurer of OPU after retirement and effectively paved the way for Mickey Murfet to become Honorary Secretary of OPU as a member of Portora staff.
- Retired initially to Wales and was replaced as Head of Science by Henry Scales, 1925.

Tetley could never understand how a person showing such intelligence in other areas of the curriculum didn't seem able to understand the simplest scientific concepts. Beckett was continually making sketches of Tetley in class in such an unflattering way that they made him look, Anthony Cronin suggests, like the murderer Dr Crippen. Beckett ended up being punished by Seale. A bitter poem published in a Paris magazine in 1930 was also said to deal with Tetley: '…*that little bullet-headed bristle-cropped red-faced rat of a pure mathematician*', and the poem also hints that he had on one occasion publicly accused the enthusiastic sportsman Beckett of behaving like a coward on the rugby field. But the Beckett view of Tetley was not shared by everybody. An obituary in the School magazine, 'Portora', described him as a '*simple, strong, kindly, unselfish, sincere…naturally reserved and retiring*' man. It recalled his services both as a cricket coach and a personal counsellor, and recorded the fact that on his retirement he had been presented, amid acclamation, with a magnificent telescope with which to pursue his scientific interests.

E E Hunt

Miss E E Hunt (S, 1915-47) was born in Roscrea. As a young girl she enjoyed a very comfortable upbringing, but as an older teenager she refused to conform to the conventional lifestyle expected of a young woman residing in rural Ireland. She persuaded her father to send her to London where she was trained as a teacher at the newly formed Froebel Institute.

In September 1915, at the age of 29, she was appointed Head Teacher to the new Portora Preparatory Department at a salary of £60 per annum, reporting directly to the Headmaster. According to a former Headmaster, Douglas Graham, who was an early young Preparatory School pupil under Miss Hunt, she ruled with a rod of iron, and '*we pupils feared and disliked her*'. Graham goes on to record that his first caning from Headmaster Seale was at the request of Miss Hunt. One of her lesser punishments, known colloquially as NJFT ('no jam for tea'), was a terrible ordeal for a starving schoolboy.

Nevertheless, she certainly 'made' the Prep and built it up until it became too large for the Upper School. In 1935, Seale persuaded the Governors to build Gloucester House as a combined boarding and teaching facility. In January 1936, Miss Hunt (or 'Lizzie' as she was known behind her back) and her 'maggots' moved to the new buildings. At Gloucester House she reigned over the 'B Set' classroom and supervised the afternoon crocodiles and walks to Rossorry for Sunday Church services over many years. Few will forget her eccentric teaching style, but everyone learned from her.

She remained at Gloucester House until 1947, when, having completed some 99 terms teaching her 'maggots' Latin, English and the Protestant work ethic, she decided to retire to Gloucestershire. Her retirement was not particularly happy, since she missed the institutional life of a boys' school and she became increasingly eccentric. However, she and Douglas Graham remained friends. He recalled that during the 1960s, while he was the Headmaster at Dean Close School, Cheltenham, he was surprised to find her one day on his doorstep, clad from head to toe in green – it was St Patrick's Day.

EILEN ELIZABETH HUNT

(s, 1915-1947)

- Native of County Tipperary.
- Graduate of Froebel Institute, London, and Royal University of Ireland, Dublin.
- Joined Portora as Head Teacher for Preparatory School, September 1915.
- Taught Latin and English at Junior School and Gloucester House for 99 terms.
- Collector of Irish watercolour paintings including some valuable items by Irish artist Paul Henry.
- Retired to Gloucestershire.

'MICKEY' MURFET MBE

(s, 1916-56)

- Native of Norfolk.
- Graduate of Peterhouse, Cambridge.
- Joined Portora as Classics Master, 1916.
- Housemaster of Connaught, 1918.
- Resurrected Boat Club and became rowing coach after World War I.
- Treasurer OPU, 1930.
- Appointed Second Master, 1935.
- Retired from full-time teaching, 1956.
- Part-time Classics Master, 1956-61.

'Mickey' Murfet in his Peterhouse College blazer.

A T M Murfet, MBE

A T M 'Mickey' Murfet (S, 1916-56) was a distinctive figure who commanded general respect and often real affection. He was born in Norfolk, the son of a gentleman farmer, and attended the Royal Grammar School, Lancaster, from 1903 to 1910. Whilst there, he not only took part in many school plays and was a member of the school debating society, but also took prizes in Greek, Latin, History and Divinity. He also played rugby and in his last three years was a forward in the 1st XV.

In 1910, 'Mickey' was awarded an Open Scholarship in Classics at Peterhouse, Cambridge. Although he was a brilliant scholar, his time there was marred by a strange accident while rowing in the College VIII. He had been awarded his Colours and had bought the appropriate socks, but the dye in them caused blood poisoning, which turned to septicaemia. In those pre-antibiotic days the treatment was long, so he missed the whole of the Summer Term and was unable to take his Tripos examination. However, his work previous to this was sufficiently excellent that he was awarded an Aegrotat Honours degree.

In 1914, having completed his convalescence, he found a job working at Galway Grammar School. Initially he had thought he was going to Galloway in Scotland and was astonished to be booked on a ferry to Dublin (Geography did not feature in his list of prizes). His lameness meant that there was no possibility of his joining up on the outbreak of World War I, so he stayed in Galway until 1916. He moved to Portora on a reported salary of £75 per annum, doubled some few years later when he threatened the Headmaster, Seale, with finding a place in another school. Seale's parsimony recalls his similar reluctance to pay an adequate salary to Tetley, and it has been suggested that in this case the cause was his Aegrotat degree. It was while at Galway that he was given a nickname he hated, so he arranged for a staff colleague to call him 'Mickey', his own choice, out loud. It caught on and was transferred to Portora via the schoolboy grapevine.

He was appointed Housemaster of Connaught (it was he who insisted on the anglicised spelling, rather than the more recently accepted and certainly more correct Gaelic 'Connacht'). His accent was supposed to have saved him when he was arrested in Dublin by the Black and Tans and, with its cultured Oxbridge tones, it was easily imitated by boys, fellow Masters and friends.

His sayings too were passed down through generations of boys, including 'Bunkum', or 'You get nought for that!', when a boy's translation fell below Mickey's exacting standards. If you softened a hard 'c', changing it to 'ch', you were likely to be called 'a greasy Italian'. 'Enlightened citizens' were always those who worked hard at Classics, while 'Barbarians' were those who failed to do justice to his teaching, or actually dropped out of his classes altogether. He was a strict but fair teacher who made lasting friends with those in close contact with him. Few would agree with Beckett's cousin John, also at Portora, and quoted by James Knowlson, that his sarcasm did his popularity no good, but even he had to agree that he was an outstanding teacher.

His appointment as Second Master under Seale made many people believe that he would succeed the latter as Headmaster, but it was not to be. Later, it was expected he would succeed Stuart, but it is said that he refused so as not to stand in the way of his former pupil, Douglas Graham.

'Mickey' also resurrected rowing at Portora. In 1914 a storm had blown down the boathouse and destroyed the racing boats, so after the war two second-hand fours and two training tub-pairs were bought. He undertook the training of the 24 club members. Later, when this job was taken over by G V Butler and N A Keen, 'Mickey' continued the tub-training for several decades.

He was in charge of School rugby for twenty-six years. His lameness meant that he never played, but as a referee he was outstanding, always fair, even, some said, to the point of being too fair to visiting teams. Another facet of the School that 'Mickey' made his own was the production of the School play, featured as the second part of the Annual Speech Day at the end of each Christmas Term. He was a good producer, calm but decisive, unobtrusive but not at all bossy, unless one started overacting. His ability to encourage younger boys to take female parts, much against their wishes, was astonishing.

After more than forty years at Portora, 'Mickey' retired in 1957 and was awarded the MBE for 'a life of service to education'. He taught Classics for a further four years on a part-time basis, living in Enniskillen and being looked after by his manservant, William. At the age of 77 he died quietly in his armchair with his cat asleep on his lap.

Major G V Butler, TD

Major Butler (S, 1926-49) taught History and English from 1926, as well as organising the Officers' Training Corps (OTC). For almost all of that time he was the Housemaster of Leinster, and also acted as the School Bursar. He continued to be the Officer Commanding the OTC, before handing over to Captain Henry Scales during World War II.

During that war, he also turned out to be a skilled handyman at plumbing, electricity and the like, helping to make up for the local wartime shortage of such tradesmen, earning himself the nickname of 'The Man'. No School play or other production was possible without his help in constructing and setting up stage scenery.

During all his years at the School he occupied the fourth of the Lower Classrooms below the Steele Hall. As a teacher, 'The Man' needed no stern discipline to keep order in class; such was his personal enthusiasm for the subject being taught that he caught the attention of every student. There were occasions, though, when his sense of humour lightened the moment, such as the hot Summer's day when, with the windows wide open, a large bumble-bee flew in, attracting the attention of the boys. Barely pausing in his discourse to the class, Butler looked at the bee and, pointing in the right direction, said to it, '*No, two windows down, please*', whereupon the bee obediently flew out the window and headed off towards the room of Mr Barnes (then nicknamed 'the Bee'). It was ten minutes before gravity was restored.

Born in England, Butler served in the Royal Engineers during World War I. He became involved in promoting the development and deployment of the first military tanks in 1917, and thereafter served in the Royal Tank Corps until the Armistice in November 1918. As an interesting historical note, he and his

MAJOR GERALD V BUTLER
(s, 1926-49)

- Graduate of Queen's College, Oxford.
- Joined Portora teaching History and English, January 1926.
- Housemaster of Leinster, January 1926.
- Commander OTC from arrival in 1926.
- School Bursar 1940-49.
- Received the Territorial Decoration (TD) for services rendered to OTC.
- Retired to assist his brother with his Preparatory School in Lake District.

crew ditched their tank shortly before the end of the war and left it where it was. Some four years later, he and another crew member went on holiday to France to visit the old fighting areas. To their astonishment they found their tank exactly where they had ditched it, but now covered in brambles. They got inside and everything was just as they last saw it; his fellow crew member even found a little teddy-bear mascot which had been left behind.

He was a thoroughly likeable man and a superb teacher as well as a respected Housemaster. Like so many Masters of that time he never married, but lived in Liberty Hall with his boarders. He instilled patriotism, duty and loyalty to the Crown, and an OP recalls that, during the 1930s, Butler insisted that Empire Day (24 May) was always celebrated. *'The OTC turned out on the cricket ground, a flag-pole was erected for the occasion and, after the Union flag had been broken, a visiting VIP spoke of our roots and heritage of loyalty to Monarch and Country, followed by everyone singing "Land of Hope and Glory".'*

Butler left Portora in 1949 to join his brother who was Headmaster of Huyton Hill Preparatory School, overlooking Lake Windermere.

H S Scales, TD

Henry Scales (S, 1924-60), always known as 'Yak' (because of the distinctive noise he made when expressing disapproval: 'huwgh'), was born of a Dublin family in 1896 and educated at Dublin High School. When he finished school, World War I was eighteen months old and he volunteered for the Army. He joined the North Irish Horse as a trooper and was sent to France. Why the cavalry? He always said that if he was going to have to cross France, he preferred to ride rather than march. Rapidly promoted to the rank of Corporal, he applied for a commission, was accepted and returned to OCTU in England. The War Office apparently mislaid the file for his class of trainees for two months, and as a result he missed the dreadful battles on the Somme. Having been commissioned into the Royal Dublin Fusiliers, however, he returned to battle and saw out the war.

Returning to Dublin on demobilisation, he obtained a place to study Science with the old Royal University of Ireland. Before he could start his final year, the new Irish Free State Government took over the University buildings, and he and his fellow undergraduates had to complete their degrees at Birmingham University.

With many thousands of newly qualified young men seeking work after the war, jobs were difficult to find, especially as he had set his heart on doing chemistry research. However, he had become engaged to Dorothy Aylward, and quickly had to find a place somewhere. He saw an advertisement for an Assistant Science Master at Portora, applied for it and joined the staff in 1924, intending it to be a temporary position until he could get another. He married his fiancée, and since he found that he loved teaching and was good at it, he stayed there until his death, at the age of 63, while attending the London OPU Dinner at which he was the Master of Honour for that year.

The newly formed Portora OTC attracted his attention and he initially became its second-in-command, with a Territorial Army commission in the Royal Inniskilling Fusiliers. He thoroughly enjoyed this side of his job, taking

HENRY STANLEY SCALES

(s, 1924-1960)

- Native of Dublin City.
- War service with Royal Dublin Fusiliers.
- Undergraduate of Royal University of Ireland and subsequent graduate of Birmingham University.
- Joined Portora as Head of Science, September 1924.
- Second-in-Command OTC, 1926.
- Housemaster of Munster, May 1933.
- Commander OTC, 1939.
- Received Territorial Decoration (TD) for services rendered to OTC.
- Second Master, 1956.

the boys on Summer camp, rehearsing them with the help of the Permanent Staff Instructor (PSI) in drill and putting on a splendid parade through Enniskillen each Remembrance Day. Taking command of the unit when Major Butler stepped down, he saw it through World War II and as a result was honoured with the Territorial Decoration (TD).

As a young man he had played for Lansdowne Road Rugby Club, and was famous for his ability to collect a pass behind his back, confusing the opposition more than somewhat. When he went to Portora, he took his turn teaching on the rugby field along with 'Mickey' Murfet. His other sporting love was tennis, and he became the NW Ireland champion, thereafter becoming President of the Enniskillen Lawn Tennis Club for many years. Golf, too, he enjoyed, and this was the only sport left to him when he became diabetic in the early 1930s, only ten years after insulin had proved a life-saver. At very much the same time as he became a diabetic, he was appointed Housemaster of Munster.

Hal was always a popular member of the Staff Room, and he was well known for his magnanimous but firm style of arguing at staff meetings. *'You may be right,'* he used to say, *'but I know I am!'*

A W Barnes

A W **'Barney' Barnes** (S, 1932-66) served Portora in many different ways for no less than thirty-four years. An Oxford graduate, after teaching for short periods at Bromsgrove and Bruton, he came to Portora in 1932. In 1933 he was appointed Housemaster of Ulster, a job he relinquished in 1936 to become the first Headmaster of Gloucester House. The undoubted success of what many regarded at the time as a daring, not to say rash, venture was in no small measure due to the care and wise guidance that he, and no less Mrs Barnes, devoted to it in its first years. During the war years he founded and commanded the Air Training Corps (ATC), and many future RAF officers owed their start to him in this capacity. For eight years, he took very seriously the management of the tuck shop, and in this period its profits were a welcome contribution to many good causes in the School.

He was a formidable teacher of Mathematics and many pupils found on leaving that they were very much ahead of their contemporaries from other schools. From 1957 to 1961 he was Housemaster of Connacht, and thus achieved the unique distinction of having been Housemaster of three different houses in the School. All through his period at the School he showed enthusiasm for both cricket and tennis, continuing to play the latter until well into retirement, not a normal practice at that time. Much of the good he did was done quietly; for example, unknown to other staff members at the time, he marked every Summer Term by buying a large basket of strawberries to be distributed to the boarders at their evening meal.

He and his wife later retired to Hampshire and he became a part-time teacher at Millfield School in Somerset. He then retired to New Milton on the edge of the New Forest. 'Barney' died aged 94 in February 1996, just a month after his wife Clarice.

ALFRED W BARNES
(s, 1932-1966)

- Graduate of New College, Oxford.
- After junior teaching appointments at several English schools, arrived at Portora as Head of Mathematics, 1932.
- Housemaster of Ulster, 1933.
- First Headmaster of Gloucester House, 1937.
- OC Air Training Corps and started Portora RAF Section, 1941.
- Returned to Upper School in 1945, handing over Headmastership of Gloucester House to Mr Pilkington.
- Housemaster of Connacht in succession to 'Mickey' Murfet, 1957.
- Returned to England for family reasons and became part-time teacher at Millfield School, 1966.
- President OPU (London Branch), 1982.

GEORGE ANDREWS, CdeG

(s, 1933-76)

- Native of Nuneaton.
- Graduate of Sidney Sussex College, Cambridge.
- Joined Portora as Head of French, 1933.
- Took over running of Portora Scout Troop from 1934.
- Housemaster of Ulster from 1938.
- Commissioned RNVR for duties with Royal Navy and seconded to Free French Forces.
- Received Croix de Guerre for services rendered to Free French Forces.
- Commanded Naval Section of post-war CCF.
- Founding member of Portora Masonic Lodge.
- Endowed scholarship for Portora students to attend Cambridge.

G C Andrews, CdeG

George Andrews (S, 1933-76), always known, at least behind his back, as 'Tich', was born in Leicester but from an early age was brought up in Nuneaton where he attended the local Grammar School. From there he went to Sidney Sussex College, Cambridge, obtaining a degree in Modern Languages. During his time at university he wrote for *Granta* magazine, which was then under the editorship of Alistair Cooke, who, when he went to the USA, appointed Andrews in his place. His love for his College remained with him, and many Old Portorans can thank him for directing their paths there after schooldays.

George came straight from university to teach French at Portora in 1933. From the start, he laid down the law, accepting no misbehaviour in his classes. One Old Portoran (OP) recalls that his first lesson on going to Upper School in 1940 was French. Early on that September morning, still feeling his way round, he was waiting along with some twenty-five others, when the door burst open, a little man strode in, leapt on to the podium and, looking every one of the pupils in the eye, declared, *'If any of you misbehave or don't attend, I'll skin you alive!'* He meant every word and we certainly learned French, recalls the OP.

A man skilled in many directions, George soon joined 'Mickey' Murfet in running the Boat Club, passing on his knowledge learned at Sidney Sussex, where he coxed. Again, the discipline he applied ensured that Portora was one of the best Irish school crews. They raced in IVs then; it was not until after World War II that VIIIs were bought, and it was not too long afterwards that Portora was racing against the best at Henley in the Princess Elizabeth Cup. The Erne Head of the River race was later instigated by George, and still draws crews from all over Ireland. In fact, he played a prominent role in Irish rowing as a whole, regularly taking crews as far afield as Galway, Athlone and Athlunkard, and umpiring the national championships at Blessington.

Another of his enthusiasms was scouting, and he ran the 1st Portora Troop for many years. (An account of these activities is covered in chapter six.)

While still a schoolboy in Nuneaton, George had played an active part in his parish church, becoming a Server in the 'high' church of St Mary's Abbey. Later he became a Lay Reader and retained that position actively to the end of his life, clocking up sixty years' service. Nearly half of that time was spent in Lisbellaw, to which he retired, indulging his love of France by calling his house 'Nuits St Georges'. Another of George's abiding passions was Freemasonry. He had joined a Cambridge Lodge, the Isaac Newton University Lodge No. 859, while studying there. On coming to Enniskillen he joined a local Lodge, The Star in the East No. 205, rising to become Master. He was a founding member of the Old Portoran Lodge, also numbered 859, which was limited to those with Portora connections.

In 1943 George joined the Royal Navy, and was immediately commissioned and given the task of liaising with the French Navy. He distinguished himself sufficiently in motor torpedo boats to be awarded the Croix de Guerre. Like many servicemen, he rarely spoke of his wartime service. It is rumoured that he spent time in Occupied France with the Resistance prior to D-Day in 1944. George returned to Portora as the war ended and resumed his teaching duties.

A E Cranston

Come rain, hail, wind or snow, seven days a week in term-time, the Big Bell inevitably rang out its morning message. At the end of the bell-chain was the man who was the mental curse of many a lazy Portoran. **Albert 'Bert' Cranston** (S, 1935-85) was born in Enniskillen in 1902. He joined the Special Constabulary ('B Specials') in 1920, at the time of the Troubles, and served for six years before going to Manchester. After five years in England he returned home, and spent a few years farming before starting work at Portora.

'Bert' did not become bell-ringer until 1937, the bell previously having been rung by the School porter. 'Bert' maintained that a definite knack was required for bell-ringing, and especially the possession of a good sense of rhythm. In this respect he had been a bandsman for over fifty years, having been a drummer in the Enniskillen Pipe Band, and the tutor of generations of Portora CCF bandsmen.

One of the heavy tasks that 'Bert' had to perform was the cleaning of the boys' shoes, up to a hundred pairs on a Saturday night, though the whole process was suspended during the war owing to the shortage of polish. Another of his old duties was the operation of the gas-pump that supplied the kitchen and laundry shed, later the Biology Lab, with water.

Many Old Portorans will have their own memories of Albert. The ornaments and photographs in his room were proof of the regard and affection in which he was held throughout the years. The great thing was that 'Bert' was always there. His love for the School was evident. He would often be seen by the terrace or down at the Sanatorium, surveying his domain. There was always a wave to all who passed. Most of all he loved the boys and was always interested in their welfare. A gentle man, he had that quality of inspiring affection from all who worked at Portora.

He was also a devoutly religious person. He regularly read his Bible and said his prayers. On Sunday he listened to morning service on the radio, and finished the day watching and joining in 'Songs of Praise' on the television.

Lieutenant Colonel H G Halpin, OBE, TD

Grattan Halpin (S, 1936-76), nick-named 'Hairy' in his younger days at Gloucester House but later known as 'Buddy' when his hair receded, joined the staff at Portora after teaching in Wesley College, Dublin.

He then joined the Portora Officer Training Corps as a 'Common Room' cadet, and on the outbreak of the World War II enlisted with the Young Soldiers Battalion of the Royal Irish Fusiliers. After initial training in Belfast, the 70th Battalion, as it was known, moved to Cornwall where he was promoted to Lieutenant. It was there he met his wife, Marie.

He later joined the 6th Battalion of the Royal Irish Fusiliers and served in North Africa, where he fought in the battles of Tangouche and Long Stop Hill. He also took part in the Centuripe Battle on Sicily and in several engagements around the foothills of Mount Etna. He received rapid promotion to Captain and then to Major. It was during a fierce battle to form a bridgehead at the Sangro River on the Italian mainland that he was seriously wounded in the neck by a German sniper. The scar of that bullet, which passed through his

ALBERT CRANSTON
(s, 1935-85)

- Janitor and bell-ringer.
- A very early photograph soon after his arrival at Portora.

Lt Col Henry Grattan Halpin, OBE, TD
(s, 1936-76)

- Native of Co Wicklow.
- Graduate of Trinity College, Dublin.
- Joined PRS for Geography and as Junior Master for Gloucester House, May 1936.
- Assisted Andrews with Junior Scouts and Wolf Cubs.
- Commissioned Royal Irish Fusiliers for wartime service and was badly wounded in Italy.
- Took over post-war JTC and then commanded newly formed CCF, 1945-46.
- Received the Territorial Decoration (TD) for services rendered to CCF.
- Awarded the Order of the British Empire (OBE) for services rendered to the Territorial Army (TA).
- Housemaster Connacht dayboys, 1963.
- Retired locally.

body before emerging in the centre of his back, remained with him ever after. He spent the next 15 months in hospital in Algiers and at a rehabilitation camp in Naples before returning to England where he was demobbed.

After the war, he returned to Portora and later became Housemaster, first of Connacht dayboys and later Connacht boarders. His greatest interest outside the Geography Department was the Combined Cadet Force (CCF); under his command and owing to his firm discipline and strict code of conduct, the CCF remained an integral part of School life. Part of his work in the Geography Department led him to an intensive study of the limestone areas of South Fermanagh. He produced a detailed article on the limestone features of the Marlbank region, which was published in the Queen's University magazine.

Grattan was also responsible for teaching Irish to those boys from the South of Ireland whose career plans required it. One Old Portoran described him as '*a seriously quiet man with a lot going for him*', but he always had a smile, an easy Dublin manner and was much respected. He died in July 1982.

J V Tapley

Victor Tapley (S, 1942-80) came to Portora to teach Geography. In 1946 he became Headmaster of Gloucester House. In those simpler days, his wife acted as Matron; and under their guidance Gloucester House flourished and grew. In 1954 he moved back to Dublin, as Headmaster of Morgan's School in Castleknock. He returned to Portora in 1958, to the Geography Department, in which he remained for twenty-two years, at first under 'Buddy' Halpin, and latterly as Head of Department. Victor, with a firmness of discipline and clear sense of right and wrong, contributed greatly to the wellbeing of the School in general, and individually to the development and progress of all boys under his care.

As Scoutmaster, from 1942 to 1965, he aided the Scout Movement, not only in Portora, but throughout the county. However, his great love was hockey, which he organised for all his 34 years at Portora. At that time hockey was a minor sport at Portora, but was played with great spirit and determination. It is worth mentioning that David Judge, one of the great names in Irish hockey, and an automatic selection for the Irish XI from 1960 to 1978, developed his hockey skills under Victor's direction.

In hockey, a player who can play in any position is called a 'utility' man, and such players are invaluable in any team. Tapley was Portora's ideal 'utility' man. Whenever there was an urgent need, successive Headmasters called on his services. In this way, he found himself Housemaster of three of Portora's four Houses.

In 1958 he was appointed Housemaster of Ulster dayboys; from 1962 to 1964 he took charge of Leinster boarders; from 1964 to 1974 he was Connacht dayboy's Housemaster; and just when he thought that he could escape the demands of Housemastership, he was asked by Headmaster Garrett to return as Housemaster of Ulster dayboys for a second time. He retired in 1980.

F E Rowlette

Francis Edwin 'Ed' Rowlette (S, 1943-81) came from Ballina, County Mayo, and was educated at Trinity College, Dublin. Arriving at Portora, he quickly became fully involved in life at the School. His move to his room in 'Tops' in 1945 meant a close association with Munster boarders that lasted over thirty years until his retirement in 1981 and, indeed, to this day. Effectively, 'Ed' became an assistant to 'Yak' Scales and it was, perhaps, no surprise that he took over as Housemaster from 'Yak' in 1951.

His great interest in sport found an outlet when he coached the First XV, and success was achieved in the mid-1940s when the School reached the semi-finals of the Ulster Schools Cup. In the early days he played for Enniskillen and later, in the 1960s, he refereed School matches. A First XV forward once commented: *'Do you know that every school we play thinks he is the fairest and best referee they have encountered? – they just don't spot where he bends the rules in our direction!'* This comment may have been a matter of opinion, but it was certainly a fact that he exerted unobtrusive and unruffled control, something only the very best referees achieve.

'Ed' ran the School tennis team throughout his time at Portora and was synonymous with the game at Portora. One highlight was when the School team progressed to the final of the Ulster Schools Cup in 1951, unfortunately losing to Methodist College. Outside of school 'Ed' competed in point-to-point racing in Mayo and Sligo, and was one of the best bridge players in Fermanagh.

Although originally employed to teach both English and French, it was for the former that he will be remembered by most Old Portorans. He was an efficient head of the English Department, in particular encouraging the writing of straightforward English. One OP, later a distinguished scientist, wrote, *'Ed tried to teach me to write unscientifically – as he would put it, "It's not a scientific journal – it's English. Just write plain English". A gentleman with a lot of patience as far as I was concerned'.*

He was well known as having time for everyone. Conversations with 'Ed' might extend to girlfriends, relatives, motivation, ghosts or anything that could be pertinent. His interest was always genuine and seemingly endless: in many ways this is what made him famous. During the 1960s, during the fashion for long hair, and before Rogers' imposition of short hair rules, a boy might be greeted by 'Ed' with: *'Goodness, you look like an inverted bog-brush'.*

'Ed' established a culture and style very different from that of the other more Anglicised Housemasters; but then he was totally Irish and that was his enduring hallmark. It is recorded in chapter three that, when news broke that he would be guest of honour at the 50th Anniversary Dinner of the Old Portora Union (London Branch), numbers increased and former charges appeared from all around the world. His 80th birthday party at the School attracted even larger numbers and both events were a testament to the affection and respect in which he was held.

Since retiring he keeps in touch and travels extensively to meet up with Old Portorans and not just those from Munster House.

FRANCIS EDWIN ROWLETTE
(s, 1943-1981)

- Native of Ballina, Co Mayo.
- Graduate of Trinity College, Dublin.
- Taught at Sligo Grammar School.
- Joined Portora to teach English and became Head of the English Department.
- Housemaster of Munster, Nov 1951.
- Rugby Coach and Referee for First XV fixtures.
- Tennis Master.
- Retired locally and to Portnoo, County Donegal.

JOCK McCARTHY

(S, 1944-85)

- Boilerman, keyholder and handyman.

MAJOR JACK WHEELER

(S, 1948-94)

- Joined Portora staff after Army service in World War II with the Rifle Brigade (RB) and Army Physical Training Corps (APTC).

- After demobilisation, completed one of the first Physical Education Diplomas from Loughborough College (DLC).

- Multi-purpose fitness coach for rowing and rugby, as well as Class 1 (Army) instructor for athletics, boxing, fencing, gymnastics and swimming.

- Joined CCF contingent as Lieutenant and progressed through the commissioned ranks to Major, and he finally took over command of the CCF from Lt-Col Grattan Halpin.

- Talented carpenter, draftsman and electrician; could build anything and everything when required at short notice for School activities, eg drama.

- He and his wife Kay trained thousands of children from Enniskillen and Fermanagh to swim at the Portora Holiday Swimming Club.

- Well into his eighties, he never really retired from having some sort of association with the School.

T McCarthy

T 'Jock' McCarthy (S, 1944-85) was born in Glasgow in 1896. The most outstanding events in his memory were those of World War I when he fought with the Royal Scots Fusiliers at Ypres and the Somme. He had to retire from the front after receiving a gunshot wound in the shoulder at Delver Wood just outside Arras. He left the Fusiliers after the war but did not, he said with amusement, receive a war pension until 1960. In 1940 he came to Ireland for a holiday and always claimed that he still possessed the other half of his return ticket. He started work at RAF St Angelo, and served with the ground staff of 422 Squadron, Royal Canadian Air Force (RCAF). It was near the end of the war, in 1944, that Jock came to Portora. He worked under three Headmasters, all of whom he held in high esteem. He continued to communicate with Douglas Graham after he became Headmaster of Dean Close School, sending him a shamrock on St Patrick's Day.

In the early days he knew the names of all the boys, but later, he said, they came and went so often that he knew only a few. When asked if he liked the new Stone Hall colour-scheme, he said he could barely distinguish one colour from another, as he was absolutely colour-blind. He grew a beard because he had *'taken a notion'*, and when asked if he had any thoughts of retirement, he always replied with an emphatic *'No!'* and added, *'I'll die with my boots on.'*

A Haslett

Alex 'Fusty' Haslett (S, 1947-81) came to Portora from Sligo Grammar School. At first he took History and PE and some of the PE displays he organised with Jack Wheeler for Speech Days are still remembered by those fortunate enough to have seen them – and those who took part in them.

He also contributed help with rugby coaching, which had been one of his main activities at Sligo. He possessed a remarkable adaptability and taught widely varied academic subjects such as Mathematics, Latin and English. He had an exceptional flair for understanding the difficulties of the plodding student and this made him invaluable in cases where individual tuition was required; many had him to thank for progressing them through exams that they had previously failed.

Major J T Wheeler

Major Jack Wheeler, (S, 1948-94), came to Portora after regular service in the Rifle Brigade, in which he became the youngest RSM in the British Army. He was a superb rifle shot, and coached several teams to compete at Bisley.

When he first arrived, some members of the Staff Common Room were unsure how to receive him. This was still the age when amateur sportsmen were clearly differentiated from professional players (hence the Gentlemen versus Players match at Lord's), and previously non-commissioned officers employed in Public Schools were treated as a kind of superior school servant. However, he received a 'Common Room Commission' in Portora CCF, and ultimately commanded it. Unlike the rest of the staff, he did not have a degree, but remedied this by attending Loughborough College and acquiring an academic diploma in Physical Education (PE). He soon overcame the initial reserve of some of the more traditional members of staff by force of his personality and abundant natural talents.

His initial responsibilities were for PE, Woodwork and Drawing, but his enthusiasm spread into many other fields of school activity: boxing, fencing, rowing (he was the first to organize weight-training), scenery-construction and the new subject of Technology. He was still on the payroll as Technology Assistant in 1994 – that was Jack's idea of retirement. When a School Chapel was required, it was Jack who refurbished the old hay-loft, and so it was fitting that his memorial service was held there.

His greatest achievement was to establish the Portora Holiday Swimming Club, through which he and his wife, Kay, taught over 12,000 children from all communities in Enniskillen to swim, over a period of 32 Summer holidays.

W P Barbour

William P 'Bill' Barbour (S, 1952-83), Housemaster of Munster dayboys and later of the newly recruited girls, was a Northerner with a special family background. His middle name was Pirrie, and he was connected with the shipbuilding family who not only built the Titanic, but also embraced the cause of Irish Home Rule in the years before World War I. After Trinity, where he was a Scholar in Classics, he began his career with the British Foreign Office which was followed by service with the Army in Egypt. However, he decided to turn to teaching and eventually returned to Ulster, with a young English wife and two children. In 1950, when the Reverend Douglas Graham interviewed Bill for the post of Classics Master at Portora, he was told at the end of the interview, *'I will have great pleasure in appointing you, but before I do I must ask you what is your religion?'* 'Bill' replied, *'I am an atheist'*, to which Graham added, *'Had you been a Roman Catholic, I should have had some trouble making the appointment'*.

Outside the classroom he also had success in coaching rugby and cricket, particularly with the younger teams. But it was not just the skills of passing a rugby ball or wielding a cricket bat that interested him; his skill on the chess board and his ability to fire the imagination of young enthusiasts culminated in Portora's winning the O'Sullivan Cup for ten consecutive years.

Over the years, Bill became increasingly involved in politics, first with the Ulster Liberal Party and then with the Alliance Party, of which he eventually became the provincial Chairman.

Dr R Simpson

Dr Robert 'Doc' Simpson (S, 1957-64) was one of the most colourful characters to have taught at Portora in the post-World War II era. Always immaculately dressed, he would arrive in the classroom in a green velour jacket, with a huge linen handkerchief stuffed up one sleeve and sporting a yellow bow tie as he expounded his deep knowledge of biology. In those days, Biology was an unusual subject at a boys' school and Simpson inspired an enthusiasm for the subject in many of his students. A distinguished OP scientist recalls being asked into the office of Professor Maxwell in the Zoology Department of Queen's. There he was told that, having been at Portora and obviously

WILLIAM P BARBOUR
(s, 1952-1983)

- Graduate of Trinity College, Dublin.
- Initially joined Portora, as Assistant Classics Master, from Foreign Office.
- Succeeded 'Mickey' Murfet in Classics Department.
- Coached countless boys in School Chess Club, which won the O'Sullivan Cup for ten years in succession.
- Housemaster Munster dayboys, 1955.
- Housemaster of Head's House.
- Active in Ulster and community politics.

Dr Robert Simpson
(s, 1957-64)

- Graduate, London University.
- Postgraduate, Manchester and New College, Oxford.
- Deacon, 1924 and priest, 1925.
- Chaplain and Master at Cranleigh, 1928-32.
- Royal Military School, Lovedale, Nilgiri Hills, 1933-37.
- Rector of Mellis, 1939-43.
- Head of Zoology, University College, Gold Coast, 1943-48.
- Headmaster of Woolmer's School, Jamaica, 1949-53.
- Prolific publisher on zoology and various educational subjects.

under Dr Simpson's tuition, Maxwell would certainly look to him if he needed additional help.

Equally, Simpson had no time for those who looked to his classes for an easy break in routine: time-wasters, he called them. On one occasion two boys were obviously more interested in the antics of the workmen outside the windows than the lesson, so he went out and spoke to the foreman, came back and sent the two boys out to learn how to shovel sand and cement. On another occasion, at the beginning of a class, he went round without a word, touching several boys on their shoulders, returned to the front of the class and told those whom he had touched to go to the library, since trying to teach them biology would be a waste of his and their time.

Another aspect of education that 'Doc' Simpson controlled was the astronomical telescope mounted on top of the new Science laboratories. Astronomy was not officially on the School curriculum, but carefully selected boys were allowed to use it. Evenings spent trying to see the stars in an average Fermanagh sky were often disappointing, but maps of what might have been visible added to the interest.

'Doc' Simpson's classroom was in the wing where the laundry was situated during the war, and on its end wall an old chimney stack had been modified to hang the school bell. This was rung by 'Bert', who would emerge from his cubbyhole by the kitchens at the end of each class, to pull three rings and four for the end of the last class of the day. He then retired to his den where he was often joined by 'Doc' carrying a bottle of wine. They would then share a glass or two, chatting of the old days and enjoying each other's company.

Simpson had spent much of his earlier life as a Headmaster in India and the West Indies, and he had been Head of the Zoology Department at a university in what was still the Gold Coast. In the course of his Portora career, his tropical connections allowed him to acquire for the new laboratory items not usually found in Irish schools, the embryo of an elephant, for example.

Simpson's family had originated in Dungannon, and in taking the post at Portora he had wanted to re-establish his personal links with Ireland. As an Oxford graduate he took advantage of the long-established rule allowing Oxford and Cambridge degrees to be commuted 'ad eundem gradum' as Dublin degrees 'by incorporation'. From then on, he regularly wore a Trinity tie on formal occasions.

He was not particularly interested in any School sport except swimming, but he enthusiastically helped with drama activities, doing make-up and helping with transport. He played an active role in Enniskillen life, being particularly keen on helping to establish more links between the School and the Roman Catholic community; although it was not immediately apparent, he was in fact an Anglican clergyman and helped out at services in the area. But his churchmanship was very broad and modernist, and of a type very rarely encountered in the Church of Ireland, especially in a remote rural diocese like Clogher. The opinions expressed in his sermons, as well as his beliefs and personal life, continued to raise pious eyebrows, especially as he never wore proper clerical dress.

The Rogers era and beyond

As we turn to the second half of the twentieth century and move into a more familiar world, it is not always easy to discern who will prove to be enduring and outstanding personalities in the history of Portora.

One major contributor to school life and to the good reputation of Portora in the surrounding community was **Mary Rogers** (S, 1954-73), wife of Headmaster Val Rogers, and also member of staff. Although she had been born in India and had spent much of her childhood in Belfast, her development had been very much influenced by her time at Oxford. She was a strong supporter of her husband's aims for the School, and she also took a lively interest in many of its internal activities, organising Sunday evening play readings for staff and senior boarders, and giving dinner parties for young bachelor teachers.

But her main mark on Fermanagh was probably made outside the School. She published two popular books on local history, *Prospect of Erne* and *Prospect of Fermanagh*. She supported much local archeological work, and was a founder-member, with Val, of the Fermanagh Field Club. But her major achievement was to take the lead in founding a new Fermanagh Literary and Debating Society. Such a title would probably have sounded innocuous and even banal anywhere else in the British Isles, but its sudden appearance and achievements in Fermanagh in the 1950s were astonishing. She even persuaded the local Nationalist MP at Stormont and Lady Brookeborough to be joint Presidents and to take part in the actual debates, something that would probably have been impossible anywhere else in Northern Ireland. Unionists, Socialists, Liberals and members of Sinn Fein all joined and supported it, and it continued to thrive until the Troubles of the 1960s finally swept it away. But in its heyday it had much Portora support, and staff members such as Bill Barbour and Bob Bell were keen participants.

Two other figures appointed in the early 1950s had a considerable influence on the School. One was **Tony Smith** (S, 1952-65), Director of Music, who not only played a major part in school activities (for example, as the Musical Director for Mrs Benson's productions of Gilbert and Sullivan) but also initiated a major Fermanagh music festival, which included performances in Enniskillen Cathedral and in Florence Court. His work was ably developed by Billy McBride, one of Smith's own pupils (for further details see chapter six). The other influential appointment was **Mike Tovey** (S, 1955-66), Director of Art, who was responsible for planning the new Art Room. He set new standards in designing scenery and programmes for school plays, and provided evening art classes for his fellow members of staff. He left to become Art Master at Rugby School, but sadly died very soon after his appointment.

The Rogers era was eventually to prove a watershed in the staffing of Portora. Up to that point most teachers had come either from the Republic or England, mainly from Oxford and Cambridge. Dublin was still very much the centre of Portora's Ireland. Being a Church of Ireland school, it sought Trinity graduates for staff and saw Trinity College as the major destination for its university candidates. Until the 1950s there was still a direct rail link to Dublin. Belfast and the Stormont government played a far less significant role in the School's life than they do today.

MARY ROGERS

(s, 1954-73)

- Graduate of Oxford, where she met her husband, Headmaster Val Rogers.

- Joined the staff at Portora where she taught English Language and Literature.

- Wrote several books on County Fermanagh.

- Founded the Fermanagh Literary and Debating Society, which was initially very successful in cross-community activities.

- Retired to Oxford with her husband, where they worked together for the blind by producing 'speaking books' from selected volumes at the Bodleian Library.

Rogers continued the Trinity tradition: for example, he appointed a married couple from Cork, the **Reverend Terence Benson** (S, 1956-79) and his wife, **Rene Benson** (S, 1957-78). Terence was a Church of Ireland clergyman who taught Mathematics, but he was even more useful as a sailing instructor. Rene was a lively influence in the School, not just as a perceptive selector and inspirer of mathematical scholarship candidates, but also as the very successful producer of two Gilbert and Sullivan operas.

We have already covered many Masters from this period, but there are others who warrant our attention. One is **Neville 'Necky' Peterson** (S, 1949-65), from Trinity, and Housemaster of Leinster boarders, who was one of a succession of cricket coaches who battled with the Fermanagh weather. He was even more successful with his stage productions. He had been a professional actor and distinguished himself particularly by ambitiously bringing to Portora André Obey's 'Noah', with its challenging array of humans and animals.

D A R 'Darcy' Chillingworth (OP, 1934-41; S, 1949-66/67), a former Headboy and Trinity graduate, as Head of History brought a liberal viewpoint that was unashamedly Nationalist rather than Unionist. He was Housemaster of Leinster dayboys, and despite his political views, which were totally at odds with those of many dayboy parents, he managed to inspire general confidence, not least because he was particularly successful at preparing candidates for Trinity. He was also impressive as an organiser of athletics, an area of sport in which he himself had shone. He was a distinguished debater, as well as an enthusiastic organiser of choral music and a diligent official of the OPU.

Victor Brennan (S, 1952-62), another Trinity graduate, was a rugby coach and a teacher of German and French. One OP recalls the conditions under which Victor Brennan had to teach during the School's rebuilding programme of the mid-1950s. He was allocated a Nissen hut generally known as the 'Beaujolais Room' or the 'French Hut', a green, rusty, corrugated-iron building which stood apart from the School on the road to the lower playing fields. It was fitted with two paraffin heaters, but the windows were broken and Stanley, the School's odd-job man, had done his best to put them together to keep the cold out. One Old Portoran remembers having French lessons there, with frosty fingers, looking at the ice on the broken windowpanes. Fortunately, Victor had an optimistic sunny personality which overcame such privations.

Martin Schrecker (S, 1953-75), a Cambridge graduate, was a prominent influence at the School during the 1950s and 1960s. Martin not only taught French and German, but also introduced his pupils to the culture of those two great nations. He was involved in all aspects of School life. He sang in the School choir; he never missed a concert, whether in the Steele Hall or Enniskillen Town Hall; he encouraged visits to exhibitions in the school Art Room; he took a keen and critical interest in School and House plays; he was the sole producer of the first Portora revue in 1954; he even coached rugby. In the 1960s he was Head of Modern Languages and Housemaster for Ulster.

R E 'Bobby' Bell (S, 1956-62) taught English and succeeded Barnes as Housemaster of Connacht. He had a Cambridge trial cap as a cox and was naturally enlisted to help George Andrews with the Boat Club, but he made a bigger mark, perhaps, as a drama producer. He helped Rene Benson with her Gilbert and Sullivan productions, while he also produced 'She Stoops to Conquer' and, for the Dublin Theatre Festival, 'Waiting for Godot'. These two plays featured in particular Billy Murtagh, a dayboy actor with a strong Fermanagh accent and distinctive personality, who considerably impressed the Guardian critic Peter Lennon (see chapter six).

Jim Spence (S, 1953-58), Housemaster of Ulster dayboys, brought a breath of modern science into the School. His arrival heralded an influx of Queen's graduates whose numbers were to increase considerably as years went by; they would be joined by graduates of universities in Britain other than Oxbridge.

Other notable staff members in the 1950s included the **Reverend Donald Caird** (S, 1954-57), who served as Chaplain and took over the task of teaching Irish from Grattan Halpin. A distinguished Trinity graduate, he was later to return to full church duties and to become Archbishop of Dublin.

Two Masters with backgrounds from Northern Ireland came to the school in the 1950s and were to remain for long periods. **W R M 'Ronnie' Moore** (S, 1955-85) had been a master at Campbell College and became generally known as 'Happy'. Sadly, he had lost an eye in World War II. He was a huge man with patience and intellect, who taught Physics brilliantly. One OP notes how, as a result of Moore's teaching, he knew more of fundamental points of Physics than any of those sitting around him in university lectures. 'Ronnie' later became Vice Principal. The other master was **T A 'Tom' Elliott** (OP, 1948-55; S, 1959-2000), one of the first Queen's graduates, who served as a teacher of Mathematics for some forty years. A Housemaster and highly successful rugby coach of the 1st XV, he was responsible for bringing Jimmy McCoy to the fore, and for the early introduction of computing into Portora. Throughout his career he was a very keen supporter of table tennis, one of the sports played equally by both boarders and dayboys.

Montague 'Monty' Ainslie (S, 1959-72) came to Portora from Cambridge. His classes were conducted under difficult circumstances in the old byre under the present Chapel, and were apparently enjoyed despite the trench in the floor that had something to do with the room's previous occupants. One OP recalls: *'I remember smelling creosote in that room. It was better than the bovine stuff and from that day I remember French lessons with that smell. Monty Ainslie, creosote and French in the old byre – but he was fantastic. He often brought his two whippets to school in the back of his rusty car and I was often asked to exercise them during lunch.'*

But Monty was remembered for more than creosote. A product of the same Cambridge college as 'Bob' Bell, Pembroke, he introduced the increasingly fashionable subject of Russian to the School and his teaching of that subject was outstanding. The apogee of his success was coaching three Portora pupils to achieve Open Exhibitions to Cambridge.

At Portora, 'Monty' was heavily involved with cricket, in spite of what he saw as the hopeless climate and conditions in Fermanagh. One can remember teams of people out with mops and buckets attempting to remove puddles of water in the hope of getting play started. While he was synonymous with cricket in a School dominated by rowing and rugby, he also took an interest in the general welfare of boys not directly under his tutelage.

Ian Knox (S, 1960-70), also a Queen's graduate, was recruited into the Chemistry Department in the 1960s. An intense and dedicated teacher, Ian took a keen interest in coaching tennis and promoting the sport in the School.

He was followed in the mid-1960s by **John Mills** (S, 1962-65), another Queen's graduate, who arrived to teach Physics. As described in chapter three, John subsequently went on to be Headmaster of Gloucester House in the 1970s. Together, he and 'Ronnie' Moore made a strong team in their subject, which was also boosted by the new and slightly infamous laboratory built on stilts, which has just recently been demolished.

Peter Ritchie (S, 1961-66), a graduate of Birmingham University, along with Mrs Benson and A W Barnes, formed the core of the Mathematics Department. They worked closely with the Physical Sciences Department and saw many boys go up to Cambridge, including one particular year when four boys reading a combination of these subjects were successful. He departed for Millfield in 1966.

One other teacher of a scientific subject, Biology in this case, to arrive at Portora was **Brian Morwood** (S, 1964-86). Brian was a Cambridge graduate who took over from 'Doc' Simpson and stayed for many years, eventually taking over from 'Ronnie' Moore as Vice-Principal. Brian had also received the Military Cross during his Army service.

The influx of Oxbridge masters continued unabated but before returning to that theme one can mention an attempt to boost the sport of rugby when **Peter Knowles** (S, 1965-67), a Durham County wing-forward (Durham were county champions at that time) was recruited as rugby coach. Rugby, therefore, became the only sport in the School to have a full-time coach, which may indicate the pressure that Rogers felt he was under to improve performance in that area.

A major recruit in 1963 was **Robert Hort** (S, 1963-83). At first there was really no post for Robert, but he responded with such enthusiasm to life at Portora that he was asked to organise the 1964 appeal for £100,000. With this money, the Castle Lane houses were built, together with the new kitchen and stores, the fives courts, the Chapel, the Murfet Cloister, the Gloucester House boarding block and the Headmaster's house. The appeal also provided funding for a new gallery in the Steele Hall, dayboys' House rooms and the transfer of Leinster to Willoughby Place. While he was still working on the appeal, the need arose for a new school drama production and, with his Cambridge Footlights experience behind him, he produced O'Casey's 'The Shadow of a Gunman'. This was the first of many dramatic achievements including 'Richard II', Frisch's 'The Firmraisers' and 'The Dragon' by Schwartz. This last was a powerful anti-Soviet allegory, which had run for a fortnight in Leningrad before the authorities tumbled to its real meaning.

Andrew Tod (S, 1965-69), a Scot from Oxford University, and **Christopher Toase** (S, 1965-75), from Cambridge, also arrived during the mid-1960s to make significant contributions to life at Portora; Tod was a keen rugby enthusiast and Toase occupied rooms in the Ulster boarding area of the School and also coached rowing.

In 1967 **David Robertson** (S, 1967-83) arrived. David had a distinguished career at Durham University. He was cox of the first eight, captain of golf and President of the Union. He took over the Boat Club from George Andrews and developed the Erne Head of the River race and the Portora Regatta, both of which became major events in the Irish rowing calendar. He also revived the Henley tradition for the Boat Club. Perhaps his greatest achievement was the development of the Portora Historical Society, to whose meetings he attracted many well-known personalities; for fuller details see chapter six. David left Portora to become Headmaster of King's Hospital School, Dublin.

During 1971 **C H Dawkins** (S, 1971-76), an Oxford graduate, arrived at the School. Rejoicing in the nickname of 'The Whizzkid', he was obsessed by computers, calling up mainframes in California and Belfast. One of his students won the Aer Lingus 'Young Scientist of the Year' competition, with a computer program modelling populations of rabbits and foxes coexisting under varying conditions.

Other new members of the staff joining the School in the 1970s and 1980s had quieter but no less useful careers. **David Kingston** (OP, 1952-59; S, 1970-2001) was Chaplain, Housemaster and Head of Careers for over thirty years, while **R G McNeill** (S, 1976-) has been involved in pastoral care up to the present. **T R Smith** (S, 1972-89) established Technology as a subject for the first time, and co-operated with Sixth Formers in building a hovercraft. **Martin Todd** (S, 1979-2007) taught Biology and became Housemaster of Connacht in 1986 for many years. He was undoubtedly one of Portora's most respected and well-liked teachers during his time at the School. Although a teacher who instilled initially an element of fear in his pupils by following tradition and addressing each of them by his surname, he quickly earned the respect of all he taught. Todd achieved excellent examination results. In his latter years at Portora, he assumed the role of Careers Master, taking a genuine interest in the future careers of all pupils.

One of Portora's teaching institutions, **James Pratt** (S, 1970-93), taught Mathematics; not only a fine teacher, he had an excellent sense of humour. He also played an active role, both within the boarding department at Portora, where he was the Housemaster of the combined boarding house from 1983, and in local amateur dramatics, displaying his talents by treading the boards on more than one occasion.

One of the most influential members of the last thirty years must be **Robert Northridge** (OP, 1955-62; S, 1973-). Unfortunately, as a serving member of staff, we have not included him. Robert's achievements must wait for a future history. Who can say which of these more recent Portora personalities will be remembered, as 'Mickey' Murfet and the other early twentieth-century figures with whom we opened this chapter, are now remembered?

Former staff attending the 50th Anniversary Reunion, September 2005: (l-r) Bill Barbour, Ed Rowlette, Rene Benson, Archbishop Donald Caird, Bobby Bell and Victor Brennan.

Eight

Some Old Portorans – past and present

For a small school in a distant part of Ireland, Portora has over the centuries produced more than its fair share of pupils who have distinguished themselves in later life. It has also turned out a number of rebels and eccentrics who demonstrate that, however much it may have been an establishment School for the greater part of its history, there was never such a thing as a Portora stereotype.

It is impossible to cover more than a tiny minority of Portora alumni in the confines of one chapter. Accordingly, what follows can be only illustrative rather than comprehensive. The focus is unavoidably on the nineteenth and twentieth centuries, because earlier records are sadly very sparse. Without the large number of unsung Portorans, there would, of course, have been no Portora, and consequently the lives of many of those mentioned here would have been significantly different. To the many Portorans still with us who are not mentioned for reasons of space, and who may justly feel that they should have been, we can only offer our apologies.

From the early days there has been a strong tradition of service to the Crown and to the Church, particularly the Church of Ireland. This is hardly surprising, given the origins of the school as a Royal Foundation and its close connections with the Church, not least through a succession of clerical Headmasters. Beyond this, it is striking how many old Portorans have made a mark in a wide variety of fields, from politics to law, science, medicine, sport and, more recently, to the world of business and finance. But above

Left: Henry Francis Lyte (OP, 1803-09).

Lt Frederick Harvey, VC.

Lt Frederick Harvey, VC, receiving the award
of the Victoria Cross from King George V.

all, Portora can claim to have enriched the arts, literature and the theatre through the work of Henry Francis Lyte, Oscar Wilde, Samuel Beckett and many others.

Wartime service

The record of old Portorans in wartime is second to none. Over 400 saw service in World War I, of whom 71 lost their lives. During World War II, 389 Portorans volunteered, of whom 38 were killed. The record in World War II is particularly remarkable, as there was no conscription in Northern Ireland, and the Irish Free State, as it was then, whence many of the volunteers came, remained neutral throughout the war.

Many decorations were won, including the Victoria Cross awarded in World War I to **Lt Frederick Harvey** (OP, 1902-06), who had emigrated to Canada before the war and joined Lord Strathcona's Horse. Harvey, who was commanding the leading troop of the cavalry regiment and was riding well ahead of his men, became the prime target for a machine-gun firing from a trench protected by barbed wire, which threatened to wipe out the entire troop. Harvey dismounted and hurdled the triple wire entanglement. Firing as he ran, he shot the machine-gunner dead. As a result of his action, the Strathconas were able to occupy a key position and capture the town of Guyencourt. Harvey, who survived this encounter and the war, went on to become a Brigadier, and to have a mountain in Canada named after him. At school he captained the 1st XV, which won the Ulster Schools Cup for the first time in 1905. He is described in the school magazine as 'a half very much above the average' who is '*very fast and makes good openings…and is a certain scorer*

World War I Roll of Honour which is

mounted on the wall in the Seale Room.

near the line'. Apart from his outstanding bravery, these abilities were probably critical to the success of his action at Guyencourt.

Other Portorans who distinguished themselves in the services both in peace and war include **Brigadier R C Jellicoe, CBE, DSO** (OP, 1893). During World War I he was mentioned in despatches no fewer than five times. He subsequently became Director of Supplies and Transport in Egypt in the late 1920s.

Vice-Admiral Sir Nicholas Archdale, 2nd Bart, CBE (OP, 1892-96) served in submarine flotillas during World War I, and held a number of senior naval appointments after the war, before retiring with the rank of Vice-Admiral. In 1929 he was Naval ADC to King George V. He also commanded the battleship HMS Malaya. From 1931 to 1946 he was General Inspector at the Ministry of Home Affairs, Northern Ireland.

Lt General Sir Ian Harris, KBE, CB, DSO (OP, 1924-29) commanded the 2nd Battalion the Royal Ulster Rifles on D-Day in 1944. His distinguished career culminated in his appointment as GOC Northern Ireland in the late 1960s.

General Sir Charles Jones, GCB, CBE, MC (OP, 1919-26) won the Military Cross in World War II, when he destroyed two German tanks during the retreat of the British Expeditionary Force to Dunkirk in 1940. After the war he commanded the 7th Armoured Division in Germany and, after a spell as GOC Northern Command, he was appointed Master General of the Ordnance and ADC (General) to the Queen. In so-called retirement he became National President of the Royal British Legion for eleven years from 1970. At School Charles 'Splosh' Jones played for both the 1st XV and the 1st XI, and was described as '*the best wicket keeper the school has had in recent years'*.

General Sir Charles Jones' son **Sir Edward Jones, KCB, CVO, CBE** (OP, 1949-54), like his father, went on to become a general and was also knighted. His service included action in Malaysia in the early 1960s, and command of the 6th Armoured Brigade in Germany while the Cold War was at its most intense. As Commander of the British military training team in Zimbabwe in the early 1980s, he established a good working rapport with all sides. Subsequently, Sir Edward had a brief spell as Commander of the 3rd Armoured Division, before being promoted to the hot seat of Quartermaster General during the Gulf War of 1991. His last appointment in the Army was as the UK's military representative at NATO Headquarters in Brussels, a post well suited to his undoubted diplomatic skills. Finally, on retirement he was for six years Gentleman Usher of the Black Rod at Westminster. He died suddenly in 2007, and in a glowing obituary the Times described him as enjoying '*wide esteem and affection'*.

At School, in a foretaste of things to come, Edward Jones was a senior NCO in the Combined Cadet Force (only staff, not pupils, could become officers). He was also a School Prefect and Head of Connacht House.

After the war many old Portorans continued to serve in the armed forces. Two were killed in the Korean war during 1951-53, and two more died on active service in Oman in the 1970s, after secondment to the Sultan of Oman's forces.

General Sir Charles Jones, GCB, CBE, MC, as Master General of the Ordnance.

General Sir Edward Jones, KCB, CVO, CBE as Gentleman Usher of the Black Rod.

Paul Maxwell.

The Red Arrows display team with Sqdn Ldr
Tim Miller, RAF (4th from right).

The Rt Hon J G Gibson, PC.

William Hearn.

During Northern Ireland's Troubles many old Portorans served at various levels in the Royal Ulster Constabulary, and six of them lost their lives, as did the schoolboy **Paul Maxwell** (OP, 1975-79), who was a victim of the bomb that killed Lord Louis Mountbatten in 1979.

Yet more recently **Tim Miller** (OP, 1964-71) was appointed Team Leader of the Royal Air Force Aerobatics Team (Red Arrows), 1988-90, having previously served as a pilot with the formation in 1982-84.

The law

A third member of the Jones family, **Sir Edward Jones, QC** (OP, 1925-31), served as a Northern Ireland High Court judge from 1968 to 1973, before becoming a Lord Justice of Appeal. For a number of years before becoming a judge, he was the Unionist member for the City of Derry at Stormont, and in 1964 was appointed Attorney General for Northern Ireland, a post which he held for four years. Sir Edward, who retired in 1984, was a younger brother of General Sir Charles Jones and uncle of General Sir Edward Jones (see above).

Many other old Portorans have had distinguished careers in the field of law as barristers, as judges and in the academic world. One such in the nineteenth century was **William Hearn** (OP, 1842), who became the first Dean of the newly created Faculty of Law at Melbourne University in 1873. But Hearn was also a remarkable polymath. After serving for five years as Professor of Ancient Greek at the new Queen's College, Galway, he was selected as one of only four original professors at Melbourne. Before becoming Dean of the Law Faculty there he had taught a range of subjects, including Modern History, Literature and Classics. In 1886 Hearn was briefly Chancellor of the University. As if all this were not enough, he was also for several years an elected member of the Legislative Council of Victoria (at that time there was no Australia-wide parliament) and played an active part in drafting state legislation.

The first President of the Old Portora Union was another distinguished jurist, **The Rt Hon J G Gibson** (OP, 1857-63), who was a judge of the King's Bench in Ireland for thirty-three years until his resignation in 1921. He was also active in politics, and represented the Walton Division of Liverpool for several years in the 1880s. During this time he was appointed successively Solicitor General and Attorney General for Ireland.

A recent President of the OPU, **Sir Anthony Hart, QC** (OP, 1955-64), has been a judge of the Northern Ireland High Court since 2005.

Another distinguished lawyer was **Michael T Knight** (OP, 1949-54). A brilliant Classics scholar at Portora, he won the Seale Scholarship in 1949 and subsequently the Steele Medal in 1953, when he was also awarded a NI State Exhibition (see photograph of Intermediate Exhibitioners board on page 122). He read Law at Trinity College, Dublin, from 1953 to 1958, where his oratorical gifts were quickly recognised in both the University Law Society (he won the Impromptu Speech Medal in 1957-58) and in the College's oldest society, the Historical Society ('The Hist'). He represented both The Hist and the College in the Final of the Observer Mace Debating Competition, and was elected Auditor of The Hist in 1958: his inaugural meeting in 1959 is remembered by many for attracting, as speakers, some of the most prominent personalities of the 1950s. After graduation (he gained an LLD from Trinity some years later), he taught Law at University College, Cardiff (Neil Kinnock, PC, Leader of the Labour Party, 1983-92, was one of his students); the rest of his academic career was spent at QUB, where he taught many of Ulster's barristers and solicitors, and became Reader in Law. He died in 2003.

Jeffery Switzer (OP, 1934-41) also made his mark in the academic world. He began early, gaining distinctions in each of the seven subjects that he took at Senior Certificate level, and winning the Tetley Gold Medal for Science twice. After the war, in which he served in the Royal Navy, Switzer read Estate Management at Sidney Sussex College, Cambridge. Following a period in town planning, he returned to his old college, where he eventually became Vice Master. He also served on the University's Financial Board, the Council of the Senate and as Chairman of his Faculty Board, where he established a new Honours degree in Land Economy.

Michael Knight.

The Church

Over the centuries Portora has produced many leading churchmen and clerics. One of the best known was the fiery **Charles Leslie** (OP, 1660-64). He refused to take the oath of allegiance to William and Mary because he believed that their accession to the throne broke the principle of the divine right of succession. He remained loyal to the Stuarts and went into exile in France and Italy.

In the early nineteenth century **William Magee** (OP, 1781), one of many polymaths produced by Portora, was Professor of Mathematics at Trinity College, Dublin, before going on to become successively Dean of Cork, then Bishop of Raphoe and finally, in 1822, Archbishop of Dublin. He was known as an outspoken opponent of Catholic emancipation. His grandson, William Connor Magee, was also Dean of Cork and Chaplain to the Lord Lieutenant of Ireland, before being appointed Bishop of Peterborough, and, in 1891, Archbishop of York, a position which he held for only four months before he died.

Charles Leslie.

In recent years there have been no fewer than seven bishops from Portora in the Anglican Communion – **James Moore** (OP, 1946-50), **Samuel Poyntz** (OP, 1939-44), **Henry Richmond** (OP, 1949-54), **David Chillingworth** (OP, 1962-67), **John Conlin** (OP, 1946-52), **Archbishop Walton Empey** (OP, 1944-52) and the present Chairman of the Board of Governors, **the Right Reverend Michael Jackson** (OP, 1967-75), Bishop of Clogher. In addition **Archbishop Donald Caird** (S, 1954-57), though not a former pupil, had taught at Portora.

Portora can also claim to be the alma mater of at least one Roman Catholic bishop, **Dr Edward Kernan,** (OP, c1790), who was Bishop of Clogher, 1824-44. He was one of a number of Catholic boys from Enniskillen and Fermanagh who attended the School in the late eighteenth century.

One of the most remarkable clerics to emerge from Portora was **Father John Sullivan** (OP, 1873-79), whose father, the Rt Hon Sir Edward Sullivan, was Lord Chancellor of Ireland. At the age of 35 John Sullivan decided to become a Roman Catholic, the faith of his mother, and subsequently took his vows as a Jesuit priest. In one of his writings Father Sullivan records that the

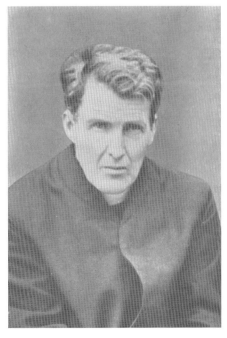

Father John Sullivan, SJ.

Old Portoran bishops at the Lambeth Conference, 1979: Archbishop Walton Empey (OP, 1946-50), Archbishop Donald Caird (S, 1954-55), Bishop Sam Poyntz (OP, 1939-44) and Bishop John Conlin (OP, 1946-54). Bishop Henry Richmond (OP, 1949-54) was a serving Bishop but was unable to attend the conference.

Headmaster, Dr William Steele, whom he greatly admired, '*on his appointment, at once opened the classes at Portora to the sons of Catholic parents, and in my own class there were several Catholic day boys…*'. This is not only an interesting reflection of the ecumenical nature of Portora at that time, but it also suggests that the seeds of his later conversion to Rome might have been sown there. At all events, as a priest he went on to serve the community of Clongowes for many years with great devotion and holiness. Such is his reputation that in 2002 his name was put forward to the Holy See for canonisation. Father Sullivan fondly remembered his old school as a place to which he went '*bathed in tears*' but which he left weeping '*more plentiful tears*'. Among the many sinners who have left Portora over the centuries here at least is one who has come close to being a Saint.

Overseas Service

During the nineteenth century and the first part of the twentieth, Portorans ranged far and wide in the service of Empire. **Robert Bourke, GCIE** (OP, c1840), created Baron Connemara in 1887, was Governor of the Madras Presidency from 1886 to 1890, after serving for eighteen years as the Conservative Member of Parliament for King's Lynn. He was instrumental in the development of the east coast rail link between Madras (now Chennai) and Calcutta (Kolkata), and founded a major public library in Madras. The library and one of the city's leading hotels are still named after him. His elder brother, the 6th Earl of Mayo, was Viceroy of India.

Still in India, **Sir Charles Tegart, KCIE** (OP, 1897-1900), after many years of police service in Bengal, became Commissioner of Police there in 1923. He spoke fluent Bengali, and had a reputation for going about in disguise to monitor the activities of criminals in the state. He later advised on security in Palestine and arranged for the building of a two-metre high fence along the border with Lebanon and Syria, and some fifty fortified police stations, which came to be known as 'Tegarts', a chilling forerunner of things to come both in Israel and Northern Ireland. All we know of him at School is that he won a swimming prize and a prize for English. He also rowed in the School VIII.

Sir Charles Tegart, KCIE.

On the other side of the Indian Ocean, the **Rt Hon Sir Albert Hime** (OP, 1857-58), after distinguished service in the Royal Engineers, settled in South Africa, where he eventually became Premier of Natal Province from 1899 to 1903. More recently, **Charles Abbott** (OP, 1913), who rowed in the 1st VIII at Portora in 1913 and was called to the Bar in 1921, became Chief Justice in Aden for two years, and then successively Puisne Judge in Nigeria and Chief Justice in Malaya. **Sir Colville Deverell** (OP, 1921-25), who was Head Prefect at Portora in 1925, became Governor of Mauritius from 1959 to 1962. **Randal Sadleir** (OP, 1938-41) left School to join the Irish Guards, and was the very last expatriate Administrative Officer to leave Tanzania after independence. In a preface to Sadleir's book, *Tanzania, Journey to Republic*, the late President Julius Nyerere wrote '…*his ill-concealed sympathy for the nationalist cause before independence in 1961 was only matched by his forthright opinions after it*'.

In the contemporary world we find old Portorans who hold, or have held, senior positions in Her Majesty's Diplomatic Service. These include **Clive Newell** (OP, 1967-70), still in the Service, and **Charles Cullimore** (OP, 1946-52), who was the UK's Deputy High Commissioner in Australia, and then High Commissioner in Uganda from 1989 to 1993.

Politics and rebellion

Portorans also ranged far and wide over the political landscape, not always on the side of the Establishment. **William Irvine** (OP, c1757) settled in America in 1763, having been a naval surgeon. He took the side of the colonists in the War of Independence and led the 2nd Pennsylvania Brigade in various actions against the British; he later became a member of Congress. **William Hamilton** (OP), who was the son of an Enniskillen solicitor, became a prominent member of the United Irishmen in Ulster at the end of the eighteenth century, and a co-leader of the rebellion led by Robert Emmett in 1803.

A more recent old Portoran who fought 'agin the government' was **George Irvine** (OP, 1891-95), a native of Enniskillen. He was Vice-Commandant of the 1st battalion, Dublin Brigade of the IRA, and was sentenced to death for his part in the Easter rising of 1916. The sentence was, however, commuted and, following a spell in Lewes prison, he returned to Dublin. After the signing of the 1922 Treaty, Irvine again took the Republican side and consequently found himself interned in Mountjoy prison by the Irish government.

In the closing decades of the nineteenth century, **Jeremiah Jordan** (OP) was an active member of the Land League, the Tenants Association and the United Irish League successively. He also sat at Westminster as the Nationalist MP for West Clare, then South Meath and finally South Fermanagh.

In the last century, Portorans continued to be active in politics in one way or another, both at Westminster and Stormont. **Sir Maurice Dockrell** (OP, 1860-70), a prominent Dublin businessman, sat as the Unionist MP for Rathmines at Westminster from 1918 until partition ended representation from the South in 1922.

Sir Thomas Moore, 1st Bart, CBE, MP (OP, 1901), who attended Portora as a dayboy in the early 1900s, sat as Conservative MP for the Burgh of Ayr for 25 years until 1950, and for the Ayr Division of Ayrshire for another 14 years up

William Irvine.

Sir Thomas Moore, 1st Bart, CBE, MP.

to 1964, by which time he had become the longest serving MP at Westminster. Previously he had been commissioned in the Army and saw action in France in World War I, and with the White Army in Russia after the war. In World War II he played a significant part in the formation and development of the Home Guard.

Another dayboy who went on to make a mark in politics was **Harry West** (OP, 1929-35). He sat as the Unionist MP for Enniskillen in the Stormont Parliament from 1954 to 1972, and was Minister for Agriculture for seven years in the 1960s, and again briefly in the early 1970s. He succeeded Brian Faulkner as leader of the Ulster Unionist Party in 1974, but resigned in 1979 after failing to win a seat for the party in the elections for the European Parliament. During this period he consistently opposed proposals for power-sharing. In 1971 he was narrowly defeated by Bobby Sands in a by-election for the Westminster constituency of Fermanagh and South Tyrone. Some political analysts believe that, ironically, Sands' victory in that election was a watershed, which helped to persuade the IRA and Sinn Fein that they had a better chance of achieving their political ambitions through the ballot box than by the bullet.

The Right Honourable Harry West, MP.

A near-contemporary of West's was **Sir James Kilfedder, MP** (OP, 1941-45), who represented West Belfast at Westminster from 1964 to 1966, when he lost his seat to Gerry Fitt in the election of that year. He won the Westminster seat of North Down in 1970 and held it until his death in 1995. Initially a member of the Ulster Unionist party, he left it in the late 1970s, and for a time sat as an Independent Ulster Unionist. In 1980 he founded the Ulster Popular Unionist party, now defunct.

Desmond Boal (OP, 1946-47) was a prominent Unionist politician in the 1960s. After Portora, he went to Trinity College, Dublin, and had a successful career as a barrister before entering politics as the Unionist member for the Shankill constituency in 1960. After a series of disagreements with O'Neill and subsequent Unionist leaders he became one of the founding members of the Democratic Unionist Party (DUP) in 1971. He was its first Chairman, although he suddenly left politics in 1974, ultimately returning to a legal career.

Two Portorans who figure on the political scene today are **Sir John Gorman, MC, MP** (OP, 1939-41) and **Nigel Dodds, OBE** (OP, 1971-77). Sir John had a distinguished War record in the Irish Guards. He won the MC for outstanding bravery in ramming a German Tiger tank. After the war he joined the RUC and then BOAC, where he became Personnel Director before moving on to take up an appointment as Chief Executive of the Northern Ireland Housing Authority. He represented North Down as an Ulster Unionist MP in the Northern Ireland Assembly, and was also Deputy Speaker of the Assembly from 1999 until he resigned in 2002. He is one of very few Catholics to have been elected as a Unionist representative. At Portora he was a School Prefect and played for the 1st XV.

Sir John Gorman, MC, MP.

Nigel Dodds, who has twice been Lord Mayor of Belfast, is the sitting DUP member at Westminster for Belfast North, and is also General Secretary of the DUP. He has also represented Belfast North in the Northern Ireland Assembly since 1998, and has recently been appointed Deputy Leader of the Democratic Unionist Party.

One of the school's most unusual alumni is **Julian Kulski** (OP, 1946-47), who came to Portora just after the war at the age of 16, through the good offices of George Andrews. His father was Mayor of Warsaw when the Germans invaded Poland, and the young Julian joined the Polish resistance. Despite being jailed by the Gestapo, released and then re-captured and interned in a POW camp in Germany, Kulski survived and made his way to England and eventually to Portora. He subsequently went on to join his father, who was by then in America. After qualifying from Harvard he has become a well-known architect in the States. He must be the only pupil to have arrived at Portora with a lifetime of experience already behind him.

Julian Kulski.

Medicine and science

Portorans have also made a significant contribution to medical research and development and the sciences. **Dr Lombe Atthill** (OP, 1841-44), who wrote a scathing account of his time at Portora in the 1840s, did much in later life to advance the practice of gynaecology as a specialist area of medicine. In 1875 he was elected Master of the Rotunda Hospital in Dublin, and later became President of the Royal Academy of Medicine in Ireland. His *Clinical Lectures on Diseases Peculiar to Women* was long regarded as the best text-book in English on the subject.

Francis Rynd (OP, 1817), who left Portora for TCD, is credited with the invention of the hypodermic syringe. There is a record of his carrying out in 1844 what was probably the world's first-ever subcutaneous injection. Two generations before that, **Naval Surgeon John White** (OP, c1774) had been a pupil at Portora before sailing as the fleet's surgeon with Captain Arthur Philip's First Fleet to Australia in 1787. Through his insistence on strict hygiene he kept the death rate among passengers and crew from fevers and other illnesses to a remarkably low level. According to Captain Philips' report, there were only 23 deaths among the total complement of some 1,300 souls. White subsequently became Surgeon General to Australia's first settlement in Sydney and played no small part in its success.

Dr Lombe Atthill.

Another old Portoran doctor, **C C de B Daly** (OP, 1877), after working at the Rotunda Hospital in Dublin and then as a ship's doctor, went on to organise the Red Cross in the first Sino-Japanese war in 1893 and a Red Cross hospital in the Russo-Japanese war in 1905. In between he was Medical Officer to a number of Cossack regiments in the army of the Tsar. In 1910 he was asked by the Chinese government to return to combat an outbreak of pneumonia in Manchuria. When he eventually retired he had been awarded the Chinese Order of the Double Dragon 1st class, and had been made an honorary mandarin. He also had the Russian, Japanese and Chinese Red Cross medals, a silver cup presented by the Tsar, and the OBE for his service with the Royal Army Medical Corps during World War I.

Later in the century **Denis Burkitt** (OP, c1922), who was born in Enniskillen in 1911 and was briefly at the Preparatory School for Portora, became a brilliant and dedicated surgeon and epidemiologist. Through his work in Uganda, notably in Lira district and at Mulago Hospital in Kampala, he identified a new cancer, Burkitt's Lymphoma, and mapped its distribution

Dennis Burkitt.

A unique display of three British banknotes bearing the signatures of Old Portorans who were Cashiers of the respective banks. At the top Robert Fry, Cashier of The National Bank Limited (Belfast), William Guthrie, Cashier of the Bank of Ireland and lastly, John Fforde, Chief Cashier of the Bank of England.

and incidence. His work contributed significantly to a better understanding of cancer in general and to the recognition that modern processed diets are partly responsible for many of the illnesses that are more common in the West than in Africa. In a memorable introduction to one of his publications, which says much about the man, Burkitt wrote:

> *Attitudes are more important than abilities.*
> *Motives are more important than methods.*
> *Character is more important than cleverness.*
> *Perseverance is more important than power.*
> *And the heart takes precedence over the head.*

A researcher and explorer of a different ilk was **Henry Chichester Hart** (OP, 1862-65). He was a leading Irish botanist and ornithologist who was best known for his work on the flora of Donegal, and as a botanist with an early British polar expedition. He is also remembered as the originator of the Hart walk from Terenure to the top of Lugnaquilla, the highest peak in the Wicklow mountains, and back within twenty-four hours. This walk, the result of a wager which he won with a few minutes to spare, has inspired many similar challenges elsewhere.

Another old Portoran, **Dr Charles Nelson, FLS** (OP, 1960-68), is an outstanding contemporary Irish botanist who has published many works on the flora of Ireland, especially in the Burren region.

Business and finance

Perhaps because of the strong emphasis on the teaching of Classics in the eighteenth and nineteenth centuries, there are few known examples of successful Old Portorans from that time in business and finance. However, the deficit has been made good since then. In a rare coincidence in the 1920s and 1930s, three old Portorans, **Robert Fry** (OP, 1919), **William Guthrie** (OP, 1923) and **John Fforde** (OP, 1932), went on to become the Chief Cashiers of the National Bank in Belfast, the Bank of Ireland and the Bank of England respectively. One of the School's most unusual pieces of memorabilia is a frame containing bank-notes bearing their signatures.

After the war **Sam McGredy** (OP, 1942-48) built up one of the world's great rose nurseries, initially in Portadown and subsequently in New Zealand. He has won virtually all the top rose awards in Ireland, the UK, New Zealand, the US, Australia and the Netherlands. In 1977, the Year of the Rose, the Post Office in the UK issued a commemorative stamp featuring one of his best-loved roses, Elizabeth of Glamis. He cultivated a rose named Mary Rogers, dedicated to the wife of the Headmaster, Val Rogers.

Another Old Portoran, **Sir Roy McNulty** (OP, 1948-55), is currently Chairman of the Civil Aviation Authority. He is also Vice-President of the Engineering Employers' Federation and a member of the Olympic Delivery Authority for the London Olympics 2012. Previously, as President of the Shorts Group, he had been instrumental in transforming it from a loss-making government concern into one of the UK's leading industrial success stories.

Dr Michael West (OP, 1949-55) was until recently Chairman of Keller Group plc, having earlier been its Chief Executive from 1981 to 1995. During that period Keller expanded three-fold. In 1990 he led a management buy-out of the company.

One of the recent Presidents of the London branch of the Old Portora Union, **John Brady** (OP, 1962-69), became a Director of McKinsey and Company, one of the world's leading firms of management consultants. Previously he had qualified as a civil engineer, designing dams, bridges and skyscrapers around the world from Hong Kong to Saudi Arabia. **Liam Strong** (OP, 1956-63), another recent London OPU President, has had a spectacularly successful business career, including spells as Marketing Director of British Airways and Managing Director of Sears, the retail conglomerate that owns Selfridges. He is now leading a private equity group. Both John Brady and Liam Strong were dayboys and have varied but mainly happy memories of the School. They have also been very generous with their support to the Old Portora Union (London Branch) over the years.

In Ireland, **David Kingston** (OP, 1956-61) was CEO of Irish Life for many years before becoming Chairman of the Irish Stock Exchange in Dublin in 1998. On his departure in 2007 his successor, Padraic O'Connor, said of him that '*his leadership was a significant factor in the successful evolution of the Exchange over the past nine years*'. David Kingston remains Chairman of a number of financial services companies and Adjunct Professor of Mathematics at TCD. He is also a past President of the Faculty of Actuaries.

A fellow Old Portoran in Ireland, **Patrick McAfee** (OP, 1951-58), who is a co-founder of the annual Beckett Joyce Award, was a Director of the then Morgan Grenfell for many years, and subsequently Chairman of Deutsche International, Ireland.

Sporting heroes

No account of Old Portorans could fail to recognise the outstanding sporting achievement of **Dickie Lloyd** (OP, 1904-09), the leading international fly-half of his generation. He won 19 caps for Ireland and captained Ireland on 11 occasions. Before that, under the rugby-fanatical Headmaster, Alister McDonnell, he had helped to build at Portora what has been called the greatest school side of all time. Five of that side went on to play for Ireland. It is less well known that Lloyd was also no mean cricketer. He played for the Gentlemen of Ireland and for Lancashire on a number of occasions, notably against the powerful Australian touring side of 1921.

Dickie Lloyd.

Equally outstanding in its field was the achievement of **David Judge** (OP, 1949-54), who was perhaps the greatest Irish hockey player of all time. He amassed 124 Ireland caps over a period of 21 years, and captained his country 31 times. He also played for the Great Britain hockey team on 15 occasions, and competed with them in the 1964 Tokyo Olympics. His achievement is the more remarkable given that hockey was only a minor sport at Portora, played occasionally in the Easter Term.

Other sporting alumni include **John Armstrong** (OP, 1975-80), who rowed for Ireland for a number of years and won Bronze at the World Championships in 1999 in the Lightweight Double Sculls. **James McCoy** (OP, 1970-76) played rugby for Ireland in the 1990 inaugural Rugby World Cup Series in New Zealand, and of course many old Portorans have played for TCD. In his school days at Portora, **Brian Sloane** (OP, 1946-52) had the unique distinction of being selected to play for the Gentlemen of Ireland. In a report of the match, *The Irish Times* commented, '*The Portora schoolboy Sloane made his runs well*'. Ironically, at Portora he was considered to be mainly a very effective fast bowler who could also bat.

Language, literature and the arts

Lastly, but arguably most significantly, old Portorans have made a lasting contribution in the world of literature, the theatre and art. Here three names stand out – **Henry Francis Lyte** (OP, 1803-09), **Oscar Wilde** (OP, 1864-71) and **Samuel Beckett** (OP, 1920-23). It is tempting to think that all of them derived part of their early inspiration from their teachers at Portora, and from the School's beautiful location at the top of a steep hill overlooking the town of Enniskillen, the river and the lake. Describing the scene, **Vivian Mercier** (OP, 1929-36), who became Professor of English at the University of Colorado, writes, '*I do not believe there are ten schools in the world with such a view from their playing fields*'.

We know little of Henry Francis Lyte's time at Portora, which he attended from 1803 to 1809, except that he was educated thanks to the generosity of the Headmaster, Dr Burrowes, after his parents had separated. But we do know that he won the Chancellor's prize for English verse three years in a row at Trinity College, Dublin, which he entered from Portora. Ordained as an Anglican priest in 1814, Lyte served first in the parish of Taghmon, near Wexford, and then as rector of Brixham in south Devon, where he wrote most of his hymns and poetry.

Lyte is best known for the wonderful hymns 'Abide with Me' and 'Praise, My Soul, the King of Heaven'. 'Abide with Me' is reputed to have been the favourite hymn of both King George V and Mahatma Gandhi. It used to be sung every year at the FA Cup Final, and is still played by the massed bands in the Indian army at the Annual Beating of Retreat ceremony in New Delhi, which is the climax of India's Republic Day celebrations. The dramatic spectacle as the sun sets behind the ramparts of Baker and Lutyens' Presidential Palace, and the haunting music, create an unforgettable experience.

Oscar Wilde, whose father was a well-known Dublin surgeon, was at Portora from 1864 to 1871, when he won a Royal Scholarship to TCD. He is

This portrait of Oscar Wilde was painted by M. Rene Thuyns, LetL (Brux) (S, 1942-47) who arrived at Portora during World War II to become the Art Master. Both he and his wife were given residency in England as 'displaced persons' (DPs), because they were friendly allies who had fled from Brussels during the Nazi advance into Belgium. Initially the School Governors declined to display his painting, but attitudes have changed and the portrait now hangs proudly in the entrance hall of the North Wing, adjoining the Seale Room.

The memorial window to Oscar Wilde in
Poets' Corner, Westminister Abbey.
(© Dean and Chapter of Westminister)

remembered by his contemporaries as a rather solitary boy with a penchant
for telling fantastic tales. They could hardly have guessed that he would go on
to become such an iconic literary figure, and perhaps the second most-quoted
writer in the English language after Shakespeare. Could his *'punctuality is the
thief of time'* have been a late protest at the strict timetable imposed by the
Headmaster of his day, the redoubtable Reverend William Steele?

If Wilde was never noted for his sporting prowess, Samuel Beckett, who
was at Portora in the early twenties, excelled at sport. He was the School Light
Heavyweight boxing champion, and also led the 1st XV to the Ulster Schools
Cup Final. He was also a fine cricketer and subsequently played for Trinity
College, Dublin. But there is no record of his having won any literary awards at
School, nor any hint that he would go on to write one of the most important
plays of the twentieth century and become a Nobel Laureate.

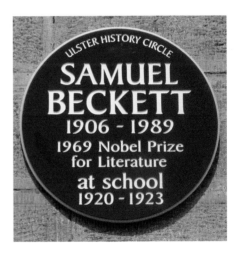

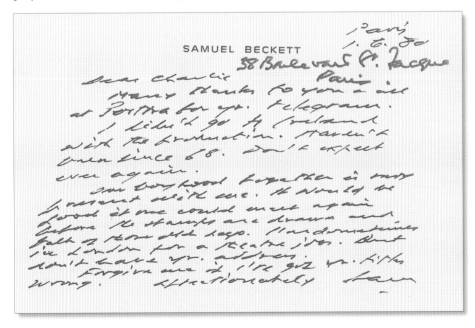

Postcard (dated 1 June 1980) from Samuel
Beckett to General Sir Charles Jones (former
President OPU) who were contemporaries at
Portora during the 1920s.

'Dear Charlie.

*Many thanks to you and all at Portora for
your telegram. I didn't go to Ireland with the
… Haven't been since '68. Don't expect ever
again.*

*Our boyhood together is very present within
one. It would be good if we could meet again
before the stumps are drawn and talk of
those old days. I am sometimes in London for
a theatre idea but don't have your address.
Forgive me if I've got your title wrong.
Affectionately, Sam.'*

Max Adrian.

James Bourchier.

One of Beckett's near-contemporaries at Portora who subsequently graced the stage, not as a playwright but as an actor, was **Max Adrian** (real name Guy Bor; OP, 1918-21). He took a number of leading parts with the Royal Shakespeare Company and the National Theatre Company. Perhaps his best-known screen performance was as the Dauphin in Laurence Olivier's film version of Henry V.

Other noteworthy writers from Portora, though less celebrated than Lyte, Wilde and Beckett, include **James Bourchier** (OP, 1865-68) and **Professor Cyril Falls** (OP, 1902-06).

Bourchier first made his name as *The Times* correspondent in the Balkans and then went on to play an important part in the foundation of the Balkan League, and in championing the Bulgarian people in their struggle for independence from Turkey. When he died in 1920, he was given a state funeral by the Bulgarian government in recognition of his contribution, and a set of stamps was commissioned bearing his portrait and a picture of the monastery where he is buried.

Cyril Falls, who was the son of an Enniskillen solicitor and attended Portora as a dayboy from 1902 to 1906, became military correspondent for *The Times* in World War II. After the war he was elected to the Chichele Chair of the History of War at Oxford. He wrote numerous books of military history, including two on Elizabeth's Irish wars. Apart from distinguishing himself as a professional historian, Falls had also experienced the horror of war at first hand, having served in the famous 36th Ulster Division in World War I when he was twice mentioned in despatches. He was also awarded the Croix de Guerre with two citations.

Brian Harpur, MC (OP, 1931-35) made his mark in the world of the media, not as a writer but as an organiser. He joined Associated Newspapers in London in 1935 as a classified advertising representative and rose to be a Director of the company in 1964, his service there interrupted only by wartime service, during which he won the MC in Italy. He was responsible for expanding the Ideal Home Exhibition to its national fame; he organised the London to New York Air Race in 1969; at the request of the Duke of Edinburgh he organised the first national conference on human values; and after he had retired he formed a club and company to celebrate the passing of Halley's Comet, ready for its return in 1986. This club still exists and sells memorabilia – ashtrays, T-shirts, china, books, wine, ties and such – to raise money to benefit one of the many charities he continued to support.

Today, **Leo McKinstry** (OP, 1977-81), who was Head of School, is well known as a biographer, columnist and political commentator, and **Keith Baker** (OP, 1952-62) is a successful author of contemporary thrillers; he is also a former Head of News and Current Affairs for BBC Northern Ireland. **Norris Davidson** (OP, 1922-29) first made his name as a pioneering film-maker of the silent years, and later as a founding figure of documentary films. He presented an opera programme on radio for RTE for nearly half a century, and is regarded as a central figure in the history of Irish broadcasting and film.

In the world of the arts, **Leslie Waddington** (OP, 1947-52) became one of London's best-known art dealers, with four galleries in Cork Street, while **John Leighton** (OP, 1970-77) has recently become Director of the National Gallery of Scotland. In the world of music, **Neil Hannon** (OP, 1982-89), son of the former Bishop of Clogher and Chairman of the School's Board of Governors, is well known as the founder and leader of the band Divine Comedy. Finally, from the select company of girls who attended Portora in the 1980s, mention should be made of **Zara Turner** (OP, 1977-85), who is making quite a name for herself with a long list of television and film credits to her name.

As the School continues to attract and motivate boys from all walks of life in Fermanagh, and perhaps again in due course girls as well, there is every reason to expect that the proud record of achievement briefly illustrated here will continue in the future.

Neil Hannon.

Finally…

On 10 June 2007, a group of distinguished Governors, former Governors and Old Portorans, gathered at Clogher Cathedral, to attend the annual service of rededication of the Commandery of Ards in Northern Ireland of the Order of St John. From left to right: Patrick Corkey (OP, 1939-44), Knight of St George, former Headboy of Portora; Right Reverend Dr Michael Jackson (OP, 1967-75), Bishop of Clogher, current Chairman of Governors of Portora; Sir John Gorman (OP, 1939-41), Knight of Malta; Right Reverend Gordon McMullan, former Bishop of Clogher, former Chairman of Governors of Portora; John Hughes (OP, 1950-57), Knight of St John, past President of the Old Portora Union (1999).

Zara Turner.

Nine

Reminiscences of School life

When we put out our letter to all known Old Portorans in October 2006 announcing our project, we asked for reminiscences of school days. We know the letter was at least received and read, for well over a hundred replied, some with a hastily written letter, others with several pages beautifully typed, yet others with what appeared to be extracts from their autobiographies; one even sent a hardbacked published book of his life, though he did accompany it with about twenty pages of typed copy relating to his days at Portora, which proved more pertinent.

In our letter we encouraged memories by saying contributors would be able to see their name in print in the final publication, and this was our intention. What has changed from the original idea is that it is not possible to attribute each reminiscence to the contributor by name: some as supplied are too long, while others relate to only part of a story and have needed to be supported by combining contributions. What we have done is to relate as many tales as we can, keeping them grouped by subjects or chronology. We have, of course, listed all those whose stories we have used in the Acknowledgements section at the back of the book.

Please note that some of these reminiscences may repeat or duplicate information covered in previous chapters. You should also remember they are the personal observations and opinions of various Old Portorans at differing times; some of the sentiments and opinions expressed have changed with the passage of time and may not reflect modern thinking.

Left: 'Mum is late' – waiting to be collected at the end of the School day from outside the entrance to Stone Hall.

The mid-nineteenth century

Inevitably most of the information we have gathered relates to the last seventy years, but published memoirs by famous Old Portorans go back further. Lombe Atthill, in his book, 'Recollections of an Irish Doctor', devotes several pages about his three years at school between 1841 and 1843. He was sent to Portora around the age of 13 because of the School's high reputation, but having been at an English Public School he found things were very different here, where pupils were taught only Latin and Greek, with a view to their being prepared for entrance to Trinity College, Dublin. English was hardly taught at all; there was a little ancient history plus some geography. A knowledge of mathematics was assumed and no modern languages were even attempted.

Strangely, there was no automatic promotion to a higher class at the end of each year, so you could (as Atthill did) stay in the same class for three years or more. He wasn't stupid, just not prepared for such a system, and many times he was caned and kept in during the break for not being up to scratch. The headmaster did the caning and from what Atthill says, he enjoyed drawing blood from the hands of idle pupils. Punishment sessions for errant boys were a daily event.

Food at the long tables in the dining hall was plentiful and wholesome, but dreadfully boring. Breakfast, after an hour and a half of school work, comprised hunks of dry bread washed down with milk. No plates, knives or forks, just a usually clean tablecloth to eat off. Lunch after finishing lessons for the day was the same, but without the milk. Dinner at 5.00 pm consisted of joints of roast or boiled meat and potatoes, with never a green vegetable to be seen. Supper at 8.00 pm was breakfast all over again. Every day.

Dormitories held anything up to forty beds. No basins or jugs were allowed there. The lavatory and washing facilities were down in the basement of the building, where wooden bowls were used as basins. There you stood on a saturated wooden plank and washed in cold water from a large tub; all this in pitch dark during winter months and in half-light for the rest of the year since there was only one small window at one end.

Boarders were not allowed out of school bounds at all, unless parents or adult friends visited, and there was no attempt at arranging organised sports. Atthill did introduce cricket as an after-school hours relaxation, but the ground was impossibly bumpy and the game unknown in Northern Ireland at that time; when he left, his cricket club died and the game wasn't reintroduced for many years.

Despite this negative report, Portora must have had a good educational reputation to attract over a hundred boarders in the days before the railway had reached Enniskillen. Certainly Atthill learned enough there to encourage his ambition to enter the medical profession. He did not immediately go to university but served an apprenticeship with a doctor first; he then went to Trinity College, Dublin, for his MD degree, later achieving Mastership of the Rotunda Hospital in Dublin and Presidency of both the Royal College of Physicians and of the Royal College of Medicine in Ireland.

Getting to school

Before the coming of the railway to Enniskillen in the late 1850s, boarders arrived by the only public transport available, the Bian Longcar daily service, centred on Clonmel but running from Cork, Dublin, Sligo and Omagh amongst many other towns. The longcars were a service set up after the Napoleonic wars, using some of the thousands of horses suddenly available. There were also the mail coaches, of course, and though rather more expensive, these were nevertheless often loaded with boarders from all over Ireland, even if this meant several days' travelling. What to do to pass the time on such a long journey? One boy was reported for firing at passers-by with his pea shooter, easy when you shared the driver's seat on top, though his taking of hot strong ale at the many horse-changing stops went unremarked, since at least such thirst-quenching had much less chance of causing illness than drinking the local water. (In the 1930s several small-beer pots were dug up at the School which had been used for such supping, but of 'small beer' in the nineteenth century and for the same reason.) Whether this induced behaviour worthy of a flogging or not, many tales are told of undisciplined behaviour in the nineteenth century, such as the boy who pulled a knife on the Headmaster and was horsewhipped and expelled. The cane was the more usual implement for punishment but, wielded with unnecessary violence, it could rebound on the caner, being grabbed from his hand and used against him.

With more boys arriving from across Ireland after the railway came through, there was a greater likelihood of infectious diseases, such as measles, scarlet fever and diphtheria being imported, so in the 1860s an isolation hospital was built in the grounds about a hundred yards from the School. Later, after World War I, when a war memorial sanatorium was built, the isolation hospital became Liberty Hall.

Being caught out of bounds was a regular reason for punishment. Enniskillen town was out of bounds for boarders, but that is where the local hostelries were, as were young girls, and both were good reasons for breaking out. Getting back in unobserved was part of the game, but occasionally this had its problems too, especially if too much liquor had been taken, such as the occasion when two boys, returning late at night, attempted to climb over the wall and one fell and knocked himself unconscious, lying bleeding on the ground. His mate found him there being tidied-up by a pig from the school farm which was licking the blood.

Upper School in the first half of the twentieth century
The earliest reference to away sporting fixtures was in 1896, with a report of matches against Derry Academical Institution and Sligo Grammar School. These appear to be football matches and possibly soccer rather than rugby, since the result of one of them is mentioned as being a win for Portora, 'one goal to nil'. In 1908 Portora took a rowing team to the Boyne Regatta, winning the Corporation Cup. Taking the boat and oars by train must have been a difficult exercise and indeed on this occasion the team had to miss the last race since they were running late and would have missed their train back to Enniskillen had they waited.

Portora, c1882. An informal photograph showing staff and pupils. It is interesting to note items for extra-curricular activities. Pupils were allowed bicycles and several are sporting racquets for fives and tennis.

Ruins of Portora Castle looking towards Lower Lough Erne from the left bank of the Narrows.

The railways didn't always work, as was the case during the Irish Civil War in 1922, when the trains to Cork had been stopped, and boys going home on holiday had to go by train to Belfast, ship to Liverpool and another ship from there to Cork.

From the time of World War I until they ceased in the 1950s, railways were the usual way for boarders to arrive from all parts of Ireland. A special coach marked 'Portora' was attached to the train in Cork, transferred across Dublin and added to a train leaving Amiens Street Station for Dundalk, to be attached to another train for the third part of the journey to Enniskillen. Heavy luggage was put in the hands of a carrier there, who took it up to the School while the boys made their own way through the town.

Following World War I, with boarders coming from all over Ireland, the School introduced a House system for the first time, allocating boys to one of four Houses (Ulster, Munster, Leinster and Connaught), regardless of which province they actually lived in. It is interesting to note that Connaught was spelt the Anglo-Irish way right up to the period after World War II, before being changed to the more geographically correct Connacht. Each House had its Housemaster, who was usually unmarried and who lived on the premises so as to be available at all times. Most masters in those days were unmarried, and it wasn't until the 1930s that married Housemasters were introduced. The introduction of their ladies, married though they were, added to the pleasures

Combined Cadet Force (CCF) parade during the late 1940s. At this time the CCF was over 120 strong with four platoons, a band, and Naval and RAF sections.

of school life. Headmaster Stuart's wife, Barbara, was a stunning blonde, and twenty years later Captain Jack Wheeler's wife would join him at school dances and concerts to give a superb exposition of the tango.

The curriculum had moved with the times and the term report form from 1923 lists, amongst the more usual and still current subjects, Commercial Subjects and Shorthand, the 'Information Technology' of those days.

Instant news from the outside world

Other than carefully selected daily newspapers, news of the outside world was hard to come by, until in 1924 Captain Campbell installed a four-valve radio set for the use of the school Radio Club, through which they were able to hear news and other programmes from the BBC, once they had overcome the difficulty of rigging up an aerial and earth. They were able to listen also to European broadcasts from as far away as Rome and Madrid. In the following decade Major Butler set up loudspeakers in the dormitories in Liberty Hall and relayed the BBC programmes there in the evenings; not only the news, but dance bands playing in London, too. There must have been, in addition, the official School Wireless, for the 1936 School Rules state that boys will be allowed to listen only to the news, nothing else.

Dr Kidd, Medical Officer to the School for over 50 years.

A pre-war OTC camp at Tidworth Pennings, 1938. Cadet Tom Milligan makes some last minute adjustments to a kit lay-out prior to the arrival of the Inspecting General.

The school doctor

A character from this period that must be mentioned is the school medical officer, one Dr Kidd, an elderly local GP of good report. 'Boozy', as he was always known from his rather red nose, though he never touched a drop, was of the old school of medicine as indeed he had to be, having trained under the Joseph Lister of late Victorian days who introduced the idea of antiseptic surgery. Boozy's life as a GP had introduced other rules to his practice and one of them was widely broadcast throughout the school: *"Every boy"*, his notice in every toilet read, *"shall have a movement of the bowels every day before breakfast. Failure to do so must be reported to matron."* A dose of syrup of figs would be administered, or at best a couple of squares of Exlax medicinal chocolate; indeed a reminiscence of that time recalls that a whole bar of this was given by a boy to another who was greedy for chocolate, resulting in quite serious illness for a week. Dr Bryson replaced 'Boozy' during the War, and any bug remotely likely to be catching would be prescribed a dose of M&B 693 in those pre-antibiotic days. On arrival for their first time, all new boys would be asked for a 'specimen' by Dr Bryson. By some, this was simply not understood and was likely to produce a spit into the specimen jar, or tap water, until the good doctor made his needs clear by using a more basic description.

The Officer Training Corps (OTC) and its successors

Major Butler and Captain Henry Scales ran the OTC, an organisation that proved to be vital when World War II broke out. Both men had served during World War I in variously the Royal Engineers, the Royal Tank Corps, the North Irish Horse and the Royal Dublin Fusiliers. OTC camps were held in England during the summer holidays. The Headmaster, the Reverend E G Seale, through the Headmasters Conference of which he was a member, had ensured that any boy gaining his Certificate A would be assumed to be officer material in the event of war, and so it proved. One boy received his calling-up papers while still at school in 1941; within a week he was in camp in England, and within a further month had set sail for India to attend an Officers' training camp.

The OTC became the Junior Training Corps (JTC) during the War. The Lee Enfield rifles were taken away for real soldiers to use and were replaced with ancient carbines; military training went on as before but with more immediate intent. In 1941 the Air Training Corps (ATC) came to Portora and was under the management of two masters, Flying Officer A W Barnes and Pilot Officer J M Malone, who received commissions into the Royal Air Force. All ATC cadets were able to use and enjoy the facilities of the RAF stations on and around Lough Erne. The members were taken for short flights in flying boats, Sunderlands and Catalinas, at Castle Archdale and at Killadeas, while really scary trips in Swordfish and Wellington bombers were to be had at St Angelo airfield. During the summer holidays, dayboys would put on their uniforms and cycle out along the road, calling at each station in turn until, with luck, they scrounged a flight. It helped if you had Sergeant's stripes on your arm. The aerodrome was originally put there in 1940 as an emergency landing ground for American Flying Fortresses and Liberators which were being lease-loaned to Britain, but which could not make it to landings in Scotland and England; there were inevitably many crashes in the vicinity, when boys would cycle out to see the sometimes dreadful remains scattered over a hill.

With so much air activity suddenly available, the ATC was never short of members. Potential aircrew cadets were taught navigation and the like, while those with poor eyesight or with other reasons for not being able to join the RAF as aircrew, were let loose on a huge radial aero-engine delivered to the School and kept in the room next to the Scout hut, where it was dismantled easily enough but never made airworthy.

Boy Scouts

There have been a few reminiscences about the 1st Portora Scout Troop, run before and at the start of World War II by George Andrews. One contributor recalls the summer camps in the grounds of Lord Mountbatten's castle, Classibawn in Mullaghmore, when fishing for mackerel produced hundreds of fish for supper; another, the camps on islands on Lough Erne, when Andrews insisted on just a single match being allowed to pass one's 2nd Class firelighting test, *"because there's a war on"* he would explain; building rafts from young trees to attempt to get to the next island; camp fires in the evening before retiring to old World War I bell tents for the night; and occasional forays to set-up a 24-hour camp by just two boys.

This last was part of the 1st Class test, when the aspiring scout would take along a tenderfoot. On one of these, during the war, 'Twinky' Miller (later killed in the Korean war), the son of the Officer in Command of the RUC training depôt in Enniskillen, took his tenderfoot up into the hills near the Border. They put up their tent and lit a cooking fire, by which time it was dark. Next thing they knew an RUC constable was yelling at them to put the fire out: had they not heard of the blackout? Twinky apologised, the constable recognised him for who he was, the son of the boss, and, embarrassed, said no more, though the fire was quickly extinguished.

Boarders and dayboys

The war changed a lot of things, both for the School and the pupils. Other facts of life remained the same, such as the attitude of dayboys towards boarders and vice versa. Boarders tended to take a rather arrogant attitude towards not only dayboys but also new boys of either category, and even against some of the teaching staff. *Beati Pacifici*

German 12 inch Howitzer Trophy gun which stood on the School terrace during the inter-war years. A popular but unsubstantiated rumour covering the origin of World War I trophies was that the War Office distributed trophy guns to those schools that had been attended by a pupil who had been awarded the Victoria Cross. At one stage the Howitzer was positioned outside the School gates, but was later moved to the School terrace. It was returned for high-grade scrap metal as part of the munitions effort during World War II.

Scout camp in the late 1960s.

(Blessed are the Peacemakers) may have been the school motto then, but it didn't always show. Maybe there were no peacemakers.

Boarders had parents who were prepared, or could afford, to spend considerable amounts of money on their sons, while dayboys were largely the sons of local farmers or shopkeepers. The latter spoke with a Fermanagh accent that was difficult for a boy from Dublin or Cork to decipher. 'Daydogs', as the boarders referred to them, were seen as unsophisticated 'country boys', while the boarders were known by dayboys not to be sensible enough to be allowed out of school bounds into Enniskillen unless accompanied by a 'responsible adult', as the school rules put it. With wartime shortages of public transport, dayboys were regularly able to blame it for absence from morning prayers: *"The bus was late"*, was their eternal excuse. A dayboy had to be outstanding either in the classroom or on the sports field to be truly accepted. In earlier days there had been open warfare between the two tribes but during a World War there were other, more important things to think of.

Two boarders in pre-war days owned horses that were stabled near Enniskillen, and they were allowed to hunt with the Fermanagh Foxhunt. One of them was allowed to keep his three-wheeler car in the school yard so that they could get to the hunts. This was no passing schoolboy phase either, for one is now, after seventy years, the longest-serving Master of Hounds in the British Isles.

Not all dayboys were ignored by boarders, especially if they were useful, such as a family that lived in Willoughby Place. The houses had outbuildings behind them and these made a perfect place to which boarders could creep out of school in the middle of the night, there to convene for a smoke and to drink cider and gin.

The years leading up to the War in 1939 saw a trickle of non-Irish boarders, this time from across the British Empire, whose parents felt it necessary to leave places such as Hong Kong, India and Egypt. When war actually began, there was another influx of boys from England, either as evacuees to a safe area or the sons of military men posted to Northern Ireland. The Belfast blitz in 1941 also brought some boys from schools there.

Rationing during World War II

Another fundamental wartime difference was the rationing of food. Fed by an institution, the boarders felt the full force of shortages; meals, which had never been the most pleasant side of school life, took a downward turn, especially when the long-serving caterer left to marry a teacher, and in turn moved out of the district on war service. Dayboys, on the other hand, many coming from a farming food-producing background, felt little effect, with the possible exception of tea (2oz a week each); they could make up for that with milk from their father's herd. Two Scouts, camping at the Marble Arch, once took a night away to assist a professional smuggler by traipsing over the mountains to the Free State, with sacks of Ulster-rationed tea for the half-ounce-a-week South, returning with bags of butter for the rationed North. Egg-rationing was another unknown to dayboys but felt hugely by boarders; should one achieve a place on a school sports team, however, bacon and eggs were given once a week. During summer the Scout Troop took part in assisting with the harvest on local farms.

Early in the war, Headmaster Stuart decided to keep some hens, in order, he said, *"to help the war effort."* As near as could be told he and his family were the only beneficiaries. One day a few boys got into the hen-house and hypnotized all the hens by laying the hen's head flat on a long board and drawing a straight chalk line away from its beak. For a week or so the hens stopped laying. Boys were not the only enemy the hens had: rats soon discovered the source of eggs and some boys were paid by the Head to catch them. Temptation is a dreadful thing and an egg a lovely thing to eat, so no doubt those that went missing were blamed on the rats, none of whom had anything to do with it.

Travelling away from school had its advantages if it took one across the Border into the Free State. A rugby team visit to Sligo meant that one could buy butter, jam and other rationed food, smuggling it back to the North. The journey was by train to Sligo via the Sligo, Leitrim and North Counties Railway. On the way back to school, at the customs post there was a platform on one side of the train only, so bags of smuggled food were hung from the outside door-handles on the blind side, or at least they were until the customs men learned of the trick.

The jam could be added to the bread and margarine supplied by friendly school maids, so the Sunday picnics held down by the Narrows near the Castle in self-made huts built of sticks were all the tastier. Sweets and chocolate, also smuggled from the Free State on cycling trips across the Border, added to the illicit pleasure. Biscuits, purloined from the Staff Common Room located just below a junior dorm, added still more essential sweetness to wartime rations.

From 1942 to 1944 County Fermanagh was a training ground for the American Army; indeed their soldiers outnumbered the local population at one time. With time on their hands and a new country to explore, with cheap cigarettes in their pockets, these doughboys found their way to Portora, where they would stand on the Terrace and gaze in awe at the main School building, having been told by helpful students, in return for a packet of chewing gum, candy or a packet of Lucky Strike or Camel cigarettes, that the building was just one year younger than their own United States.

The Americans used the lower playing fields on Sundays to play baseball, and many made friends with boarders watching the game whilst stuck there over the weekends. Other American-watching, also often on Sundays, could be carried out round the Portora Castle ruins, where the soldiers could be seen entertaining local girls, undisturbed except for boys noisily chucking sticks at or near the action.

Wartime staff changes

From early in the War several teachers left the staff to join the armed forces, and as a result the level of education in some subjects dropped as temporary wartime substitute 'gangers', the school slang for teachers, of both sexes and often straight out of university without any previous teaching experience, took on the job. Some left after a short while, others settled in and were later appointed

Pupils enjoying an informal photo-call during a School trip to Paris in 1936; see page 174 for further information.

Rugby 1st XV, before their semi-final match against Royal Belfast Academical Institution, 1948: (standing) D J Connell, H R R Fry, C S M Kilroy, W D Kinley, S S Brown (captain), B E Reid, C N G Bruce, W Allen, S J Shanks; (sitting) N J Shelley-Smith, D R Fullerton, P T P Homan, J B Quigg, W J Crowe, W G S Spence.

Changing fashions for schoolboys at Gloucester House: (above) top hat and tails from Stuart's time as Headmaster in the 1940s, (bottom) herringbone suit from Graham's time as Headmaster, 1947.

to the permanent staff. One was there because he had been a refugee from Hitler's Germany. The addition of female teachers in the Upper School at this time has also given rise to a number of memories. One such tale relates to Miss 'Clapper' Bell, a maiden of uncertain years and an excellent teacher of Maths and Chemistry, who was believed to have a crush on a good-looking student who did not reciprocate her passion. One day the boy was searching for some paperwork in a filing cabinet when Clapper saw him and ill-advisedly cried out, "*You! Take your hand out of my drawers!*"

Discipline

Discipline under Seale and his successor Stuart was, by modern standards, harsh but effective. In Seale's time the cane was used by the Headmaster. He had three canes which he kept behind the door in his study. They were known as Tom, Dick and Harry, varying from thin, to medium, to thick, and were always administered by him in multiples of three whacks. As well as Seale, the Deputy Head (Mickey Murfet), Housemasters and School Prefects were allowed to beat errant boys. Boarders who were late for morning roll call more than twice in a week were caned on a Saturday night by the Deputy Headmaster ("*Bend towards the window*", he would say in a Cambridge accent). Under Headmaster Stuart, caning was much rarer and only he could administer it. A copy of the Rules and Bounds was given to each boarder and their breach meant a caning. Being caught smoking was a caning matter too, proving that the 'perfect cover' was anything but. This so-called cover was to smoke in the piggery while it existed, on the theory that the smell of the pigs would drown the smell of tobacco. Wrong. The dayboys' bicycle shed by the entrance gates was another hideout, and probably safer. Detention after school hours meant missing sport and anyway was rarely applied, since it meant the master responsible would have to oversee the culprit. Impositions were more likely, to be done in one's own valuable time.

Located so close to water, the School has had a boat club for many years and its history is recalled earlier in this book. Water, however, can be used for more than just organised sport. There have been many reminiscences of unofficial sport, very much against the rule that boarders shall not, in any circumstances, boat or swim there unless under strict supervision. At night, the boathouse, conveniently well away from dormitories, could be opened, and a training tub slipped into the water for a row down the Narrows, to Devenish even, possibly forgetting the harder row back against the current. Other boys would creep out in the dark and swim across the Narrows into Frying Pan Lake and back. Usually at night, these forays were seldom if ever discovered.

The Prep School and Gloucester House

The Prep School, founded in 1915 in a successful attempt to increase the number of boarders, was under the control of Miss E E Hunt, newly arrived on the staff and known to all as Lizzie. The boys were provided with Spartan accommodation in a dormitory on an upper storey of the main building, next to the Headmaster's house. Wood flooring, metal beds, no curtains was the order of the day; personal cleanliness was enabled by providing each boy with his own bedside washing facilities, unlike those of sixty years earlier. Unfortunately for the pupils, Miss Hunt's bedroom was immediately above their dormitory, with just a thin wooden floor between her and the boys' changing room and WC, so there were few secrets she did not share with them. During the Spanish 'flu epidemic of 1918 she proved to be a real warrior, helping Matron for long hours in the sick room.

Saturday night was bath-night in preparation for church the following morning. The two baths were filled and Mrs Mavitty, the matron, and Aggie, the maid, supervised the scrubbing. No high jinks or horseplay were permitted by Matron; a solemn, if cleansing, occasion.

A 6th form Prefect was in charge of the dormitory, and he was allowed to use the cane if boys did not settle down to sleep, though this was rare. The Duty Master visited all dormitories to say good night and to ensure that peace reigned. The morning wake-up bell was rung by Tom Ashe. He was a 60- or 70-year old (in the early 1930s) who lived with his wife on the ground floor of Liberty Hall and also ran the tuck shop.

Sunday morning meant getting dressed in Eton suits; the putting on of the starch-stiffened collar was made easier by sucking the stud-holes until they were soft. Breakfast was followed by writing home to parents and, afterwards, donning straw hats (in the summer term) or top hats and joining the crocodile to walk to St Macartin's Cathedral, where the boys occupied one of the galleries. There they could spot Lord Belmore, who arrived in his horse-drawn carriage, noticing that he dusted each page of the Prayer Book with a white linen handkerchief.

After church and lunch, Prep boys had to sit and read a book for half an hour, and afterwards be taken for a country walk by Miss Hunt, to Kinawley Quarry, Rossorry or the lake shore road. Never through the town, say several correspondents, but the author of this chapter recalls Miss Hunt and her crocodile passing his father's house at the other end of town and learning to scrounge a square of chocolate from her, so they must occasionally have taken the liberty of being walked through Enniskillen.

Following the Sunday evening meal there was a church service in the Dining Hall, with the whole school attending and the Headmaster's wife, Margaret Seale, playing the harmonium. The last hymn was always 'Abide with Me'. Each night, not just on Sundays, Prep School boys went to Matron's room where they knelt down to say their prayers.

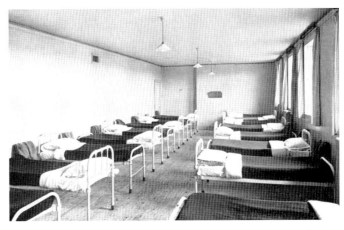

Gloucester House dormitory, 1950s. Note the regimentation and the sequence of beds ranged head to tail. Health and Safety Regulations of those times.

Gloucester House boys pose informally for the camera, c1950s.

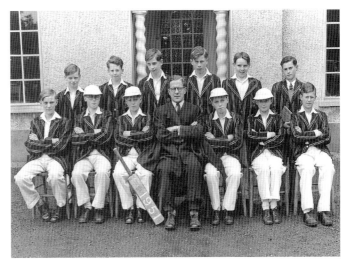

Gloucester House Cricket team, 1951. Seated in the middle is PL (Paddy) Rice, a former pupil at Portora and pre-war member of the staff, who enlisted in the army at the beginning of hostilities. On demobilisation, he rejoined the staff as Headmaster of Gloucester House, in succession to Mr J V Tapley. He was a popular Headmaster in the Junior School and well known in the Upper School for his strong support of activities in the Combined Cadet Force. He resigned as Headmaster of Gloucester House to join the Royal Army Education Corps (RAEC).

Food in the 1930s was adequate. The school had its own herd of Friesian cattle which supplied milk, as well as having pigs and poultry, all kept in outbuildings. Apples in season were pilfered whenever seen. If you found an egg in a hedgerow, that was a bonus and was handed to a maid at tea time to be boiled. If there were any spare slices of bread, these were tucked under your jacket and toasted in one of the several coke-fuelled boilers. The best of these was in the Sanatorium, usually empty, which could be got into via a window that didn't close properly. Jam or spreads were never on the menu; for such luxuries one relied on the tuck box brought each term, though even these could be denied by Miss Hunt if she saw misbehaviour at table.

At much the same time that Seale retired in 1936 (and died two months later), when Stuart became Headmaster, the Prep School became Gloucester House, located in a lovely new building at the bottom of the hill. Mr Barnes was appointed Headmaster, assisted by his wife Clarice, but Lizzie Hunt remained in charge of the largest class, 'B' set. She had a sitting room located right by the classroom where she would take her morning break, able to watch errant boys doing 'Terrace Parade' outside her French window. Round and round they would go, wasting away perfectly good break-time just because they had misbehaved in her class. Lizzie wore plain Bakelite bangles on her wrist, one in each of the School House colours plus a black one; if the black one was worn closest to her hand, she was in a particularly bad mood and liable to lash out for the smallest offence. Her method of teaching the noun-endings in the 1st and 2nd declensions in Latin was to use a model telegraph pole with three cross beams, and one learned to recite the correct endings as she pointed to each in turn. It worked, as several recent correspondents have told us, for they remember them seventy years later.

Discipline in Gloucester House was, in those pre-war days, firm but fair. Apart from 'Terrace Parade' there was 'The Slipper'. This worn, shiny bedroom slipper was the ultimate weapon and was wielded by the Headmaster, Barnes, who alone had the authority to use it, with two, four or at worst six smacks at a time across the bottom. It hurt, but no lasting damage was done, and why it had been deserved tended to remain in the memory. Much joy was expressed by all when Mr Barnes' dog stole it and chewed it beyond further use. It was, of course, immediately replaced.

Also on the Gloucester House Staff from 1936 was a young Mr (later Colonel) Halpin, in those days with a hugely thick head of hair, accounting for his nickname of 'Hairy' Halpin. In later years, when his full head of hair had diminished, his nickname changed to 'Buddy' Halpin.

At the back end of the new Gloucester House, very soon after it had been opened, a temporary wooden hall was added, known officially as the Recreation Hall but called the Rec by everyone. Here were held morning prayers, and various plays and concerts featuring the percussion band, piano solos and duets, all in front of visiting parents. It was also used by the new Wolf Cub pack when Mr Jim Tapley joined the staff.

Although the Prep school was originally intended to be for boarders only, from quite early on the pupils included dayboys and, being very young, these were without exception from homes in or very near Enniskillen. The transition

Another memory, relating to the sexual attitudes of the day, concerns Headmaster Stuart who at some time before coming to Portora had edited a special Schools edition of Shakespeare's plays. These were the official versions used in the School when studying for Junior or Senior Certificates, and had been varied from the original by the total exclusion of any reference to sexual activities between characters, even if this meant wiping out several lines from a speech and almost killing off its meaning. In this, dayboys had an advantage over boarders, since many knew girls from the Collegiate school and had the opportunity to read their unexpurgated editions.

from kindergarten to Prep school was usually marked by their being given their first 'grown-up' bicycle; the fact that an eight year old boy would be allowed to cycle through the town in all weathers and – during World War II – with heavy army traffic, is a comment on the Health and Safety attitudes of those days.

There was fun to be had during the daily journey and one recollection is the 'initiation' ceremony each went through. It took place at the 'Round 0', where a gentle incline led from the road to the lake side. The game was to whiz down the incline and through a large, deep puddle that always formed at the bottom. With foreknowledge one knew one could build up enough speed to get to the other side before stopping, but new boys were ignorant of this: they would approach the puddle carefully and inevitably come to a stop in its middle, whereupon anything up to half a dozen lads would come tearing down, though the puddle and soak the innocent stuck beside his bicycle.

Those living on the Pound Brae had the pleasure of dashing down the hill, over the railway bridge with two sharp bends and onto the main road at the bottom, regardless of traffic, pride insisting that this be done without brakes. One boy recalls that his speedometer touched 40 mph. No serious accidents are recalled. The disadvantage came at the end of the day with the long push up the steep hill to home.

Team sport was restricted to cricket and soccer. The only away cricket matches that can be recalled were those against Sion Mills. Otherwise two form teams would be selected to play against each other. There was another version of cricket played in break times, with a tennis ball and a stick like a broken stump acting for the bat. Fast and furious is the only description of play; the only two ways to be out were by being caught or bowled, whereupon the catcher or bowler took the bat.

Soccer was the only football played in Gloucester House, and a regular fixture was against the boys from the Enniskillen Model School who always trounced us; 12–0 would be a usual sort of score.

Boxing, too, was encouraged at Gloucester House, under the control of the Sergeant Major, and more than one boy from those days recalls having a couple of teeth loosened in friendly bouts in the C-Set classroom or the Rec.

The Enniskillen Lawn Tennis Club, under the Presidency of Henry Scales, opened a junior section available to those who had reached ten years old and quite a few Prep school dayboys – and later, in the 1950s, boarders – took advantage of this.

The Gloucester House sports day featured cross-country, running, jumping and tug-o'-war, as well as the Fathers' Race. Medals were awarded to the winning boys and the silver Dickson Cup given by Mr 'Dentist' Dickson was won by the best overall athlete.

All boys were taught to swim by Sergeant Major Ingham. This took place in the old pool down beside Portora Castle. The water in the pool was regularly refreshed by the ups and downs of Lough Erne's level, brought on by changing weather. A boy still learning to swim would be strapped into a safety harness which was hooked to a sort of fishing rod held by the Sergeant and led up and down the length of the pool. It worked.

With modern furnishings throughout the new Prep School building, both food and personal comfort were a huge change from the old arrangements. The two new dormitories had fewer, but more comfortable, beds, lockers were part of the furniture and generally things were right up to twentieth century standards.

Early post-war years

In the Upper School, the arrival of Douglas Graham as Headmaster, following both the end of World War II and Stuart's leaving, produced many changes. Firstly, Graham was himself an OP (as a boy he had been kicked out of the Rowing Club for smoking in the boathouse). Secondly, his appointment was a reversion to having a 'Man of the Cloth' as the Head. Thirdly, he had had an excellent war as a Chaplain in the Royal Navy. In his youth he had been boxing heavyweight champion of the British Universities and bore the appropriate cauliflower ears to prove it. This sport was encouraged by him at first, though in later years, in schools for which he was responsible after he left Portora, he banned it when it became common knowledge that it could cause brain damage. However, while he was at Portora there were regular inter-House boxing matches. Some boys had learned the rules of the game, but many tended to use the ring to settle a score in the same way as they did amongst themselves outside the ring, roughly and toughly.

Headmaster Graham's attitude to discipline was strong. He had not only served in the Royal Navy, he had taught at English Public Schools including Eton, so despite his calling to the Church he used the cane just as his forebears had over the centuries. One boy was caught wearing brown shoes instead of the regulation black, was called to the Head's study and given six strokes, wielded by a strong, physically large man: the memory stays with him to today. Other recollections from that time include Lizzie Hunt giving you a rap over the knuckles for crossing your legs ("*You will grow up with a crushed spine!*") and Henry Scales making you stand in the corner of the laboratory, facing the wall, for the whole of the period if he caught you using foul language; he would also make you stand up on the bench for inattention. Well, the tiny spiders that wove their webs across the water taps in front of you were often doing more interesting things and could be encouraged to crawl over your hand. An offence deserving punishment, though rarely committed, was to connect the water tap to the gas tap with rubber tubing and turn on both. This flooded the gas pipes and meant a major exercise to clean them out. Even then the gas would sometimes blip and belch with uncleared water. Laziness in class, if reported and repeated often enough, was sufficient ground for a caning from one's Housemaster.

Little has been reported in the many reminiscences we have received about initiation rites for new boys. One such relates in some detail to the large dormitory on the top floor of the old block where new boys slept for their first year. The dorm was divided down the middle by a low partition with washbasins along its length, and new boys on their first night were made to do a circuit or two round the length in the nude, while Prefects and other older boys flicked heavy wet towels at the passing flesh. Another, in the 1950s, was the

With the coming of peace in the mid-1940s, overseas visits were once again possible, and groups of boys went to France or Switzerland to improve their French, while similar groups came to Portora from Europe in exchange. One remarkable and most un-Irish teenage boy to arrive in 1945 had spent the war in Warsaw as a commando, fighting the German Wehrmacht and SS on the streets of his native city. His memories of Portora make it sound like a paradise after all he had been through; no doubt he was admired by his fellow students for what he had done and experienced, but he was also especially welcomed when his ability to box and row became clear.

ducking in the lily ponds with the head held right under, or, as a variation of this, having the face held under the water in the drinking fountain by the Murfet Cloisters. None of these was 'official', just expected.

The OTC reinvented as the CCF

The OTC, which had become the JTC during World War II, now became the Combined Cadet Force (CCF), taking in the ATC and the newly-formed Sea Cadets, these last encouraged by the arrival of Graham and the return of George Andrews. All were under the command of Col Halpin, who eventually earned his Territorial Decoration for years of this work. The day he was to be presented with the medal was marked by the arrival at the school of the GOC Northern Ireland, who having had the CCF paraded for his inspection, discovered that he had left Halpin's TD on his desk in Belfast. *"No matter"*, said Captain Scales, who had received his TD some years before, *"I have one of those at home; give me twenty minutes."* He dashed the full length of Enniskillen to his home, returned in no time and Col Halpin was duly decorated.

Once a year there was an official 'war' between the JTC and the Sea Cadets, when the JTC were dug in at the top of the hill and the Sea Cadets went to battle with them, arriving from the shores of the lake. On one occasion, when the JTC had settled in for the night and were asleep (even the sentries, one supposes), two Sea Cadets, no doubt using Boy Scout training from George Andrews, crept up and stole the rifles conveniently piled for use the next morning. The loss was reported to the police, the rifles reappeared and the two Cadets were duly chastised, though the Headmaster and the Police DI congratulated them for winning the war.

The Duke of Edinburgh gold awards provided the excuse for another CCF expedition, this time to the Mourne Mountains. Six cadets set off for Castlewellan and were required to visit several summits and make a record of their achievements thereafter. To prove there had been no short cuts, they had to record the date of a penny left in a tin at the top of each mountain. It was Easter time, at the end of a cold, snowy winter, and the two-man tents they shared did little to keep out the cold and damp. Basic food rations had to be prepared on a methylated spirit stove, which ran out of fuel before cooking was completed. The descent next morning, a Sunday, was down a steep mountain track, with deep snow lying on high heather which obliterated the track, and two lads lost

Armistice Day, 1950. Portora CCF bugles and drums assembled outside the dayboys' shed prior to marching onto the parade ground.

CCF wireless demonstration for the Annual Inspection by the General Officer Commanding (GOC), c1950.

Rowing IV in the 'Narrows', late 1940s.

Rowing past Enniskillen Castle.

their way, ending up stumbling into a small church where a dozen parishioners were waiting to start the service. The boys were directed back to base, only to learn that the mountain rescue teams had been alerted and a helicopter dispatched from Aldergrove to find them.

When World War II ended, the ATC began to lose the opportunities for flying from Lough Erne because the flying boats were taken away. At first the occasional flight was still possible, and the airstrip at St Angelo added the opportunity for gliding lessons, but the peacetime highlights were the trips abroad that were now possible. These included a tour of Germany to see the dreadful results of our wartime bombing. On another trip a few lucky cadets were chosen to act as cabin boys by RAF Transport Command flying in York planes, converted Lancaster bombers with up to forty passengers, to such places as Gibraltar, Malta, Fayed on the Suez Canal and Iraq.

An International School again

The 1950s saw another influx of boarders from all over the world. The British Empire was gradually being dismantled and Britain was getting back some of its good name for living standards. For these reasons the School attracted boys from countries such as Malaya, Hong Kong, Sarawak, Tanganyika, the Gold Coast, Kenya, Northern and Southern Rhodesia, Arabia and South America, along with exchange students from the USA and Canada. These, mixed with boys from all over the UK and Ireland, melded into one reasonably happy brew. Some of these overseas boarders found themselves residing in The Redoubt, little improved since it had been a hospital for shell-shocked soldiers of the Great War. Not only was it unheated, frost on the bed covers in the morning being not unknown, but the World War II emergency water tank was still there, something that would not be acceptable nowadays. Getting to school required a walk along the full length of Willoughby Place which had to be made before breakfast, with the threat of a caning if one was late more than twice in a week.

Conditions get better

However, with the removal of wartime rationing, food served in the dining hall gradually improved, in variety if not in the cooking. The old subsistence diet of pots of porridge and piles of soda bread washed down with

…continued on page 232

The silent piano…

On the last evening of Summer Term 1955, there was a well attended 'musical extravaganza' held in the Steele Hall, with parents and the cultural elite of Enniskillen Town as guests. There were performances by visiting artists, including the internationally known local duet of Joan and Valerie Trimble, as well as by talented pupils and selected members of staff. In addition, there was an excellent rendition of 'Les Beaux Gendarmes' by **Ronnie Frazer** (OP, 1947-55), a well known and talented international amateur opera singer.

The final act of the evening was to be a another piano duet, this time by two members of the staff, **A (Tony) E Smith** (S, 1952-65), the Director of Music, and **J W Bunting** (S, 1953-56), who taught languages. Amongst the boys, Smith was considered to be rather strict, whilst Bunting was new and very popular, but not known for keeping order. All evening there were rumours that Smith might be the target of a musical incident.

Anyway the audience, which had enjoyed the programme so far, was now listening to the opening bars of the duet, when abruptly there was a loud plunking noise from the bass section of the Bunting piano, followed by total silence from both performers. Smith strode over to Bunting's piano and lifted the lid; we all expected him to apologise to the audience and say that a string had broken – that would have been the most sensible thing to do. Instead, he stalked to the front of the stage and announced loudly in his pronounced and distinctive Oxford accent: *"It's been sabotawged!"*. It was really quite a dramatic moment and definitely signalled that the evening was at an end. The assembled guests did not appear to be particularly upset; *"boys will be boys"* seemed to be the amused attitude.

However Rogers, who had been Headmaster for only about a year, was incandescent. He immediately ordered the Headboy, **G W (Bill) Strahan** (OP, 1950-55), to gather all senior boys into their respective House classrooms, where they were to be thoroughly interrogated by School Prefects.

Rogers had a rather short temper and, although he later became a much respected Headmaster, he was not yet entirely tuned into the Irish way of life or the Portora wavelength.

He made all boys stay behind and decreed that nobody would be allowed to go home on holiday, until the perpetrators had been found. During the interrogation, there was a great deal of speculation concerning the method of sabotage and curiosity about the identity of the perpetrators. Eventually it transpired that a section of the bass strings, in one piano, had been tied together rendering the notes totally unplayable. It then seeped through that culprits had owned up and all could now go to bed.

However, even to this day the identity of the real culprits has never been fully established. There are no accurate accounts that anybody was actually interviewed or punished by the Headmaster and since most of the alleged suspects were leaving, there wasn't much Rogers could do.

As the Headmaster, Rogers must have felt that he had made a sufficient fuss to impress his guests with firmness. However, another impression given by the audience was they disliked his explosion of rage and there was some sneaking admiration for the daring prank. After all, not much harm was done and it was well known that the end of summer term is a time for liberties from leavers and a difficult time for school discipline.

The overpowering impression of the incident was that most of the boys, including the culprits (whoever they may have been), felt sorry that Mr Bunting turned out to be the victim.

(Editor's note: we have been supplied with a list of suspects, but feel that their names should continue to be a secret and shared only by the individuals themselves and the former Archbishop of Dublin, as indicated in his Foreword)

The people who linger in the memory are often not the most talented but the most unusual and eccentric. One such figure was **Albert Johnston**, an Ulster boarder of the 1960s, who is said to have run a profitable fishing industry during the night from a base in the dormitory where younger boys were employed in mending nets. He is said to have sold some of his fish to the unsuspecting wife of the Headmaster. Such stories remain when lessons have been long forgotten.

'Fishing' down by the boathouse during the 1960s!

tea continued to be served for breakfast, though corn flakes were included at weekends, but other meals started to include mountains of potatoes and potato bread, usually with tepid, greasy fried eggs, and dreadful fish on Fridays. Tuesday was prunes day (shades of Dr 'Boozy' Kidd). Some of the Prefects attempted to cook their own meals in their tiny studies, leaving the filthy burnt dishes to be washed up by junior boys.

One boy, more adventurous than most, brewed his own ginger beer in his locker. However, he left the old screw-top lemonade bottles too long and one exploded in the night, setting off all the others, so that in the morning there was a smelly pond of fluid on the floor to be cleaned up.

While there was a reasonably adequate supply of hot water for showers and washing, the weekly bath night had its limitations. Each dorm had three full-size bath tubs which were filled to the brim, then leaped into, sending a tidal wave across the tiled floor. No matter: for the boys from warmer climates it was a change from the damp cold winter weather outside.

The 1950s and 1960s

The wonderful countryside and the Lough just outside the School gave boarders a freedom unknown during the war, when, with so many soldiers from many nations all over the place, whole areas had been out of bounds. There were rules governing the use of boats, but even these were reasonably lax, requiring only that a list of those participating be given to one's Housemaster before setting out.

Illicit visits to boats and water were frequent and many were never spotted. One was, though, when Val Rogers was Headmaster in the 1950s. He kept an old converted lifeboat lashed to a buoy beside the boathouse, and one Saturday night a group of boys swam out to it and enjoyed some of the beverages they found on board. On the following Monday morning, when Assembly had finished in the Steele Hall, the platform group left the Hall and the door was locked behind them. Rogers threatened that they would stay in the Hall until those guilty admitted their crime. Nobody did; an hour later the door was unlocked and school work took over, but nobody ever owned up.

The War Memorial swimming pool near the gates, where Major and Mrs Wheeler could often be found with some of the thousands of children they taught to swim, was the location of an unofficial event. The dayboys' cycle shed was near it and a spate of tyres being let down was causing fury. Tyres had to be pumped up at the end of a tiring day and the joke went sour. The culprit was spotted however, and physically carried to the pool, thrown in and left on his own, no doubt working out what he would tell his parents about his wet clothes when he got home.

To visit Enniskillen town, boarders required a pass from a master stating the reason for the visit, but once past the West Bridge, the back streets were clear of Gangers and Prefects and one could wander, free from being watched.

By contrast, dayboys had an automatic freedom to all areas in and around what was after all their home town. Many lived well outside Enniskillen though, and they relied on an improved school bus service that came in with the closure of the railway in the 1950s. If they were the sons of farmers they could have a difficult journey to and from school, possibly having to cycle several miles in driving rain to the bus and then walking through town from the bus stop to School. They may well have had a home-cooked breakfast, but at an unholy hour if they were to help with milking the cows and still be in time for School. For some, various harvests (hay, potatoes, corn at differing times of the year) meant they had to have time off from school to help out just when exams were looming.

A day in the life of a dayboy from the country

One dayboy recalls his extreme daily journey to school in the early fifties, telling of having to leave home at 7.00 am, cycle four miles over a rough country road to Newtownbutler, and catch a train to Enniskillen which picked up other dayboys at Lisnaskea, Maguiresbridge and Lisbellaw on the way. They then had to walk a long mile to school, often in rain, wind, or snow. On arrival they went to the ugly dayboys' shed at the back of the School, a building that looked like a typical hay shed, except that the sides had been filled in with corrugated iron; its earthenware floor had had a sprinkling of gravel which helped to fill in the potholes. There they found rows of dark green lockers, many of them unlocked or with unlockable doors where they stored books and belongings.

Rarely getting there in time for Assembly in the Steele Hall, they went to their first classroom for the day. Two or three classes later, a break for mid-morning was taken in the Dayboys' Dining Room, two steps up from the Stone Hall, where they were given a glass of milk and

During the 1960s Headmaster Val Rogers embarked on an extensive building development programme. Hand-in-hand with this programme was the development of a promotional campaign, the highlight of which was a four-page article in the prestigious magazine the *Illustrated London News* in July 1958.

That there was a noticeable cultural divide between boarders and dayboys, there can be no denying; it had gone on for generations, but with the coming of the 1944 Education Act, which gave every child a secondary education until at least the age of sixteen, it is surprising that the gap continued for so long. It wasn't based just on the economic differences between families, witness the few boys who 'changed sides' as it were while at Portora, moving from dayboy to boarder: those who became boarders were completely accepted as such almost immediately, one of the family. That they also learned much that would guide them through careers later in life, preparing them socially as well as academically, of this there is no doubt. Many more boarders than dayboys went on to university; the experience of being away from home for protracted periods no doubt contributed to their success at that later stage of their education.

a tasteless bun. The furniture comprised rows of narrow trestle tables which had to be folded away, because the room was also used as a classroom, and plain wooden benches to sit on. The table tops were covered with dark brown linoleum which looked and felt as though it had been treated with sticky oil. Though well lit it was a depressing room, with no pictures on the walls and a general air of decay. Next door they could get a glimpse into the boarders' dining hall: what a difference, with its many framed portraits of Headmasters down the centuries, a top table with handsome chairs; one stood out, that of the Headmaster, looking down on the polished wood refectory tables for the boys, their benches upholstered in dark green leather. Two glass-fronted alcoves contained an array of brightly polished silver trophies to be won in various sports.

After school, dayboys were faced with the possibility of anything up to a two-hour journey home. Few could stay on for sports or clubs such as the Debating, Gramophone or Photographic Societies unless they lived locally. Nevertheless they were Portora boys, getting the finest secondary education available, knowing that, for many, theirs would be the last generation to be farmers or shop keepers. The world beckoned and they knew it.

It needs to be remembered that we are writing of a time, over half a century ago, when a very small proportion of boys went on beyond the Senior School Certificate exam; today it is a very different world, based much more on academic ability. The secondary education at Portora is still as good as it gets, as is shown by the number who move on to tertiary education.

During the academic year 1958-59, when the railway connection to Enniskillen ceased, boarders from the far corners of Ireland often had to rely on parents driving them to school; a total of six journeys a year, each of perhaps 200 miles. The beginning of the decade saw a period of IRA insurgence, making the cross-border part of the trip a matter of close scrutiny. Many a Church of Ireland clergyman, driving his wife and children and arriving at the border post, would get strange looks from the Republic customs men, doubtfully wishing him *"Good luck, Father"* as he drove on. Advantages came with the clerical collar, since none was ever asked for a luggage check.

The 1960s began with a winter that has stuck in the memory of more than one Old Portoran. Bitter, icy weather for week after week froze the fast-running Narrows and the still Frying Pan Lake. Further down the Lough two postmen delivering mail to an island were caught in their boat by the ice and froze to death. Inevitably the weather was used by a group of some dozen boys out for adventure, so they made a slide across the Narrows between the boathouse and the Frying Pan. The duty master, strolling on the terrace, saw them and managed to get them to see sense and return without harm being done.

Charity

When the early 1960s Troubles had passed, a more unusual cross-border journey was made by nine boys who set out to walk from Portora to Dublin on behalf of the Red Cross and Third World Aid. They left the school on a Friday afternoon, accompanied by bagpipes, pushing an open cart along the road, and in towns they passed through encouraged people to throw money into it.

BBC News recorded their journey at several stops, so locals were well aware of the charities they were supporting. The money they had collected each day was lodged in a local bank. They were put up in such differing places as a local laundry one night, Headford School on another, and on their last night by Sir Gregor and Lady Sharp in Dunshaughlin. It was all well worth it, though, for they collected over £600, a considerable amount forty years ago, for which they were thanked by the Lord Mayor of Dublin at a reception especially laid on for them.

Sex education

Gather a hundred boys together away from home and at an age when their bodies are developing at an alarming rate, put them in an institution where there are few females, have them sleep in dormitories, add institution rules that forbid visiting the local town, and you have the perfect conditions for sexual experiment. Such experimentation was the subject of much serious literature, as well as of a great deal of publicity in the media, during the sexual revolution of the 1960s. According to the one reminiscence we received on this subject, homosexual encounters took place on a surprising scale at Portora.

There had of course been homosexuals at the School in the past, and one thinks immediately of Oscar Wilde in the nineteenth century, the most famous of them all. Many recall with regret that his name was erased from the Honours Board when he was found guilty in court of what was then an illegal act; happily, his name was later restored to the board. A blue plaque commemorating his time at Portora was recently affixed to the facade of the main school building, and the famous portrait now hangs in a prominent place in the Headmaster's house (see page 210).

The blue plaque to Oscar Wilde, unveiled by Parliamentary Under-Secretary of State, Angela Smith, MP, in 2003.

Our contributor tells us that homosexuality (which Wilde famously described as *"the love that dares not speak its name"*) was never mentioned officially in the School during the 1950s and 60s. It was not for the lack of opportunities, most obviously with the introduction of Biology to the curriculum, a seemingly natural context for discussion of these matters; however, the subject was never raised. There were also the Divinity classes taken by the clerical Headmaster, who appeared to avoid those parts of the Bible which he regarded as best not spoken of. His sermons, preached exclusively to boarders on Sunday evenings in the Steele Hall, would have been the perfect chance to mention, and even explore, the subject, but he never grasped it. It was the Head of the English Department who came nearest to opening up the subject, when he introduced some of Wilde's most autobiographical and most sexually explicit works, including 'Salomé', 'The Picture of Dorian Gray' and 'The Ballad of Reading Gaol' into the sixth-form curriculum, but discussion of these works never led to the exploration of the issues which inspired them.

A dramatic sun-rise over Enniskillen town – taken from the front terrace early on the morning of an historic visit to Portora Royal School, by Dr Mary McAleese, President of Ireland, October 2007.

Pupils at Portora before the Headmastership of Stuart will have sung and remember the School song, 'Floreat Portora'. As it was never popular with the boys, Stuart dropped the song and introduced 'Abide with Me', adopting it as the School hymn. It is believed that the last time 'Floreat Portora' was performed publicly was in 1977, as part of the pageant 'Two Hundred Years at the Top', as written by Headmaster Garrett.

Floreat Portora

Words by E N Cook; music by Cicely Ritchie

1   Clio, The Muse of History
Sometimes tells tales a trifle tall;
About a British Solomon
She tells the tallest of them all.
No true Portoran can believe
That Good King Jamie was a fool;
None but the wisest of the wise
Could be the founder of our School.
Chorus:
Portorans all! With might and main
Raise loud and long the glad refrain:
'Floreat Portora! Floreat Portora!'
And when you've sung it, sing again
'Floreat Portora!'

2   Three hundred years and more have gone
Since the first schoolboys came to learn
The way to work, the way to play,
Beside the waters of Lough Erne.
The vanguard of a mighty host
Of men of future worth and fame,
Whose deeds at home and far afield
Have brought the School her honoured name.
Chorus

3   From century to century
In fashion's shifting outward show,
Change follows on the heel of change
As generations come and go.
The scented curl, the powdered wig,
No more Portora's sons display;
The cocks who fought their fight in school
Have not been seen for many a day.
Chorus

4   There was a time, as we are told,
When every boy, Smith, Jones or Brown
Thought cricket merely meant a 'bug'
And Rugby but an English town:
Yet life in those benighted days
Was not unutterably tame,
Doublet and hose or rowing togs,
Portora sons are still the same.
Chorus

5   And still she stands upon her hill
Living her peaceful cloistered life,
Remote, serene, a place apart,
Above the shouting and the strife;
Not dreaming idly of the past,
But looking forward proud and sure
That many hundreds years from now
Her sons will match her sons of yore.
Chorus

Appendix B

The School's Coats of Arms

The illustrations below have been used by Portora Royal School, Enniskillen, in various forms over the last 100 years or so as the School's Coat of Arms, Crest or Insignia. It is fortunate that most of their usage has gone unchallenged, because, unfortunately, for most of the time their display has been illegal.

Before the arrival of Steele, in 1857, we can find no evidence of a School Crest and the School medals issued by Greham in 1844 and 1851 carried none. Shortly after his arrival Steele published his first photograph of Portora, which he then embellished with a small medallion of Queen Victoria, to signify the Royal connection and foundation of his School.

Steele then started to use the Royal Arms of Queen Victoria as the Arms of the School. He modified the Arms with the date of 1627, which was of course the date that Charles I had re-awarded new Land and Letters Patent to all five Royal Schools. After Steele retired in 1891, Biggs changed the founding date to 1618, which was the date

238

when the Reverend Geoffrey Middleton was appointed as the first Master of the Free School for Fermanagh at Ballibalfour (Lisnaskea).

Some time in the 1930s, Seale adopted the full Arms of King James I together with the date of 1618 as the official Arms for the School. The College of Heralds say that the use of the Arms of King James I on buildings, gates and other static objects is quite in order to show the origins of our foundation. However to use the Arms of any Sovereign is to suggest this item has come uniquely from that specific Monarch.

The situation was finally regularised in 1954, after some delicate observations were made on the various insignias displayed by our Boat Club members during their first visit to the Henley Royal Regatta. In consequence, the

School Governors applied to Norroy and Ulster King of Arms for the design of a new and exclusive Coat of Arms for future use by Portora Royal School.

The Arms granted by Sir G W Wollaston, KCB, KCVO, Norroy and Ulster King of Arms, are in the School colours of black and gold (sable and or). They are exclusive to Portora Royal School and are almost an address in heraldic symbols.

Portora is represented by a mural coronet on the banner, which stands for the Old Castle.

Royal is represented by the two fleurs de lys, royal symbols taken from the Arms of our Founder.

School is represented by the open Book of Knowledge.

Enniskillen is represented by the Castle, surmounted by the flag of St George.

County Fermanagh is represented by the 'stag trippant proper armed, collared and chained or', which is the crest of Thomas Maguire (Maguire Mor), Lord of Fermanagh, who died in 1430; it is the land of his descendants which formed the endowment lands of the Royal School.

Ireland is represented by the Harp, which again connects the School with its founder, for it was King James I who first put the Harp of Ireland in his Royal Arms.

The date in Latin of 1608 is that of the instrument of foundation, viz. the Order in Council of 1608, stating 'that there shall be one free school at least, appointed in every County for the education of youth in learning and religion'; these last two concepts being symbolised by the Book and the Cross of St George on the Castle pennant.

Appendix C

Old Portora Union (OPU)

Introduction

For many years an annual dinner in Dublin was organised by Portora undergraduates at Trinity College, Dublin, with a 'High Table' for all old boys living in the Dublin area. The first recorded function was held at the Bolton Hotel, Dublin in 1879.

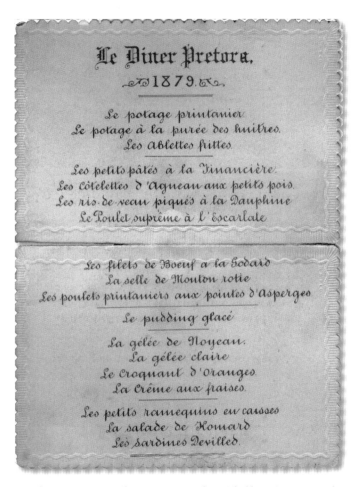

A rather pretentious gilt menu in French entitled 'Le Diner Pretora' from the function held at the Bolton Hotel, Dublin in 1879.

Old Portora Union (OPU)

However, the Old Portora Union (OPU) traces its official foundation to a committee meeting, held on 9 November 1921, at St Anne's Vicarage, Dawson Street, Dublin, when the distinguished member of the Irish Judiciary, The Right Honourable J G Gibson, PC, Chief Justice of Ireland, agreed to become the first President of the OPU.

Supporting him as Committee members were: Reverend Edward G Seale, MA, Headmaster (ex-officio); The Right Honourable the Lord Dunalley of Kilboy (Hon Henry O'Callaghan Prittie); The Very Reverend the Dean of St Patrick's Cathedral (Reverend Dr Charles Thomas Ovenden, DD); and Dr Louis Claude Purser, SFTCD, Vice Provost, Trinity College, Dublin University.

The Committee passed a motion to hold its inaugural OPU Dinner on 12 May 1922, at the Shelbourne Hotel, Dublin, priced at 8s 6d (42.5p). Discussion then turned to the design for an OPU tie, scarf, tobacco pouches and various other gentlemen's requirements, which would be stocked by Messrs Tyson Ltd, Grafton Street, Dublin. Life Membership subscriptions were set at three guineas or fifteen shillings per annum (£3.15 and £0.75 respectively), with automatic Life Membership granted after six successive annual subscriptions. These rates remained until 1953, when Life Membership became five guineas.

Shortly after formation of the OPU, W N Tetley, Second Master, was co-opted as Honorary Treasurer for the Society, a position which he held until his death in 1927, when, after a short break, his duties were assumed by A T M Murfet, new Second Master, and retained until his eventual retirement from the staff in 1956.

Towards the end of the 1920s, there was strong pressure to hold the annual dinner on alternate years in Belfast and Dublin. In the event, there were sufficient numbers and interest to form a separate 'Belfast Branch' to operate in Northern Ireland, and this was very effective for Northern-based OPs, until the outbreak of World War II. However, wartime constraints led to the closure of the Belfast Branch, and all records and unused funds were subsequently transferred back to the parent branch of the OPU.

During the 1920s the growth of OPs living deep in the South of Ireland led to an annual dinner being organised in Cork, and there are certainly reports in the *Cork Examiner* during 1935, listing 23 members dining at the Metropole Hotel.

OPU (London Branch)

During the early 1950s, when Douglas Graham was Headmaster, the OPU Committee, together with W S Gunning (OP, 1910) and R Meara (OP, 1909), organised an initial trawl of its membership living in the South of England. This revealed at least 60 names, from which some 58 members responded to a call for establishing a regular dinner and endorsing the formation of an OPU (London Branch). The first London Branch Meeting and Dinner was held under the Chairmanship of Dr William C McFetridge (OP, 1895) on St Patrick's Night, 17 March 1953. The initial plan was to hold a regular dinner function in London on the Friday night before the England-Ireland rugby match at Twickenham and, in alternate years, on the Friday night of, or as near as possible to, St Patrick's Day. Vice Admiral Sir Edward Archdale (OP, 1892) and Lieutenant-Colonel Sir Thomas Moore, MP (OP, 1901) were elected Vice-Presidents. It was recorded that Sir Thomas made a witty after-dinner speech, but was recalled by his Party Whip to the House of Commons for an important vote, before the evening finished.

The OPU (London Branch) has prospered and has regularly managed to hold an annual dinner that successfully attracts twenty-five to seventy members to its main function. The highlight at this dinner has always been a visit by the current Headmaster of the School, usually accompanied by one 'Master of Honour' and/ or if possible more staff members from the School as opportunity allows.

Locations have been many and various, the Irish Club, various restaurants, the Globe Theatre, sundry London Clubs and, of course, the Duke of York's Barracks when Colonel Noel Dorrity (OP, 1936-40) was commanding the TA Battalion of the London Irish Rifles. Although the event usually centred around a formal black-tie dinner, there were lighter moments when Dr Billy McCombe (OP, 1932-39), fresh from his appearances at the London Palladium, used to entertain the guests with his magic and witty after-dinner patter.

In more recent years informal Summer drink parties have been held at a Rowing Club boathouse on the Thames, courtesy of David Porteus (OP, 1951-59), a long-serving Branch Secretary and Treasurer. The OPU (London Branch) under a more recent Secretary, C John Brady (OP, 1962-69), together with several other London members, initiated the Irish Schools Annual Cocktail Party featuring schools from both North and South of the

One of two memorial boards recording Presidents of the Old Portora Union. These boards were partially funded from a legacy donated by 'Bert' Cranston.

border. Another scheme, devised by Charles Cullimore (OP, 1946-52) in his Presidential year, together with the Secretary John Brady, saw a team of London OPs travel to Enniskillen to support a careers conference being organised at the School and bringing some City expertise from 'across the water'.

John Brady was most generous during his period as Branch Secretary, hosting the committee meetings in his spacious office in Jermyn Street.

In more recent years, several individual London Branch members have generously subscribed to a fund which enables the Headmaster to bring the Head Boy to the dinner as a guest and introduce him as the second after-dinner speaker, covering the School's sporting achievements. The London Branch has also instituted a second prize for a Senior boy, who as an all-rounder and the Headmaster's special nomination, to accompany the Head Boy and attend the London dinner. Liam Strong (OP, 1956-63) has also been financially generous to the OPU (London Branch) and the School.

Although the original concept for the London Branch dinner was to foregather in London prior to the Twickenham match for the England and Ireland rugby international, the advent of professional players and corporate hospitality has made a visit to Twickenham a rather rare event for most OPs.

Over the last ten years, thanks to Lowry de Montfort (OP, 1937-44), we have enjoyed the hospitality of the Army and Navy Club, and the annual dinner soldiers on towards the 100th Anniversary.

Some of the seventy or more guests who attended the 50th anniversary dinner, OPU (London Branch) in 2003.

Presidents of the London Branch

1953 W C McFetridge, MA
After taking his degree practised in Hove, Sussex. He was one of the founders of the London OPU branch in 1953.

1954 Vice Admiral Sir Nicholas Archdale, 2nd Bart, CBE
Born 1881, joined the Royal Navy where he was an early developer of torpedoes. Distinguished naval career, ending as Naval ADC to King George V. Chairman of the League of Remembrance. Died 1955.

1955 Lt-Col Sir Thomas Moore, Bt, CBE, MP
Born 1886, served in the Army during World War I and Russia, 1914-1920. MP for Ayr 1925-64, created Baronet 1956. Member of RSPCA and other animal protection leagues. Chairman of the Home Guard during WWII. Died 1971.

1956 Professor J G Smith, OBE
Professor of Finance and Economics in several universities. Served on many governmental committees in the early days of the Irish Free State. Died 1968.

1957 Captain F E Manico
Entered Portora 1895. After serving in the army during the World War I, he lived in Petworth, West Sussex.

1958 Captain C Emerson-Huston, MRCVS, JP
Entered Portora 1904, practised as a veterinary surgeon in the Army and later in Barrow upon Soar, Leicester.

1959 Dr A W J Knox
Entered Portora 1908. Lived and died as a doctor in Cobham, Surrey.

1960 Major G H Wood
Entered Portora 1906. Having served in the army throughout World War II, he settled in Hornsey, north London.

1961 Reverend C F H Carroll, MA

Priested in the Church of Ireland, he served as Curate in a number of Parishes before moving to the Church of England where, after several further curacies, he was appointed Vicar of two Parishes in Norfolk.

1962 W S Gunning

A Founder and the first Secretary of the London OPU, he worked for the Ulster Weaving Co. in Belfast and London. He retired to live in West Chillington, W Sussex, where he was deeply involved in the parish church.

1963 R Meara

A Founder and the first Treasurer of the London OPU, his career was as a factory inspector and engineer with the CEGB. He retired to Hove, W Sussex, and later moved to join family in Armagh.

1964 Dr W F Whaley, MA

Entered Portora in 1907 and after university worked as a GP in Ramsgate, Kent.

1965 Major E L Mecredy, MC

A School sportsman in rugby, shooting and rowing and School Captain, he served in WWI, earning the MC and the CdeG. He went on to serve throughout WWII and died aged 86.

1966 General Sir Charles Jones, GCB, CBE, MC

Of a Dublin family, he was commissioned into the RE, served through World War II, afterwards becoming Master of Ordnance and ADC to the Queen. In retirement he became National President of the Royal British Legion and died in 1988.

1967 T E Dickson, LLB

Entered Portora in 1918. He later lived in Liphook, Hampshire.

1968 Professor C B Falls, CBE

Served throughout WWI and after frontline duties was a liaison officer with the French, when he was twice cited for the CdeG. A distinguished writer and a journalist with *The Times* and the *Illustrated London News*, he was elected Chichele Professor and a Fellow of All Souls, Oxford.

1969 B V C Harpur, MC

Served throughout WWII and awarded the MC. He became a Director of Associated Newspapers, instigating the Daily Mail Transatlantic Air Race and developing the Ideal Homes Exhibition, as well as a charity based on the passing of Halley's Comet. He died in 1990.

1970 Lt-Cdr R Ashton Clarke

From a Cork family, he was a Founder Member of the London OPU, serving for many years as the Treasurer. A keen Freemason, he was a founder member of the OP Masonic Lodge and died in 1985.

1971-72 J F Q Switzer, MA

A brilliant student at Portora, he joined the RN and having been invalided out, commenced a long and rising career with Cambridge University, ending as elected Emeritus Fellow and a Freeman of the City of London.

1973 G H S Webb, MBE

After leaving school and moving to Canada, he returned to set up an advertising company in London, then joined the Army for World War II, where he earned an MBE (Military) in Italy. He returned to join the Civil Service and died in 1996.

1974 Colonel N W Dorrity, TD

Captain of a 1st XV that won the Ulster Schools Cup, after war service he was appointed Colonel of the London Irish TA, earning his TD. He ran a hotel near Henley and was subsequently a Club Secretary in London. He retained his strong Dublin accent to the day he died in 1987.

1975 G N Taylor, MB, MCh, FRCS

Entered Portora in 1926. Sadly little can be found with certainty about this remarkably well-qualified man, though his name comes up in connection with nuclear physics.

1976 J B Musgrave, MB, BCh, BAO

A Cork man, he took his medical degree at Trinity and after house jobs in Dublin settled into general practice in Hendon, where he was also appointed medical officer to the police college. On retirement he returned to the family farm in Co. Galway and died shortly afterwards.

1977 T L Kelly, MB

Another GP. Joined the RAMC and serving in Burma, then GP in Eastcote. He retired to Rustington, West Sussex, enjoying 20 years there before dying in 1998.

1978 Kenneth McCrea, MB, BCh, BAO, JP

Following his medical degree at Queen's and hospital house appointments, he became a GP in Upminster and, despite three heart attacks, stayed on in the job until he was 56 when he had to retire; he then continued to serve as JP on the Bench until his death in 1988.

1979 J W Jackson, MCh, FRCS

Yet another medical man, but sadly we know no more about him.

1980 R D G Creery, VRD, MD, FRCP, DCH

Another medical President, he took his degree at Queen's and joined the staff of the Royal Belfast Hospital for Sick Children, then the RN Reserve, retiring as a Surgeon Commander in 1963. He took up paediatrics in Belfast, London, Bristol, South Shields and Cheltenham, continuing as such after 'retirement' in Guernsey.

1981 I H D Scales

Joined the Colonial Service as telecommunications lecturer. On return to England he ran the communications for UPI in Fleet Street, before starting up a company for telex machines, and then a consulting company. He retired to concentrate on writing local history.

1982 A W Barnes, MA

Barney's story as a Master, Housemaster and Gloucester House Headmaster is covered in chapter six of this book.

1983 J M Bliss

He moved to Surrey after School and served for 32 years with British Rail, in personnel, health and safety and welfare. Blessed with a superb voice, he has sung with several famous choirs and still found time to be the London OPU Secretary for six years.

1984 Reverend D L Graham, MA

This Old Portoran and then Headmaster is well documented in several places in this book. He died in 1990, aged 81, of a massive heart attack.

1985 R N Davidson, C Eng, MIEE

After Portora he took his degree in Queen's, leading to a career in the oil industry, then he joined the Civil Service in the Overseas Development Administration. After visiting 40 countries he has retired and plays golf.

1986 A W Gethin, MA

Born in Kenya, after School he joined the army and returned there with them. Back in the UK he took a degree in Geology, which took him to the Middle East in search of oil, before returning to the UK and the North Sea oil search. Retired, he took up fly fishing and making wine.

1987 G M Coburn

After School he went into the weaving trade and eventually chaired the Irish Linen Guild. While at Portora, he learned to play the organ, a a skill he continues to enjoy to this day, by playing for his parish church.

1988-89 Major W M Henry, FRICS

A member of the third generation of his family to attend Portora, he then joined the Army with the RE Survey Service, which led to civilian work digitally mapping many countries. He is the main writer of this book, delving deeply into the early history of the School.

1990 Lt-Cdr B H L Braidwood, MBIM, MIExpE

A second-generation OP, he joined the RN, serving 34 years, mainly in mine warfare and clearance, before retiring from the RN, but thereafter clearing the oceans of rubbish as a consultant.

1991 D F McCoy, MRIBA(I), FRTPI

Studied architecture after Portora and worked for the City of Belfast; he took exams for the Royal Town Planning Institution, becoming a Fellow. He moved to Kensington where he set up business as a Planning Consultant. He is an enthusiastic river-sailor and walker.

1992 Reverend P H Rogers, MBE, MA

His life and career as Headmaster of Portora are well covered in this book. He died in 2001.

1993 H A Schaafsma, BA, BAI

Following Portora, this Hiberno-Dutchman took his degrees at Trinity and worked in the printing and publishing trades before setting up his own successful publishing business. His vast experience is at the back of getting this book printed and through the publishing webs. He is now rebuilding a castle in Tuscany.

1994-95 C A K Cullimore, CMG, MA

Following Portora, Trinity College, Oxford and a short-service commission in the Inniskillings, he joined HM Overseas Service and later HM Diplomatic Service, ending as British High Commissioner to Uganda. Following retirement from this, he helped set up the South African Business Association. He, too, has contributed extensively to the writing of this book.

1996-97 D M Porteus, BSc

After Portora and Queen's, where he studied Physics, he decided on teaching, but at a school with a rowing tradition, and joined the staff of St Paul's School, London, where he stayed until retirement. He has served the London OPU as both Treasurer and Secretary in his time.

1998-2000 D W Learmond, BA

With a background of maths he took a job in the City of London, then became a journalist in Fleet Street with a commodities news agency; he then moved to Reuters as commodities editor. He retired to Bruton, Somerset, where he is rebuilding an old farmhouse.

2000-02 Liam Strong, BA

Following Portora and Trinity, he joined the business world, eventually running Sears, who own Selfridges. Then he went into the worldwide telecom business, living variously in Montreal, New York, London and Ibiza.

2002-04 C John Brady, MA, MBA

Following Portora, he took an MA at Cambridge, but engineering across the world didn't satisfy him; so back in London he took an MBA, leading to McKinsey & Co., advising companies, the last fifteen years as a Director.

2004-06 Gerry Lowe, OBE

After Portora entered the accountancy profession with a close connection to Queen's. Founded Lowe Refrigeration Co., one of the few NI based businesses to win a Queen's Award for Export Achievement – on three occasions.

2006-08 James E Wilson, MA, MEng

After Portora went to St John's College Cambridge. Abandoned chemical engineering after a year and entered the computer industry in sales and marketing, primarily with IBM. Other interests include being a vice-president of Richmond Hockey Club.

2008-10 Dr R G Wynn Anderson, BSc, MRCS, LRCP, AFOM

After study at Queen's and Leicester Universities, he graduated in Medicine and joined the RAMC. He retired as a substantive Major and obtained a Cabinet appointment as the Senior Medical Officer at AWE Aldermaston. Currently he is Medical Director of Trident Medical Services Limited, at AWE Aldermaston.

Appendix D

Portorans elected Foundation Scholars of Trinity College, Dublin

On 1 September 1960, former Headmaster the Reverend Douglas Graham (S, 1945-53) wrote to the new Headmaster the Reverend Val Rogers (S, 1954-73) outlining the surges and gaps in the award of Foundation Scholars at Trinity College, Dublin: '*Dunkin (the best headmaster in Ireland, friend of Swift) in mid-18th century; Mark Noble in his new buildings at Portora, 1780 onwards; Greham – a great period 1840-1860 (40 scholars), followed by Steele another great period 1861-1876 (26 scholars), then a slow decay to Biggs 1896-1904 (10 scholars), followed by McDonnell (all games) and Burgess to Seale 1920-1930 (11 scholars) then a gradual decay to Stuart and the War, both disastrous to scholarship, and to Graham (?) – what a terrible 21 years, 1939-1959, with 1 or 2 scholars!! Let us hope that the nineteen-sixties will bring a crop of "Rogers" Scholars.*'

1640	Thomas Gutrich
1673	Robert Whitelaw
1679	Robert Brisbane
1680	Nicholas Browne
1682	Adam Nixon
1684	John Connolly
1685	James Browning
1710	John Humphreys
1712	James Cathcart
1716	John Kerr
1717	George Gregory
1721	John Dundas
1727	John Forster (Fellow 1724)
1729	William Henderson
1741	Newburgh Higginbotham
	John Major
1742	Robert Argyle Elliott
	John Hamilton
	John Roscrow
1750	Lawrence Grace
1751	William Clarke
	John Gibson
	Mungo McIntosh
	William Major
1754	– Cassidy
	James Johnston
1756	Alexander Clotworthy Downing
	Hall Hartson
1757	James Dunkin
1761	William Nixon
1762	James Armstrong
	Thomas Lindrum

1763	Patrick Crawley
1772	Patrick Plunkett
1773	James Irwin
1777	James Armstrong
1780	Robert Johnston
	George Nixon
1784	Mark Chartres
	William Magee (Fellow 1788)
1785	William Thompson
1786	Edward Barton
1796	Thomas Robinson
1803	John Whitley
1807	Andrew Armstrong
1811	John Smith
1813	Henry Francis Lyte
	William Armstrong
1818	Christopher Weir
1821	Joseph Cooper
1825	Richard O'Beirne
1827	Cadwallader Wolseley
1834	William Falloon
1837	John Flanagan
1838	George Stone
1840	Henry Carr
	Michael Haynes
1842	William Alexander Battersby
	Charles Ingham Black
	Frederick Benjamin McLean
1843	William Irvine
1844	Richard Carr Kirkpatrick
	Ronald Macdonnell
	Edward Graves Mayne

1845	Richard Vigers Doyne	1872	Richard Galbraith
	Edward Willian Hearn	1873	Louis Claude Purser (Fellow 1881)
1846	Travers Adamson		Oscar Fingal O'Flahertie Wills Wilde
	William R Weir	1874	Robert Cramsie
1847	Bridges Carmichael Hooke	1875	Herbert MacCartney Beatty
	Francis Hopkins		William Chadwick Bouchier
	Henry V Mackesy		John Gilloway Garrett
	William Malam		Jeffrey Browning McDowell
1848	William Caine	1876	William Trevor Lendrum
	John Gwynne (Fellow 1853)		Edward Sullivan
1849	Frederick Greham Evelyn	1879	Hugh Latimer Haughton
	Robert Rogers	1883	Alfred Edward Russel Joynt
1850	Joseph Carson Moore	1884	James Clarence Newsome
1851	Richard Travers Smith	1894	William Harloe Elwood Dundas
1852	Robert Gwynne	1895	Frank Hannyngton
	Robert Tighe Hopkins	1896	John Chartres Molony
1853	William Bradford		Harry Frederick Hill deVere White
	Christopher John Weir	1897	William Parker
1854	Thomas William Carson		John Archibald Valentine
	Arthur Molloy Mitchell		Arthur Edwin Gray
1855	John Ellis	1900	John Courtenay Clarke
	John Thompson Henderson	1901	Arthur Haire Forster
1856	Joseph John Henry Carson	1903	Henry Francis Biggs
	Henry William Maxwell Rodgers		John George Smith
1857	Thomas Allingham	1904	David Duff
1859	David Eccles	1907	John Ernest William Flood
	Lucas Dickson	1915	Noel Desmond Trimble
1860	Thomas Brett	1918	Robert Mervyn Ferguson
	Thomas Evelyn Little	1920	William Holmes
1861	Maurice Charles Hime	1926	Samuel Barclay Beckett
	Robert Joseph Hutton		Thomas Richard Fisher Cox
1863	William Anstell Leech		Oliver William McCutcheon
1864	James MacIvor		Gerald Pakenham Stewart
	Robert Warren Symes	1927	John Alexander Wallace
1865	John George Gibson	1928	Frederick Herbert Gamble
1866	George Henderson		Douglas Leslie Graham
	Francis Hodder	1930	Ernest Deschamps Camier
	Mark Henry Little	1933	Hugh Frederic Woodhouse
	William Smith McKay (Fellow 1872)	1938	John William Hamilton McBrien
1870	James David Bourchier		Vivian Herbert Samuel Mercier
	Thomas Edmund Hackett	1949	Eldon Young Exshaw
1871	Henry Monch Mason Hackett	1955	J R Cole
	Graves Atkinson Leech	1957	F Henry A Richmond

Bibliography

Akenson, Donald. *The Irish Education Experiment*. Routledge & Kegan Paul, 1970.

Akenson, Donald. *Education and Enmity: The Control of Schooling in Northern Ireland 1920-50*. David & Charles, 1973.

Atthill, Lombe. *Recollections of an Irish Doctor*. The Religious Tract Society, 1911.

Auchmuty, James Johnston. *Irish Education: A Historical Survey*. Hodges Figgis and Co., 1937.

Bodkin, Mathias. *The Port of Tears: the Life of Father John Sullivan*. S J Clonmore & Reynolds, 1954.

Chandos, John. *Boys Together: English Public Schools, 1800-1864*. Hutchinson & Co., 1984.

Connolly, S J (editor). *The Oxford Companion to Irish History*. Oxford University Press, 1998.

Coolahan, John. *Irish Education: Its History and Structure*. Institute of Public Administration, 1981.

Crittenden, Victor. *The Voyage of the First Fleet*. The Mulini Press, 1981.

Cronin, Anthony: *Samuel Beckett, the Last Modernist*. HarperCollins, 1996.

Cunningham, John B. 'Dr Lombe Atthill and His Picture of Fermanagh Before the Famine', *Clogher Record* Vol. XIV, No. 3 (1993), pp. 29-41.

Day, Angélique and McWilliams, Patrick (editors). *Ordnance Survey Memoirs of Ireland Vol. 4: Parishes of Co. Fermanagh 1834-5*. Institute of Irish Studies, 1990.

Department of the Environment for Northern Ireland. *Historic Monuments of Northern Ireland* (sixth edition). Her Majesty's Stationery Office, 1983.

Dowling, P J. *A History of Irish Education*. Mercier Press, 1971.

Durcan, T J. *History of Irish Education from 1800*. Dragon Books, 1972.

Edwards, Ruth. *An Atlas of Irish History* (second edition). Methuen, 1973.

Ellmann, Richard. *Oscar Wilde*. Hamish Hamilton, 1987.

Fisher, Charles A. 'Evolution of the Irish Railway System', *Economic Geography*, Vol. 17, No. 3 (July 1941), pp. 262-274.

Friel, Charles and Johnston, Norman. *Fermanagh's Railways: A Photographic Tribute*. Colourpoint Books, 1998.

Knowlson, James. *Damned to Fame: The Life of Samuel Beckett*. Bloomsbury, 1996.

Luce, J V. *Trinity College, Dublin: The First 400 Years*. Trinity College Dublin Press, 1992.

MacDonald, B. 'Portora School-lands', *Clogher Record*, Vol. 15, No. 2, 1995.

McElligott, John. *Education in Ireland*. Institute of Public Administration, 1966.

McElligott, T J. *Secondary Education in Ireland 1870-1921*. Irish Academic Press, 1981.

McGrath, Fergal. *Father John Sullivan* (second edition). Longmans, 1945.

Maxwell, Constantina (editor). *A Tour in Ireland by Arthur Young*. Cambridge University Press, 1925.

Mercier, Vivian. *Modern Irish Literature: Sources and Founders*. Clarendon, 1994.

Mercier, Vivian. 'The Old School Tie', *The Bell*, Vol. XI, No. 6, March 1946, pp. 1,081-90.

Ministry of Education. *Public Education in Northern Ireland* (revised 1969). Her Majesty's Stationery Office, 1970.

O'Brien, Eoin. *The Beckett Country*. The Black Cat Press Ltd, 1986.

O'Cathain, Sean. *Secondary Education in Ireland*. The Talbot Press, 1958.

Oxford Dictionary of National Biography. Oxford University Press, 2004.

Quane, Michael. *Portora Royal School, Enniskillen*. Cumann Seanchais Chlochair, 1968.

Rogers, Mary. *Prospect of Erne*. Fermanagh Field Club, 1967.

Trimble, W C. *Enniskillen Royal School at Portora*. Fermanagh Protestant Education Board, 1918.

Trimble, W C. *The History of Enniskillen*. Enniskillen, 1919-20.

Urwick, William. 'The Early History of Trinity College, Dublin, 1591-1660', *The English Historical Review*, Vol. 7, No. 28 (Oct. 1892), pp. 747-754.

Webb, Alfred. *Compendium of Irish Biography*. M H Gill & Son, 1878.

White, Heather. *Oscar Wilde at Portora Royal School*. Principia Press, 2002.

Who Was Who 1929-1940. Adam & Charles Black, 1947.

Wood, Helen. *Enniskillen, Historic Images of an Island Town*. Friar's Bush Press, 1990.

Young, Arthur. *A Tour in Ireland*. London, 1780.

Acknowledgements

As might have been expected, producing this book has proved to be a bigger task than any of us thought. That it has seen the light of day is due to the enormous response we received from Old Portorans and staff recalling their memories of anything up to seventy-five years ago.

The book is peppered with facts that came to light in this way, many in the main chapters, but the whole of the 'Reminiscences' chapter is composed from the wonderful letters and photographs we received. We have deliberately avoided using names associated with sources, partly because the same story might have been referred to by several correspondents, with all combined into one tale. One suspects that some memories, if attributed to a name, might cause friction or even distress in their families.

The production team that did the hard work of sourcing, writing, chasing up slow contributors and producing copy that could be edited, they must be mentioned by name:

Miles Henry, who did an enormous amount of research on the compilation of the history of the School and subsequent writing of the book.

Ian Burn, whose IT abilities to compile drafts and prepare photographs for this publication was essential.

Hubert Schaafsma, whose life-long experience of the printing and publishing trade has proved invaluable.

The writing team comprising **Bobby Bell, Charles Cullimore, Robin Preston, Henry Richmond and James Wilson** who all suffered comment and correction from the nominal editor **Ian Scales.**

During the research and preparation of the book we received help and assistance from many people at Portora. In particular, **Richard Bennett**, former Headmaster of the School and author of the section on Portora Royal School in the 1608 Royal Schools book; and **Jane Fisher-Holland** proved her worth, locating facts and dates from Portora records for the Sports chapter.

We received additional support from organisations such as *The Impartial Reporter, The Belfast Telegraph, The Irish Times, The Illustrated London News,* Dean and Chapter of Westminster Abbey, Dean and Chapter of Clogher Cathedral, Trinity College, Dublin, Queen's University, Belfast, Cambridge University, the Portora Masonic Lodge and many others.

We acknowledge permission to reproduce illustrations from Dean and Chapter of Westminster, Dean and Chapter of Clogher, and the NI Environment Agency.

Although every attempt has been made to trace copyright holders of images contained herein, any unacknowledged copyright holder omitted should contact the publishers so that the situation may be rectified in future editions. The published also invite any corrections (giving background references) as frequently it has been difficult to substantiate previously published information.

Names of OPs responding to the Editor's letter of October 2006, where these have been used as sources: R F Alston, C D C Armstrong, G Armstrong, W Barbour, G A Bayne, J M Bliss, D Boyd, B H L Braidwood, C Bruce, D Caird, L W Carew, C E Carson, G M Coburn, J Connor, F McL Cox, H G W Crawford, A L deMontfort, N Dobbin, J F Douglas, G V Drought, A Evans, G E Ferguson, G T Finlay, A E D Fleming, W J Francis, D E Gentleman, J E Gentleman, G L L Henderson, R Henderson, I J Holmes, J Hughes, D N Ingram, H R B Jack, C E W Jones, W Keatinge, J L Kerr, P J Kirwan, J Kulski, C Leatham, G Leinenbach, D J Longford, D Mallinson, G Marshall, R Mathewson, J Maxwell, W J McBride, L McCombe, D F McCoy, H McKeown, A H N McKinley, A McMeekin, D B McNeill, T E Milligan, T G Molyneux, J D Morton, J F Mullan, B Murphy, H M Nelson, M Pollard, S G Poyntz, B E Reid, F H A Richmond, N Ritchie, D Robertson, M Ruddell, R Sadleir, P R Scales, R Seaman, J M F Steede, G W Strahan, J F Q Switzer, L F Tarrant, F G D Tisdall, D Trotter, P H Vaughan, G W V Whitcroft, W F Wilson.

Index

Floreat Portora